Live Wired

A Guide to Networking Macs

James K. Anders

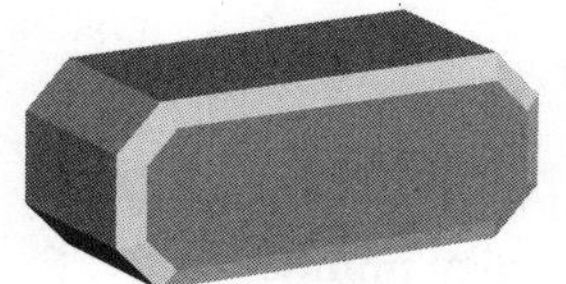

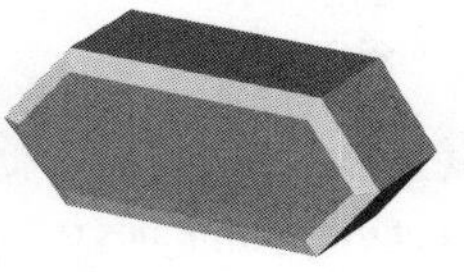

Live Wired: A Guide to Networking Macs

Library of Congress Catalog No.: 93-77320

ISBN: 1-56830-015-8

95 94 93 4 3 2 1

Interpretation of the printing code: the rightmost double-digit number is the year of the book's printing; the rightmost single-digit number the number of the book's printing. For example, a printing code of 93-1 shows that the first printing of the book occurred in 1993.

Dedication

To Ada

Time passes...
but memories remain.

Credits

Development Editor
Karen Whitehouse

Production Editor
David Ciskowski

Technical Reviewer
Richard Leach

Cover Designer
Kathy Hanley

Designer
Scott Cook

Indexer
Jeanne Clark

Production Team
Diana Bigham, Tim Cox, Mark Enochs, Tom Loveman,
Michael J. Nolan, Joe Ramon, Carrie Roth,
Mary Beth Wakefield, Barbara Webster

Composed in Utopia

About the Author

James K. Anders

Jim Anders is a Senior Consulting Engineer with Computer Methods Corporation, where, for the last five years, he specialized in desktop systems integration, focusing on Macintosh/VAX integration and CAD/CAM technologies. Through Computer Methods, Mr. Anders teaches the seminar "Integrating Apple's Macintosh into VAX System Networks," for Digital Equipment Corporation. He has provided consulting services for companies such as Apple Computer, Inc., Boeing Aerospace, Colgate Palmolive, Digital Equipment Corporation, Du Pont, Mobil Oil, and Union Carbide Corporation.

Jim Anders writes and lectures on Macintosh networking, systems integration, and CAD/CAM topics in a variety of forums, such as the Mactivity networking conference and the Macintosh Summit Conference. He is also the author of *Technical Drawing with Claris CAD* and *The Macintosh CAD/CAM Book.* He also writes reviews and articles for *MacUser* magazine.

His background includes over fifteen years experience with the implementation and administration of networked, integrated CAD/CAM systems. He was an engineering staff member of RCA Missile and Surface Radar, where in 1986 he spearheaded a successful effort to integrate Apple's Macintosh with their multivendor network. Previously, Mr. Anders worked for RCA Laboratories in Princeton, New Jersey, and for various companies in the medical and semiconductor manufacturing industries.

We Want to Hear from You

What our readers think of Hayden is crucial to our sense of well-being. If you have any comments, no matter how great or how small, we'd appreciate your taking the time to send us a note.

We can be reached at the following address:

Hayden
11711 N. College Ave.
Carmel, IN (yes, Indiana—not California. . .) 46032
(317) 573-6880 voice
(317) 571-3484 fax

If this book has changed your life, please write and describe the euphoria you've experienced. Do you have a cool book idea? Please contact us at the above address with any proposals.

Acknowledgments

Books are collaborative efforts. Even though there's one name on the cover, there are many people who deserve credit.

Guy Kawasaki deserves a special note of thanks. It was his continued insistence and cajoling that prompted me to expand and formalize a set of lecture notes that were used to help explain networking concepts to attendees of the Macintosh Summit Conference, held at the University of California at Santa Barbara.

Joe Dallatore provided valuable assistance with the Management and Troubleshooting chapter and with the technical aspects of the manuscript.

Sunny Anders spent countless hours reading and re-reading every page of this book—making sure that everything made sense.

Gloria Anders created the wonderful cartoons used throughout the book.

Thanks to Bill Sturdevant, and Silk City Software, for their timely and professional development of the PICTviewer application included on the disk that comes with this book.

I also would like to acknowledge the efforts of Garry Hornbuckle of Apple Computer, and the many representatives from the various Macintosh and AppleTalk networking companies.

Thanks also to Stephen and Maria Hull.

A special thanks to Karen Whitehouse and David Ciskowski of Hayden Books for their tireless efforts providing the necessary direction and editing to take this project from a big Microsoft Word file and a bunch of MacDraw Pro documents into the finished product that you see before you.

Finally, thanks to Al Cini (of Computer Methods Corporation), who nurtured and encouraged many of the ideas and concepts outlined in this book. I would like to offer my undying gratitude for those individuals—Frank Monzo, Anthony Caraffa, Ruth Logue and Vickie Briggs—at CMC who make my job so much easier.

Jim Anders
Feasterville, Pennsylvania
March, 1993

Foreword

For a computer that was supposed to be for "the rest of us," Macintosh has progressed (I use the term loosely) until it's now a computer for "the best of us." I often reminisce about the days when LocalTalk was AppleTalk, and AppleTalk was nothing more than a long printer cable to reduce the cost of a LaserWriter: "You see, if we buy a $7,000 printer, seven people can share it on an AppleTalk network, so it really only costs $1,000."

That was then—and this is now. IBM and Apple are allies. There's a twelve month warranty for Macs in the United States. The Berlin Wall is gone. "Macintosh Portable" isn't an oxymoron anymore. And Macs are connected on networks in organizations all around the world—even on half breed, mulatto, hapa-haole networks of Macintoshes, IBMs, DECs, HPs, and other superfluous mini- and mainframe computers.

In this confusing world, all I can say is, "Thank God for Jim Anders." I've sat through many a presentation about networking and communications and Jim is the only person I can understand. He's so good at it that I usually beg him to explain networking and communications to a Macintosh conference I run for desktop publishing weenies.

Indeed, part of the reason this book exists is because I pounded on Jim to write a book that would explain networking and communications to the rest of us. I don't know how he positions *Live Wired,* but in my mind, it's the *The Mac is Not a Typewriter* (by Robin Williams) of networking and communications books. If you know that book, you'll know how good *Live Wired* is. If you don't, trust me.

Guy Kawasaki
Macintosh Curmudgeon

Table of Contents at a Glance

Table of Contents

Introduction

Dr. Richard Feynman (see figure 1) was one of America's leading nuclear physicists. He achieved this acclaim by demonstrating his genius at M.I.T. and Princeton University, and later by playing a key role in the Manhattan Project, which produced the first atomic bomb at Los Alamos, New Mexico.

Figure 1
R. P. Feynman.

After World War II, Feynman became a professor at Cornell University, where he tackled the complexities of the newly emerging science of quantum mechanics. At the time, quantum physics was awash in competing theories, none of which effectively explained the intricacies of the sub-atomic world or satisfied the members of the physics community.

In the late 1940s, Feynman published a sequence of papers that completely redefined physics. While Feynman's writings were revolutionary, they were also full of simple examples and metaphors that made the complex subject accessible to a new generation of particle physicists.

One of the metaphors employed by Feynman was a simple diagram that depicted particle interactions (see figure 2). In fact, these "Feynman diagrams" were just a part of an entire language invented by Feynman—a language that has a complete and consistent grammar, with corresponding syntactical rules.

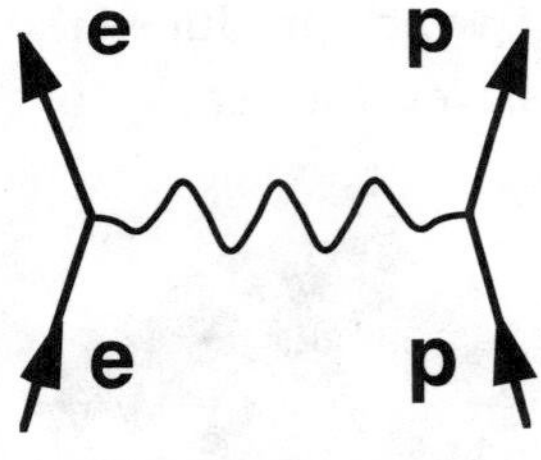

Figure 2
Feynman Diagram.

During the remainder of his years, Feynman continued his achievements: winning the Nobel Prize for Physics in 1965, and serving on the commission to investigate the Space Shuttle Challenger disaster.

Richard Feynman died in 1987 after a long battle with cancer, but his diagrams lived on and are now the *lingua franca* of the particle physics community. The symbols gave physicists the power to express complex phenomena in an elegant, graphical form.

The power of symbolic representation has been repeatedly demonstrated throughout history. From our numbers and alphabet to the iconic Macintosh user-interface, symbolic representation gives us the power to master complex concepts.

When we master complex concepts through using symbolic representation, we use a higher level of abstraction to deal with objects and events. For the programmer, it's the difference between writing a computer program in the computer's native language of assembler or in a higher level symbolic language such as Pascal or HyperTalk.

Just as the Macintosh made computing accessible to the general public, it also has made computer networking commonplace. Tasks that once were left to engineers and "authorized" networking professionals are becoming the responsibility of desktop publishers, architects, and other Macintosh end users.

At the simplest level—networking a Macintosh to a LaserWriter, for example—Macintosh networking is a plug-and-play operation that's as easy as connecting stereo components. But networks are not always this simple, and for many Macintosh users networking seems as complex as nuclear physics.

To extend beyond the simple LocalTalk network requires an understanding of basic networking principles and concepts. When the average Macintosh user tries to learn and understand these networking concepts, he or she is often confronted with confusing and ambiguous terms.

This book demystifies Macintosh networking and makes it understandable for everyone. Macintosh users, network administrators, and systems integrators will find the material presented in this book as clear and understandable as the Macintosh itself. It will bring an order and a symbolic representation to Macintosh networking by introducing a graphical language and diagramming technique that unifies and simplifies Macintosh network design and systems integration. This language is used throughout the book to introduce and define complex network protocols and components.

A disk containing a complete library of this symbolic networking language is included with this book. The disk contains hundreds of PICT-based networking symbols, called NetPICTs, that define all major networking components, computers, and software environments. These symbols also will be offered by Macintosh networking vendors and will be posted on online services such as CompuServe, AppleLink, and America Online.

Every hardware or software element that has some relevance to networking will be explained and diagrammed so that you can understand its function and role in the larger picture. You'll be able to use your favorite Macintosh drawing program to open these PICT symbols, so you easily can combine them to solve problems or diagram your Macintosh network.

The language breaks down Macintosh networking into four basic categories, or layers. Thoughout the book, obscure networking concepts like bridging, routing, and tunneling are clearly positioned and explained. Is Ethernet a networking protocol or cable? Is AppleTalk hardware or software? Is it necessary to use the same networking protocols and cabling on each networked computer? These are the kind of questions that this book readily answers. You'll learn from the diagrams that AppleTalk, Apple's networking software, not only runs on Macs and LaserWriters, but also on PCs, Unix workstations, and many other computers.

This book also provides a practical guide to designing, implementing and troubleshooting AppleTalk and multivendor networks. Numerous real-world examples are used, so it's likely that the "blueprint" of your present (or planned) network exists between these covers.

Unlike other computer books that focus solely on products and have a limited lifetime, this book will focus on making the basic Apple networking concepts clear and understandable. This book will be as relevant five years from now as it is today.

Years ago, Feynman's diagrams profoundly changed the world of physics by introducing a new graphical language that made difficult and obscure concepts understandable. For me, the goal of this book is much more pedestrian than Feynman's achievements: to provide a graphical user interface for Macintosh networking, and to make Mac networking understandable and accessible for the rest of us.

Jim Anders

March, 1993

“One”

erstandable to everyone

Part I covers the fundamentals of
networking, using concepts and
metaphors that are understandab
everyone. It establishes the found
that will be used throughout the b
describe Macintosh networking.

Part I covers the fundamentals of networking, using concepts and metaphors that are understandable to everyone. It establishes the foundation that will be used throughout the book to describe Macintosh networking.

Networking Fundamentals

shes the foundation that will
hroughout the book to
Macintosh networking.

How Does Communication Take Place?

1

Although computer networking appears to be a confusing world of terminology and buzzwords, the basic concepts can be reduced to four basic, interrelated layers. These layers apply to computer networking, spoken English, written German, sign language, smoke signals—any language you choose. This chapter describes each of these four layers, common to all communication, by starting at the top with the first layer (the Idea layer) and then proceeding down through the remaining three layers.

To make the position of the layers easy to remember, the number of lines in the ends of the layer diagram indicate the number of the layer. The Idea Layer (layer 1) has one line on its ends; the Expression Layer (layer 2) has two lines; the Transport Layer (layer 3) has three; and the Medium Layer (layer 4) has four (see figure 1.1). These end treatments will gain additional significance and will be used in other ways later in the book.

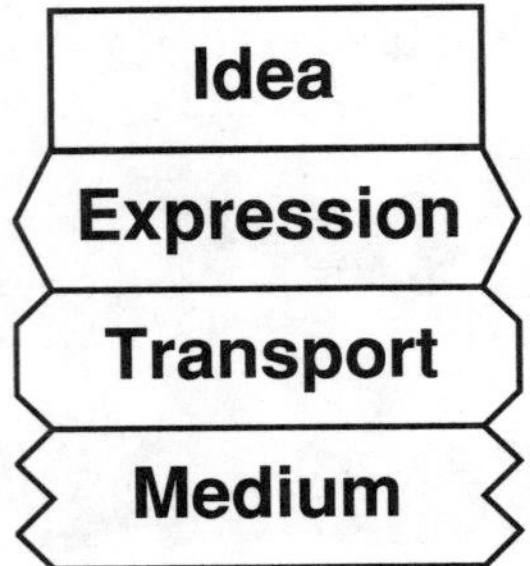

Figure 1.1
The four fundamental layers of communication.

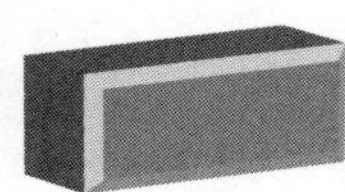

Idea

The Idea is the reason behind the communication. It's the thought or essence behind the message. It's an abstract concept that, when expressed, transforms the idea into a specific form and causes the process to move down into the next layer, Expression.

For example, if you have an idea that you would like to express, it first starts as an abstract concept in your mind. Fortunately, developing and fostering these concepts is what our minds do best. Within your mind you can entertain such abstractions as the fall of communism, the smell of morning coffee, your expectations of future Macintosh computers, and the sound of your favorite piece of music. All communications start at this abstract layer of the Idea.

Expression

Until ESP becomes a proven and reliable way to communicate, the external expression of ideas is necessary in order to prepare the ideas for conveyance. To express the idea of the fall of communism, you could use English, Braille, or a sequence of pictures. Each format of expression has inherent advantages and disadvantages that make one format better than others for a particular situation.

Transport

Once the abstract idea has been expressed in an external form, the message then can be transported from the origin to the destination. This is the function of the Transport layer. Each method of transport has certain rules, or *protocols*, that must be adhered to in order to ensure error-free delivery of the message.

Just as there are many different forms of expression, there also are many different transport mechanisms. If I decide to tell you about the fall of communism by speaking to you directly, I am using a specific, mutually agreeable protocol known as conversation. Usually, a conversation is a two-way process. One person speaks; another person listens and acknowledges the message. The order then reverses and the process repeats itself.

I could also convey my English-based message about the fall of communism using a written transport protocol. The rules for conveying written English are much different than those for spoken English. To convey ideas about the fall of communism using the written transport protocols of English, I write on a piece of paper, starting at the top, writing from left to right. I then convey the message by handing you the piece of paper.

Of course, the idea and the expression (the language) remain the same using either transport mechanism. The only thing that has changed is the method of transport.

Medium

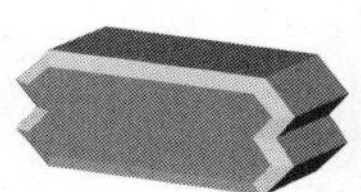

The last step in the process is the communications *Medium*—the mechanism used by the Transport layer to deliver the message.

When you deliver a message by speaking, the delivery mechanism is compressed air. Your lungs force compressed air over your vocal cords, which vibrate and in turn vibrate the air and create modulated waves of compressed air (see figure 1.2). These sound waves hit the listener's ear drum, which vibrates, causing electrical impulses to be sent to the brain where they're finally "heard."

Figure 1.2
Spoken communication uses compressed air.

> **NOTE:** So, just in case you were wondering: if a tree falls in the forest and there is no one there, it doesn't make a noise, it just compresses the air.

If I want to deliver my hand-written document on the fall of communism, I can choose from numerous delivery media—hand delivery, mail, fax, or Federal Express. Each method has distinct benefits and disadvantages, but they all do the same thing: they transmit my hand-written document.

Matching Layers

By using separate four-layer diagrams for the sender and the recipient of the message, we can better illustrate the degree of interaction between the two parties (see figure 1.3).

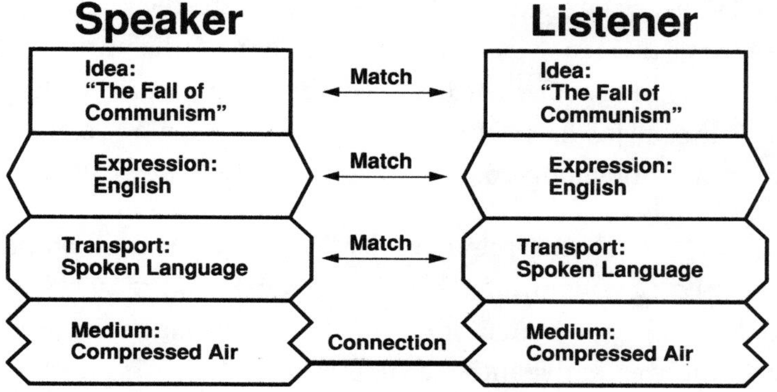

Figure 1.3
Diagramming a simple conversation.

In order for communications to be successful, each corresponding layer of the sender and the recipient must match. To illustrate this point, let's analyze a communications transaction from the bottom up.

The sender's and the recipient's chosen communications medium (layer 4) is compressed air. For this example, we'll assume that they're within speaking distance of each other in normal atmospheric conditions, and therefore would have no problem communicating over this medium. If either of the participants were deaf, then a better choice for the communication medium might be visual in nature.

Both parties are familiar with the protocol of spoken language, so the next layer up the stack, the Transport layer (layer 3), matches as well. If one of the participants only understood the protocol of spoken language and the other only understood the reading of lips, the layers would not match and communication would be unlikely.

Moving up to the Expression layer (layer 2), both parties understand the English format. Here, as with the other layers, if there was a mismatch where one person understood English and the other only French, the communication process would not occur.

Finally, even at the uppermost Idea layer (layer 1), there must be a match between the sender and the receiver. If the recipient of the message has no idea what communism is, or was, the purpose of the message will be lost. The beauty of this diagramming technique is that all forms and instances of communications can be diagrammed and analyzed.

What if the sender and recipient are too far away for the medium of compressed air to work effectively? Let's say they were 100 yards apart. In this case, the medium would have to be altered in order to support the greater distance (see figure 1.4).

Figure 1.4 If the medium of compressed air is insufficient, perhaps radio waves will work.

A walkie-talkie is such a device. It converts the compressed air waves into electrical signals. These signals are transmitted as radio waves to another walkie-talkie, which reverses the process and converts the radio waves back into electrical signals. These electrical signals vibrate the internal speaker, which in turn compresses the air so the listener can hear the message (see figure 1.5).

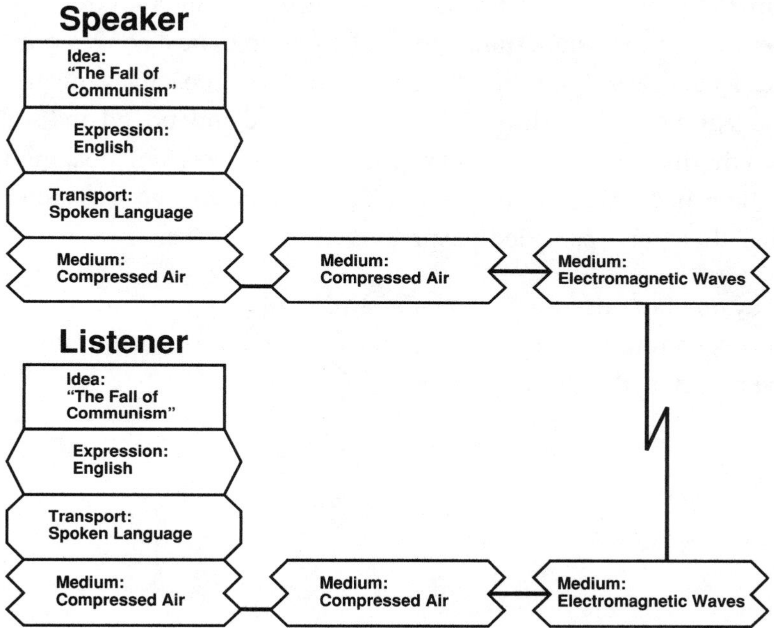

Figure 1.5
Diagramming a complex communication using walkie-talkies.

Notice how each side of the diagram matches the other. The compressed air medium of the sender's mouth matches the medium of the microphone; the compressed air medium of the walkie-talkie's speaker matches the medium of the receiver's ear.

This conversion process only happens at the Medium layer (layer 4) since it's strictly a medium conversion. Walkie-talkies are ignorant of the protocols of spoken communication and therefore the process is limited to the medium layer. You're totally free to be rude, incoherent, and ignore all the established protocols of spoken communication. Since the walkie-talkie only operates at the lowest layer, it will not attempt to police the conversation.

Conclusion

Each layer of the communication process serves a specific function, but provides us with unlimited choice. We can tailor the method of expression, transport, and medium to best convey our ideas. Each layer is connected to its neighbor, but each layer can also stand independently and can be analyzed and judged on its own merits. If English doesn't properly convey a certain idea, then perhaps haiku can do a better job. If the U.S. Postal Service is too slow, then perhaps Federal Express is a better choice.

A key tenet of this idea is that when two or more parties are involved, communication can only occur when their corresponding layers match identically.

2

How Does Networking Take Place?

This chapter introduces computer networking by defining network concepts in terms of the four basic concepts of communication (Idea, Expression, Transport, and Medium) as defined in the first chapter.

As with any communication, computer networking can be broken down into four layers (see figure 2.1). We'll use slightly different nomenclature (nomenclature that's specific to networking) to describe these layers.

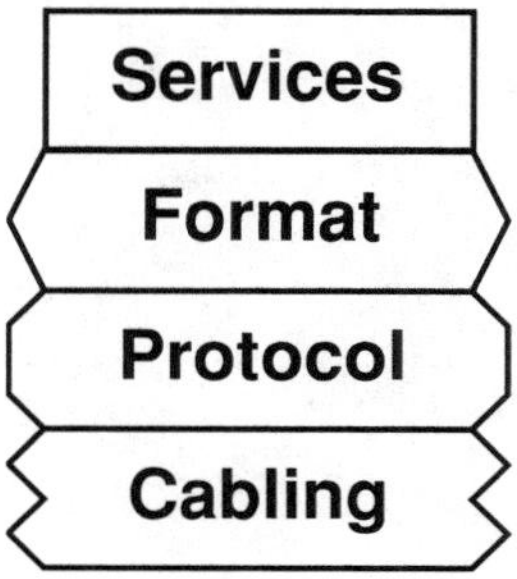

Services
Format
Protocol
Cabling

Figure 2.1
The four fundamental layers of computer networking.

Idea > Services and Programs

In Chapter 1, the first layer represented the idea—the reason behind the communication. In general, layer one embodies the purpose behind the communication. With computer networking, the purpose or reason behind the communication is to deliver services to the participants.

In a simple network consisting of a Macintosh and a LaserWriter, the LaserWriter provides a print service to the Macintosh user (see figure 2.2). Software on the Macintosh communicates with software on the LaserWriter and establishes what is known as a *client/server* relationship.

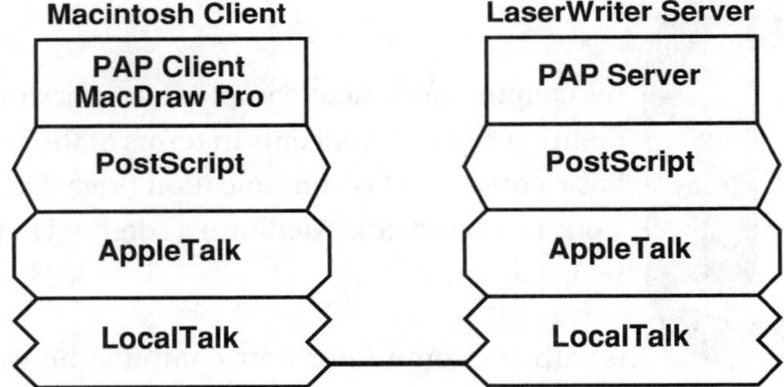

Figure 2.2
Client/Server with Mac and LaserWriter.

The client/server model has been used throughout all aspects of Macintosh networking to provide access to file, database, and mail servers. Today, the concept continues to expand to include workgroup applications such as calendar and time management programs, document librarian systems, and System 7's Publish and Subscribe capabilities.

Expression > Formats

Humans rely on standard languages to provide effective communications. We have numerous expressive formats to satisfy different situations and cultures. The same is true for computers. Information can be represented in thousands of computer formats. Some of these formats are widely adopted standards, while most of them are unique to a specific computer application.

To start with, all computer formats have at least one thing in common—they're all comprised of *binary data*. That means that all computer file formats consist of a sequence of ones and zeros. Each one and zero is called a *bit* of information. For convenience, these ones and zeros are often put into eight-bit groups, commonly called *bytes* (see figure 2.3).

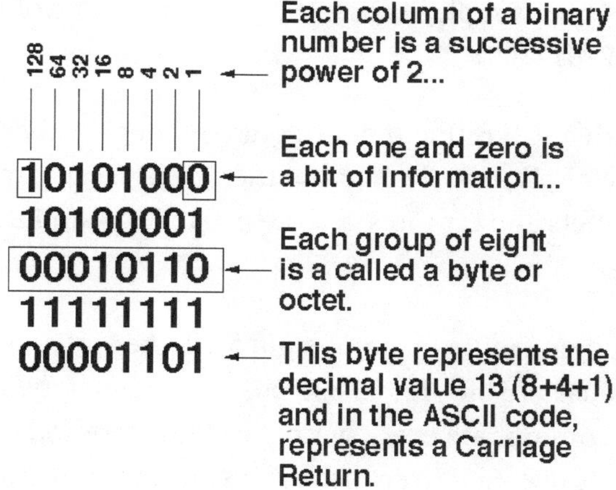

Figure 2.3

Bits and bytes.

Octets

Bytes are often referred to as *octets*, particularly in the networking community.

Early in the history of computing, it became obvious that digital information would need to be standardized. For example, ASCII (American Standard Code for Information Interchange) has been a widely used and popular standard for some time. It uses seven bits of information to represent most of the characters on an English typewriter keyboard.

Within a byte of information, there are 256 possible characters, ranging from 00000000 to 11111111. Of these, ASCII uses the first 128 characters to represent common alphanumeric characters and special characters unique to data processing. The first 32 characters of the ASCII code are special control characters that cannot be printed; these control characters are used to represent characters such as carriage returns (which have an ASCII decimal value of 13 and a binary value of 00001101), line feeds, and tabs. The remaining 128 values are used for special characters or symbols. The Greek letter "pi," for example, has an ASCII decimal value of 185 an a binary value of 10111001.

The problem with ASCII is that it doesn't have enough values to encode all the symbols used throughout the world. To accommodate other alphabets and symbols, a more expansive standard was needed.

To solve this problem, industry groups put forth the Unicode standard, which uses 16 bits, for 65,536 possible characters. This standard can accommodate every symbolic character used in the world today and is destined to eclipse the ASCII standard. Apple uses double-byte characters (but not yet the Unicode standard) in System 7.1 to accommodate these additional characters.

Today, many computer applications, particularly word processing applications, can read and write the ASCII standard. But since ASCII only encodes information about the characters and basic formatting, it is not used as a native word processing format.

Therefore, every word processor developer must devise another special binary format to handle all the other attributes common to modern word processors. With an application such as Microsoft Word for the Macintosh, these attributes can include color, fonts, graphics (of varying formats), and even sound. Of course, when you save a document that has these elements as an ASCII file, all that remains is the plaintext. The other elements are lost.

There are many other standard formats, such as PostScript, QuickDraw, PICT, TIFF, GIF, EBCDIC, QuickTime, DXF, and IGES. For the most part, these formats are independent of the computer on which they were created. A QuickTime file, composed of a specific sequence of ones and zeros, can be played on a Macintosh, a PC, or a Silicon Graphics workstation. All that is needed is an application that understands the QuickTime format.

Some formats use other formats as a starting point. For example, PostScript, DXF, and IGES files are composed of strings of ASCII text. The ASCII text is actually a series of commands or statements in the higher language. (The English format is based upon the Roman alphabet text format, as is the French format and the Italian format.)

When it comes to the native format used by most applications, nearly every one has its own unique (and often proprietary) file format. In other words, if you create identical documents in MacWrite and Microsoft Word, each application would use different patterns of ones and zeros to describe the same data. Both applications can import and export each other's format, but that's because the respective applications can translate the competitor's format.

More than any other layer, the Format layer is responsible for successful communications. A transcontinental telephone conversation is an apt analogy. It's easy to dial the phone number of someone who lives in France. The call gets routed and placed with all kinds of sophisticated technology, but the ultimate measure of successful communications is whether or not I can understand French, or if my counterpart understands English (see figure 2.4).

Figure 2.4
The expression (or format) of the message is crucial for understanding.

Establishing a common format for communications is by far the most difficult challenge in computer networking. It's the task that requires the most thought and effort to solve.

Transport > Protocols

Until this point, all we've done is establish a service and agree on a common descriptive format. No information has moved across the network. The rules for moving formatted information across the network are the function of the third level: protocols.

Networking software must solve many problems; the rules that describe the solutions are the networking *protocols.* First, the sender and recipient must be uniquely identified on the network. (This is analogous to assigning phone numbers to identify phones—you need to know the number of the phone you want to call.) Next, there must be a means to route data over complex pathways without the loss of data. This is just a sample of the functions of the Protocol layer.

Apple developed a protocol known as AppleTalk that very elegantly solved the problem of identifying the sender and the recipient. AppleTalk provides reliable, error-free transmissions, and chooses appropriate routes on the network. AppleTalk, like other networking protocols (such as TCP/IP, Novell, and DECnet), exists only in software. All Macintosh computers and most of Apple's networked printers come equipped with AppleTalk software.

Although AppleTalk is part of the Macintosh System software, it is by no means limited to the Macintosh. The AppleTalk protocols are available for many other computers and networking devices (see figure 2.5). DOS-equipped PCs can use Farallon's PhoneNet Talk PC software to gain the AppleTalk protocols. PCs running OS/2 2.0 come with AppleTalk protocols. (This was one of the goals of the Apple/IBM alliance.) AppleTalk protocols are available for other computer platforms, including NeXT workstations running NextStep 2.0 and Digital's VAX family.

Computers—the Macintosh included—are not limited to running a single networking protocol. Just as humans can deal with multiple transport methods, so can computers.

Your Macintosh can have several transport protocols loaded at one time (see figure 2.6). In addition to the standard AppleTalk protocol, you could install MacTCP from Apple and DECnet for Macintosh from Digital. These protocols would enable your

Macintosh to communicate using the native transport protocol of other computers.

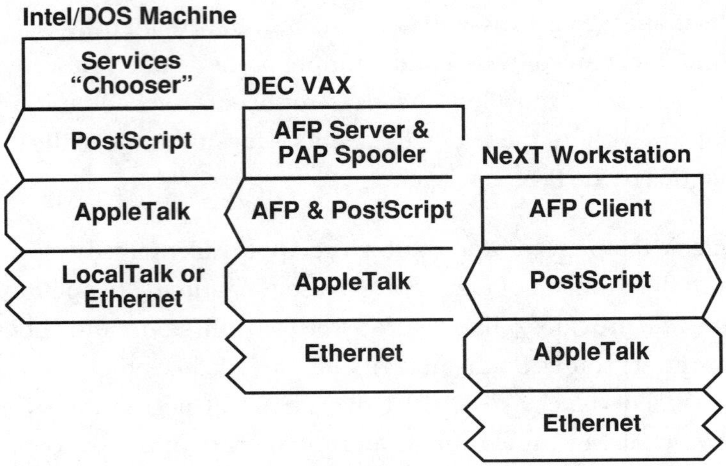

Figure 2.5
AppleTalk protocols on other platforms.

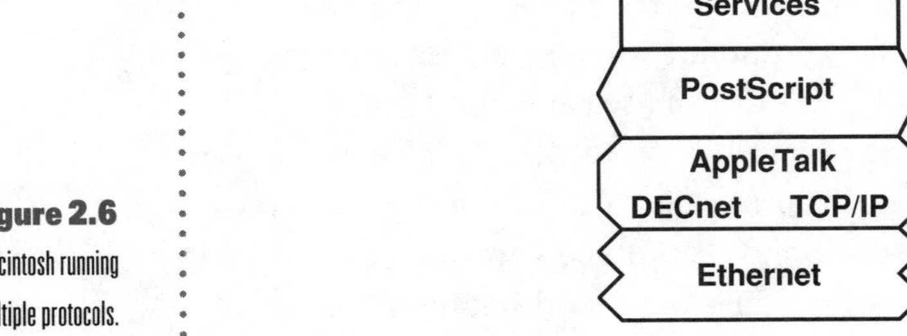

Figure 2.6
A Macintosh running multiple protocols.

MacTCP equips the Macintosh with the TCP/IP protocol used by most UNIX computers. Running DECnet for Macintosh turns your Mac into a DECnet node and enables it to communicate with DECnet-equipped computers such as PCs and VAXes.

Figure 2.7 shows another diagram depicting the concept of multiple protocols. Here, the protocols are shown as geometric shapes. Those computers that are able to send and receive these protocols have corresponding notches designed to handle the protocols.

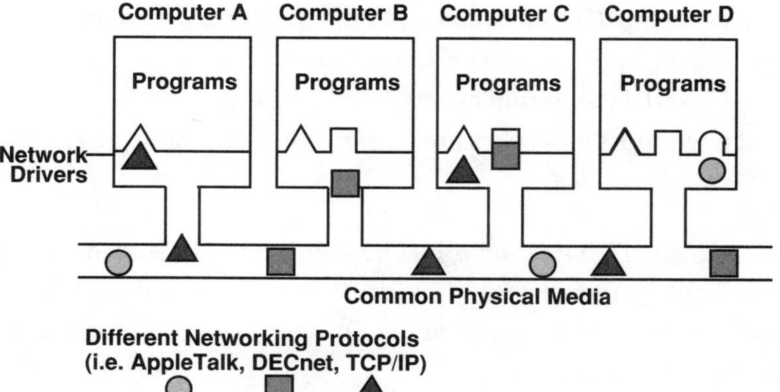

Figure 2.7
Multiple protocols.

While it's possible for a Macintosh to run multiple transport protocols, it's important to note that these transports don't always support every Macintosh service. For example, the Chooser only works with AppleTalk transport protocol. The file service of NFS is only accessible with the TCP/IP transport.

There are only a few Macintosh services that work with multiple transport protocols. The best example of such a service is MacX, which works over several transports, such as AppleTalk, TCP/IP, and DECnet. In this case, the choice of a transport depends largely on the transport protocol of other network participants.

Medium > Cabling

At some point, the networking software, or protocols, must deal with the physical world to send the message. When we speak, it's the air that carries our words. When computers speak, they rely on electromagnetic signals to carry the sequences of ones and zeros. These encode the networking protocols that contain the formatted information which ultimately delivers the service to the user. There are several ways computers can transmit electromagnetic signals, but the most common way is through a cable.

Every Macintosh has two serial ports. They are most commonly known as the printer port and the modem port. Both ports can be used for serial communications, but only the printer port can be used to connect to Apple's low-cost networking cabling medium known as *LocalTalk.*

Since LocalTalk hardware is included on every Macintosh and on most Apple printers, it is a simple task to create a basic network. Just acquire the LocalTalk connectors and connect them using the appropriate cabling.

Apple's LocalTalk was designed in the mid 1980s, when Ethernet hardware cost $750 to $1000 per node. Apple needed an inexpensive way to send AppleTalk protocols over a simple network. At $50 per node, LocalTalk networks rapidly took hold. To get the price down, Apple made some reasonable tradeoffs.

First, LocalTalk networks have a limited bandwidth, of 230,400 bits per second (230.4 Kbps). This limits the maximum number of connected nodes to 32. This was much less than Ethernet or other cabling systems, but it was reasonable for Apple's small workgroup strategy of 1985. While LocalTalk put serious limitations on large and complex networks, Apple took the necessary steps to expand the AppleTalk protocols to other popular cabling systems.

First came support for Ethernet. Apple and third-party vendors began to develop Ethernet cards for the Macintosh. Included with the cards was special driver software that enabled the AppleTalk networking software to communicate over the Ethernet card, instead of the standard LocalTalk port.

Apple decided to trademark the software that sends AppleTalk protocols over Ethernet, and called it EtherTalk. But don't be confused. It's not a new kind of cable or a different protocol. Just think of EtherTalk as AppleTalk protocols over Ethernet cabling, and it will make more sense.

Ethernet has a much higher bandwidth than LocalTalk. It's capable of carrying information at a rate of 10 million bits per second (10 Mbps). This is roughly 40 times the bandwidth of LocalTalk. There are three different implementations of Ethernet; all have the same bandwidth, but the cable type, connectors, and maximum segment lengths differ.

After Ethernet, Apple provided support for Token Ring networks. Token Ring is common in the IBM mainframe and minicomputer world. There are two implementations: a 4 Mbps version, and a 16 Mbps version. As with Ethernet, Apple included driver software to connect the higher-level AppleTalk protocols to the Token Ring hardware. The Apple trademark for this is TokenTalk. Again, just think of it as AppleTalk protocols running over Token Ring cabling.

Usually, the decision to use Token Ring as a cabling medium has more to do with IBM connectivity than it has to do with the relative merits of the cabling system. Token Ring cards are significantly more expensive than Ethernet cards, but as we'll see later on, Token Ring cabling operates in a fundamentally different way than Ethernet does, and it might make sense to consider Token Ring even if you don't have an IBM mainframe.

More recently, Apple introduced AppleTalk support for another kind of cabling. With AppleTalk Remote Access Protocol, or ARAP, AppleTalk protocols are sent over serial connections, such as RS-232 cabling used by modems. As with the other cabling choices, only the low-level drivers are affected. The higher-level AppleTalk protocols remain the same.

ARAP makes it possible for a remote Macintosh client to connect to a Macintosh or another server by calling in through a modem. The computer that receives the call acts as the ARAP server. Once the connection is made, the remote Macintosh client becomes a part of the network and is able to access the services as if the remote

Mac were directly connected to the network. Of course, since the dial-up modem connection is significantly slower than either LocalTalk or Ethernet, the trade-off is performance.

Apple's Remote Access software provides both the client and server applications for the Mac (see figure 2.8). However, third-party vendors are offering ARA servers that run on dedicated server boxes, such as Shiva's LanRover products and Computer Methods Corporation's AsyncServeR (which enables a DEC VAX to become an enterprise-wide AppleTalk Remote Access server).

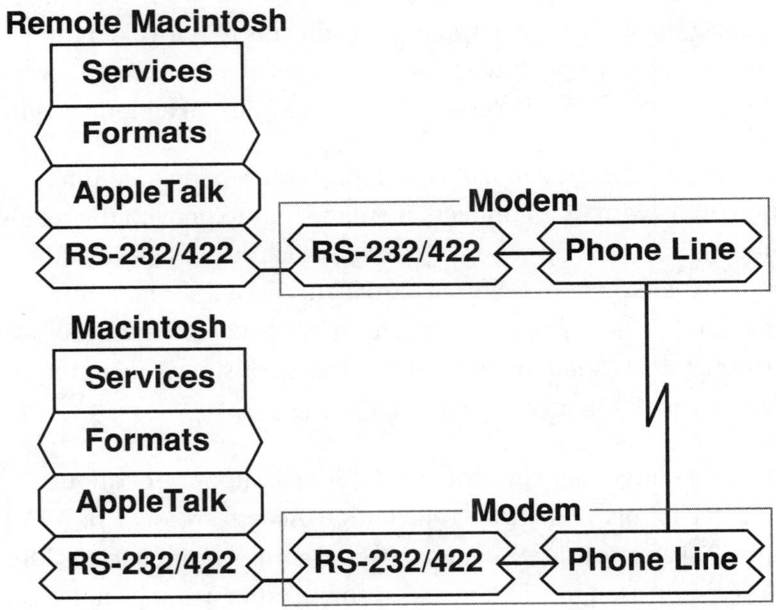

Figure 2.8
Remote access diagram.

Apple has already released the specification for the next generation of high-speed cabling systems. Fiber Distributed Data Interconnect (or *FDDI*) has a bandwidth that is an order of magnitude more than Ethernet (see figure 2.9). At 100 Mbps, FDDI interfaces should provide the necessary bandwidth for the demanding applications where voice data and real-time video are sent over the network. Several vendors are already starting to offer FDDI NuBus cards for the Macintosh, and Apple has no doubt trademarked the FDDITalk name. Prices are still high, but just as Ethernet prices have plummeted during the last few years, you can expect the same to happen with FDDI technology as well.

Figure 2.9
FDDI.

Electromagnetic communication is not limited to copper wiring or fiber optics. In fact, it seems likely that the next generation of small hand-held computers, as exemplified by Apple's Newton, will not use any cabling.

Instead, different portions of the electromagnetic spectrum will be used in place of physical cabling. Your TV or VCR remote control uses infrared waves to communicate. Your pager, remote auto alarm, and cellular phone use radio waves to communicate. All these methods will be common communications and networking mediums in the near future.

Conclusion

Networking may appear to be a a complex subject, but it easily can be broken down into four layers. *Services* are the applications, which use a variety of *formats* or data structures. These formats are delivered with networking transport *protocols,* over some kind of delivery medium, such as *cabling.* This is true of all computers and network systems. Once this concept is understood, all that remains is to determine which buzzwords belong to which layer.

3

Network Diagramming with NetPICTs

In this chapter, the symbolic language based on the NetPICT symbols and the associated diagramming technique is introduced and explained, using several basic Macintosh network scenarios. Using the four-layer NetPICT symbol as a starting point, the seven-layer OSI reference model is finally explained in an easily understandable fashion.

Introducing the NetPICT symbol

To this point, the NetPICT symbols have been used to describe fairly simple networking scenarios. Combined with a few simple rules, we will use the symbols to depict common Macintosh networking scenarios, and to solve some simple problems.

Let's start with a typical Macintosh. Out of the box, the Macintosh, combined with its System software, fulfills each of the four layers.

Starting at the top, the most familiar Macintosh service is the Chooser desk accessory. Found under the Apple menu, the Chooser application is a service that delivers other services to the user (see figure 3.1). With the Chooser, a Macintosh user can select services from the network, including file, print, mail, and other services.

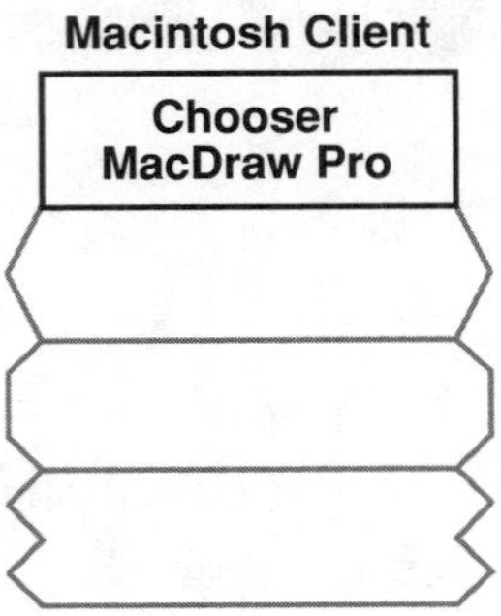

Figure 3.1
The standard Mac Service layer.

Once a service (a LaserWriter, for example) has been selected, other Macintosh applications, such as MacDraw Pro, can utilize that service and print documents. So, in addition to the Chooser, we've also placed MacDraw Pro as a typical application that appears at the Service layer.

Working our way down, the next layer is the Format layer (see figure 3.2). Here, we see that the MacDraw Pro application supports several different formats.

First, there is the native binary MacDraw Pro format that is unique to MacDraw Pro. This is the format that writes to your disk when you save a MacDraw Pro document.

Another format used by MacDraw Pro is QuickDraw, which is used as an imaging format to draw entities on the Macintosh screen.

It also can be used for printing, when combined with a QuickDraw printer such as Apple's StyleWriter. If you're using a PostScript printer instead, the MacDraw Pro application generates yet another format, known as PostScript.

Figure 3.2
The standard Mac Format layer.

As mentioned before, every Macintosh comes equipped with AppleTalk protocols as part of its System software. Thus, we've placed AppleTalk in the third Protocol layer (see figure 3.3). The PostScript generated in the second layer is now passed down to the third level for subsequent delivery.

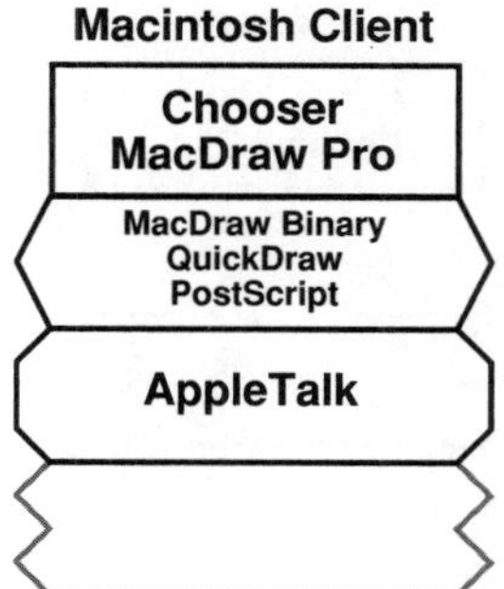

Figure 3.3
The standard Mac Protocol layer.

And finally at the fourth layer, the LocalTalk cabling, which provides the physical cabling connection to the outside world, is used to actually transmit the PostScript data, along with network and printer control data, to the printer (see figure 3.4).

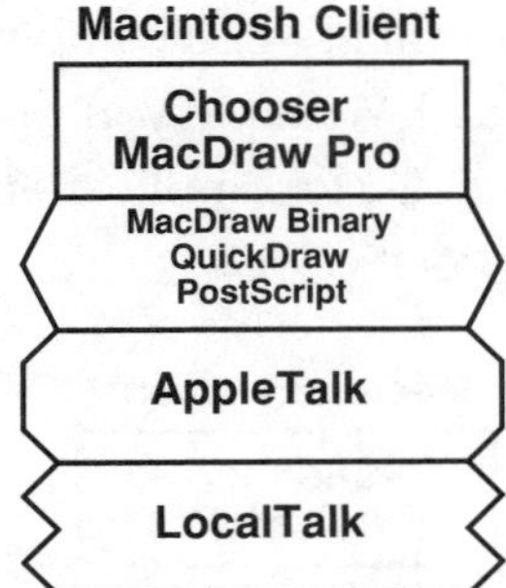

Figure 3.4
The standard Mac Cabling layer.

To further illustrate the function of each layer, let's look at a few examples of other systems. With an IBM (or compatible) PC, the layers perform the same function.

At the Service layer, the PC user chooses services in different ways, often depending on the application (see figure 3.5). Printers are usually assigned code names such as LPT1 or LPT2. With DOS, the printer selection is usually typed in as part of the command line. With Windows-equipped PCs, the printers often have iconic representations.

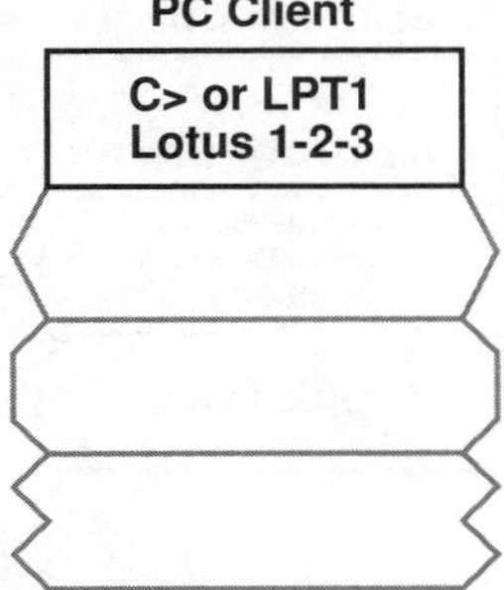

Figure 3.5
The standard PC Service layer.

As with the Macintosh example, applications also belong at the service layer. So Lotus 1-2-3 (and any other application) would be placed here as well.

Lotus 1-2-3 supports a number of formats, in addition to its own native file format. Some of these formats are used for printing.

These include Hewlett-Packard's PCL, used by LaserJet printers, and the industry standard PostScript, which is understood by many laser printers.

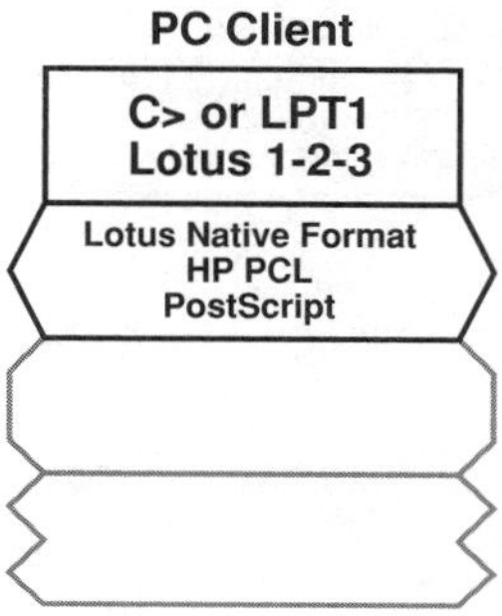

Figure 3.6
The standard PC Format layer.

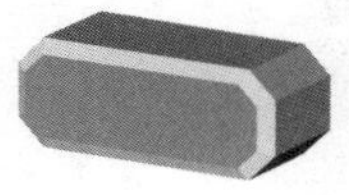

At the transport layer, the PC user is confronted with many confusing choices (see figure 3.7). Unlike the Macintosh, the PC was never designed with a networking protocol built-in, so third-party companies proceeded to fill the void. Novell NetWare, Banyan Vines, and Microsoft LAN Manager are all examples of popular transport protocols available for the PC.

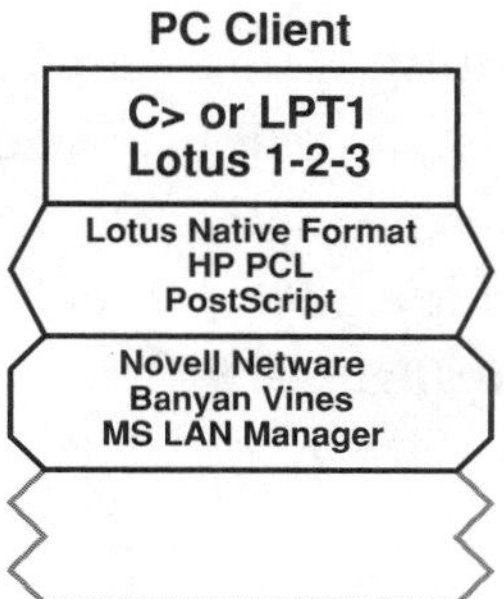

Figure 3.7
The standard PC Protocol layer.

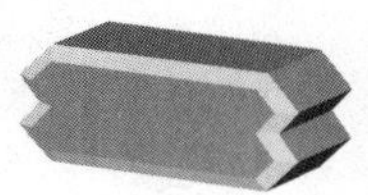

There's a similar problem at the lowest Cabling/Media layer as well (see figure 3.8). The only communications port that comes standard on a PC is a serial communications port. Serial ports are not normally thought of as networking ports, since they only support a single connection at one time. To provide a PC with a true network connection, a networking card must be purchased.

Figure 3.8

The standard PC Cabling layer.

There are several networking cards that are popular for PCs. Today, most PC networking cards are either Token Ring, Ethernet, and Arcnet. In its day, Arcnet was the LocalTalk of PCs. It was inexpensive and used standard twisted pair wiring. But as the price of Ethernet and Token Ring cards dropped over the years, these cards have come to dominate the PC market.

Swapping Layers

Let's return to the Macintosh example used earlier. Here we have a Macintosh that "speaks" AppleTalk over a LocalTalk interface. If we wanted to trade-up to an Ethernet connection, we would simply install a networking card and install the appropriate EtherTalk driver software (figure 3.9).

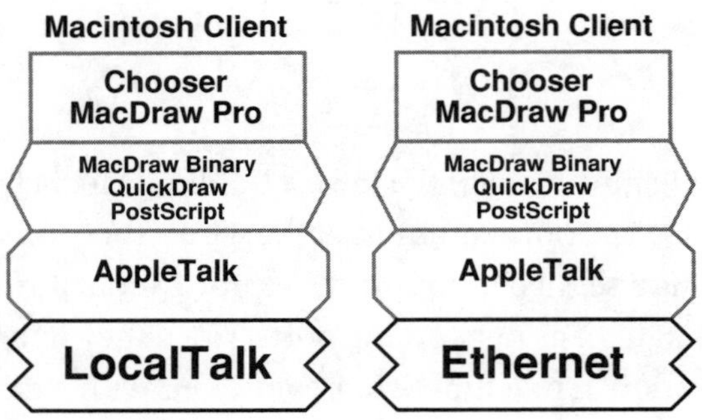

Figure 3.9

Swapping LocalTalk for Ethernet.

As far as the diagram is concerned, the only change we would need to make is to replace the current Cabling layer of LocalTalk with one of Ethernet. All the other layers remain the same. With the PC, we might want to get a bit more ambitious. Here, we might want to get rid of the Novell networking protocols and replace them with the AppleTalk protocols (see figure 3.10). This can be done with Farallon's PhoneNet PC. PhoneNet PC works with most PC Ethernet cards, or with PC LocalTalk cards that are offered by Farallon and other third-party vendors.

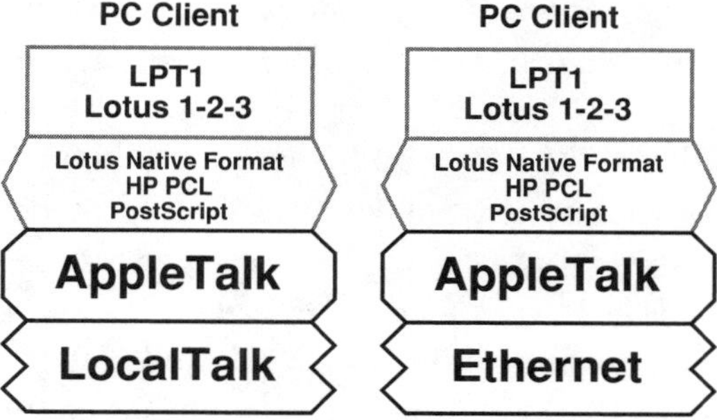

Figure 3.10
PC running AppleTalk with LocalTalk and Ethernet.

As evidenced from the prior example, the process of network design or systems integration often involves the swapping and substitution of various layers, in order to achieve the desired results.

IMPORTANT NOTE: The most important rule to remember is: Two computers can only fully communicate when each of their respective four layers match exactly, or have counterparts that can work together.

Matching Layers

Let's look at the NetPICTs of a Macintosh and LaserWriter and see why they're able to communicate. As shown in figure 3.11, the Macintosh and the LaserWriter match all four layers.

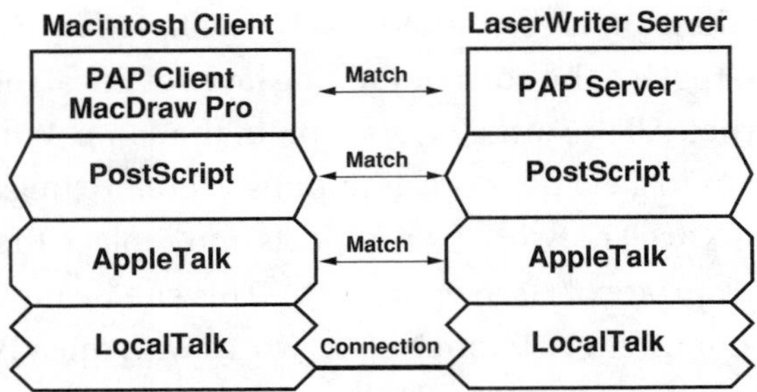

Figure 3.11
Mac and LaserWriter matching layers.

The LaserWriter icon in the Chooser represents the client portion that is responsible for printing. It matches and connects with the server application that runs on the LaserWriter.

At the Format layer, the PostScript generated by MacDraw Pro can be readily processed by the PostScript interpreter on the LaserWriter.

Both machines can speak and understand AppleTalk, which is being used to convey the printing instructions at the Protocol layer.

Since both machines have LocalTalk interfaces at the Cabling layer, they can use a common mechanism for carrying the AppleTalk protocols.

If any one or more of these layers didn't match, the printing process wouldn't be possible. For example, Hewlett-Packard offers a LocalTalk card for certain models of their LaserJet printers. They also provide AppleTalk protocol and PostScript support as well. If I were to just install the LocalTalk card into a LaserJet, without also installing the AppleTalk and PostScript software, I would be unable to print (see figure 3.12). The same situation would also exist if I installed the AppleTalk protocols without the PostScript, or vice versa.

Again, all four layers must match exactly for communications to occur.

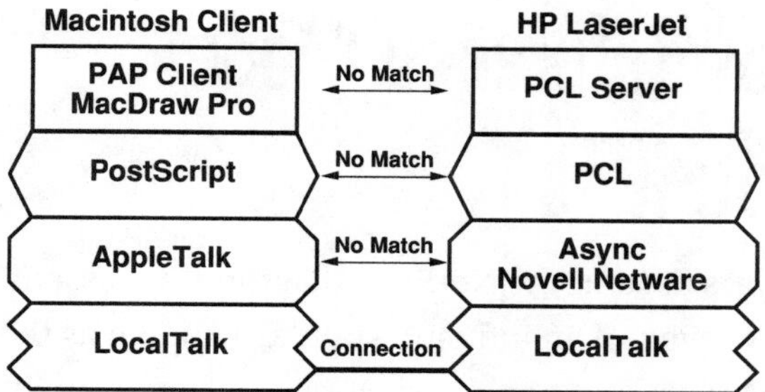

Figure 3.12
Mac and LaserJet not matching layers.

Clients and Servers

Client/Server computing is not a product or a specific application. It's a way of designing computer programs. It's a design philosophy. In the client/server model, computers and programs interact in a way that's ideal for a networked environment.

The general idea is simple. A client program submits a request to a server program, which acts on the request along with the requests of other clients. The obvious example is a file server that handles the requests of clients that desire file services. Database servers, such as Apple's Data Access Language (DAL), performs a similar function for clients desiring database services.

The client/server model even applies to the design of computer programs. The popular symbolic math program, Mathematica, was written using a client/server model. When Mathematica is running on a single computer, such as the Mac, the client and server portions of the program are running on the same machine. In a networked environment, a different server could be used. By having the option to choose different Mathematica servers, the user has the option of selecting a server that runs on a super minicomputer, while still using the client interface on the Mac.

Throughout this book, the concept of client/server computing will appear quite often. It will be used to describe the way applications work together, or how one network layer interacts with its neighbor.

The OSI Reference Model and NetPICTs

The four layers used in the NetPICT diagrams are essentially a condensed version of an industry standard known as the OSI Reference Model. The model, developed by the International Standards Organization (ISO), is used to describe the ISO's standard networking protocols and also to act as a road map for other networking protocols as the fundamental layers can be applied universally.

The OSI Reference Model uses seven layers, as opposed to the four used by the NetPICT diagrams (see figure 3.13). As we discussed earlier, the end treatments of the different NetPICT layers serve different functions.

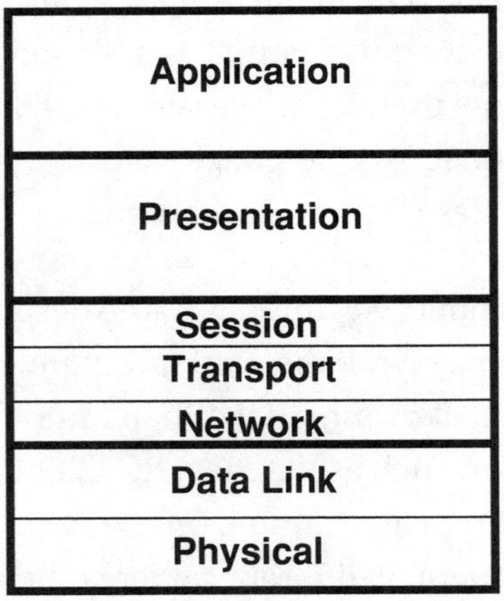

OSI layers
Application
Presentation
Session
Transport
Network
Data Link
Physical

Figure 3.13
OSI Reference Model with seven layers.

First, the number of lines in the ends of the NetPICT layers indicate their respective position on the stack. Secondly, many of the end treatment lines correspond to key layers of the OSI Reference Model (see figure 3.14).

The three lines in the Protocol layer symbolize the three layers in the OSI Reference Model that focus on the networking transport protocol. Another similarity can be found in the fourth Cabling layer. Here the four line end treatment can be readily divided in half, where the upper half represents the Data Link OSI layer and the lower half represents the Physical layer.

The only deviation from the strict interpretation of the OSI model is the two lines of the Format layer. Here, the entire Format layer is represented by the Presentation layer of the OSI model.

For the purposes of this book, however, later we'll use the two lines of the Format layer to separate different kinds of formats.

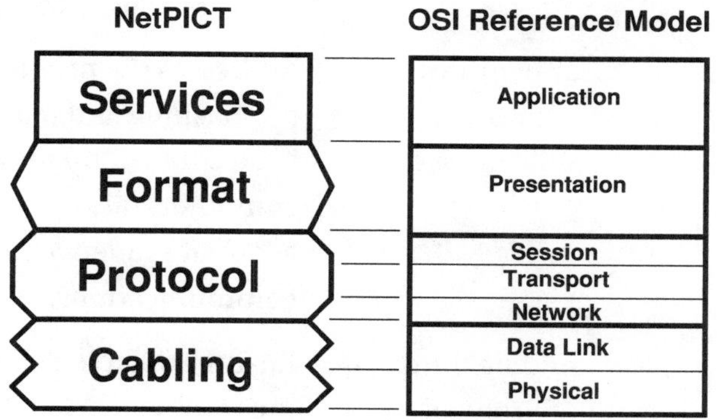

Figure 3.14
NetPICT and OSI Matching.

So, by starting with our simplified four-layer approach, you already have a basic understanding of the OSI Model. Table 3.1 describes the specific relationships between the NetPICT model and the OSI model. As the function of each layer is described, keep in mind that each layer dovetails with its neighbor in a client/server relationship.

Table 3.1 OSI Reference Model Layers

OSI Layer	*Corresponding NetPICT layer*	*Function*
Application	Service	The place where network services and applications reside; utilizes the formats established in the next layer of the stack.
Presentation	Format	These include file formats, such as PostScript, ASCII and Microsoft Word; and file access formats such as the Apple Filing Protocol.
Session	upper third of Protocol	Addresses the problem of establishing and maintaining a connection between computers; also maintains a logical sequence to the communications.
Transport	middle third of Protocol	Ensures reliable delivery of the message.
Network	bottom third of Protocol	Essentially addresses the message for delivery.
Data Link	upper half of Cabling	Concerns the specific kind of cabling or communications medium employed.
Physical	bottom half of Cabling	The level where the physical cable or delivery medium exists.

A few of these descriptions are new and require a brief explanation. The Transport layer ensures that the message is correctly transmitted. If one portion of the communication transmission is lost or garbled, it's the job of the Transport layer to re-transmit the necessary portion.

The Network layer functions as an envelope containing the message. The envelope has the address of the message recipient and the return address of the sender. These addresses are logical addresses that are specific to a particular networking protocol. This logically addressed envelope is known as a *datagram*. This concept is very important and will be covered in detail in the next chapter.

The function of the Data Link layer is to place the datagram, created at the Network layer, inside a network delivery vehicle, known as a *frame*. Network delivery frames are specific to the particular kind of cable being used. An Ethernet frame can hold the same AppleTalk datagram as a Token Ring frame, but the respective network frames are different. Another way for Macintosh users to think of the Data Link layer is by looking at the Mac's Network Control Panel. When a Macintosh user chooses a different network driver with the Network Control Panel, a different Data Link layer is being selected.

The Physical layer is the level at which the actual delivery medium is realized. The three different kinds of Ethernet and two different kinds of Token Ring cable are defined in this layer. The Physical layer often has its own form of addressing in addition to the protocol-specific logical addressing. For example, each Ethernet node, or device, has a unique 48-bit hardware address that remains constant. LocalTalk, on the other hand, doesn't use physical hardware addresses and relies on the logical AppleTalk address instead. Physical hardware addresses and their relationship to the protocol logical addresses will be covered in the next chapter.

With that quick overview of the OSI Reference Model, let's take another look at how a Macintosh prints to a LaserWriter, but this time, we'll use the full seven layers of the OSI Model.

A Seven Layer OSI Example

As before, starting at the top, the most familiar Macintosh Application is the Chooser desk accessory. Found under the Apple menu, the Chooser application delivers other services to the user (see figure 3.15). With the Chooser, a Macintosh user can select file, print, mail and other services from the network.

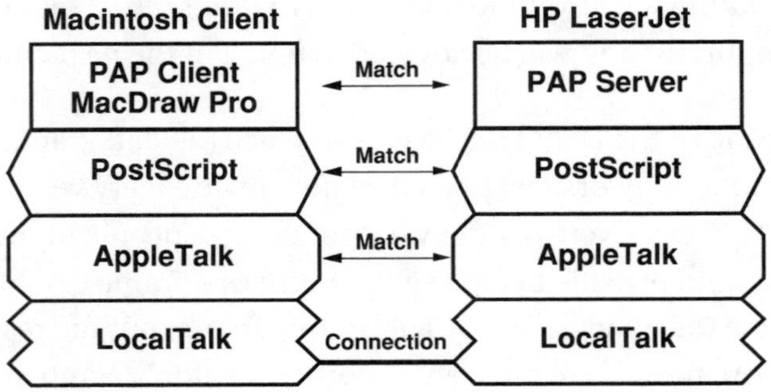

Figure 3.15
Printing described with the OSI Reference Model.

Once a service, such as a LaserWriter print server, has been chosen, other Macintosh applications, such as MacDraw Pro, can utilize that service and print documents. So, in addition to the Chooser, we've also placed MacDraw Pro as an application that appears at the OSI Application layer.

Working our way down, the next layer is the Presentation layer. Here, as before, we see that the MacDraw Pro application supports several different formats. First, there is the native binary MacDraw Pro format that is unique to MacDraw Pro. This is the format that is written to your disk when you save a MacDraw Pro document.

Another format used by MacDraw Pro is QuickDraw, which is used as an imaging format to draw entities on the Macintosh screen. It also can be used for printing when connected to a QuickDraw printer such as Apple's StyleWriter. If you're printing to a PostScript printer instead, the MacDraw Pro application generates yet another Presentation layer format, known as PostScript.

The Presentation layer of PostScript gets sent to the Session layer. The Session layer is the first layer where the AppleTalk networking protocols really come into play. At the AppleTalk Session layer, there's an Apple protocol known as the Printer Access Protocol (PAP). PAP's job is to add printer control information to the PostScript data.

Once the AppleTalk PAP Session layer has done its job, it passes the data down the stack to the Transport layer. At the Transport layer, the AppleTalk Transaction Protocol, or ATP, adds transaction-oriented commands to manage the give-and-take nature of the transmission.

With the transaction data added to the message, it's placed inside an AppleTalk datagram at the Network layer. Here, the Datagram Delivery Protocol (DDP) has the task of creating the datagram and logically addressing it for delivery.

The addressed datagram is then sent to the Data Link layer where the selected network driver—either the LocalTalk Link Access Protocol (LLAP), EtherTalk Link Access Protocol (ELAP), TokenTalk Link Access Protocol (TLAP), or another AppleTalk network driver—places the datagram into the appropriate network frame.

Finally, the Data Link layer passes the frame onto the Physical cabling layer and the message is sent to the recipient.

Conclusion

The seven layer OSI Reference Model provides a complete—but often complex—view of Macintosh networking. To address this problem of complexity, a simplified four-layer symbology has been introduced which essentially collapses some of the detail. The collapsed layers of the OSI Model have importance and significance, and will be discussed, where appropriate, throughout this book. But, for most basic Macintosh networking activities, the four layer NetPICT approach will enhance the reader's understanding and comprehension of a complicated world.

Networking Concepts

4

xtending and adding to the NetPICT concept, this chapter explores concepts such as network addressing (both logical and physical) and how digital signals are conveyed over a network.

Types of Networks

Basically, there are two kinds of computer networks: circuit-switched and packet-switched. *Circuit-switched networks* employ point-to-point links between the participating nodes of the network (see figure 4.1). The link is dedicated between the participants of the connection. This is similar to most telephone systems, where the phone company uses elaborate switching mechanisms to connect the callers.

Packet-switched networks utilize a common connection which is shared simultaneously among all nodes of the network. Members of a packet-switched network communicate by sending discrete packets of information that are identified with the network address of the sender and recipient. To better describe the differences between circuit and packet switching, let's imagine a classroom full of students.

Figure 4.1
Circuit switching.

The students aren't allowed to talk out loud, so one of them fashions a circuit-switched network with two tin cans and some string. Each time it's used, the connection is dedicated between the two participants. The switching occurs when other students need access to the network. Then, the tin cans get passed along to another pair of students. Of course, waiting for the tin cans becomes tiring, and when a number of students need to communicate, the circuit-switched network becomes inefficient.

So, in place of the tin cans, another solution was devised. The students began to pass notes to each other. To identify who receives and who sends the note, each note has the names of the sender and the recipient on the outside of the note. This networking technique is known as packet-switching.

If the sending and receiving students are sitting next to each other, they simply can pass messages between themselves. If the sender and the recipient are sitting at opposite ends of the classroom, the note has to be passed from student to student. Each student who handles the note looks at the names of the sender and recipient to determine how best to route the message. This is similar to the task that network routers perform when they route network packets from the source to their destination (see figure 4.2).

Figure 4.2
Packet switching.

One advantage of the note-passing packet-switching scheme is that multiple notes or packets can be handled at any given instant. This is in direct contrast to the circuit-switching technique, where each connection remains dedicated for the duration of the transaction.

Most LANs, such as LocalTalk, Ethernet, and Token Ring, rely on packet-switching technology. Obviously, one of the important aspects of a packet-switched network involves the identification of the sender and the recipient. This general problem is referred to as *network addressing*.

Network addressing, like the street address of where you live or the name of a note-passing student, simply means to uniquely identify the network participant. There are two different kinds of network addressing: logical and physical.

Logical addressing is software-based. It's how a specific networking protocol, such as AppleTalk, identifies the senders, recipients, and other devices on the network. *Physical addressing* is hardware-based. It's tied to a specific cabling system. Let's compare these two different addressing schemes.

Logical Addressing

Every networking protocol, such as AppleTalk, DECnet, and TCP/IP, has a scheme to identify members of its respective network. Essentially, this means every network member, or *node*, has a unique identification number.

With AppleTalk, this identifying number, or *node number*, is based on an eight-bit number. With eight bits of information, the maximum number of nodes is 2^8 or 256 (see figure 4.3). For small networks, having a limit of 256 nodes is not a problem. In fact, Apple's LocalTalk cabling system permits no more than 32 nodes. (With LocalTalk, the restriction is a physical or electrical limit, not a logical limit of node addresses.)

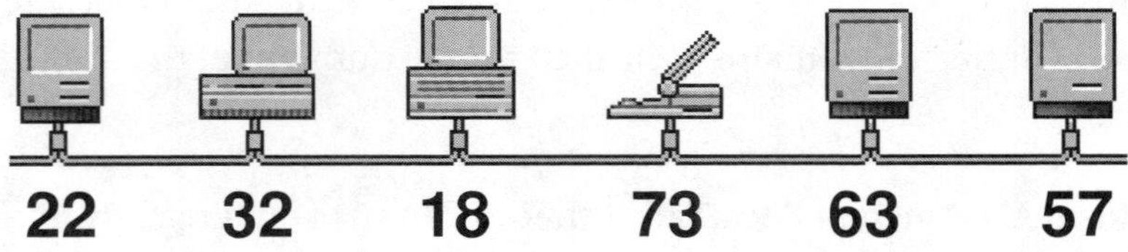

Figure 4.3
AppleTalk node numbers.

But many networks require more than 256 AppleTalk nodes, and another mechanism was needed to support these larger networks. So, Apple developed a concept that permitted groups of nodes, called "networks," to be established; each AppleTalk network would have its own range of 256 potential node IDs.

To create the boundaries between these different AppleTalk networks, Apple developed the specifications for a device known as an AppleTalk router. AppleTalk routers are the glue that connects separate AppleTalk networks into a larger whole known as an *internetwork*. AppleTalk routers separate and define the boundaries between AppleTalk networks.

Each AppleTalk network has a unique ID number that is stored inside each router connected to that network. In the simplest case of two AppleTalk networks connected by a single router, the router maintains the AppleTalk network numbers for each of the two networks. Routers will be discussed in depth later in the book.

The current AppleTalk specifications provide a 16-bit network number. With 16 bits there can be 2^{16} or 65,536 unique AppleTalk networks (see figure 4.4). And since each network can potentially support 256 nodes, AppleTalk can support a theoretical maximum of 16,777,216 devices!

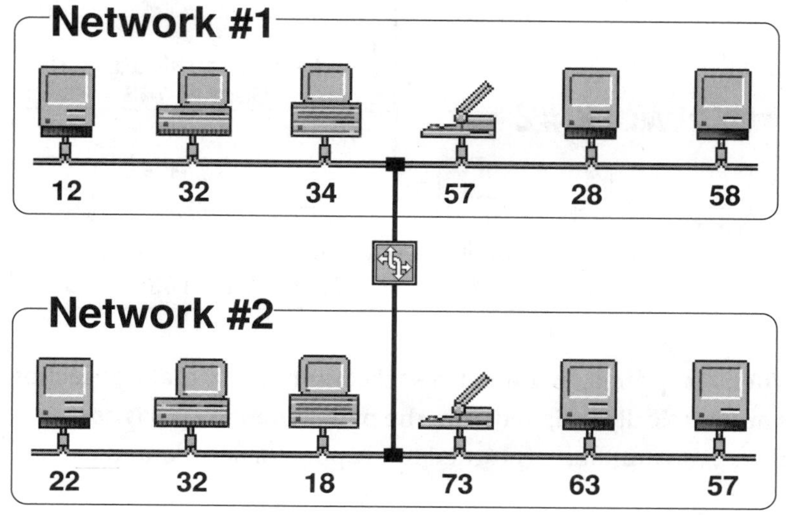

Figure 4.4
AppleTalk network numbers.

The 16-bit network and 8-bit node number make up only part of a complete AppleTalk logical address. An additional 8 bits is used to define something known as an AppleTalk socket number.

Your Macintosh can handle a number of network chores at one time. At any given instant, a Macintosh could be accessing a file server, printing to a LaserWriter print server, and receiving an E-mail message. To keep these diverse transactions separate and distinct, AppleTalk assigns a unique socket number for every logical connection. With socket numbers consisting of 8-bit values, there are 256 possible socket numbers that can be used (see figure 4.5). Socket numbers start at 0 and end at 255. Both 0 and 255 are undefined. Half of the remaining socket numbers, from 1 to 127, are reserved for special system use by Apple. The other half, from 128 to 254, are pooled resources available for general use by applications.

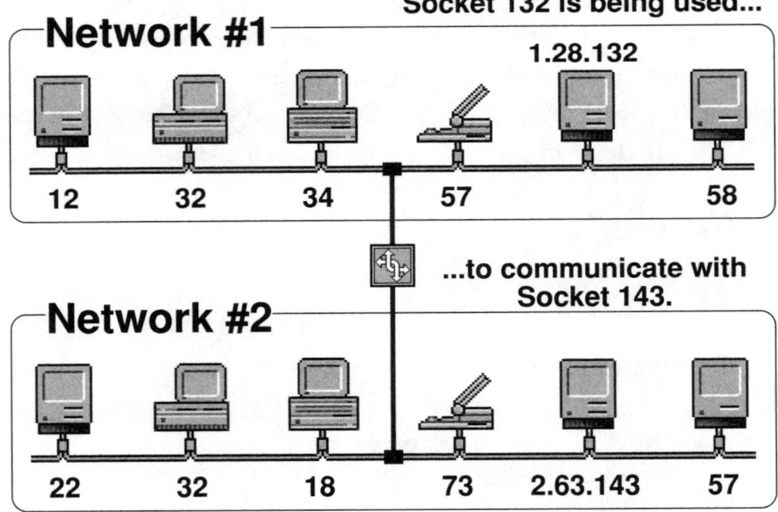

Figure 4.5 AppleTalk socket numbers.

When you print a document, a socket number for that transaction is automatically assigned from the pool. When the job is completed, the number is returned to the pool for subsequent use.

Collectively, these three numbers—network, node, and socket—make up a unique AppleTalk logical address. When a Macintosh and LaserWriter engage in printing transactions, they identify the participants using network, node and socket numbers—for instance, Macintosh node number 22, located in network 100, is communicating over socket 129 to LaserWriter node 32, in network 101, with socket 130.

The choice of three numbers—the 16-bit network number and the 8-bit node and socket number—is specific to AppleTalk. Other networking protocols, such as DECnet and TCP/IP, use similar but different numbering schemes to logically identify their nodes. The important thing to remember about these logical network addresses is that they are tied to a specific networking protocol, and they only exist in software.

Because Macintosh and other computers can often run multiple networking protocols concurrently, it's often common to have multiple logical addresses on a single computer. For example, a Macintosh that's running AppleTalk, DECnet, and TCP/IP concurrently would have three different logical addresses (see figure 4.6). Its AppleTalk address might be 12.22 (network.node), its DECnet address might be 5.2 (area.node), and its TCP/IP address might be 100.22.128.132.

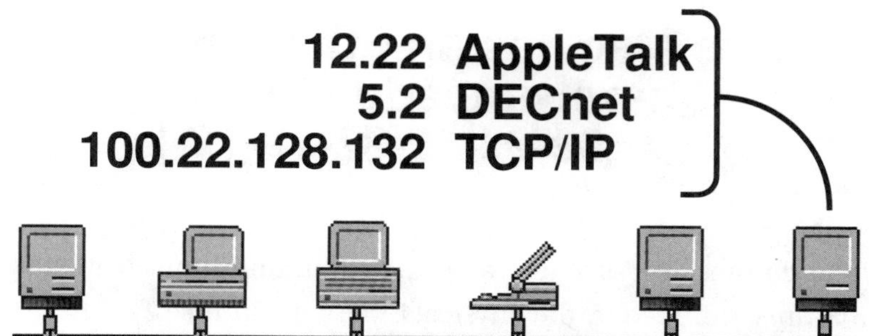

Figure 4.6
Different logical addresses on one Mac.

Every time this Macintosh sends or receives AppleTalk communications, its logical network AppleTalk address is 12.22; when DECnet is sent or received, the logical DECnet address of the Macintosh is 5.2.

Physical Addressing

Another kind of addressing is used often to facilitate the transmission of data over a physical cabling medium. For example, Ethernet uses a unique number to identify each Ethernet device (see figure 4.7). The best example of an Ethernet device is an Ethernet card. Ethernet relies on a unique 48-bit number, where the first 24 bits identify the vendor of the device and the last 24 bits identify the specific device—kind of like a serial number. These numbers are stored permanently inside the Ethernet device. If you swap Ethernet cards with another Macintosh, the physical Ethernet address remains with the card rather than with the Macintosh.

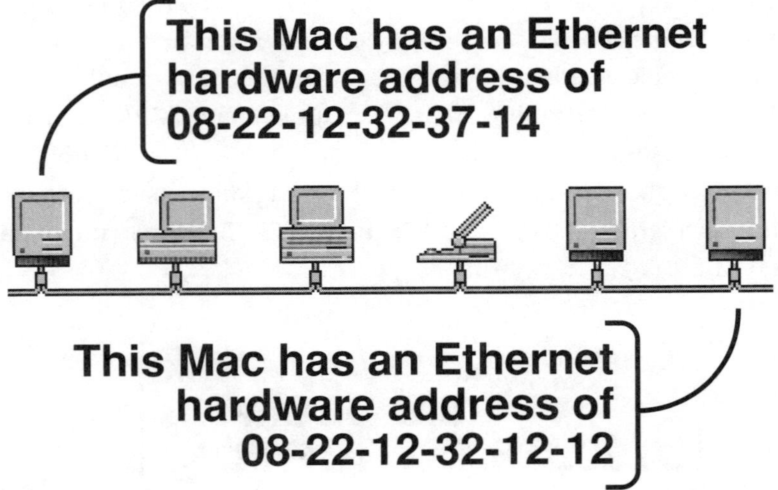

Figure 4.7
Ethernet physical addressing.

With Ethernet, access to the cable and communications over that cable are controlled by the physical Ethernet addresses. Each networking protocol is responsible for equating its protocol-specific logical address to the Ethernet physical address that is present.

So, going back to our example of a Macintosh running three different protocols (AppleTalk, DECnet, and TCP/IP), each protocol has a different logical identification number—but all must convert their respective logical addresses to the same Ethernet physical address (see figure 4.8).

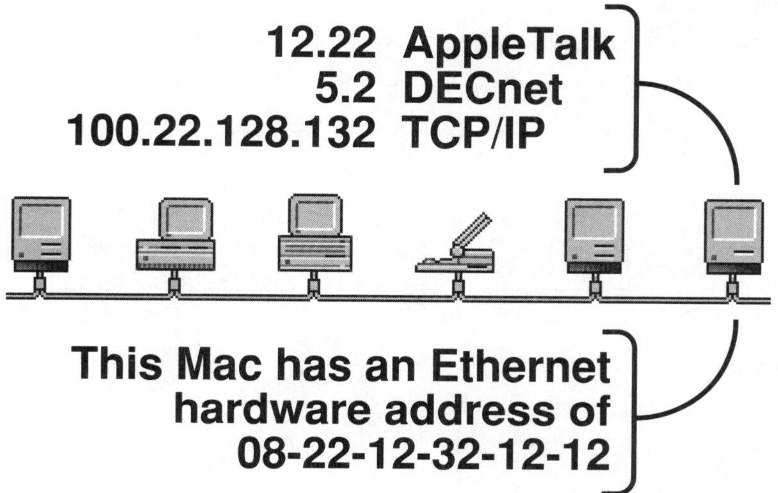

Figure 4.8
Ethernet physical addressing and multiple logical addresses.

TCP/IP uses a special protocol called ARP, which stands for Address Resolution Protocol. It resolves the different logical and physical addresses. AppleTalk uses a similar protocol called the AppleTalk Address Resolution Protocol, or AARP. AARP equates logical AppleTalk addresses with physical Ethernet addresses.

A table containing the AppleTalk addresses, along with their respective Ethernet addresses, is maintained on each Ethernet-equipped Macintosh. This table is known as the Address Mapping Table, or AMT. When a Macintosh needs to send a message to a specific AppleTalk address, the corresponding Ethernet address is determined from the AMT. Then, when the message is sent to the Cabling layer, Ethernet addressing is used to deliver the goods.

Network Frames

Each cabling system (or transmission medium) in a packet-switched network has its own method of conveying or framing information. These network frames act as "delivery trucks" designed for a specific kind of network highway (see figure 4.9).

Figure 4.9

A Network highway.

With Ethernet, a network frame is composed of a number of different components, each with its own function. The first two components are the source and destination of the Ethernet frame (see figure 4.10). These are identified with the unique 48-bit Ethernet hardware addresses. They're similar to the "From" and "To" logical addresses of an AppleTalk DDP datagram.

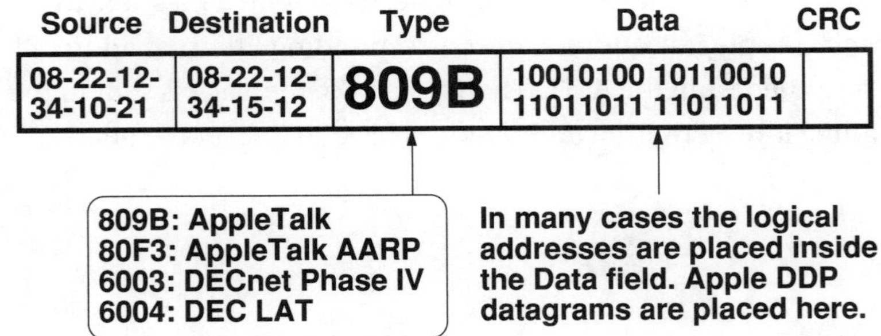

Figure 4.10

Ethernet frame diagram.

The next component is known as the type code. The *type code* uniquely identifies the networking protocol contained within the next component of the frame. Every Ethernet networking protocol has a unique type code. AppleTalk has several type codes, one for plain AppleTalk (809B) and one for AARP (80F3). A DECnet packet has a type code of 6003. Think of the type code as the sign on the side of the truck that identifies the contents held within.

The actual payload is placed within the data section of the Ethernet frame. The data are usually protocol specific. In the case of AppleTalk, the data section is the place where the DDP datagrams are stored. The data section can vary from anywhere between 5 and 1500 bytes in length.

The last component is used for error checking. A special algorithm known as a *cyclic redundancy check* is used to ensure that no transmission errors have corrupted the data.

NOTE: Because most networking frames can support multiple protocols, it's important to remember that networks, such as Ethernet and Token Ring, were designed to support multiple protocols. Therefore, it's not mandatory to restrict your network to a single protocol.

Network Signaling

When binary signals are finally sent to the Cabling layer for transmission, the software that generates the binary communications data must now interact with the "real," physical world. While a complete explanation of the physical laws and the electronics involved with these network communications is beyond the scope of this book, an introduction to the basic concepts will help you understand the capabilities and limitations of the network.

A good starting point is the concept of network speed. Ethernet is not "faster" than LocalTalk. All electrical signals travel at speeds close to the speed of light (approximately 80% of it). In order to transmit digital, or any kind of data, with electromagnetic signals, there are a limited number of choices available.

One way is to vary the *amplitude*, or strength, of the signal as time progresses. By changing (*modulating*) the amplitude, the ones and zeros of the binary data can be represented by different voltage levels (see figure 4.11). Actually, amplitude modulation was the basis for the very first radio signals; AM radio still works this way today. With AM radio, though, the source of the transmission is not digital, but analog.

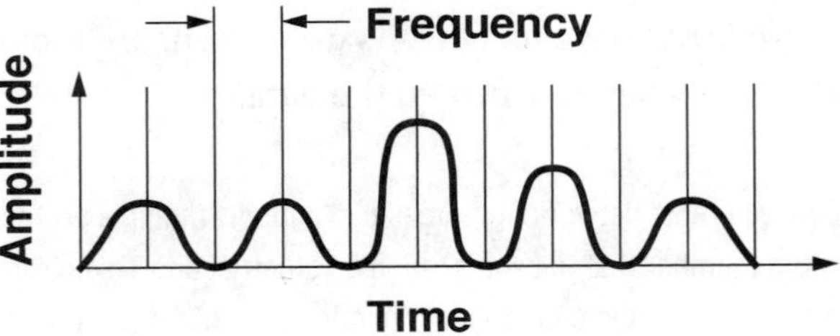

Figure 4.11 With amplitude modulation, the amplitude, or strength, of the signal varies with time. The frequency remains constant.

Another technique is to vary the frequency of the signal with time. Instead of changing the amplitude or voltage, ones and zeros are represented by shifts in frequency (see figure 4.12). This technique, known as *Frequency Modulation*, is a much more efficient and reliable way to transmit data. Just compare the broadcast quality of AM and FM radio stations and you'll begin to get the idea.

In fact, radio and television stations are a good way to describe the signaling behind computer networking. The network cable, be it LocalTalk, Ethernet, or Token Ring, has many similarities to a radio or TV broadcast.

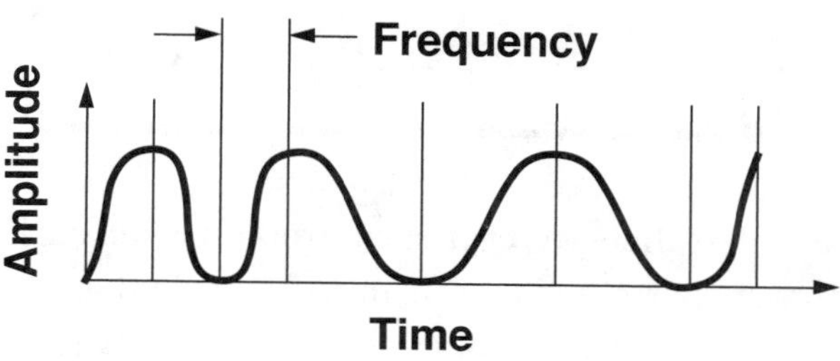

Figure 4.12
With frequency modulation, the amplitude of the signal remains constant. The frequency (the distance between the peaks and valleys) varies with time to encode the signal.

With radio and television, each station broadcasts over a specific frequency. All these different frequencies are being used simultaneously to carry the hundreds of programs that you can watch or hear. All that's required is to tune in to the appropriate frequency with the appropriate receiver.

In computer networking, this kind of multi-channel access is often referred to as *broadband networking*. Broadband networks are common in campus environments and large corporate environments where multiple communication channels are required (see figure 4.13).

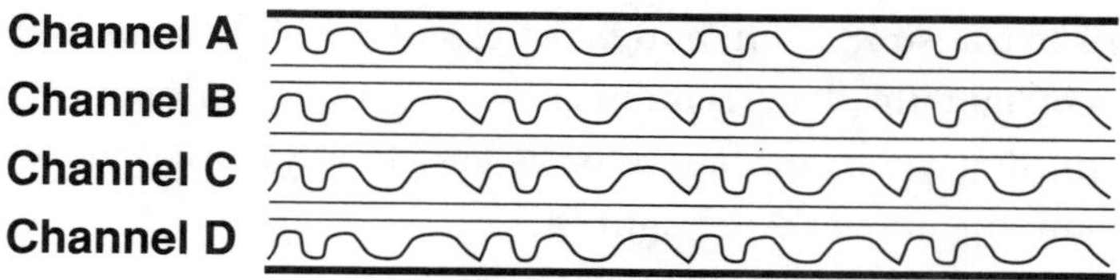

Figure 4.13
Broadband communication uses multiple channels on one signalling medium.

Most computer networks, particularly local-area networks, use a single channel technique known as *baseband networking* (see figure 4.14). To compare it to radio and television broadcasting, it's as if each station were communicating over the same frequency or channel.

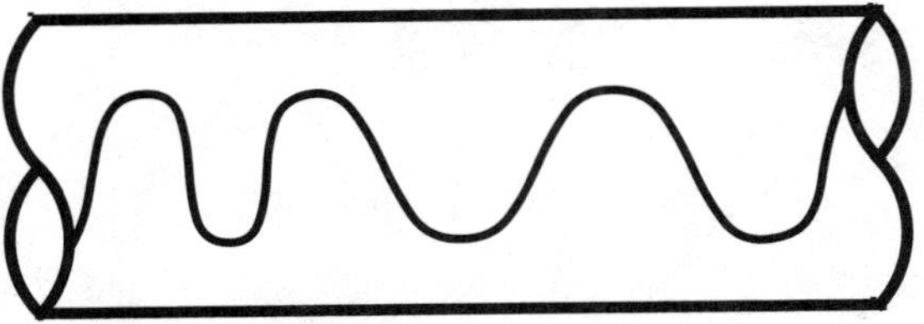

Figure 4.14
Baseband communication uses one channel to transmit information.

Of course, unless there were strict controls on when each radio and TV station were permitted to transmit, the single shared channel would be a garbled mess of colliding and interfering transmissions.

Such is the problem confronted by the designers of modern network cabling systems—how best to share the common carrier and maximize throughput. Ethernet and Token Ring exemplify two of the more popular approaches to solve this problem.

With Ethernet, the solution is to play a statistical game of listen and wait. When an Ethernet node has to send a message, it first "listens" to the network. If another station is transmitting a message, it waits until another check indicates that the channel is clear. If the channel is clear, the Ethernet station begins to transmit. The major problem with this technique is one of timing. Station A can start to transmit, but its signal might not reach Station B before Station B begins to transmit. Even though the signal travels at close to the speed of light, the delay is often enough to fool a station into transmitting when another message has already started to make its way onto the network (see figure 4.15).

When this happens on an Ethernet network, it's called a *collision.* Fortunately, the Ethernet hardware can handle and recover from these collisions. When they occur, the messages are retransmitted after a short waiting period.

One of the side effects of this collision detection technique is that the actual throughput of heavily loaded Ethernet networks will begin to degrade as the number of collisions and retransmits begins to increase.

Figure 4.15
Ethernet collisions.

To compare Ethernet networking to our radio and TV example, imagine that all the radio and TV stations share a common frequency or channel. Before transmitting, each station turns on a radio or TV to check if anyone else is transmitting. If the channel is unused, the station begins to transmit for a specific period of time.

Occasionally, two stations might start to transmit at roughly the same time, and the airwaves become garbled. But shortly after you hear a burst of static or the TV screen goes fuzzy, special circuitry kicks in, transmits the first signal, and stores the second signal for subsequent playback (see figure 4.16). Of course, as more and more stations are added, the static bursts and interruptions become more frequent, until it reaches a point where there's simply too much traffic—the listeners are getting more static than programming.

With Token Ring, the technique is a bit different. Each station can transmit for a specific period of time. The time period is determined by a *token* that gets sent around to each of the stations.

When a station possesses the token, then—and only then—is it allowed to transmit. It's kind of like the hall pass in Junior High School that establishes shared use of the rest rooms.

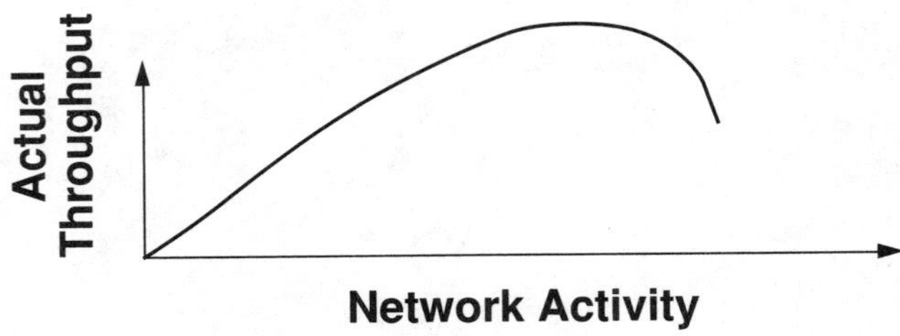

Figure 4.16 As the level of traffic increases on an Ethernet network, a point is reached where actual throughput is optimized. Eventually, as activity increases, throughput degrades.

Unlike Ethernet, it's not necessary to "listen" to the network before transmitting. A welcome side benefit is that the network performance doesn't degrade when it's pushed to the limit. With Token Ring, as more and more stations are added to the network, a point of equilibrium is reached where the network will continue to deliver its maximum throughput although each station may have to wait a correspondingly longer period of time before transmitting.

With our radio and TV analogy, Token Ring networking is made very simple. Each station is allowed to transmit only at specific times and only for so long. Every station transmits in turn and every station is assured of access to airwaves (see figure 4.17). As new stations are added, the time between a given station's transmission sessions may increase, but at least the listeners won't be bothered with interruptions and static.

LocalTalk uses a "wait and listen" approach similar to that of Ethernet. With Ethernet, this access method is called CSMA/CD. It stands for Carrier Sense (check for carrier before transmission)

Multiple Access (a number of nodes can use the cable at one time) Collision Detection (there's special circuitry built into the Ethernet controller that detects and recovers from collisions).

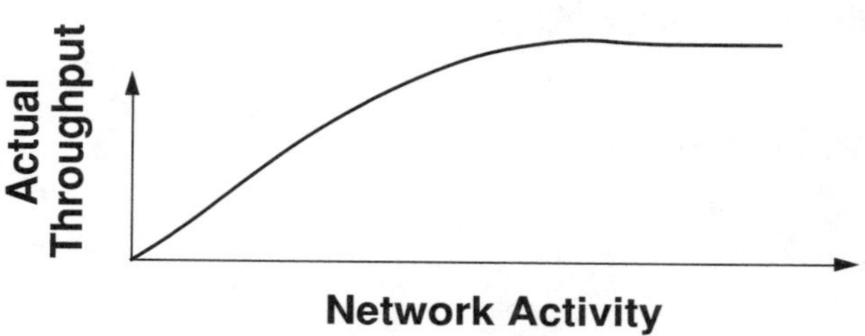

Figure 4.17
As the level of traffic increases on a Token Ring network, the throughput reaches a stable point and remains constant. Unlike Ethernet, no degredation is seen.

In order to get the cost down, Apple omitted the extra components required to detect and recover from collisions. Instead, LocalTalk tries its best to avoid collisions by waiting random periods of time. If any garbling occurs, the signal is retransmitted by the higher-level AppleTalk protocols. This technique is called CSMA/CA, where the CA stands for Collision Avoidance.

Conclusion

The fundamentals of networking can be described by the four basic layers, but certain aspects of networking require additional explanation. These technical aspects can also be easily explained using convenient and common metaphors.

The basis for most computer networking is the technique of packet switching. Discrete packets of data are sent over the networking medium from the sender to the recipient. These devices must be identified, and that is the reason for a network addressing scheme.

Depending on the physics of the cabling system, different electronic access methods must be used. Ethernet is an example of a delivery mechanism that detects for the presence of a signal, listens for traffic, and then begins to transmit. Other cabling systems, such as Token Ring, parse the available bandwidth by specifying a specific period for transmission.

Common Network Components

5

The networking industry is full of terms and buzzwords that are confusing and often misleading. Using NetPICTs, this chapter unambiguously defines and depicts common Macintosh networking components such as bridges, repeaters, and gateways. Once these basic components are defined, they will be placed in the context of various networking topologies. These various topologies and networking implementations, such as Local Area Networks and Wide Area Networks, will be discussed in Chapter 5.

LANs & WANs

LAN and WAN are acronyms, respectively standing for Local Area Network and Wide Area Network. Distance is the major difference between the two. *LANs* are usually confined to a single building or a group of buildings in the same general vicinity. When multiple buildings are involved, it's common to have a LAN network segment in each building. These segments are often connected with other segments. Underground fiber optic cable is frequently used to connect the segments.

WANs are interconnected networks that span wide geographic areas. Basically, this means distances greater than what can be supported by a LAN. While there are no definite rules, WAN distances are generally measured in miles and LAN distances are usually measured in feet.

Typically, WAN connections have a limited bandwidth when compared to LAN connections. This limitation might be one or two orders of magnitude. For example, an Ethernet network has a maximum capacity of 10 million bits per second, or 10 Mbps. T1, a popular WAN carrier, has a bandwidth of 1.544 Mbps. In this case, the Ethernet network has roughly 6 1/2 times the bandwidth of the T1 link.

WAN links, such as T1, can be very expensive. These connections are usually leased by phone companies or other service providers and may cost several thousand dollars per month to maintain. Clearly, optimization and rational use of these WAN resources is important. Later on, we'll discuss the specific issues and problems with AppleTalk protocols on wide-area networks.

Repeaters

Repeaters are the simplest of networking devices. They exist at the very bottom of the stack, functioning at the Cabling layer—the Physical layer of the OSI Reference Model (see figure 5.1). At this layer, the repeater is entirely ignorant of the higher-level protocols, such as AppleTalk. Repeaters only deal with the electrical signals that exist at the Cabling layer. As such, repeaters are often referred to as being *protocol transparent*.

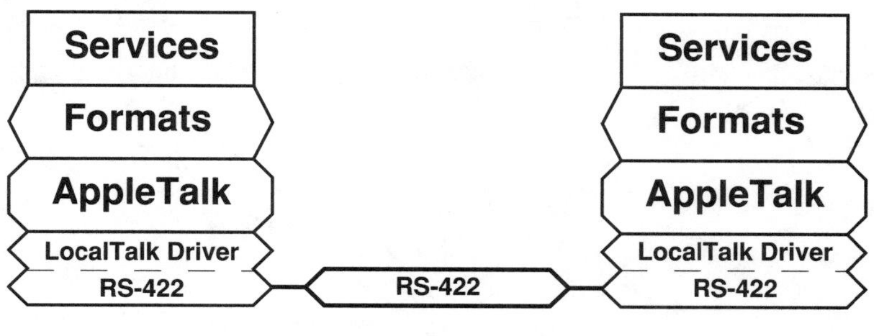

Figure 5.1
NetPICT of a LocalTalk repeater.

Repeaters are essentially signal boosters that amplify weakened incoming signals, thus extending the effective range of a cable. Since repeaters are "dumb" devices, they also will amplify noise or any unwanted signals that might find their way onto your network.

LocalTalk Repeaters

There are a number of LocalTalk repeaters on the market. Some of them, such as Farallon's PhoneNET Repeater, simply extend single segments of PhoneNET/LocalTalk. Other repeaters (for example, Farallon's StarController) have multiple ports and permit different wiring topologies.

The simplest kind of LocalTalk network is when all the participating devices are connected in a daisy-chain fashion. However, daisy-chaining can create problems for all but the smallest LocalTalk networks.

With daisy-chained networks, the wiring runs from node to node, creating the real possibility of occasional disconnects and disruptions to the network. By using a star or radial topology with a multiport LocalTalk repeater, each branch of the star is independent from the others (see figure 5.2).

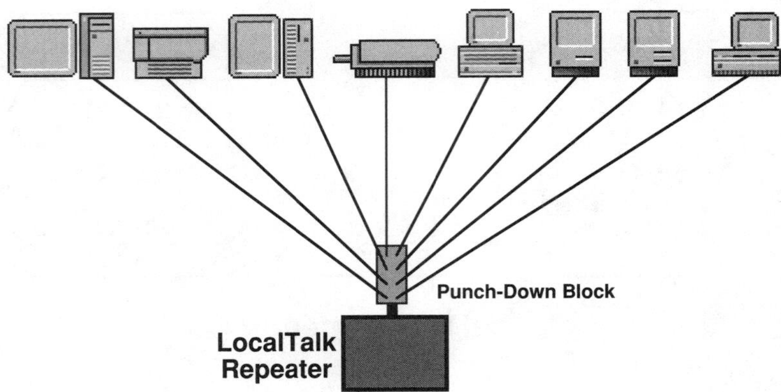

Figure 5.2
Radial repeater topology.

Think of repeaters as wiring conveniences. They do not filter or limit network traffic in any way. The same signal and network traffic is seen on all ports of the device.

It is possible to construct very large LocalTalk networks by interconnecting repeaters, but problems often occur as the available bandwidth is still being shared across all wiring segments. At some point, the limited bandwidth of LocalTalk simply cannot support the traffic that's routinely generated by an AppleTalk network. So, it's best to limit the use of LocalTalk repeaters to extending that extra long run for the people in the shipping department, and to break away from the nasty habit of daisy-chaining.

Ethernet Repeaters

Like their LocalTalk cousins, Ethernet repeaters are protocol-transparent wiring conveniences. Like the multiport LocalTalk repeater (such as Farallon's StarController and Focus's TurboStar), Ethernet repeaters let you avoid the daisy-chain network. There are Ethernet repeaters for all flavors of Ethernet cabling: thick, thin, and twisted-pair (see figure 5.3).

In fact, with twisted-pair Ethernet (otherwise known as 10Base-T) repeaters or hubs are mandatory. All 10Base-T connections are made through a hub.

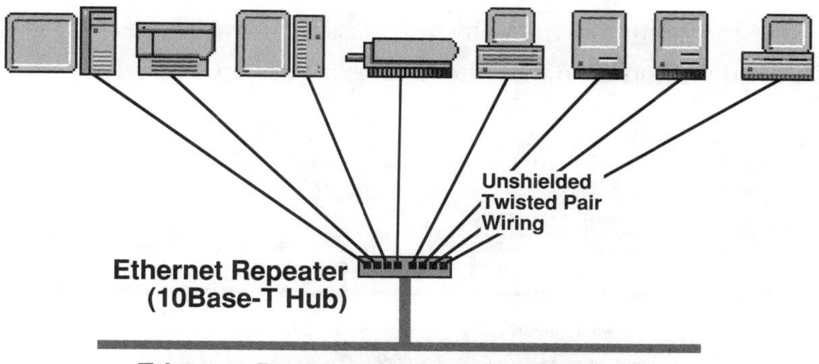

Figure 5.3

Ethernet repeater.

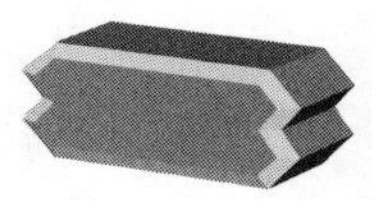

Bridges

Bridges function at the upper Cabling layer, or the Data Link layer of the OSI Model. They are one step higher than repeaters on the network evolutionary scale.

Bridges use the layer that connects a specific networking protocol to a specific cabling system. Because they function one layer higher than repeaters, and thus know about physical hardware addresses or cable-specific addressing, bridges are often able to use these addresses to optimize traffic (see figure 5.4).

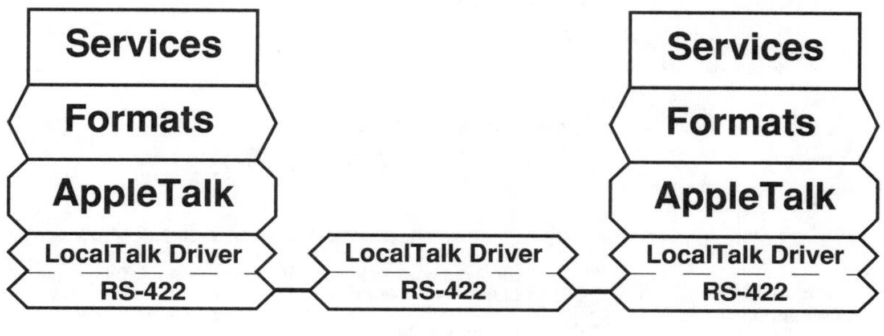

Figure 5.4

Bridge NetPICT.

Bridges can examine the source and destination of network frames and maintain a listing of which nodes are on which port. Then, the bridge can minimize traffic by only passing those frames that are destined for nodes on the other side (see figure 5.5).

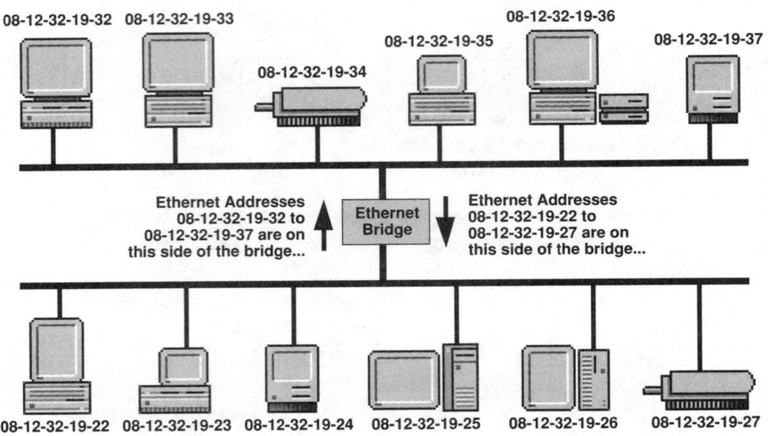

Figure 5.5
Ethernet bridges.

Like repeaters, bridges are often used to extend a particular type of network. Unlike repeaters, some bridges also can use the cabling-specific information to filter packets based on their protocol type.

Certain Ethernet bridges are capable of examining the Ethernet Type Code of a frame. These bridges also can be programmed to pass or block a network frame based on the Type Code. These bridges are often referred to as *filtering bridges* (see figure 5.6).

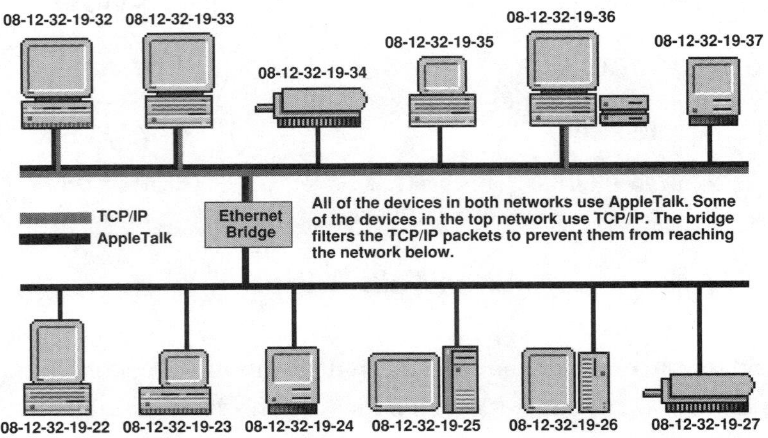

Figure 5.6
Ethernet bridge filtering.

Remember, bridges are cable-specific and, like repeaters, are essentially protocol-transparent. Bridges don't inspect the datagram to see the logical address data. They can only infer, as in the case of Ethernet Type Codes, the networking protocol contained within.

LocalTalk Bridges

At this time, there is only one LocalTalk-specific bridge. Tribe's LocalSwitch uses the LocalTalk-specific node number to keep track of node locations. It then uses these numbers to limit traffic to only those segments containing the valid nodes.

For example, if segment A of the Tribe bridge has LocalTalk nodes 1 and 2, and segment B has nodes 3 and 4, then whenever nodes 1 and 2 communicate, the resultant traffic will only be seen on segment A and not on segment B.

Ethernet Bridges

Historically, Ethernet bridges have been used to interconnect large corporations and organizations over long distances. By using bridges that connect to Ethernet on one side and wide-area network services on the other, organizations easily could connect two geographically remote Ethernet LANs and make them appear as a single connected entity (see figure 5.7).

Unless some form of packet or frame filtering is employed, these devices logically connect the segments. Certain types of traffic seen on one segment will eventually be seen on the other segment. Of course, if the traffic represents frames destined for the other side, this makes sense. All too often, however, the traffic seen on one side of the bridge is local and is not destined for the other side. This unwanted passage of traffic particularly creates problems when the interconnection between the two networks is at a restricted bandwidth. This often creates a bottleneck between the higher bandwidth of the LANs.

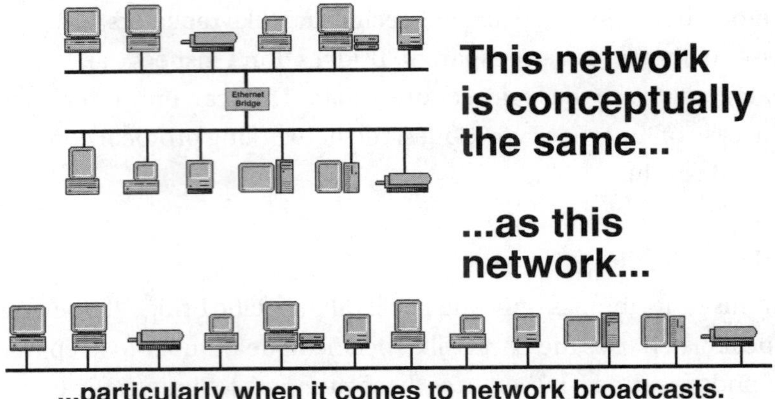

Figure 5.7
One big Ethernet.

For example, it is a common practice to connect two Ethernet LANs with a leased telephone line, with a bandwidth of 56 Kbps. Considering that Ethernet has a bandwidth of 10 Mbps, it's like having a 179-lane freeway being reduced to a single lane of traffic (see figure 5.8).

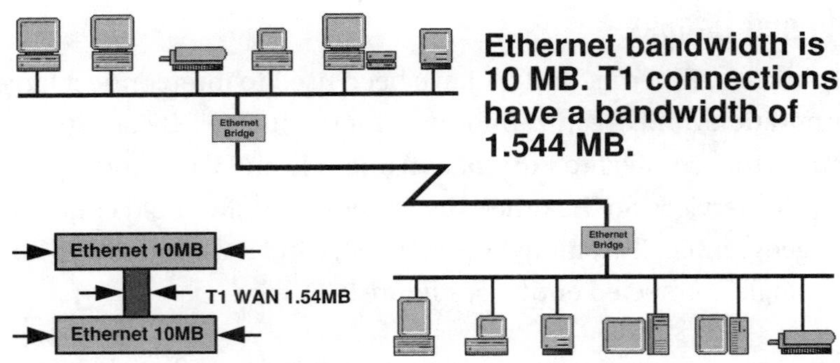

Figure 5.8
WAN bottleneck.

Therefore, if you're using wide-area bridges over modest bandwidth connections, it's very important to keep unwanted or unneeded traffic to a minimum. This shortcoming, inherent with wide-area network bridges, is one reason why the wide-area router is fast replacing the bridge as the wide-area network device of choice.

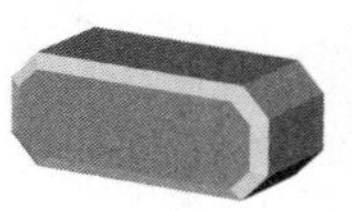

Routers & Brouters

Routers do their work at the Protocol layer, inspecting the source and the destination of a specific protocol's datagram. Routers, like the children passing notes in the classroom, make decisions on how best to route messages based on the source and destination address. This is fundamentally different from bridges, which process network frames without regard to the networking protocol contained within.

Because routers operate at the Protocol layer, they are often referred to as being protocol-specific. There are AppleTalk routers, DECnet routers, TCP/IP routers, and Novell routers. There are even routers that can route multiple protocols concurrently.

Each connection on a router is called a *port* (see figure 5.9). These ports may be the same cabling type, or they may be different. For example, there are many AppleTalk routers that have a LocalTalk port and an Ethernet port.

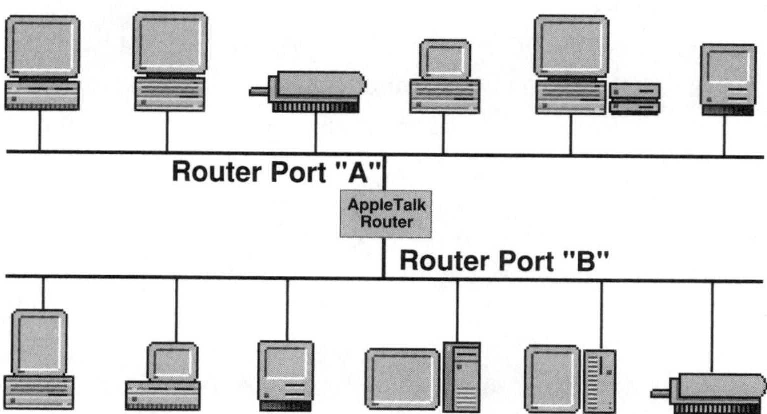

Figure 5.9
Ports of a router.

Because of this, it is often assumed that these devices are simply used to connect a LocalTalk network to an Ethernet network. In addition to providing this basic cable conversion, as shown in figure 5.10, routers also possess a special capability. Routers can be used to isolate traffic.

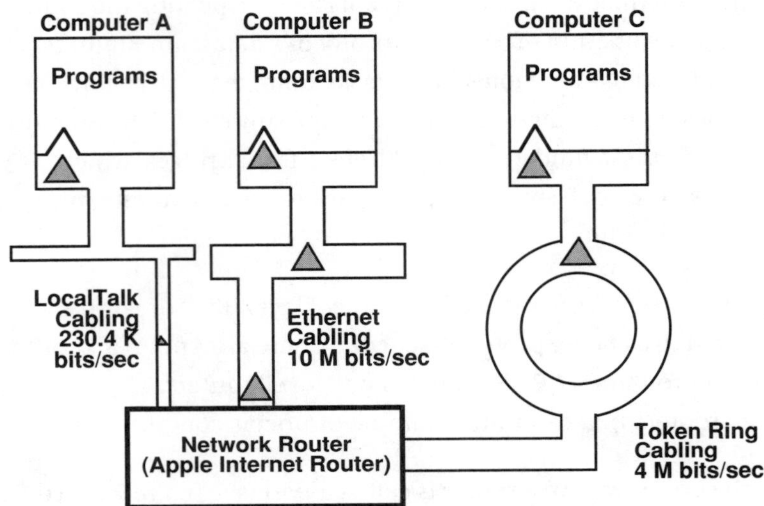

Figure 5.10
Routers connecting multiple cable types.

Similar to the filtering bridges mentioned before, routers are able to keep local traffic local. For example, if a Macintosh and a LaserWriter are connected to a network on port A, the network traffic generated between these two devices will be limited to that network (see figure 5.11). The router will forward a datagram to another network only if the destination of the datagram is on that network.

So, routers perform two basic functions. They provide a fundamental way to connect one network to another, and they effectively isolate network traffic.

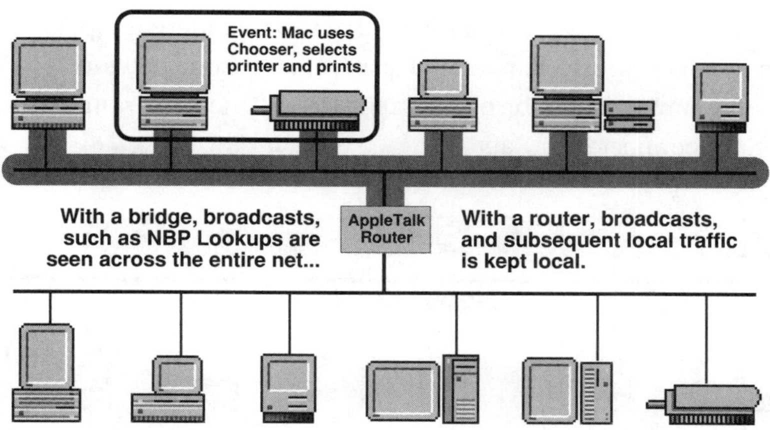

Figure 5.11
Network traffic isolation with routers.

AppleTalk Routers

What started in 1985 with the Kinetics FastPath has evolved into a crowded and competitive market with dozens of AppleTalk routers. While these routers support different cabling choices, unique configuration software, and value-added options, every AppleTalk router works on the same basic principles. All AppleTalk routers use AppleTalk network numbers to differentiate their ports. In fact, for most AppleTalk networks, the network numbers originate in the router.

Let's use a simple example of two LocalTalk networks connected by a two-port LocalTalk-to-LocalTalk AppleTalk router. In this example, we've used the configuration software that came with the router and established unique network numbers for each of the ports. It's crucial that each network number be unique. This can be a challenge for a very large network. With large networks, it's necessary to plan and administer AppleTalk network numbers. If an AppleTalk network number is duplicated anywhere on the collective network, unpredictable results may occur.

AppleTalk routers can be connected in several different topologies. They can be arranged in a serial fashion, where one network is simply connected to the other. In Figure 5.12, network number 2 is serially connected to 1 and 3.

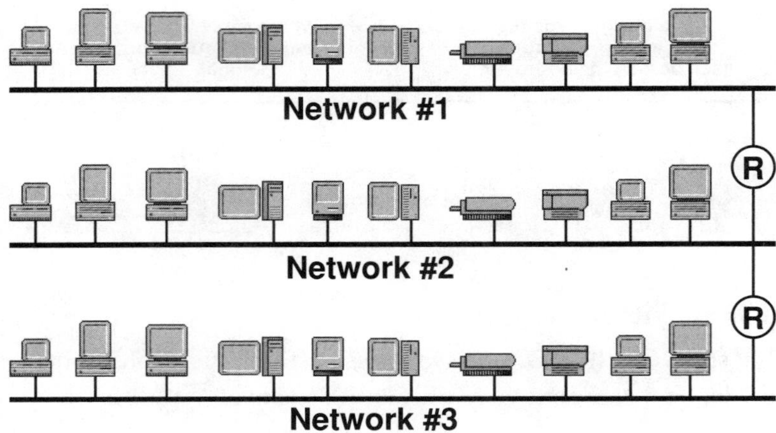

Figure 5.12 Three serially connected AppleTalk networks.

Therefore, in order for an AppleTalk datagram to travel from network 1 to network 3, it must go through two routers. Each time a datagram passes through a router, it is called a *hop*. A hop is a unit of measurement that is used to measure the distance between the sender and recipient. AppleTalk has a maximum hop count of 15.

Using serially connected routers to build large AppleTalk networks can be problematic because every time a datagram travels through a router, it must inspect the network address, which takes a certain amount of time. In a large serially-routed network, these delays accumulate. Another problem with this topology is that networks that are located between the sender and recipient have to deal with all the network traffic.

A better way to build large AppleTalk networks is to use a backbone topology (see figure 5.13). Here, a common backbone network acts like a common network that connects a number of routers. With this topology, no network is more than two hops away. Backbone topologies are very common in large AppleTalk networks, where the backbone is often an Ethernet network and the routers are used to connect a number of LocalTalk networks to the backbone.

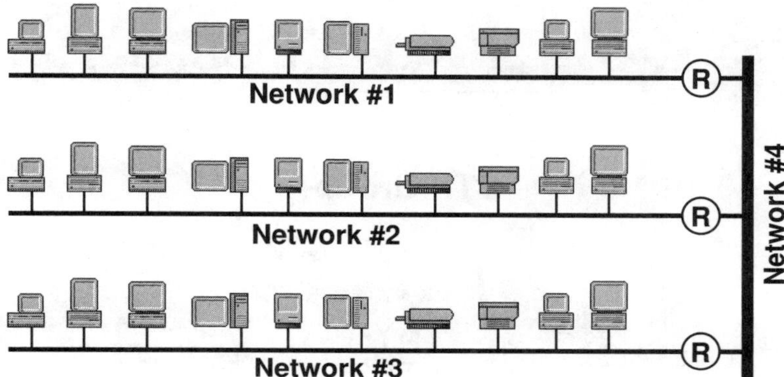

Figure 5.13
Three AppleTalk networks on a backbone.

As the cost of Ethernet connections continue to plummet, and since Apple now offers computers and printers with built-in Ethernet connections, LocalTalk networks and routers are becoming less popular. Instead, Ethernet-to-Ethernet routers are beginning to displace the sales of LocalTalk-to-Ethernet routers. These routers are not used to connect dissimilar cabling; the goal is simply to isolate network traffic.

For many networks, routers provide a convenient way to isolate areas of high network traffic. Let's use the example of an organization with an Ethernet backbone. Each department within the organization has its own Macintosh computers and LaserWriter printers connected to the Ethernet. The desktop publishing group is continually taxing the network with demanding print jobs and the transfer of large image files. The other departments and users have started to complain about poor network performance. One way to alleviate the problem is to place the DTP group on a separate Ethernet, connected to the primary network with an Ethernet-to-Ethernet router (see figure 5.14). With this approach, the extensive traffic associated with the DTP group will be kept to its own network.

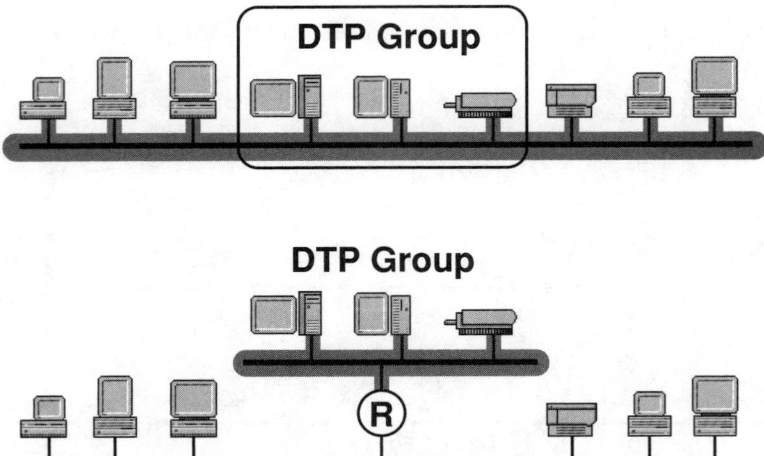

Figure 5.14
Ethernet to Ethernet solution.

The network numbers maintained by the routers are the primary determinants of an AppleTalk network. As mentioned before, the network numbers are used by the AppleTalk software to assist with the routing of datagrams. The problem with network numbers is that they're not the best way for users to locate network services.

To help users find services, Apple devised a way to associate names with networks. These names are called *zones.* AppleTalk zone names are stored in the router along with the network numbers. Unlike AppleTalk network numbers, which must be unique, AppleTalk zone names can be duplicated throughout the network. This feature makes it possible to organize network services in logical groups.

As an example, imagine a ten-story building with a backbone Ethernet running up through the building. In the wiring closet of each floor, a LocalTalk-to-Ethernet AppleTalk router is used to connect a number of Macs and LaserWriters to the backbone. Each LocalTalk network has a unique network number and a zone name. The LocalTalk network on the first floor is network number 1, and the zone name is "1st Floor."

The Ethernet backbone also carries AppleTalk traffic, and therefore is also considered an AppleTalk network. In this example, the backbone is assigned network number 1000 and given the zone name of "Backbone." This is accomplished by configuring the routers so that all routers agree that the backbone is defined as network 1000 and has the zone name of "Backbone."

Most floors only have a dozen or so devices, so the theoretical limit of 32 LocalTalk devices per network does not matter. But on the tenth floor, there are more than 50 devices that need to be connected to the network. Since this is too many devices to be placed on a single segment of LocalTalk, another LocalTalk segment and router will be required.

Like the other routers, this additional router on the tenth floor must have a unique network number. Since it will be convenient for the users to refer to this new network with the same zone name as the other network, the zone name also will be "10th Floor" (see figure 5.15).

What's interesting about this process of zone grouping is that the AppleTalk protocols will combine all like devices by zone. So, if there were five LaserWriters in each of the two networks on the tenth floor, the Chooser would combine the devices and display a list of ten printers for the "10th Floor" zone.

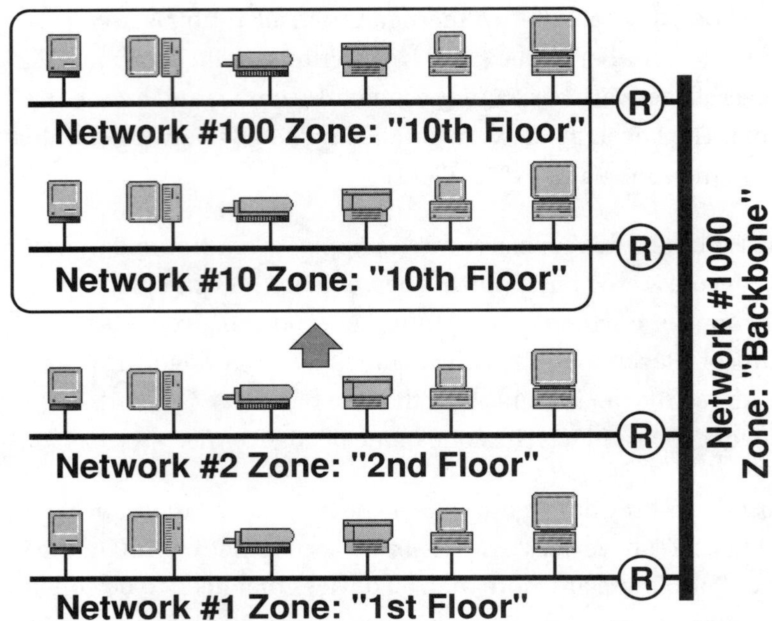

Figure 5.15
Zone grouping.

Multiprotocol Routers & Brouters

Certain routers are capable of routing multiple networking protocols at the same time. These are generally known as *multiprotocol routers.* A good example of such a device is the Shiva FastPath.

The FastPath is a LocalTalk-to-Ethernet AppleTalk router, but in addition to AppleTalk, it can also route DECnet and TCP/IP protocols. A multiprotocol router does not convert one protocol into another; it simply routes each protocol that comes along according to the protocol type.

When the FastPath encounters DECnet datagrams, it routes them in accordance to the DECnet routing rules and configuration data maintained in the router's program and memory. When an AppleTalk datagram appears, it's routed using the AppleTalk rules. It's as if three separate routers—one each for AppleTalk, DECnet and TCP/IP—were merged together as a single unit, sharing their hardware and portions of their configuration software.

With a multiprotocol router, each protocol must be configured separately. So, in order to set up a FastPath to route all three protocols, you must configure each protocol independently using the FastPath Manager application that comes with the router.

While AppleTalk, DECnet and TCP/IP are all different protocols, they do have something in common. They all can be routed. This is because all three protocols utilize the concept that large networks can be broken down into smaller pieces.

With AppleTalk, large networks, called *internetworks*, are subdivided into networks by network numbers. The AppleTalk protocols support more than 65,000 networks, each potentially supporting either 253 or 254 nodes (under Phase 2 or Phase 1 AppleTalk, respectively).

DECnet uses a similar technique where large networks are broken down into areas. DECnet supports a maximum of 64 areas; each area can potentially support 1024 nodes. TCP/IP, like AppleTalk and DECnet, also breaks down large networks into smaller groupings (see figure 5.16).

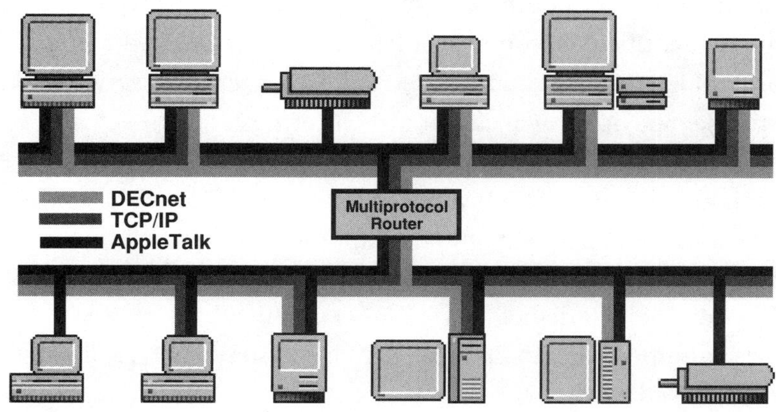

Figure 5.16
Multiprotocol routers.

Each of these protocols utilize numbers that will be used by their respective routers to subdivide large networks. Each subdivision enjoys the benefits of traffic isolation, so that unneeded and undesirable traffic is kept within each subnetwork.

Returning to our analogy of students passing notes in class, imagine that the students form three cliques, and members of each clique never talk to the other cliques. To accommodate the note passing, the students decide that each clique will use a different color of paper for their notes. Also, each clique develops certain rules and idiosyncrasies for passing its notes. Those students who are allowed to pass all three colors of notes know the rules for each clique's notes. For example, the red notes have the last name first and have to be passed with the palm held down; the blue notes are addressed with just initials and have to be transferred within a closed fist.

The students that know all the rules act as multiprotocol routers. Each clique has their own protocol with addressing differences that have to be managed by the routing student. He has to be able to deal with notes that use different protocols in order to send them along to their proper destination.

Some protocols don't use routing numbers at all. These protocols rely on a single monolithic network, with each node having a unique identifier. One such protocol is DEC's Local Area Transport, or LAT. LAT is primarily used to provide terminal services to networked devices, such as "dumb" VT terminals, connected to an Ethernet network with a device known as a terminal server. The terminal server takes the asynchronous communication from the VT terminal and places it onto the Ethernet within a LAT frame. The terminal server is a computer that can direct the LAT traffic to any available host (usually a DEC VAX) on the Ethernet. PCs and Macs equipped with an Ethernet card can also speak LAT directly to networked hosts.

Unlike AppleTalk, DECnet, and TCP/IP, however, LAT was designed to run over a single, logical segment of Ethernet. There is nothing equivalent to a LAT network number or area number. Therefore, LAT is an example of a non-routable protocol. There is no such device as a LAT router—there is no network or area number that the router could use to route datagrams. Since LAT cannot be routed, it is often difficult to expand LAT terminal services beyond the confines of a single Ethernet LAN.

One way that a LAT network can be expanded to another LAN is with a bridge. Since bridges only look at the Cabling layer—and do not care about the protocol-specific datagram information—they can be used to extend an Ethernet and to bridge LAT services between remote Ethernet segments. As mentioned before, Ethernet bridges can be used to essentially create one large Ethernet.

What if we wanted to design a network providing AppleTalk, DECnet, TCP/IP and LAT services to two sites: one in New York City and the other in San Francisco (as in figure 5.17)? Each site has a backbone Ethernet.

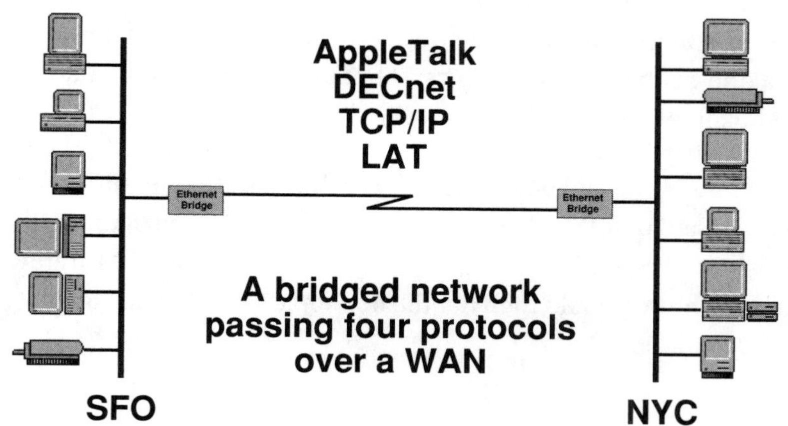

Figure 5.17 NY to SFO with bridged Ethernet.

If we simply connect these two networks using Ethernet bridges and leased telephone lines, everything would work, but we would have essentially created one big Ethernet. All the protocols will freely traverse both networks via the phone lines. This might create a problem. Every time someone prints a document or sends a mail message in New York City, the traffic generated by those activities is sent through the phone lines and reproduced on the San Francisco network. Filtering bridges would help somewhat, by keeping track of what Ethernet devices are on what side of the connection, but certain kinds of traffic (known as *Ethernet broadcasts* or *multicasts*) would still be seen on both sides of the network.

To really solve the problem, a pair of multiprotocol routers could be used to subdivide our AppleTalk, DECnet, and TCP/IP networks into logical segments on each side of the connection. This would effectively isolate any unwanted traffic, preventing it from traversing the expensive and restrictive leased phone lines.

If we simply added the routers in addition to the Ethernet bridges, we would have a problem (see figure 5.18). The AppleTalk, DECnet, and TCP/IP traffic would still be able to sneak through the bridge and get to the other side. We simply can't do away with the bridge because that's how LAT is getting to the other side. And since LAT is a non-routable protocol, it can't be routed through the multiprotocol router.

One solution would be to configure each bridge to filter out and ignore the AppleTalk, DECnet, and TCP/IP traffic (see figure 5.19). This would essentially limit the bridge to only carrying LAT traffic, and the router would then handle the AppleTalk, DECnet, and TCP/IP traffic.

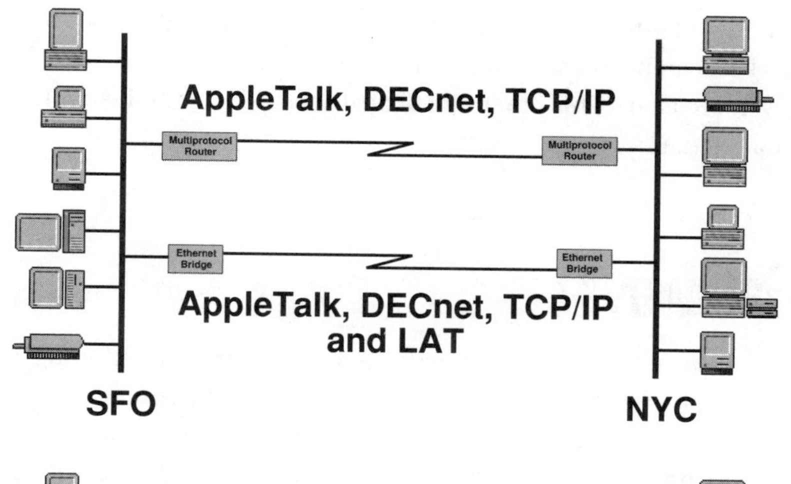

Figure 5.18 The router is passing AppleTalk, DECnet, and TCP/IP, but so is the bridge.

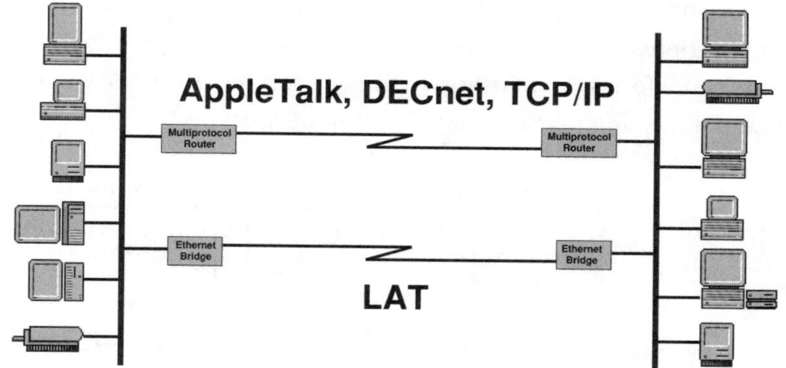

Figure 5.19 AppleTalk, DECnet, and TCP/IP are filtered at the bridges.

Router manufacturers, in an attempt to solve this problem, have designed hybrid routers and bridges. These devices, sometimes referred to as *brouters,* route all the routable protocols and bridge the non-routable protocols. Most of the high-end routers (such as Cisco and Wellfleet) can be set to act as multiprotocol brouters.

Another approach to solve this problem is to place the non-routable protocol inside another protocol that can be routed. This general practice is called *tunneling,* and can be used to solve a number of different problems in addition to LAT. AppleTalk packets can be tunneled inside DECnet and TCP/IP packets for several reasons. This practice will be discussed later in the book in more detail.

Gateways

Gateways are the most complex of network devices, functioning at the upper-most layers where the format of the data comes into play (see figure 5.20). Simply put, gateways provide translation services on the network. They can be used to connect different kinds of network cabling, but most important is that gateways convert the format in addition to the networking protocol. Gateways are the language translators of the network.

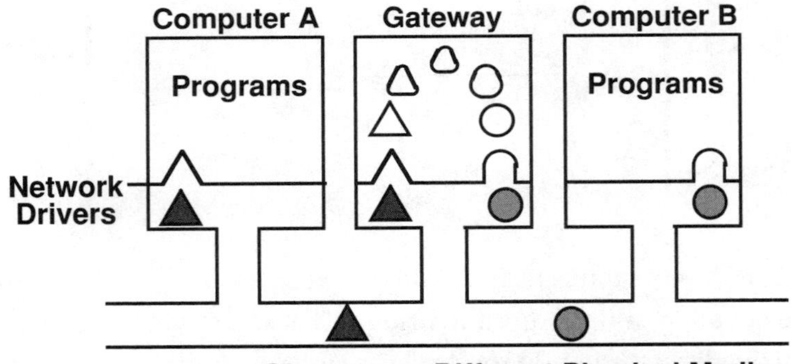

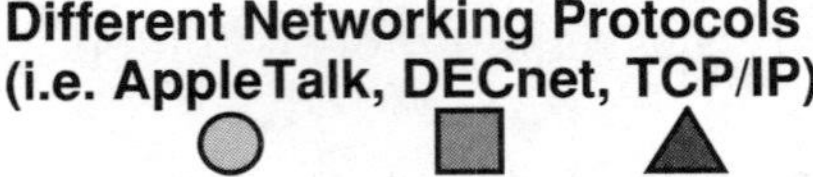

Figure 5.20
Gateway theory.

Since gateways build upon the bottom two layers, it's common that most gateways also function as multiprotocol routers. Some gateways can even be exclusively set up as routers, thus ignoring their higher-level conversion capabilities.

The main advantage and purpose of gateways is to provide a centralized alternative to placing a "foreign" transport and service on your client computers.

AppleTalk Gateways

Suppose you needed to connect a Macintosh to a UNIX-based workstation, perhaps to share files. One approach would be to simply equip your Macintosh with the TCP/IP protocol stack, and then choose a file service that works in concert with TCP/IP, such as NFS (Network Filing System).

Once equipped, the Macintosh would match the UNIX workstation at all layers, and therefore would be able to transfer files. Of course, the other solution would be to equip the UNIX machine with AppleTalk and its file sharing software, AFP (Apple Filing Protocol).

But, if we wanted to stick with TCP/IP and NFS on the UNIX machine, we would still have another option. With an AFP-AppleTalk/NFS-TCP/IP gateway, the Macintosh would use the gateway to convert AFP and AppleTalk protocols into corresponding NFS and TCP/IP protocols.

To the Macintosh, the AFP-AppleTalk side of the gateway looks like any AFP or AppleShare file server. To the UNIX workstation, the NFS-TCP/IP side of the gateway looks like an NFS client. The gateway handles the complete conversion between the different filing systems and network protocols (see figure 5.21).

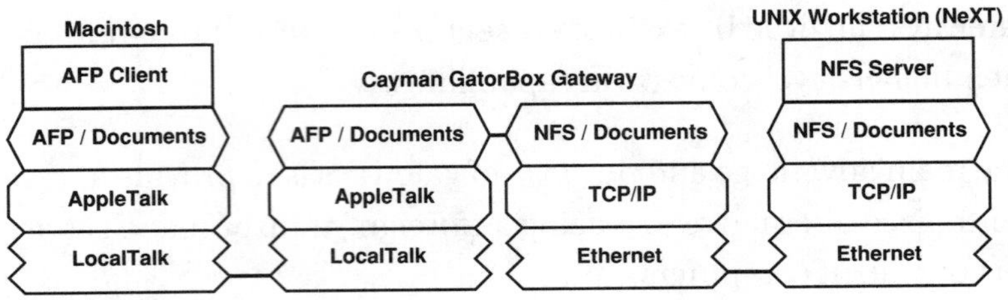

Figure 5.21
NetPICT of NFS gateway (Cayman Gatorbox).

One appeal of a gateway is that no special software is required on either the client or the server. The gateway performs all necessary functions. This approach may not be as fast as placing the same native protocols on each machine, but it can be a simple and cost effective way to share dissimilar network services. There are several different kinds of gateways for the Macintosh. In addition to the AFP/NFS gateways, which are available from several vendors, there are AppleTalk gateways that work other protocols as well.

In DEC's PATHWORKS for Macintosh product, there are two such gateways. One gateway is the AppleTalk-DECnet gateway. This gateway runs on the VAX, in conjunction with AppleTalk for VMS and its native DECnet. Macintosh services, such as DEC's All-In-1 Mail for Macintosh, can use the AppleTalk protocol to communicate with the VAX. However, DEC's mail server doesn't communicate over the AppleTalk for VMS protocol stack—it uses DECnet. So the gateway converts the protocol and service calls from AppleTalk to the corresponding DECnet calls (see figure 5.22).

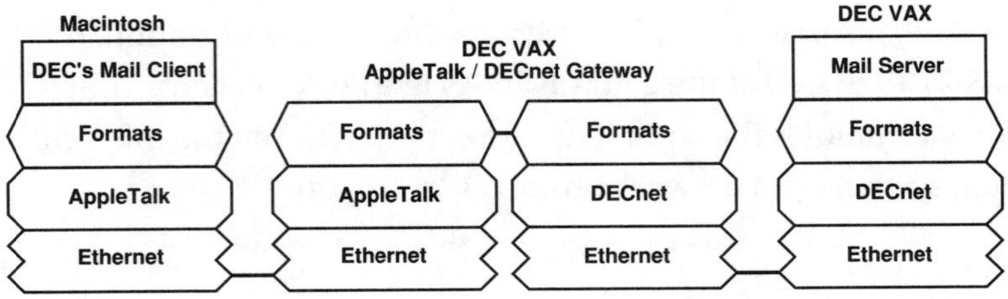

Figure 5.22
NetPICT of AppleTalk/DECnet gateway.

The other PATHWORKS for Mac gateway is the AppleTalk LAT Gateway (see figure 5.23). It enables LocalTalk-equipped Macs (or any non-Ethernet resident Macs, such as dial-in AppleTalk Remote Access Macs) to access LAT-based terminal services. This gateway runs in the background of an Ethernet-resident Macintosh. Client Macs use the AppleTalk-LAT tool to connect to the gateway; the gateway takes the incoming AppleTalk data, converts it to LAT, and sends it out over the Ethernet.

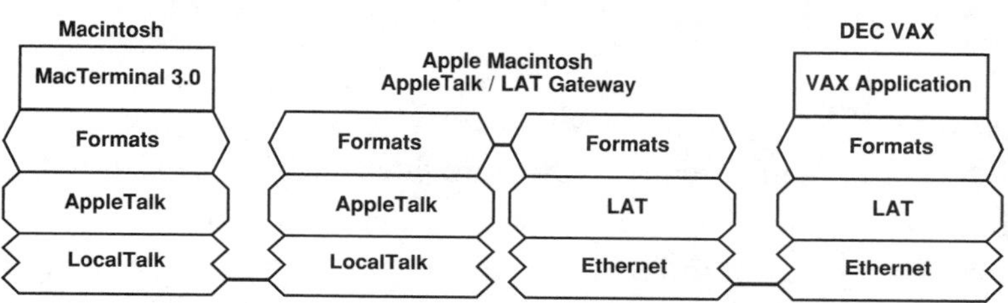

Figure 5.23
AppleTalk/LAT gateway.

In all these examples, one protocol has been converted and transformed into another. To help with the basic idea behind gateways, let's return to the analogy of students passing notes in a classroom. Before, we discussed how packet-switched networks could be likened to students passing notes in a classroom. When a student looks at the "To" and "From" on the note and passes the note along, she is essentially performing the function of a router. But let's imagine a situation where one of the students, Sonia, can only understand Polish and does not understand English.

For Sonia to communicate with the other students, she can learn English, or the other students can learn Polish. Until this happens, however, Sonia must rely on a gateway. Her sister, Patrizia, understands both Polish and English. Notes that are sent to Sonia must first be sent to Patrizia, who converts the English to Polish, and then passes the note to Sonia. When Sonia sends a note to one of the other students, Patrizia reverses the process and converts the Polish into English.

In this brief example, we can see the difference between a router and a gateway. Those students who merely passed the notes along acted as routers. Patrizia, who converted from one format to another, acted as a gateway for Sonia.

Miscellaneous: Hubs, Concentrators, and So Forth

Hubs and *concentrators* are wiring conveniences that essentially perform the same function—they provide a central attachment point for network devices. Unless they incorporate bridges or routers, they do not interact with the networking addressing or protocols in any way. Most large network installations employ some sort of network concentrators in order to implement a radial or star wiring topology. The specifics of the various networking topologies will be covered in the next section.

Usually, network hubs and concentrators are installed in a standard 19-inch rack. These racks are standardized metal frames that hold electronic equipment and permit easy access and maintenance. Often, other networking components (such as modems, bridges, routers, and gateways) are also stored in the rack with the concentrator. This makes it easy to interconnect the LAN with the desired devices.

Many hubs and concentrators come with diagnostic software that assists with the management of network devices and performs fault diagnosis. This software should not be confused with the protocol-specific configuration software that comes with routers and gateways. Instead, this software is often able to turn on and off the concentrator's ports, perform line quality checks, and even perform rudimentary traffic analysis.

Network Topologies

One topic that's covered in all networking books is topology. The topology of a network is simply the form and sequence of connections. The topology does not depend on the kind of wiring or protocols used. There are several different kinds of networking topologies, each with their own benefits and disadvantages, and these can be combined to create hybrid networks.

Daisy Chain

One of the simplest network topologies is the daisy chain. As the name implies, a *daisy-chain* network is created by simply connecting one node to the next. Perhaps the best example of a daisy-chain network is LocalTalk.

With LocalTalk cabling, the connections are made with segments of wire, in a serial fashion—one after the other (see figure 5.24). Daisy-chained networks are fine for small workgroups where the wires can be conveniently routed. The problem with daisy chaining is that the entire network can be easily severed and disrupted if the cable is broken or disconnected at any point along its length.

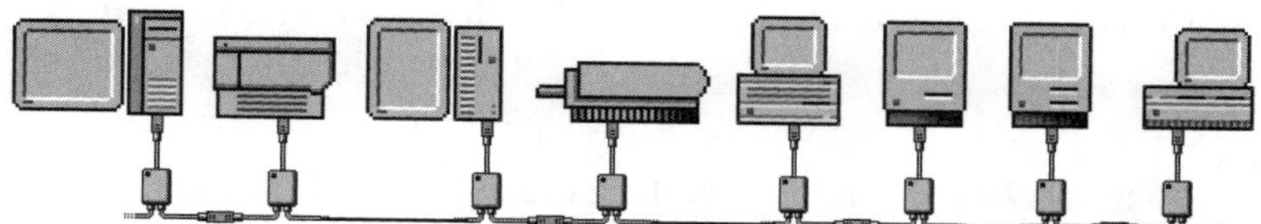

Figure 5.24 Daisy-chain topology, with LocalTalk.

This often happens when someone disconnects their Mac from the LocalTalk segment by disconnecting either of the two network segments instead of the single attachment point at the printer port. It also happens when a new node is added to the network and cannot be added to one of the two free ends of the network.

Thinwire (or 10Base-2) Ethernet networks can also be set up in a daisy-chain topology, but the same problems exist (see figure 5.25). The network can be easily severed by a careless disconnection. The end points of a thinwire Ethernet network must be terminated with resistive end caps. If the network is broken at either of the two network connections on the tee, the resistive load is missing and the network is disrupted.

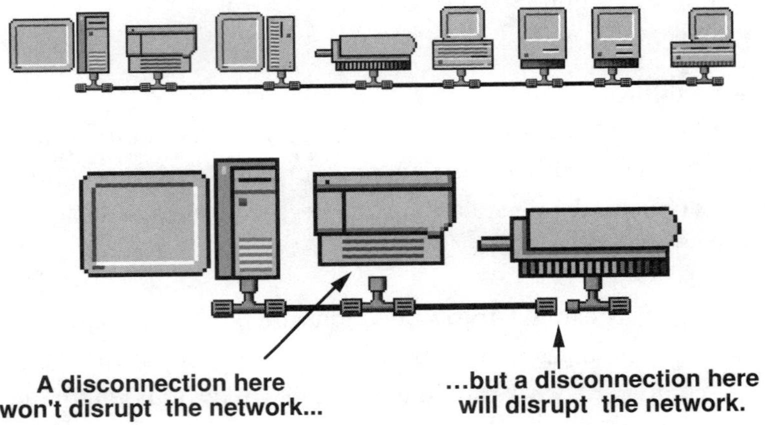

Figure 5.25
Daisy-chain, thinwire topology.

Apple recently introduced a version of thinwire Ethernet, where the resistive loads are automatically maintained in the event of a disconnection. (At least this way you'll still have two functioning network segments.)

For most office and business settings, daisy-chained networks are usually avoided because of the problems associated with frequent disconnects and maintenance of the wiring.

Common Bus or Backbone

A common bus, or backbone, network is similar to the daisy-chain network except that the cable connecting all the participating devices is one entire segment. The nodes connect to the backbone with an attachment unit.

The most common example of a backbone network is a thickwire or 10Base-5 Ethernet cable. A thickwire Ethernet backbone can be as long as 500 meters (1600 feet). Nodes and other network devices attach to the thickwire Ethernet with transceiver devices that clamp onto the cable.

These transceiver connections are somewhat expensive (ranging anywhere from $100 to $300) and take some time to install. Because of this, these transceiver connections are very often used to connect hubs or other devices where multiple connections can be made at a single location.

Most large network installations that use Ethernet utilize Ethernet backbones that are connected to other devices. These backbones often run up through the stories of the building, between the wiring closets where the connections are established (see figure 5.26).

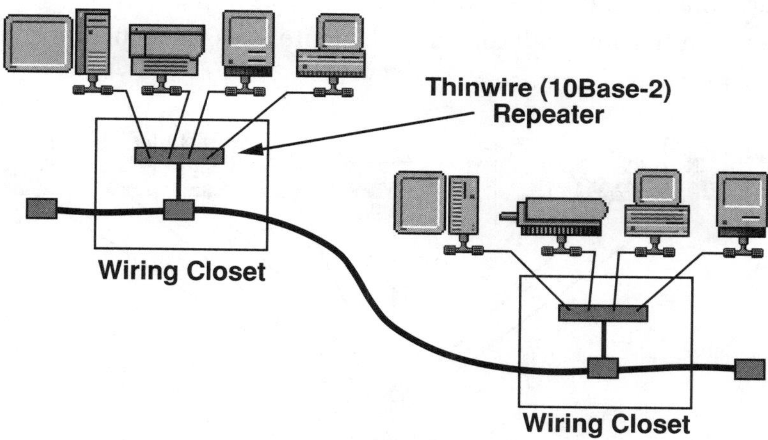

Figure 5.26
Backbone or bus topology.

Radial or Star

A radial, or star, topology has connections that radiate from a single location. Usually there is a single node on each branch of the star. Some configurations of star networks support the daisy-chaining of devices, but this often defeats the principal advantages of the star topology.

One advantage of star networks is ease of wiring. Each node (or office) is wired so that all connections converge at a single point—usually a concentrator located within a wiring closet. Then, when wiring changes are needed, they can take place within the closet. This avoids the hassle associated with daisy-chaining. Another advantage is that connections and disconnections can be easily made without disrupting the other members of the network. A node could blow up and it still wouldn't affect the traffic on the other segments of the star.

Star networks are common in the Macintosh world. With LocalTalk networks, there are several repeaters that permit the use of star topology (see figure 5.27). Farallon's StarController and the TurboStar from Focus are two well-known examples. These devices also come with software which provides some measure of network maintenance.

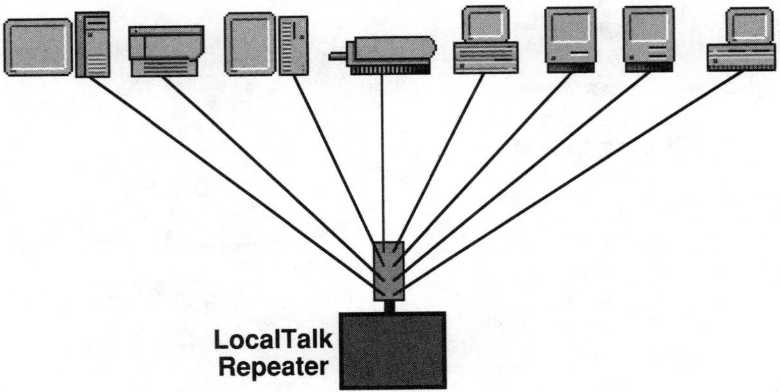

Figure 5.27
Star topology.

There are also Ethernet devices that permit the use of a star topology. There are thinwire Ethernet hubs that can be used to get away from the problems associated with thinwire daisychaining. The most popular Ethernet hubs today are the 10Base-T (or twisted-pair) Ethernet hubs. These hubs typically attach to a backbone Ethernet and provide several (usually eight) connections for twisted-pair Ethernet nodes.

Twisted-pair Ethernet has a maximum range of 100 meters (320 feet) and uses inexpensive four-conductor telephone-style wiring. Each node must connect to the hub.

Ring

A ring topology (see figure 5.28) connects all the devices in a circular manner. Ring networks are typified by Token Ring and by FDDI, which uses dual rings for redundancy and increased throughput.

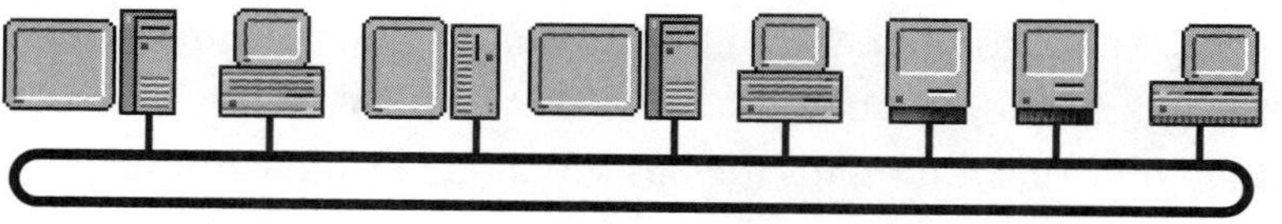

Figure 5.28
Ring topology.

Composite

Most large networks use a combination of topologies (see figure 5.29). Each topology is used for a specific reason and purpose. Performance, maintenance, and cost are all factors that determine the choice of a comprehensive networking topology. For example, it's common to see star and ring networksthat connected to a backbone network, that's in turn connected to another backbone in a serial fashion.

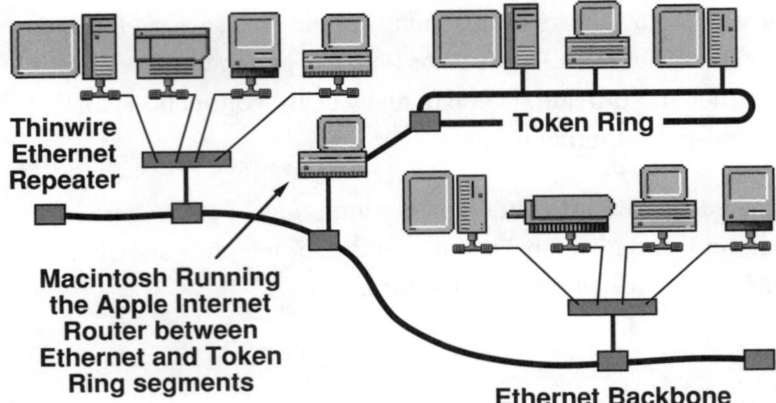

Figure 5.29
Composite topology.

Conclusion

Part of the difficulty in understanding networking is the plethora of networking black boxes that perform unknown or mysterious tasks. These components fall into a number of categories, such as repeaters, bridges, and routers. Of these, one of the key devices is the AppleTalk router. It's the basis for creating large AppleTalk networks and isolates traffic to a specific segment. Many AppleTalk routers are also capable of routing other protocols, such as DECnet and TCP/IP. These are known as multiprotocol routers.

These routers, along with other devices (such as bridges, repeaters, and gateways), are connected in specific arrangements referred to as topologies. These topologies are often dictated by the choice of a cabling system. Small networks, such as LocalTalk networks, are comprised of a single topology. Most large networks employ several topologies, such as a combination of backbone and star topologies, to meet specific networking and wiring requirements.

"Two"

mats, Transports, and Media.

Part II introduces Macintosh spe

networking by breaking the topi

four basic components: Services

Formats, Transports, and Media.

Part II introduces Macintosh specific networking by breaking the topic into the four basic components: Services, Formats, Transports, and Media.

Macintosh Networking

ng by breaking the topic into

basic components: Services,

Transports, and Media.

Macintosh Services

6

This chapter covers the reason why Macintosh and AppleTalk networking is so popular: the services. The only reason to network your computers is to supply services, such as file and print services, to the users. The common Macintosh and AppleTalk-based services will be described.

AppleShare (AFP)

To many Macintosh users, access to an AppleTalk network means shared, controlled access to files. To provide such access, Apple developed a Service layer (Presentation layer in the OSI model) protocol called the *Apple Filing Protocol*, or AFP. The AFP server at the Service layer represents an implementation of the AFP protocol, which can be described as a Format layer protocol in the NetPICT diagram, or as a Presentation layer format in the OSI model. Figure 6.1 shows a NetPICT diagram of an AFP Server. In this example, the AFP server is running on a Macintosh with an Ethernet card.

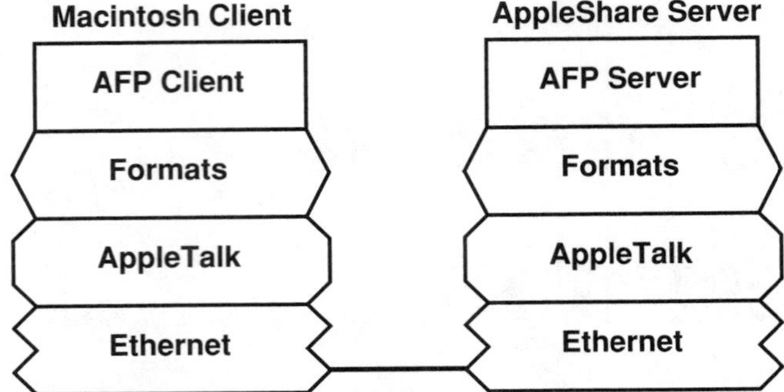

Figure 6.1
NetPICT of a Macintosh running AppleShare.

When Apple introduced AFP, Macintosh users were introduced for the first time to such radical concepts as user names, passwords, groups, ownership, and protection. AFP provided a mechanism whereby Macintosh users could find AFP servers on the network, log on these servers, and create, edit, and share files. Apple called this product *AppleShare*. AppleShare was easy to use, because the files stored on the server appeared as an extension of the user's local hard disk. All the techniques learned in creating and naming folders and files were immediately transferable to the file server environment.

AppleShare is a textbook example of a client/server connection. A user on a client Macintosh identifies and connects to a Macintosh that is running the AppleShare server software. This is done by clicking on the AppleShare icon in the Chooser.

AFP Server

Actually, it would be more correct if the icon were labeled AFP Server, because all AFP servers on all platforms will be searched for—not just the Macs running AppleShare.

Once the AppleShare icon is highlighted, as shown in figure 6.2, the Macintosh sends out a series of special inquiry packets that look for all the AFP servers in the current zone. The AFP servers, hearing this request, respond to the sender with their network address and name. The names are displayed in the Chooser and the addresses are remembered for future communications.

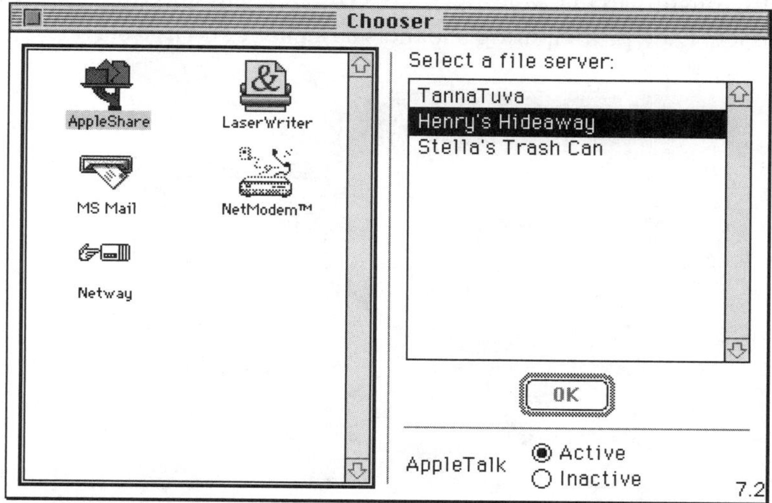

Figure 6.2 The Macintosh Chooser, showing AppleShare servers.

The user then selects the desired server and enters a user name and password in order to gain entry to the server. Once the user has successfully logged onto the server, a list of volumes—shared disks—appears in a dialog box. Multiple volumes can be created to address the particular needs of the workgroup. AppleShare comes with a management utility that is used to add and delete users and perform other necessary administrative tasks.

System 7 File Sharing

Starting with System 7, Apple expanded the concept of AFP services so that any Macintosh can be an AFP server and client. This is known as Macintosh File Sharing. Assuming your Macintosh is running System 7, you can grant or deny access to your Macintosh on a user or group (a collection of users) basis. You then designate folders on your local hard disk that you wish to make available to certain users or groups. Figure 6.3 shows several of the Macintosh dialog boxes, under System 7, that control or monitor File Sharing. With Macintosh File Sharing, there is no dedicated, centralized file service. Each participating user acts as a client and as a server.

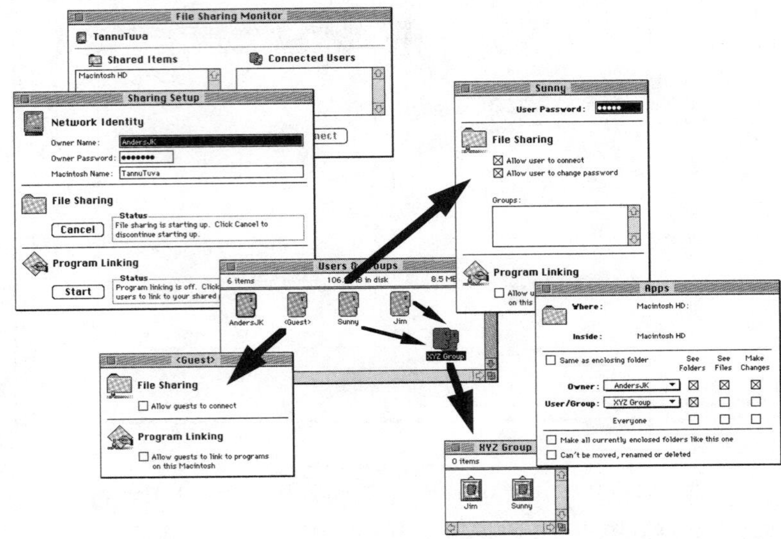

Figure 6.3

With System 7's Macintosh File Sharing, each Macintosh can be an AFP client or server.

Other AFP Clients and Servers

The AFP standard is not limited to the Macintosh platform. In fact, Apple made sure that AFP was an open standard that could be implemented on other computers. As shown in figure 6.4, there are AFP servers available for most popular platforms, including DEC VAX, IBM PC, UNIX, and even dedicated hardware boxes.

For the most part, AFP services on platforms other than Macintosh appear to the user exactly like a Mac running the AppleShare or File Share software (although there may be some differences with filename limitations, or the number of nested folders). An example of this is found in the VAXshare component of PATHWORKS for

Macintosh, from Digital. VAXshare is software that enables a VAX/VMS computer to appear as a AFP server (or servers). The AFP volumes, or disks, can correspond to any VMS directory. Macintosh folders on these volumes correspond to VMS subdirectories.

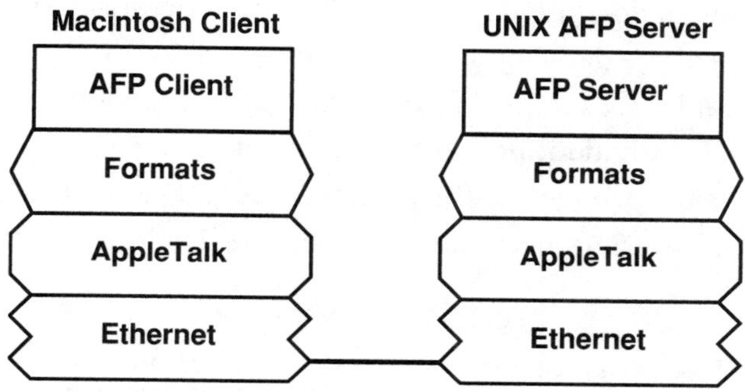

Figure 6.4
AFP Servers aren't limited to Macintosh.

One simple problem that often happens with mixed-platform environments is filenames. VMS filenames cannot contain spaces, so VAXshare must maintain a conversion map that translates Macintosh filenames into acceptable VMS filenames. Another problem might occur if the VAX is also used to store and share DOS files. While the Macintosh and VAX/VMS environments support long filenames, DOS filenames are restricted to an eight-character limit. Therefore, if you intend to share Macintosh files with DOS users over a shared filing system, you may need to restrict your Mac filenames to eight characters.

Print Services (PAP)

For many Macintosh users, the act of network printing is not normally viewed as a client/server activity. In fact, the print services provided over AppleTalk networks are an excellent example of client/server computing. While the Macintosh supports many printers and printing protocols, the most common print service is provided by Apple's *Printer Access Protocol* (PAP).

Apple LaserWriter Family

Perhaps the most popular Macintosh client/server application is the printing of documents to an Apple LaserWriter printer. Just as in the case of the dedicated AppleShare file server, the Apple LaserWriter is an example of a client/server transaction, where the client Macintosh identifies and selects a networked print server, then sends the print job to the printer for subsequent queuing and printing. Figure 6.5 shows the corresponding NetPICT of a LaserWriter.

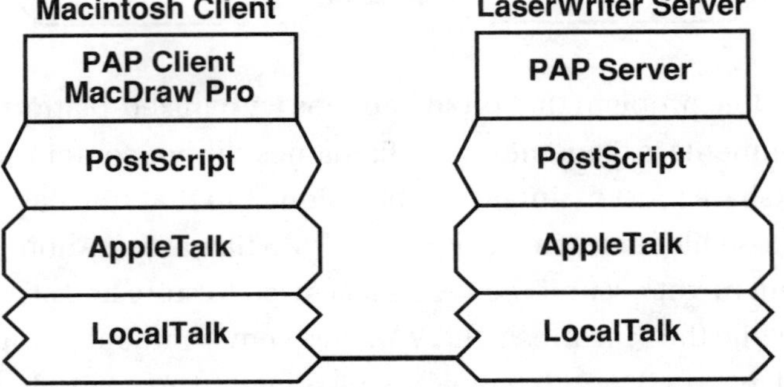

Figure 6.5 NetPICT of an Apple LaserWriter.

As was the case with AFP, a special protocol called the Printer Access Protocol (PAP) was developed to handle the unique and specific requirements of networked laser printing. PAP manages the printing specifics, provides the queuing, downloads fonts when required, and even informs the user if the printer is out of paper or if the paper tray is out of the printer.

Other PAP-Compliant Printers/Spoolers

PAP print services aren't limited to Macintosh. They also can be found on UNIX and VAX/VMS hosts as well. There are numerous products that allow these computers to accept and spool Macintosh print jobs. Spooling relieves the Mac of the burden of locally spooling print jobs on its hard disk. This practice causes the annoying delays seen when the Print Monitor application is used. Instead of local spooling and continual polling to check the printer's status, the remote PAP spooler accepts the print job as fast as the Mac and network can send it. Figure 6.6 shows a NetPICT of the PATHWORKS VAXshare PAP spooler running on a DEC VAX. To the Macintosh client, the spooler program appears exactly like a LaserWriter. The program queues the print job and forwards it to the LaserWriter.

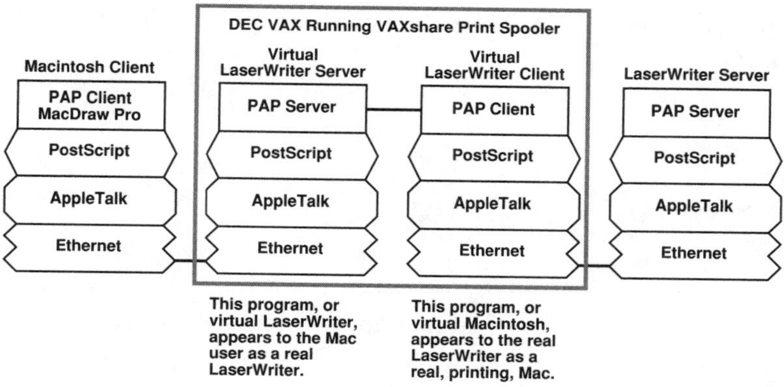

Figure 6.6 Print spooling under DEC's PATHWORKS for Macintosh.

Apple Open Collaboration Environment (AOCE)

AOCE is a new set of Apple services that integrates a wide variety of services necessary for collaborative activities. These services will let the Macintosh manage personal communications, workgroup collaboration, and enterprise-wide workflow. An important part of AOCE is the extensible directory services that will provide personal or distributed listings of users, network services, and even phone numbers.

Network security is always a concern, and AOCE provides tools that ensure private and secure communications. A new AppleTalk protocol, the AppleTalk Secure Data Stream Protocol (ASDSP), encrypts network traffic to prevent packet snooping. Another technique offered by AOCE, digital signatures, will provide a way for users to sign electronic documents. These electronic signatures will be tamperproof and provide users the assurance that their messages and authorizations are secure.

Starting in 1993, AOCE will lay the foundation for a new generation of shared, cooperative applications. Messages such as voice, fax, mail, and even video will be managed through a consistent interface.

Terminal Services

Although terminal emulation is a throwback to an earlier time, there are still a number of application services that require the use of terminals. The Macintosh offers a number of terminal emulators that work with DEC, UNIX, IBM, Prime, Data General, and many other hosts. The types of terminals supported include most of Digital's VT series (that is, the VT100, VT220, VT340…), IBM 3270 and 5250 terminals, Tektronix graphics terminals, and many others. These emulators are able to connect with direct serial connections, or through network connections such as LAT, TCP/IP, DECnet or SNA. Figures 6.7 and 6.8 use the NetPICT diagrams to illustrate the difference between a terminal emulator (VT220) running over a conventional serial connection and a network connection using LAT over Ethernet. A more detailed description of terminal services can be found in the platform-specific chapters later in the book.

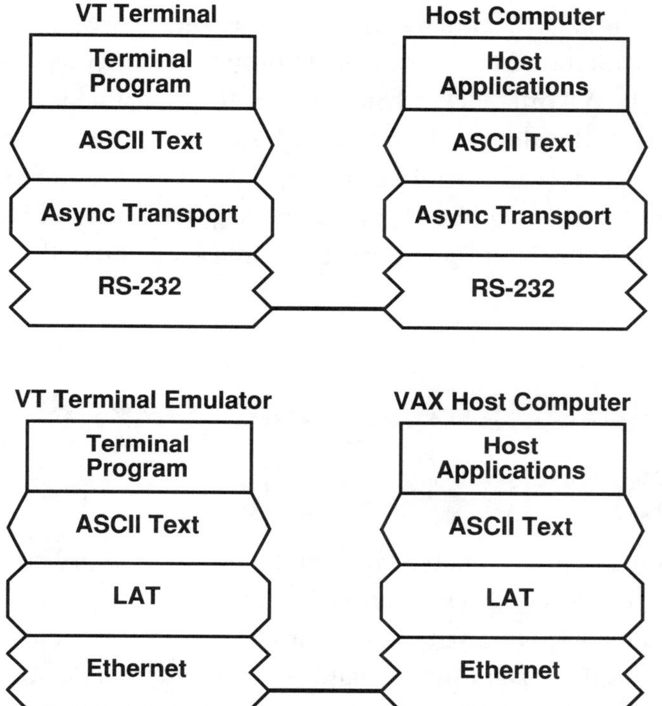

Figure 6.7

A VT220 connected over a serial connection. The serial communications line is a single-use connection only. Unlike a network connection, it cannot be shared.

Figure 6.8

A VT220 connected over a LAT network. Terminal access through a network connection can be shared by many users.

In the past, most terminal services were provided over serial transmission lines (RS-232) that used an asynchronous protocol. Today, terminal services are often delivered over LAN connections and protocols. Figure 6.8 shows terminal access with DEC's LAT protocol, which is part of their PATHWORKS for Macintosh product.

Alternatives to conventional terminal emulation include those products that create a front end to terminal-based services. As an example, products from Apple, Avatar, and DCA offer programming interfaces so that programmers can build Macintosh applications that have the look and feel of a Mac application, but utilize terminal traffic as a communications medium.

Other examples that build atop a terminal session are MacWorkStation from United Data Corporation and MitemView from Mitem. With MacWorkStation, a host application sends simple ASCII codes to a Macintosh. The Mac interprets these codes as commands that control various aspects of the Mac interface. MitemView uses standard terminal messages or MacWorkStation codes, together with HyperCard, to act as a front end to the host.

Data Access Language (DAL) and Other Database Services

DAL's purpose is to enable Macs (and other DAL clients, such as PCs) to uniformly access relational databases (see figure 6.9). Extending the SQL language, DAL provides a standard that can be used on different computing platforms and different databases.

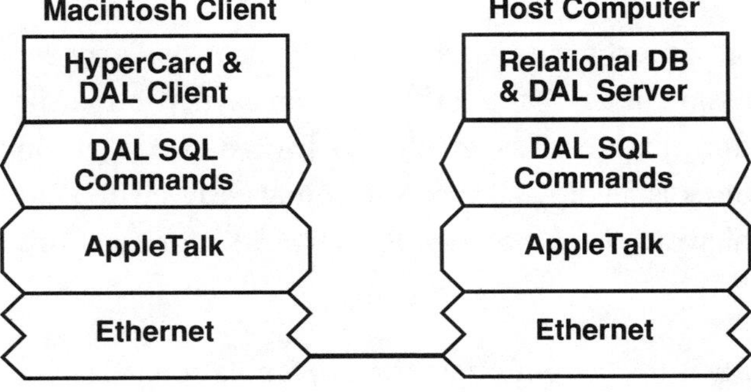

Figure 6.9
NetPICT of a Client/Server DAL relationship.

The DAL software on the client side is implemented as an optional extension for System 7 (it used to be part of System 7 software, but Apple recently unbundled it). DAL client applications can be written as Mac applications or as HyperCard stacks. These stacks contain the DAL XCMDs that give the HyperTalk programmer access to the necessary DAL commands. In addition to HyperCard,

DAL is supported by other development environments, such as Andyne's Graphical Query Language (GQL) and the iconic, object-oriented development environment from Serius.

There are also many Mac applications that have built-in DAL client capabilities. Spreadsheets such as Microsoft Excel and Lotus 1-2-3 are DAL-equipped and can be used to access and retrieve data managed by relational databases. Clear Access, from Fairfield Software, is a desk accessory that can be used to construct ad-hoc database queries.

DAL servers are currently sold by Apple, DEC, Tandem, Novell, and Pacer Software. Apple offers DAL servers for DEC VAX/VMS, IBM mainframes, IBM AS/400, and Macs running A/UX (Apple's version of UNIX). The VAX/VMS version supports DEC's Rdb, Ingres, Oracle, Sybase, and Informix databases. The IBM mainframe version supports IBM's DB2 and Teradata's DBC/1012 databases. Pacer offers a DAL server for HP UNIX computers, DEC Ultrix, and Sun's SPARCstation. Tandem has a DAL server for their line of computers, and Novell has added DAL support for NetWare's SQL NLM.

The appeal of DAL is that the client applications are insulated from the host database. This makes it easy to switch the database and host server as needed. DAL also provides a single standard so that software developers can offer database access without having to deal with each database vendor's own proprietary access language. Since DAL uses a common-denominator approach to database connectivity, some specialized features, such as database triggers, may not be available through DAL.

Other products get around this limitation. SequeLink (by TechGnosis) doesn't rely on DAL; instead, it uses specific database connections for each host database. Database companies, such as Ingres, Oracle, and Sybase, have also gotten into the act by developing Macintosh client tools that work with their specific database languages. Figure 6.10 shows an Oracle database being accessed by a Macintosh client running the Oracle client software.

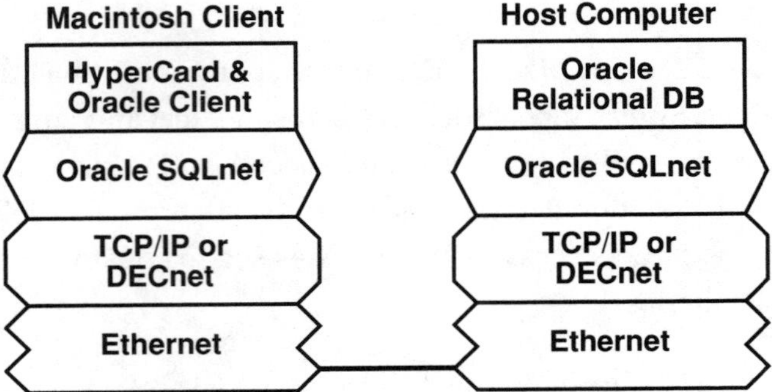

Figure 6.10
NetPICT of an Oracle database connection.

Mail Services

Perhaps more than any other Macintosh service, E-mail has the potential for truly transforming an organization. Users can finally quit the annoying game of telephone tag and enhance their communications with their co-workers. E-Mail can be used as a communications framework where voice, textual messages, and binary file attachments are sent and tracked over the entire network. In fact, many companies are now starting to view E-mail as the engine that will power the drive toward the elusive goal of workflow automation. Using custom-designed electronic mail forms, a company can replace its current paper-based operations with a system that eliminates many of the inherent shortcomings (time delays, manual records keeping, loss of data, transcription errors, and so forth) of the past.

During the past five years, support for Macintosh E-mail has become widespread. As mentioned before, Apple's AOCE initiative will set the foundation for a new generation of mail applications, where various message formats (mail, fax, voice, and video, for example) are integrated and presented to the user within a consistent interface. AOCE will also provide the security and authentication required by collaborative applications.

Today, the Macintosh is supported by most of the popular multiplatform E-mail systems. Two of the most popular Macintosh mail programs are Microsoft Mail for Macintosh and CE Software's QuickMail. Both of these products offer client and server components that work in an AppleTalk network environment (see figure 6.11). The challenge begins when other mail systems, multiple platforms, and different transport protocols are used.

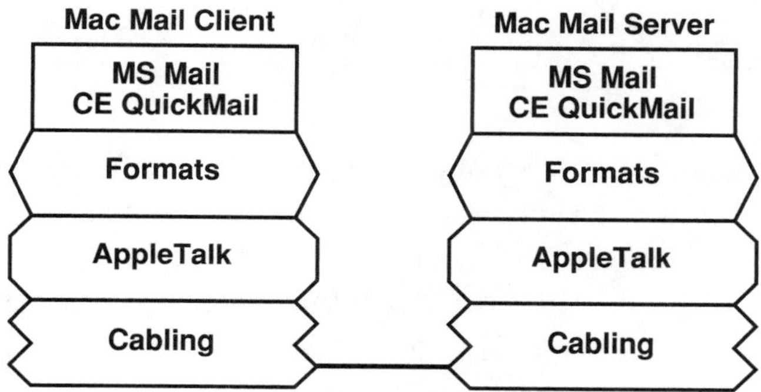

Figure 6.11 AppleTalk-based mail services for the Macintosh.

Many Macintosh mail vendors offer mail gateways for their products that are used to meld different mail formats or transport protocols. These mail gateways are similar to the other transport gateways mentioned earlier in this book. A mail gateway deals with all aspects of the mail message. This includes the formatting of the message as well as any changes required in the transport protocol used to deliver the message.

The most common Mac and PC gateways are used to connect to these LAN mail systems to the UNIX mail standard SMTP (which stands for Simple Mail Transfer Protocol) or to the emerging industry-standard of X.400. Other less-common gateways provide access to other mail environments, such as IBM PROFS, DEC All-In-1, MCI Mail, and Novell MHS. There are even mail gateways that forward mail messages to a networked fax server (see figure 6.12)! These mail gateways run on the computer that's running the mail server application, or on a separate computer that's connected to the mail server.

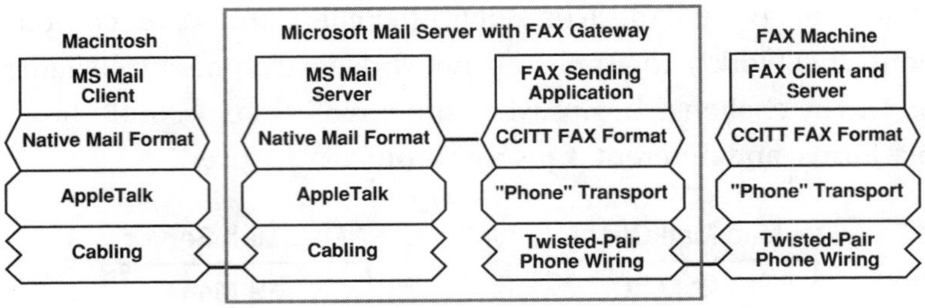

Macintosh: MS Mail Client / Native Mail Format / AppleTalk / Cabling
Microsoft Mail Server with FAX Gateway: MS Mail Server / Native Mail Format / AppleTalk / Cabling — FAX Sending Application / CCITT FAX Format / "Phone" Transport / Twisted-Pair Phone Wiring
FAX Machine: FAX Client and Server / CCITT FAX Format / "Phone" Transport / Twisted-Pair Phone Wiring

Figure 6.12
A Macintosh mail server to fax gateway.

As an example of a shared mail server and gateway, figure 6.13 shows a Macintosh QuickMail server that is also acting as a gateway to VMS Mail running on a DEC VAX computer. In this case, the Macintosh users are using the AppleTalk protocol to communicate with the server, and the server is using the DECnet protocol to communicate with the VAX. The product that delivers this gateway capability is Alisa's MailMate QM.

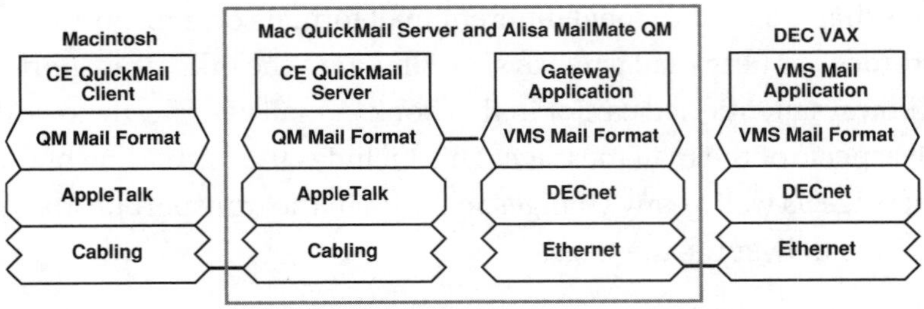

Macintosh: CE QuickMail Client / QM Mail Format / AppleTalk / Cabling
Mac QuickMail Server and Alisa MailMate QM: CE QuickMail Server / QM Mail Format / AppleTalk / Cabling — Gateway Application / VMS Mail Format / DECnet / Ethernet
DEC VAX: VMS Mail Application / VMS Mail Format / DECnet / Ethernet

Figure 6.13
A Macintosh mail server to VAX gateway.

Macintosh E-mail systems that support multiplatform access can be very complex—they probably deserve a separate book to adequately describe their capabilities. Hopefully, the descriptions and diagrams found in *Live Wired* will place the elements of these systems into a clear and comprehensible form, opening the door to future discovery.

Conclusion

Of course the services listed previously only scratch the surface. The Macintosh offers hundreds of networkable applications, such as time management, resource management, backup/archival, and even games that work over AppleTalk networks. Since the Mac was designed at the outset to operate in a networked environment, most Mac applications naturally take advantage of network capabilities. Today, with the System 7 features of Publish and Subscribe and AppleEvents, the Macintosh has gone beyond mere client/server applications, using the AppleTalk network to automatically update shared objects and to enable applications to directly control and manipulate other services available on the network.

Macintosh Formats

7

Often overlooked or underestimated, the data format is the single most crucial aspect of the network. More important than cabling or protocols, the formats and data structures that encode our file access methods, word processing documents, spreadsheets, drawings, sounds, and multimedia presentations represent the true measure of success when it comes to network interoperability.

The binary underpinnings of all computer formats are platform-independent. All computers express information in the same way—with binary numbers. The only difference is that computers and programs have different coding schemes to represent the data. It's important to realize that any computer can read, write, and store any sequence of binary numbers. This means that any binary computer can read, write, and store any other binary computer's data. The difficulties start to arise when one computer is able, through its programming, to act on and manipulate that binary data in a manner that another computer is unable to do. This is one of the central problems in computing today.

For every unique computer application or service, there is usually a unique binary representation for its data. This is why MacWrite documents are different from Microsoft Word documents, even though they might have identical content. The choices for interoperability are limited: either agree on a common data format, or provide interchange utilities to convert one format to the other. In all likelihood, we will always have a mix of these approaches. There will be continued pressure for data standards, but as innovation continues to fuel the industry, new formats and data structures are inevitable. Let's look at some of the predominant data standards and interchange utilities that are available on the Macintosh.

ASCII Text and Word Processors

As stated earlier in Chapter 2, "How Does Networking Take Place," ASCII text is a standard that uses eight bits of data to encode the English alphabet, numbers, symbols, and special computer control characters (such as line feeds and carriage returns). Although text editors and word processors offer the ability to change the displayed font of an ASCII text file, the ASCII format doesn't support fonts or special attributes such as bolding or underlining. Therefore, using ASCII as an exchange medium will only preserve the text; any font information or special formatting will be lost. All Macintosh word processors and spreadsheets can read and write ASCII text. Many other Macintosh applications can also read and write ASCII text. For example, HyperCard can read and write ASCII text through its HyperTalk scripting capability. Most Macintosh programming environments, such as Apple's MPW and Symantec Lightspeed C, also use ASCII text files for source code files.

Macintosh word processors usually rely on proprietary formats for their documents. Word processors that are available on multiple platforms usually use the same file format for all platforms, or contain built-in translators that convert one platform's format to the other. Microsoft Word has translators that translate documents between the Mac and Windows versions of Word. Word also has built-in translators for other competing Macintosh word processors, such as MacWrite and WordPerfect. Figure 7.1 shows the wide range of formats supported by Microsoft Word 5.1.

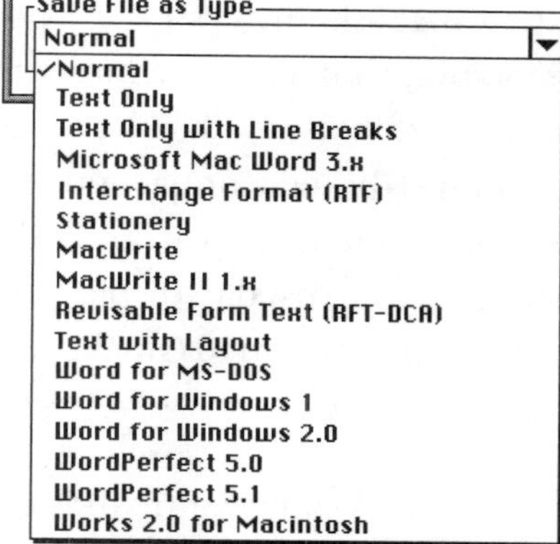

Figure 7.1
Microsoft Word can read and write a number of different formats.

Claris uses a technology called *XTND* that can be used to translate between different word processing formats. With XTND, for example, MacWrite users can read and write Microsoft Word documents using options found in the Open and Save As dialog boxes.

If a word processing document is truly foreign (Wang, for example), then a dedicated conversion program such as MacLinkPlus from DataViz is often required. MacLinkPlus supports hundreds of formats from many different platforms.

MacPaint and PICT Formats

The Macintosh introduced a number of new graphic formats. MacPaint was one of the first Macintosh applications. It introduced paint programs and bitmaps to the world. The MacPaint-style bitmap data structure is still in widespread use today. The original bitmap definition was 72 dots per inch and one-bit color (either black or white). Today, Macintosh bitmaps exist in a range of resolutions and millions of colors.

Another Macintosh format is known as *PICT*. The PICT format is an outgrowth of the Macintosh imaging environment. The Macintosh System contains a programmers' toolkit known as *QuickDraw*. It is a two dimensional, integer-based world where programmers can create lines, arcs, circles, rectangles, text, and Mac bitmaps. The QuickDraw data structures are used to display these objects on the Mac monitor, and to print them to QuickDraw-based printers such as the Apple StyleWriter II.

A PICT file is a series of QuickDraw commands organized in a special resource. Thus, PICT files are limited to the objects and precision found in QuickDraw. Because PICT files are so intimately linked to the display environment of the Mac, the PICT format has become a standard for the storage and management of graphics. There are two implementations of PICT: the original, and PICT2 (which contains color and grayscale support).

Because the QuickDraw standard supports both object-oriented graphics (that is, lines, arcs, rectangles, and text) and bitmaps, the PICT standards support these elements as well. A PICT file can contain only objects, only bitmaps, or a mixture of both. One potential problem with PICT is its limited precision. As mentioned, QuickDraw is integer-based. Under certain circumstances, when PICT files are scaled or resized this limited precision can cause a certain amount of distortion. This problem doesn't occur with

PostScript images, because PostScript uses a higher precision floating-point world.

Since Macintosh has made inroads into the graphic and publishing worlds, the PICT standard has become an industry standard; many drawing, illustration, and publishing applications on other platforms include PICT support.

PostScript

When Apple introduced the LaserWriter, it also introduced Adobe's PostScript imaging language. *PostScript* is part programming language and part data sructure. PostScript instructions can be used to drive laser printers, display graphics on monitors, or to serve as a graphical format suitable for inclusion in published documents. PostScript soon became a standard in the computing world, both as a printer language and as a display language. While other companies (most notably NeXT) have adopted PostScript as a screen display language, Apple has continued to support and enhance QuickDraw. Because of this, Apple has two imaging standards: QuickDraw for the display and certain printers, and PostScript for other printers (see figure 7.2). PostScript, like PICT, can contain lines, arcs, rectangles, text and bitmaps. It uses floating point numbers to locate objects; this provides a higher degree of precision.

A variation of PostScipt, called *Encapsulated PostScript* or *EPSF*, has become another industry standard for graphic files. EPSF files are essentially PostScript files with the addition of "bounding box" data that defines the size of the graphic. Most Mac illustration, drawing, and publishing programs are able to read and write the EPSF format.

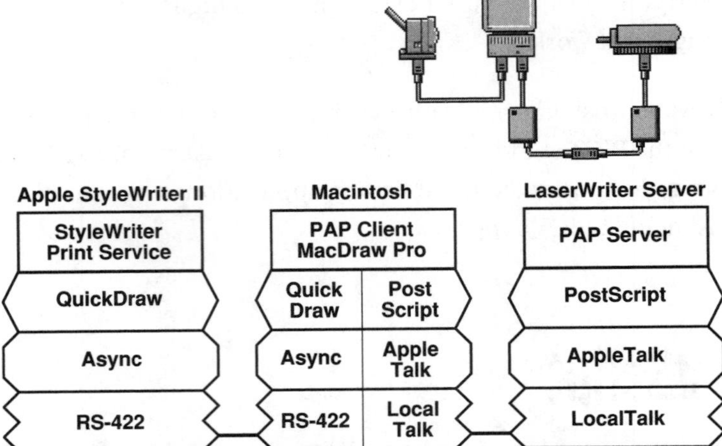

Figure 7.2

A Macintosh can generate either QuickDraw or PostScript output.

IMPORTANT NOTE: One word of caution about EPSF files. There are two versions: a generic version, and a Mac-specific version that contains a special PICT preview file resource. This additional resource, sometimes referred to as a "thumbnail," is used to provide an onscreen display image which approximates the real PostScript image. When the file is finally printed, the real PostScript is used.

With many Mac applications, if you insert an EPSF file without the PICT preview, you'll only be able to see a rectangle that represents the border of the image. The image will still print properly. Some applications can convert generic EPS files into Mac-specific EPS files, and DataViz also provides a MacLinkPlus translator for this purpose.

TIFF and GIF

TIFF and GIF are raster formats (that is, bitmap formats) that are commonly supported on many platforms. *TIFF* (Tagged Image File Format) is a standard format that's frequently used by digital scanners. TIFF files are often used to store high-resolution images that have been scanned from photographic sources. *GIF* (Graphic

Interchange Format) is similar to the TIFF format, but it's popularity seems to be limited to storing images of bikini-clad females on bulletin board services.

Because both TIFF and GIF are raster formats, they are usually viewable and editable with Macintosh paint/bitmap programs such as Adobe Photoshop. There are also numerous viewing and conversion utilities (Macintosh and PC) that are able to handle these formats.

Binary

By far the largest category of Macintosh formats are those that rely on a proprietary binary structure. Most Mac applications use their own binary format to store data. As more vendors start to offer cross-platform versions of their programs, the trend of binary compatibility is likely to increase. PageMaker for the Mac uses the same file format as PageMaker for Windows, so it's simply a matter of transferring the document from one machine to the other. This can be done with a floppy disk, or over a network. Figure 7.3 shows a NetPICT of a PageMaker file that is shared between a Mac and PC. The real problems start when you try to exchange documents between incompatible applications.

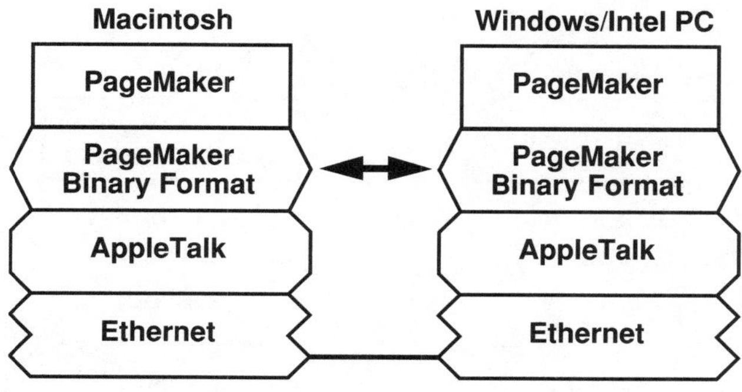

Figure 7.3
PageMaker uses the same binary file format on both Mac and Windows versions.

Document Interchange

The problem can be simply stated: Most application developers design a unique binary file format to represent and store the data created within their applications. These formats are designed using many criteria, which include file size, application performance, and memory requirements. Formats are rarely designed with the goal of inter-vendor binary compatability. This is due to valid technical reasons, as well as those pragmatic business concerns associated with true binary cross-vendor compatibility. However, there are many initiatives from vendors and industry standards organizations that attempt to bridge the long-standing language barrier between different computer applications.

MacODA

MacODA attempts to solve the problem of document interchange. It does this not through conversion but through a standardized file format. MacODA is based on the Open Document Architecture, which is an ISO standard (standard #8613, to be precise) for the interchange of compound documents. (A *compound document* is a document that contains fonts and graphics, both bitmap and object.) ODA preserves the formatting and structure of documents, so chapters, paragraphs, headers, and footers are maintained. Figure 7.4 uses NetPICTs to illustrate ODA use as a common interchange format.

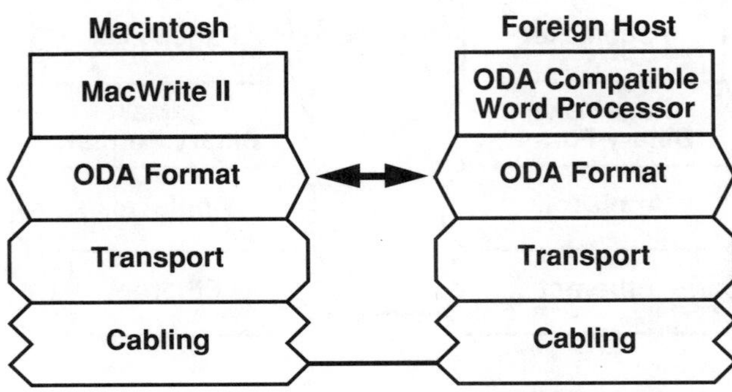

Figure 7.4
MacODA supports the ISO Open Document Architecture Standard which standardizes compound documents.

The ODA standard specifies three implementation levels.

- Level 1: Textual data
- Level 2: Textual and Graphical (word processing)
- Level 3: Textual and Graphical (desktop publishing)

At the present time, Apple's (and most other vendors') implementation of ODA supports Level 2, so effective transfers are limited to basic word processing documents. For example, at this time, MacODA only supports the Helvetica, Courier and Times typefaces. The OSI standards continue to evolve and it's expected that MacODA will be continually enhanced.

Adobe Acrobat and PDF

Another document interchange standard is being developed by Adobe Systems. With Acrobat, they plan to extend their PostScript standard to support a new file format called the Portable Document Format (PDF). PDF will support fonts, graphics, text and color in a platform-independent file format. PDF, like ODA, will be a common interchange format, supported by Macs, PCs, and UNIX. (A NetPICT of the PDF standard is shown in figure 7.5.) Initially, PDF will be a view-only format; users won't be able to edit the information contained in a PDA document. Adobe may add this capability sometime in the future.

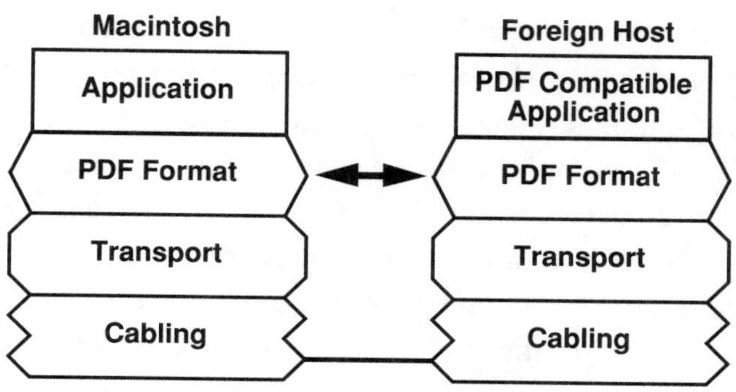

Figure 7.5
The PDF Standard from Adobe promises a unified, platform independent, interchange format.

Conversions

We have just discussed one approach to document interchange; using a mutually agreed-upon standard that is supported by many applications. The other approach is to simply convert one format into another.

Both approaches have their tradeoffs. With the common format standard mentioned before, each application must support every element and entity in the common format. This places quite a burden on the common format, as it must accept or adapt to a rich superset of elements used by all participating applications. This is why common file standards are so difficult to standardize. The benefit of this common format is that each vendor need only implement a single converter, or translator, for their application.

The other approach is through conversion. Here, each format is explicitly converted into another. The advantage is that the conversions can be explicitly tailored and tweaked to accommodate the two participants. Explicit conversion often provides a greater degree of conversion accuracy. The problem is that the number of required conversions begins to multiply with each aditional format. We'll now look at two examples of utilities that facilitate the direct, seamless conversion between different applications.

Claris XTND

Claris's solution to the problem of file translation is an open exchange architecture known as *XTND* (pronounced "extend"). XTND translation has been offered with MacWrite II, and with most other Claris applications as well. It has also been adopted by other software developers because Claris has licensed the technology. With XTND, additional translation modules are simply added to a folder (figure 7.6), after which they appear in the Open and Save As dialog boxes (figure 7.7). XTND is also used by those Claris applications that offer a Place command. For example, you can place an EPSF or TIFF file into a MacDrawPro document; the appropriate XTND translators automatically convert and import the graphic.

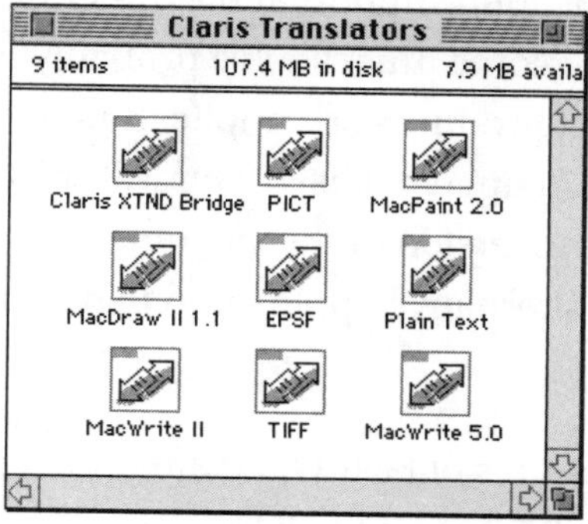

Figure 7.6
XTND filters.

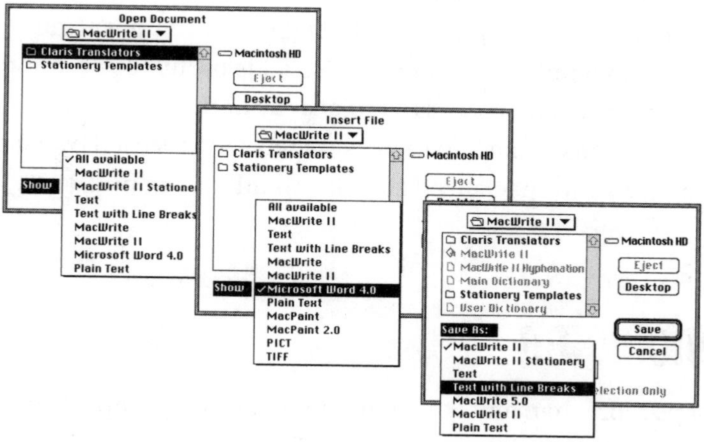

Figure 7.7
XTND Open/Save options.

Claris' XTND architecture is modular. Each translator is a separate document that can be added or deleted to the "Claris" folder as required. Once the XTND translators are added, they automatically appear in the Open and Save As dialogs of XTND-compatible applications.

Apple Easy Open

Easy Open is a new Macintosh developer's toolkit that incorporates seamless file translation into the operating system of the Macintosh. It provides a standard interface for translation software and alternate application support at the System level. If you've been a Mac user for some time, you've probably seen the plain document icon that produces an "application not found" message when you attempt to open it. Easy Open will solve this problem by coordinating the conversion of this document into another form, or by selecting an alternative application that is capable of opening the file.

The translation features of Easy Open are not limited to file access. The Claris XTND environment will be managed under the auspices of Easy Open. It will also provide transparent data conversion during copying, pasting or publishing (System 7 Publish and Subscribe) operations. Easy Open also adds useful file descriptions and informative color icons to replace the annoying generic document icons. Expect to see Easy Open services used by general applications and specialized conversion utilities by mid-1993.

Conclusion

Perhaps more than any other computer company, Apple Computer has addressed the issue of data format portability. Starting with the Macintosh Clipboard, Apple has continued to provide mechanisms to seamlessly share information between applications and platforms. Unlike its rivals, the PC-compatibles, which have a myriad of application-specific file formats, the Macintosh has a few key formats that are supported by many applications.

8

Macintosh Transport: AppleTalk

The Transport layer is where the networking protocols reside. Apple's networking protocol is called AppleTalk. It consists of many separate protocols, each performing a specific function or task. This chapter explains the various components of the AppleTalk protocol family and discusses why it is destined to be one of the most important networking protocols for the future.

The AppleTalk Protocol Family: An Overview

AppleTalk, the networking protocol, actually consists of many separate protocols that work in conjunction to deliver services to the Macintosh user. This collection of protocols is often referred to as the AppleTalk *suite* of protocols.

AppleTalk and the 7-Layer OSI Model

The easiest way to describe and explain the AppleTalk protocol suite is to use the 7-layer OSI model. Each AppleTalk protocol exists at a certain layer in the stack. Sometimes, there is more than one protocol at a given OSI layer. The AppleTalk protocols span the layers from the Presentation layer down to the Data Link layer of the model. Remember from the printing example at the end of Chapter 3, "Network Diagramming with NetPICTs" that each layer in the stack has a client/server relationship with its neighbor. Figure 8.1 shows the entire suite of AppleTalk protocols, using the 7-layer OSI model.

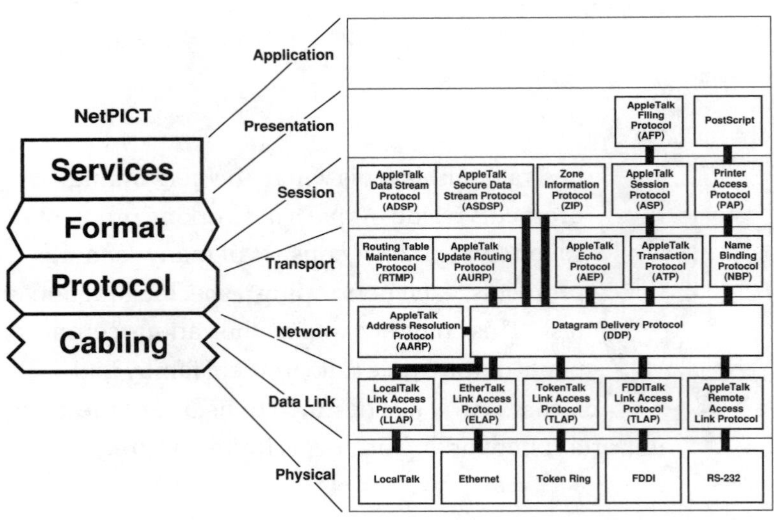

Figure 8.1
The AppleTalk protocol stack.

Let's take each AppleTalk protocol and describe its basic function, starting at the top and working our way down to the bottom. Unless you plan to develop and program AppleTalk applications, it's not important to understand in detail each of these protocols. Instead, it's only necessary to understand the basic function of the protocol and where it fits into the larger scheme.

Presentation: AFP, PostScript, and QuickDraw

As mentioned earlier, the OSI Presentation layer is the same as the NetPICT Format layer. At this layer, as shown by figure 8.2, the protocols deal with the format of the data. For example, Apple developed the AFP protocol to address the needs of shared file service. PostScript and QuickDraw solve the problem of device-independent imaging.

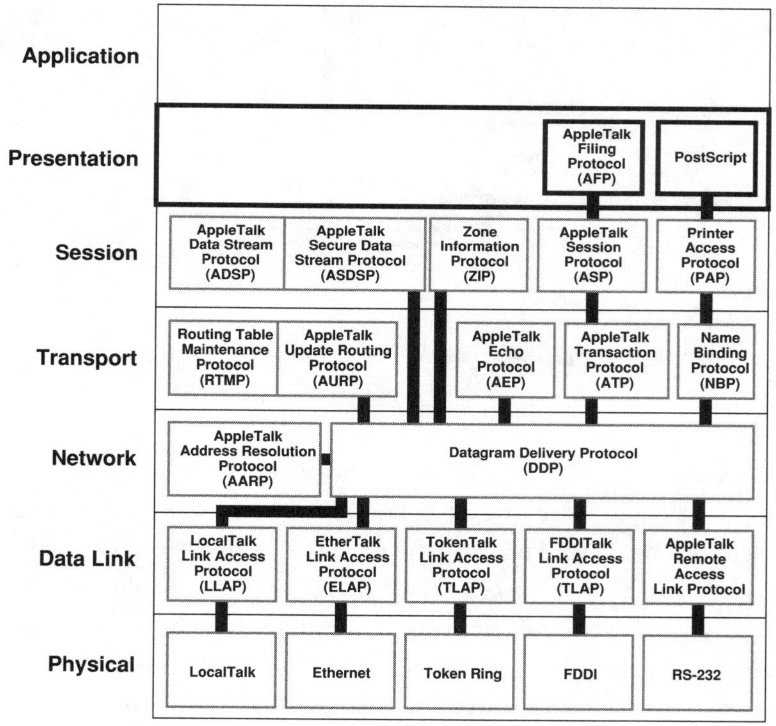

Figure 8.2
The Apple Filing Protocol (AFP), PostScript, and QuickDraw are all examples of AppleTalk Presentation layer protocols.

Session: ZIP, ASP, PAP, ADSP, and ASDSP

At the Session layer, the Macintosh uses ZIP, ASP, PAP, ADSP and ASDSP (see figure 8.3).

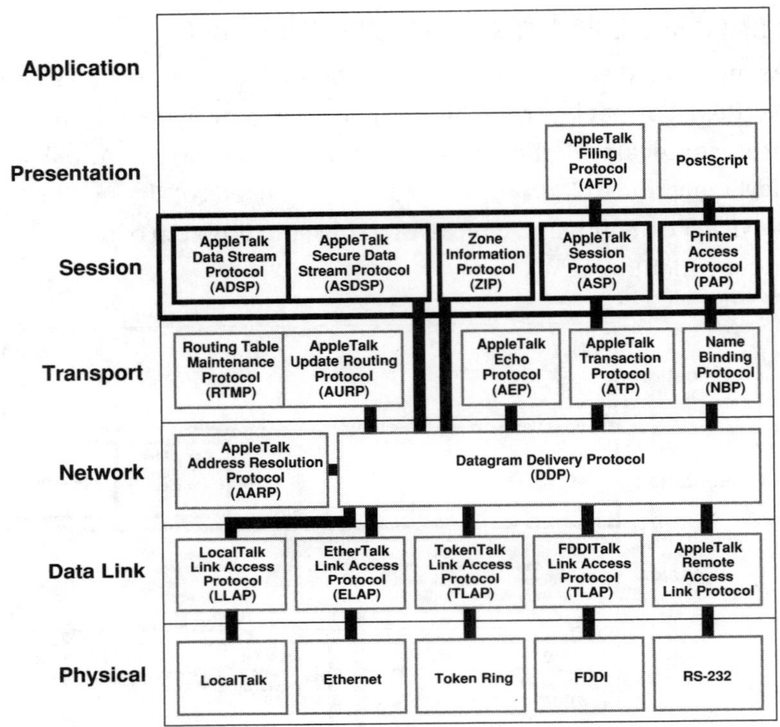

Figure 8.3
Macintosh Session layer protocols.

ZIP stands for *Zone Information Protocol.* Its purpose is to determine which networks are associated with which zones. To accomplish this task, ZIP is used by the AppleTalk routers on the network to maintain a Zone Information Table (or ZIT). This table, exemplified by Table 8.1, maps networks with their corresponding zone names. The table is stored within each AppleTalk router on the network. ZIP also has the facility to make changes to the table when the configuration of the network is altered. A good example of the use of ZIP is the Macintosh Chooser. When the Chooser is opened on a network with zones, ZIP is used to get the current list of zone names from the router.

Table 8.1 Zone Information Table

Network Number	*Zone Name*
10	Philadelphia
20	Wilmington
21	Philadelphia
22	Dover
119	Paris

ASP, or the *AppleTalk Session Protocol,* maintains a logical network connection between an AppleTalk client and server. ASP is responsible for starting and stopping each session, as well as maintaining *sequencing.* ASP can be likened to the page numbers of a document. If I were going to send you a document by copying every page and sending them one at a time, you would use the page numbers to reassemble the document in the correct sequence. The page numbers would also eliminate the potential of missing or duplicated pages. For example, if I sent you a 20-page document, and you received two copies of page 5 and didn't receive page 6, it would be an easy matter for you to discard the extra page and request page 6 from me.

Session management and sequencing control is crucial to maintain a reliable connection between network partners. ASP doesn't provide a service directly to the user; instead, it's used by the higher level protocols, such as AFP, to keep things in order.

PAP is an acronym for *Printer Access Protocol.* It manages communications with network printers, usually LaserWriters. PAP is sandwiched between the Presentation layer of PostScript and the Transport layers of ATP and NBP. Basically, the function of PAP is to open, maintain, and close a network session with the printer, and to send the print instructions (the PostScript code). PAP is also responsible for determining the printer's status. These printer status indicators are often displayed in the Print Monitor, or in a print status window that appears across the top of the Macintosh screen after print invocation.

ADSP is the last of the Session protocols. It stands for *Apple Data Stream Protocol.* Because ADSP is a Session protocol, part of its job is to open, maintain, manage and close connections between two network devices. In addition, ADSP provides for efficient, bidirectional delivery of data without loss or duplication. Unlike the other Session layer protocols, which connect to various Transport layer protocols one layer down, ADSP skips a layer and connects directly to the Network layer of DDP. This is because ADSP duplicates some of the functionality of the Transport layer. A new alternate version of ADSP, called ASDSP (Apple Secure Data Stream Protocol), has recently been added to the AppleTalk suite. It is part of the Apple Open Collaboration Environment (AOCE) and provides secure communications through encryption techniques.

In some ways, the combination of PAP and ATP (discussed next) provide functionality similar to that of ADSP (and ASDSP). PAP and ATP work in concert to provide a reliable, sequenced, and managed connection to printers; ADSP (and ASDSP) provide the same capability for general network connections.

Transport: RTMP, AURP, ATP, NBP, and AEP

At the Transport layer, the Macintosh uses RTMP, AURP, ATP, NBP, and AEP (see figure 8.4).

RTMP stands for *Routing Table Maintenance Protocol.* RTMP is a protocol spoken by AppleTalk routers, designed to keep AppleTalk network routing tables current. Briefly, an *AppleTalk routing table* is a listing compiled by a router, consisting of each AppleTalk network, its corresponding distance, which router port is used to access that network, and the AppleTalk node number of the nearest router used to access that network. RTMP packets are exchanged by the routers on a regular basis.

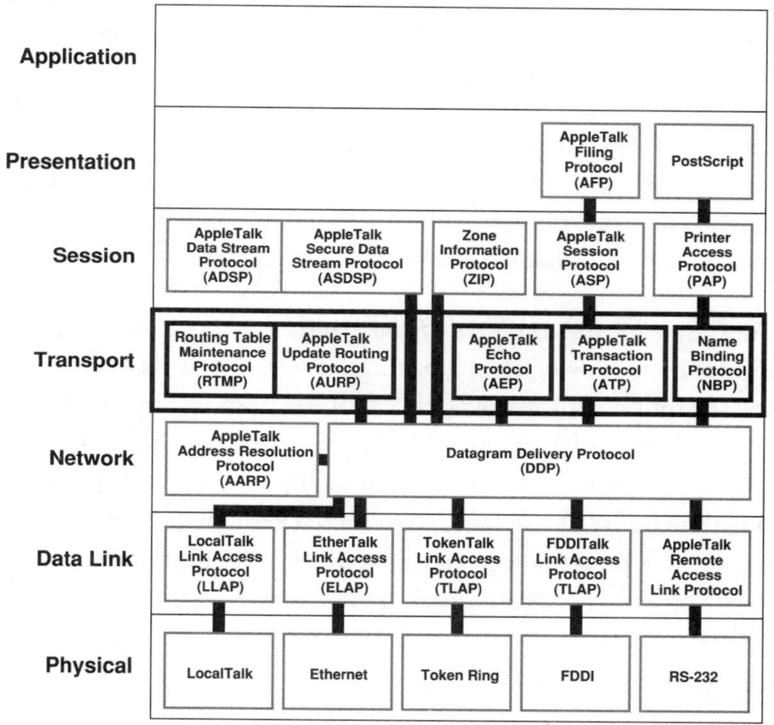

Figure 8.4
Macintosh Transport layer protocols.

RTMP is about to be supplanted by AURP. AURP, the *Apple Update Routing Protocol,* is a new routing protocol that only sends out routing tables when a network change occurs. This new protocol, first introduced with the Apple Internet Router 2.0, will make AppleTalk better suited for use over wide-area networks. Since routing is so important in an AppleTalk network, RTMP and AURP will be discussed in greater detail later on in the chapter.

ATP, the *Apple Transaction Protocol,* provides reliable transport services between the source and destination sockets. Three different types of ATP packets ensure this delivery. First, a *transaction request* gets the attention of the destination socket. The destination socket replies back to the source with a *transaction response,* and the source finishes the transaction with a *transaction release.* As an example, ATP is used by PAP to provide reliable printing to a LaserWriter. It's as if the Mac was saying, "Here's some PostScript," followed by the LaserWriter saying, "OK, I got it," followed by the Mac saying, "OK, here's some more."

NBP is the *Name Binding Protocol.* It's purpose in life is to link names (such as "Joe's LaserWriter" or "Bob's Mac") to AppleTalk addresses. This protocol will be discussed in depth when we analyze how the Chooser works.

AEP stands for the *AppleTalk Echo Protocol.* This is a simple protocol that is used for diagnostic and testing purposes. AEP can be used for two purposes: to check for the presence of another node, or to get an estimate of the round-trip delay time between two nodes on the network. A prime example of AEP is Apple's Inter•Poll utility. It can be used to send a variable number of echo packets to another device on the network. The minimum, maximum and average transit times are displayed.

Network: DDP

At the Network layer, the Macintosh uses the Datagram Delivery Protocol to address the message (see figure 8.5).

The *Datagram Delivery Protocol,* or DDP, is the primary protocol at AppleTalk's Network layer. DDP places AppleTalk communications into a suitable "container" and addresses them for delivery on the internetwork. All the higher-layer data is encapsulated within a DDP datagram.

The datagram is labeled with the source and destination AppleTalk address. This means that the datagram will have two 32-bit AppleTalk addresses that contain the network, node, and socket numbers of the sender, or source, and the recipient, or destination. When routers route AppleTalk packets, they look at the source and destination network numbers in order to determine the best way to route the packet.

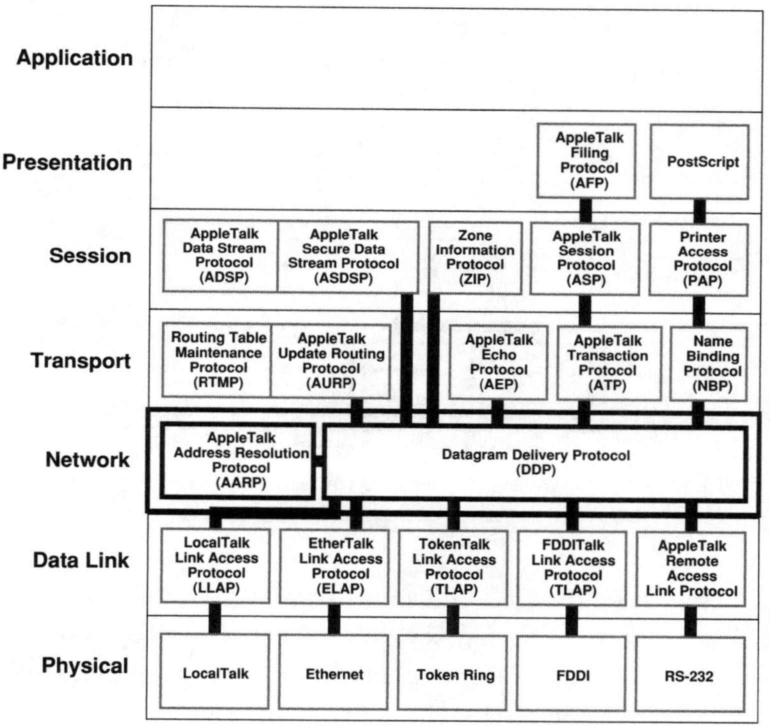

Figure 8.5
Macintosh Network layer protocols.

The datagram is independent of the cabling. Only at the next layer down—the Data Link layer—is the datagram placed within the appropriate cable-specific network frame.

Data Link: LLAP, ELAP, and TLAP

The various data link protocols (see figure 8.6) correspond to the different cabling systems supported on the Mac.

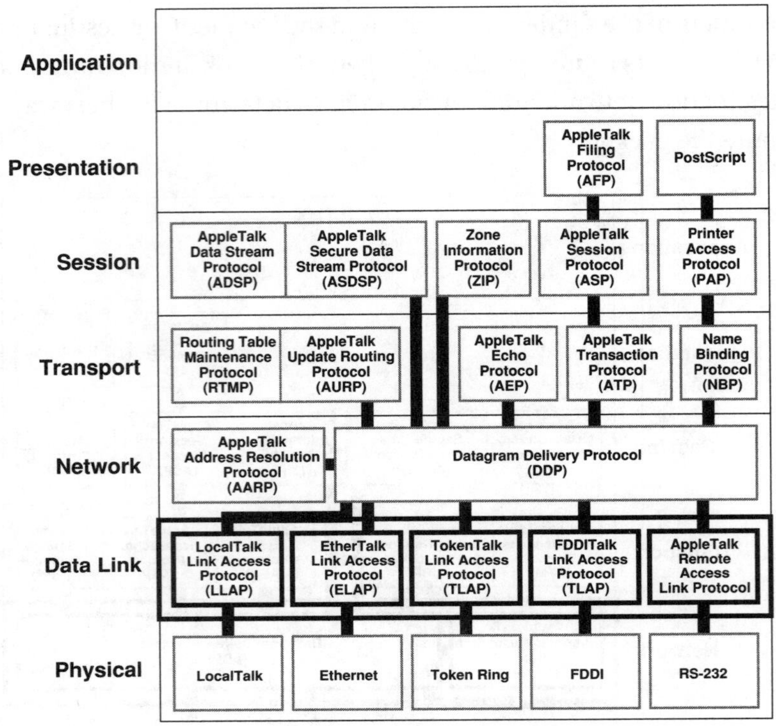

Figure 8.6
At the Data Link layer, the Macintosh uses a number of protocols, such as LLAP, ELAP, and TLAP, to handle different kinds of cabling.

LLAP stands for the *LocalTalk Link Access Protocol* and is the built-in driver that comes with every Mac and networked LaserWriter, and with many LocalTalk peripherals. The LLAP driver takes the DDP datagram and places it in an LLAP frame for subsequent delivery over a LocalTalk network.

ELAP stands for the *EtherTalk Link Access Protocol* and is present on Ethernet-equipped AppleTalk devices. The ELAP driver takes the DDP datagram and places it in the data field of an Ethernet frame.

TLAP stands for the *TokenTalk Link Access Protocol*, and places the DDP datagram within the data field of a Token Ring frame.

How Does AppleTalk Work?

As mentioned in Chapter 4, "Networking Concepts," AppleTalk communication is based on the premise that all devices and network processes are uniquely identified. For AppleTalk, this requires network, node, and socket numbers.

AppleTalk Addressing

AppleTalk network numbers are 16 bits in length; there are 65,536 potential network numbers available for use (see figure 8.7).

Figure 8.7
With 16-bit network numbers, AppleTalk supports more than 65,000 networks!

In the simplest of networks, consisting of a Mac and a LaserWriter connected with LocalTalk, the network number is somewhat useless. There are no routers to maintain the network numbers, and therefore in this case there *are* no network numbers (see figure 8.8). With a single non-routed LocalTalk (or PhoneNET) network, the network number is always 0.

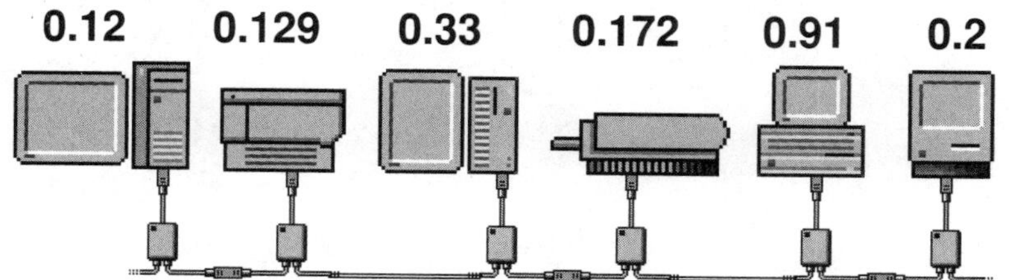

Figure 8.8
In a simple LocalTalk network, the network number is always 0.

In actual network transmission, the 16 bits consisting of all zeros aren't even included in the source and destination of the communications. Why carry 32 bits of "nothing" with every transaction? When these all-zero network numbers are omitted from the source and destination of the DDP datagram, it's known as a *Short DDP*. In cases where the network number is non-zero (and is therefore necessary), the DDP datagram is referred to as a *Long DDP*. Additional addressing details will be covered later in this chapter, when AppleTalk Phase 1 and Phase 2 are described.

The Importance of Dynamic Addressing

Imagine moving into a new house. One of the first things you need to do is to get a new phone. Normally, when you get a new phone, the phone company assigns you a number from their registry of phone numbers. But imagine a phone company that doesn't want to be bothered with the tedious administrative details of assigning unique phone numbers.

This phone company has a system, whereby you simply dial any phone number at random. If someone answers the phone (see figure 8.9), you apologize and hang up. If there's no answer, then that number becomes your new phone number.

Figure 8.9
Someone answers the phone...

This imaginary scenario is the mechanism that Apple uses to dynamically assign AppleTalk node addresses. With other protocols, such as DECnet and TCP/IP, the node ID number is determined and assigned by a human. This human usually has a big list or spreadsheet of node assignments in order to determine which numbers are available for use.

Apple tried to avoid this problem with AppleTalk by implementing a dynamic node-addressing scheme. When a LocalTalk-connected Macintosh boots up on a network for the first time, it chooses a node number at random (see figure 8.10). The Macintosh has no way of knowing whether this random number is already in use by another node, so it sends a special packet (known as an *enquiry control packet*) to the node in question. If the enquiry reaches its destination, the node responds to the inquiring Mac with an *acknowledge control packet.* Of course, this means that the number is in use and cannot be used as the node number for the new Mac on the network.

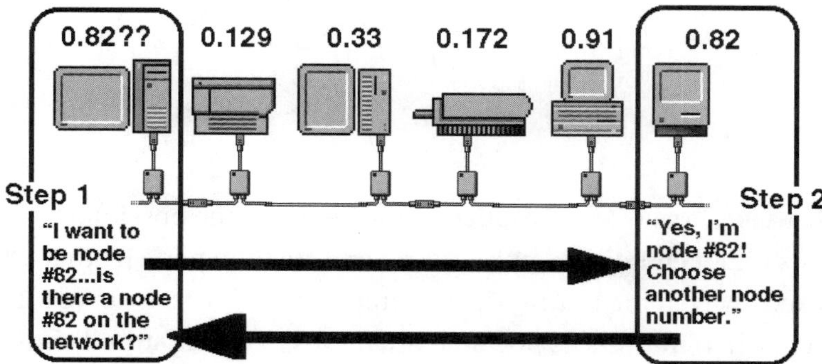

Figure 8.10
A Mac on a LocalTalk network generates its own node address at random.

Therefore, another random node ID and enquiry control packet is generated. If no acknowledge control packet is received, then the new Mac is free to use the number. Once a Macintosh determines a unique node ID for itself, it stores the number in the Mac's PRAM. (The PRAM, or Parameter RAM, is special memory that is non-volatile—a battery is used to maintain its contents even while the

Mac is turned off.) The Macintosh will use the stored node ID as an educated first guess the next time the machine is booted. This minimizes the node ID contention during startup.

Generally, a Mac's node number remains with a given Mac, but this is not always the case. When a Macintosh, or any AppleTalk node, is turned off, it's unable to respond to the enquiry control packets sent out by the other machines. Using the phone example, it's as if the receiver of the message was asleep or out of the house—he would be unable to answer the phone (see figure 8.11).

Figure 8.11
No answer—even though there's a phone with the requested number.

Likewise, if a new Mac is added to the network, the possibility exists that it could randomly guess—and steal—a node ID that is locked away in the PRAM of a powered-down Mac (see figure 8.12). Then, when this Mac is powered on, it tries to use its stored node ID as its first guess, and the other Mac responds with the acknowledgment packet. This causes the original Mac to establish a new node ID. Therefore, it's quite possible for your Mac to be node 44 on Monday and node 32 on Tuesday. With AppleTalk, it's not important that a node number be permanently associated with a given Macintosh.

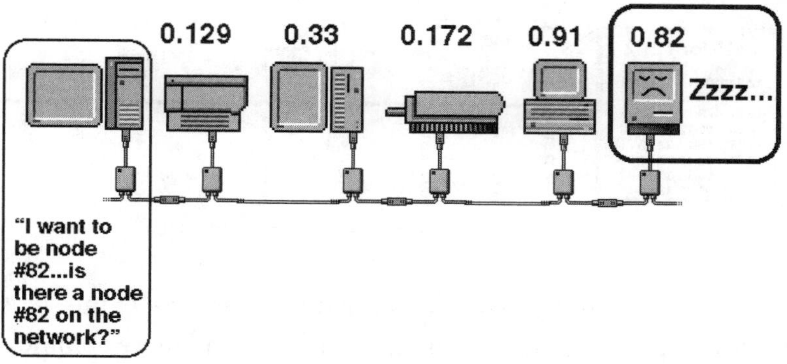

Figure 8.12

In this case, there is a node #82 on the network, but that Mac is not running and therefore is unable to respond to the enquiry control packet. The Mac on the left will "steal" the sleeping Mac's node number.

If the Mac is connected to an EtherTalk network, the process for establishing a unique number is a bit different. As we discussed in Chapter 4, "Networking Concepts," each Ethernet card has a unique address stored in its hardware. AppleTalk must create a standard AppleTalk logical address and associate it with the Ethernet hardware address. Because of this, the Mac uses another protocol—the *AppleTalk Address Resolution Protocol*, or AARP—to create a logical AppleTalk address, instead of using the LLAP Enquiry technique. Upon booting a Mac onto an EtherTalk network, your Mac broadcasts a series of AARP probes. The AARP probes contain a tentative AppleTalk logical address and the physical hardware address of the Ethernet card. After the receiving nodes compare the logical addresses and report back any conflicts, the Macintosh obtains a unique logical AppleTalk address.

AARP is also used to construct an Address Mapping Table (AMT), which links the logical AppleTalk address to the physical Ethernet address. This dynamically generated and updated table, exemplified in figure 8.13, contains recent AppleTalk addresses and their corresponding Ethernet hardware addresses.

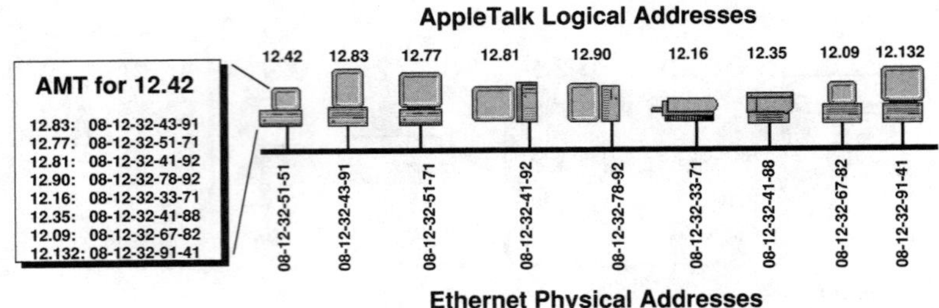

Figure 8.13
AARP is used to construct an Address Mapping Table, which equates logical AppleTalk addresses with physical Ethernet addresses.

In fact, this is a very important and significant feature of the AppleTalk protocol. As computers get smaller and more commonplace, and as wireless networking catches on, dynamic node addressing will become crucial. It would be ridiculous to have to stop at the front door of a company that uses a wireless LAN simply to receive a network node ID for your Newton personal digital assistant (see figure 8.14). These node numbers don't possess any intrinsic meaning—they're simply unique numbers, and it just so happens that computers can do an excellent job of assigning unique numbers.

Figure 8.14
I need a node number?!?

Zones

Zone names are simply names assigned to networks. They, along with network numbers, are stored within the AppleTalk routers. In the case of LocalTalk (Phase 1 AppleTalk) networks, there can be only one network number and one zone name per network. Imagine a simple internet, figure 8.15, consisting of two LocalTalk networks connected by a router. Each network has a unique network number and different zone names.

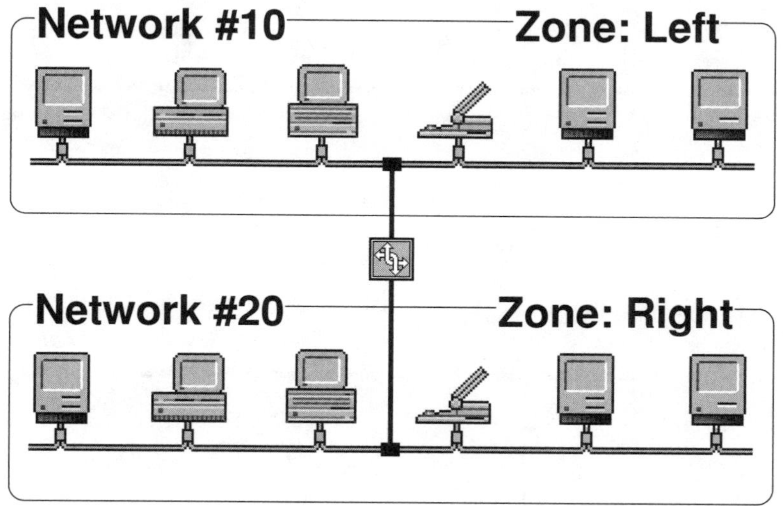

Figure 8.15
Two LocalTalk networks connected with a router. Each network has a unique network number and different zone names.

Each network has a unique network number (10 and 20), and each network has a zone name (Left and Right). Here, the zone name Left is used to identify the devices in network number 10; Right is used to identify devices in network number 20.

There's no uniqueness requirement, however, for zone names. It's perfectly fine to have duplicate zone names in order to logically organize services. Therefore, networks 10 and 20 could have the same zone name of "CAL." In figure 8.16, each network still has a unique network number, but the zone names are the same.

When networks have the same zone name, similar devices are grouped together. So, if there were two LaserWriters in network 10 and three LaserWriters in network 20, there would be a total of five LaserWriters in the "CAL" zone. Keep in mind, however, that when there's only one zone, the Macintosh Chooser does not display the zone list. This is true even when there are multiple networks with the same zone name.

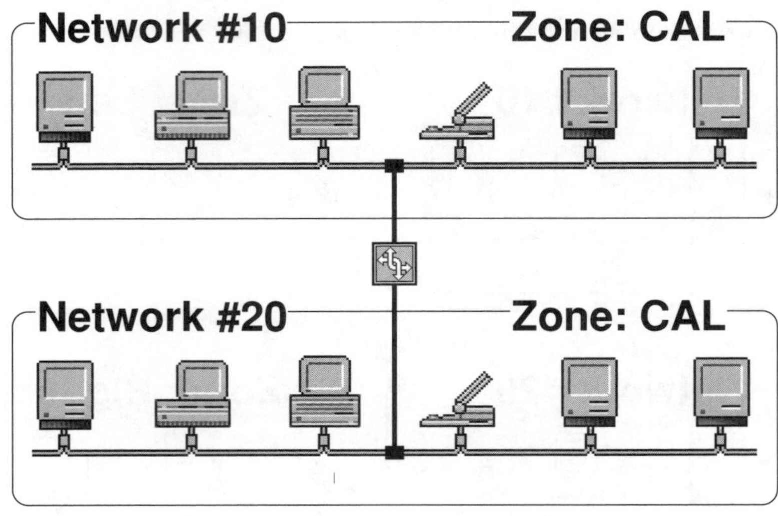

Figure 8.16
In this example, each network still has a unique network number, but the zone names are the same.

In the case of Ethernet and Token Ring networks (Phase 2 AppleTalk), a cable segment can be assigned a range of network numbers and multiple zone names. In figure 8.17, the zone names are not associated with any specific network number.

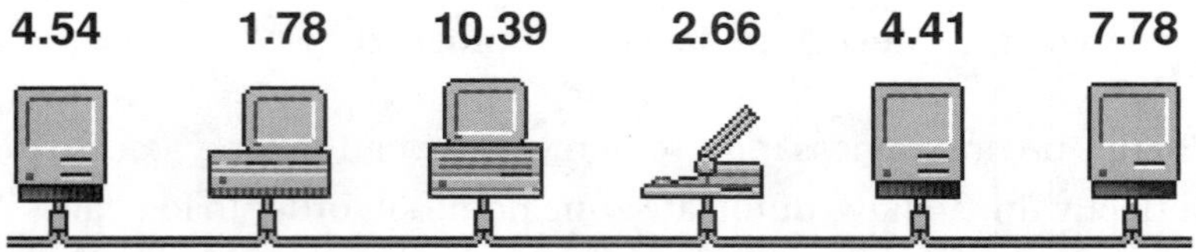

Figure 8.17
Ethernet and Token Ring AppleTalk networks can use a range of network numbers.

With Phase 2 networks (described in the next section), the zone names are defined for the entire network segment. When a

Macintosh (or other AppleTalk node) is added to the cable, it automatically belongs to the Default zone.

The Default zone is a designated zone where AppleTalk nodes appear by default. It's established by choosing a zone from the list of defined zones maintained by the router configuration software. If there are multiple routers on the cable, as in figure 8.18, all routers must agree on the network range, zone list, and default zone assignment for the cable. Mismatched net numbers and zone lists are the most frequent causes of network problems.

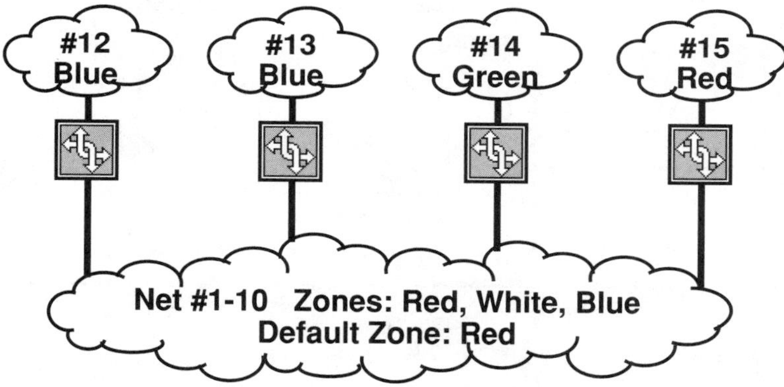

Figure 8.18
All routers on a given segment must agree on the network number range, zones and the default zone.

As shown in figure 8.19, you can change your Mac's default zone assignment by opening the Network control panel and double-clicking on the EtherTalk or TokenTalk icon. A zone list will appear, along with a prompt to change the Mac's zone. From then on, your Mac will belong to that zone—until you decide to change it again. If you're unsure which zone your Mac belongs to, simply open the Chooser. The highlighted zone is the zone to which your Macintosh belongs.

It's important to realize that the choice of zone names can affect network performance. For example, consider a wide-area network that connects two AppleTalk-Ethernet LANs. As shown in figure 8.20, one network is in Washington and the other is located in

Little Rock. One could assign zone names geographically by creating a "Washington" and "Little Rock" zone, or functionally by creating an "Administrative" and "Judicial" zone. However, if you group by function, instead of geography, there is a potential for increased traffic.

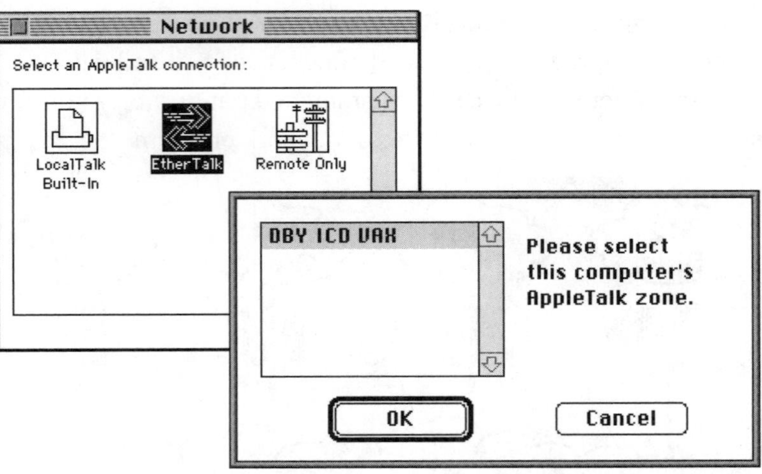

Figure 8.19 The default zone assignment of a Mac can be changed by double-clicking on the EtherTalk or TokenTalk icon in the Network Control Panel.

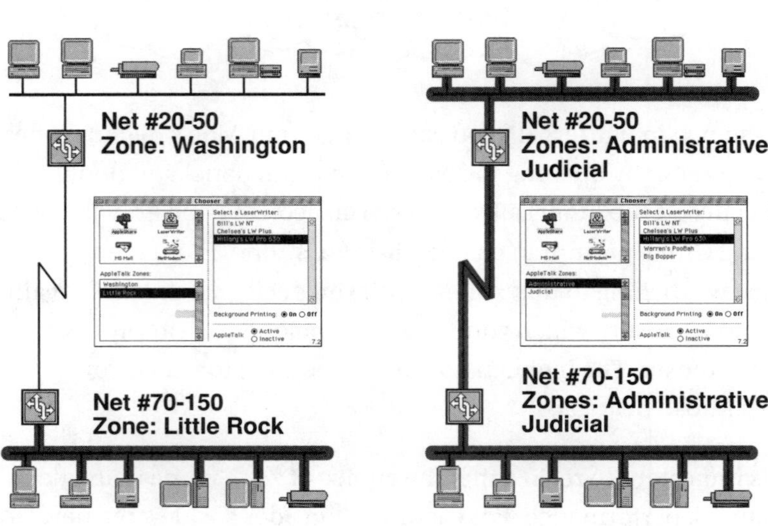

Figure 8.20 AppleTalk zones can be set up geographically or functionally. However, there can be a performance difference.

Let's look at an example of functional grouping. Suppose there are three LaserWriters located in Little Rock on the Administrative zone, and six LaserWriters located in Washington on the Administrative zone. Every time I select the Administrative zone from a Mac in Washington, AppleTalk must not only poll for the printers in Washington, but it must also poll over the wide-area connection for printers in Little Rock. Eventually, I'll see nine LaserWriters in my Chooser. The problem with this functional approach is that large AppleTalk networks over limited-bandwidth links can bog down with the polling traffic. If the zones are arranged geographically, then the polling traffic remains local and doesn't burden the wide-area connection.

NOTE: Zone names can be up to 32 characters in length. They are case-insensitive. This means that zone "Little Rock" and zone "LITTLE ROCK" are the same. Zone names are much easier to read, however, if the standard sentence case is used. Spaces are significant, so be careful not to type an extra space between words or to add an unwanted space at the end of a name.

If you're creating a zoned network, try to establish a meaningful zone-naming convention prior to router installation. Remember that network numbers are for the computer's convenience; zone names are for the users' convenience. Your zone-naming standard should help users find networked printers and file servers, and should be flexible enough to support future expansion.

Zone names of "First Floor" and "Second Floor" only make sense if your organization has a single building. Avoid the practice of naming zones after the room number of the wiring closet where the router is located. Zone names should also be coordinated with device name conventions (such as AFP servers and LaserWriters). If your zone-naming convention consists of a city, building number, and floor, it's not necessary to repeat this information at the device level. Instead, try to include information that pinpoints the final location or function of the device.

AppleTalk Phase 1 and 2

In the beginning, when Apple designed AppleTalk and LocalTalk, there was no distinction between Phase 1 and Phase 2. When Apple developed EtherTalk, which is nothing more than AppleTalk protocols on Ethernet cabling, they simply carried the original AppleTalk protocol used on LocalTalk networks over to Ethernet.

Apple developed AppleTalk Phase 2 to address certain shortcomings that were present in the initial EtherTalk implementation. Phase 1 EtherTalk networks were restricted to a maximum of 254 devices and were inefficient when it came to certain aspects of routing and broadcasting. Phase 2 fixed these problems, and also provided the first version of TokenTalk, which is Apple's implementation of the AppleTalk protocols on Token Ring networks.

Phase 1

Phase 1 networks, as mentioned before, can only have a single network number per cable segment. Because AppleTalk only supports 256 potential nodes per network number, each cable segment was therefore limited to 256 devices (see figure 8.21).

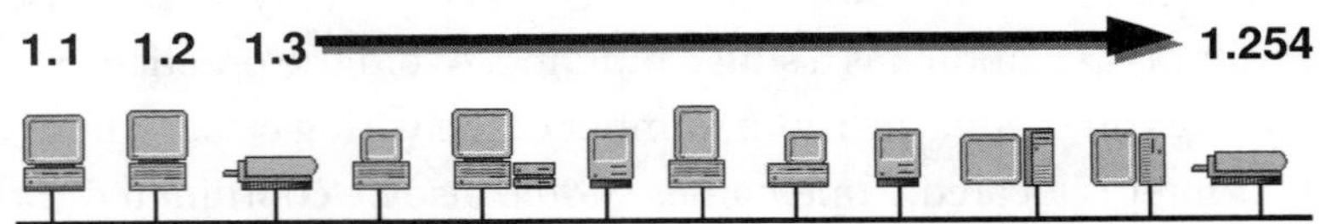

Figure 8.21
Each AppleTalk network can potentially support 256 devices. Phase 1 and Phase 2 reserve different values.

Phase 1 Limits

Actually, the limit is 254 devices. With Phase 1 networks, node numbers range from 0 to 255. 0 is not used and 255 is reserved for broadcasts heard by all devices.

With LocalTalk, this is hardly a problem. LocalTalk networks have electrical and isolation restrictions that limit the number of nodes to a recommended limit of 32 devices. When Apple introduced the first version of EtherTalk, it too was limited to a single network number and 254 nodes per segment. This was bad news for large organizations that wanted to start populating their Ethernets with Macs. This was particularly bad news for those organizations that had bridged Ethernets that spanned many locations. They were limited to a grand total of 254 EtherTalk devices throughout their entire organization (see figure 8.22). Apple addressed this problem in 1989 with the introduction of AppleTalk Phase 2.

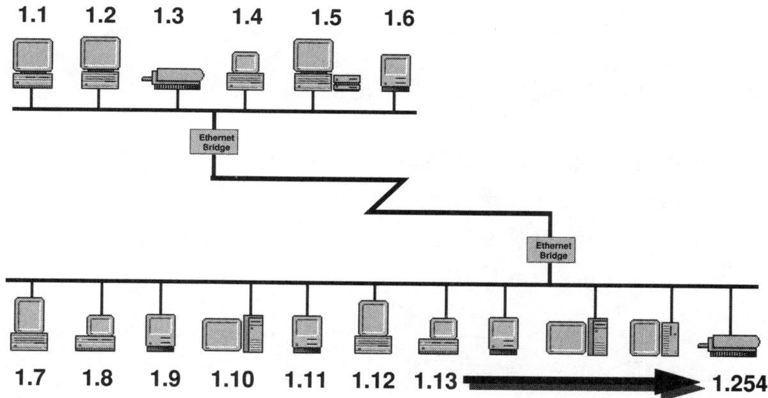

Figure 8.22
It was easy to reach the 254 node limit of EtherTalk Phase 1, particularly with large, bridged Ethernet networks.

Phase 1 and 2 Network Number Assignment

Phase 2 broke the 254 node limit by avoiding the restriction of a single network number per cable segment. Instead, the cable (either Ethernet or Token Ring) can be assigned a range of values. In a Phase 2 network, the network numbers range from 0 to 65,534. Zero (0) is undefined and not used. A special range, called the *startup range*, runs from 65,280 through 65,534. This leaves the numbers 1 through 65,279 for general assignment.

Let's review the network number assignment rules.

- Phase 1 (LocalTalk, and the now-extinct first version of EtherTalk) with no routers (see figure 8.23).

  The network number is always 0. In practice the 16-bit zero network number is omitted from the address to conserve space. This is known as a *Short DDP* address.

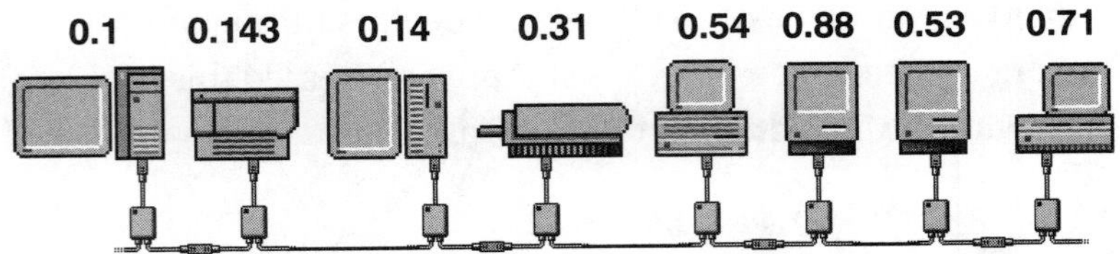

Figure 8.23
Phase 1 with no routers.

- Phase 1 with routers (see figure 8.24).

  The network number is a single number between 1 and 65,536. Each network segment, either LocalTalk or the old EtherTalk, must have a single number assigned. No duplicates are permitted.

Figure 8.24
Phase 1 with routers. Network numbers can be 1 through 65,536

- Phase 2 (the current version of EtherTalk and TokenTalk) with no routers (see figure 8.25).

The network numbers fall in a range between 65,280 and 65,534. This is known as the Startup range. There are 254 numbers in this range that are used by AppleTalk nodes as they come onto the network.

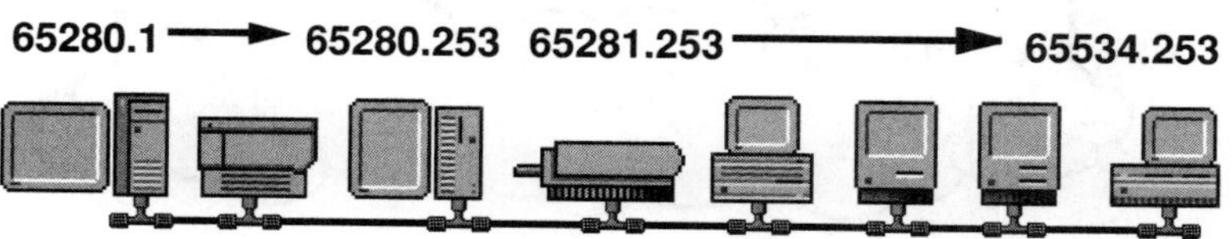

Figure 8.25
Phase 2 with no routers. When no routers are present, Phase 2 devices assign network numbers in the startup range—65,280-65,534.

The choice of network number, like the node number, is made at random. One Macintosh could be in network 65,288 and be node 23; an adjacent Mac could be in network 65,500 and be node 23.

> **NOTE:** In Phase 2 networks, there is an additional reserved node number, so there can only be 253 nodes per network. This means that for a single, logical segment of Ethernet, there can be 254 networks each having 253 nodes. This multiplies for a total of 64,262 AppleTalk devices per segment. If you need more than this, an AppleTalk router will be required.

- Phase 2 with routers (see figure 8.26).

  The network numbers are a range between 1 and 65,279. 0 is not used and 65,280 through 65,534 are reserved for the startup range. Theoretically, you could use the entire range of numbers for a single segment, but this would be wasteful. Instead, it makes sense to assign a modest range of numbers to a cable. This way, growth and expansion can be easily accommodated.

Figure 8.26
Phase 2 with Routers. Network numbers can be 1 through 65,279.

For example, in a large organization, it might make sense to assign ranges to the various divisional locations. Houston can have 1-100, Dallas 101-200 and San Antonio 201-300. Then local network managers can add routers using network numbers in their pre-assigned range. We'll see later how Apple's new routing protocol, AURP, extends this concept even further and provides additional flexibility in network number assignment.

Phase 2 Transition Routing

Before 1989, EtherTalk networks were Phase 1. As mentioned before, they were limited to a maximum of 254 AppleTalk devices. When Phase 2 was introduced, Apple chose a different Ethernet frame format and type code. From an Ethernet perspective, this meant the Phase 1 and Phase 2 packets could be readily distinguished by network devices. It also meant that Phase 1 and Phase 2 protocols could coexist on the same cable.

The coexistence of Phase 1 and Phase 2 was originally deemed as desirable, since large organizations making the switch would find it difficult to upgrade all at once. The only problem with this coexistence technique was that the Phase 1 and Phase 2 devices could only communicate with like devices. A Phase 1 node could not communicate with a Phase 2 node. Apple addressed this problem with an interim solution called *transition routing*.

A router (either a Mac running the AppleTalk Internet Router, or a dedicated router, such as a FastPath) could be configured as a transition router. The transition router's function was to accept all Phase 1 packets and retransmit them as Phase 2 packets, and vice-versa. This unfortunately doubled the traffic, but at least the Phase 1 and 2 nodes could communicate during the transition process.

Today, Phase 1 EtherTalk networks are rare. Almost everyone has converted to Phase 2. Those sites still running Phase 1 EtherTalk are at a significant disadvantage. In addition to increasing the number of devices and zones per segment, Apple made other significant improvements with Phase 2.

Phase 1 Broadcasting versus Phase 2 Multicasting

Starting with AppleTalk Phase 2, Apple altered the broadcasting mechanism (used by NBP Lookups and other AppleTalk services) to utilize a more specific technique known as multicasting. Let's first review the concept of broadcasting, using Ethernet as an example.

Often, a networking protocol (such as AppleTalk) must make an announcement to all the devices on the network. Imagine that you work at a large company and you need to contact someone. If you know that person's phone number, you simply dial the number, but what if you don't know that person's number, or they don't answer the phone? Then, you'll need to have that person paged (see figure 8.27). Loudspeakers all over the company send out a "broadcast" message. Of course, this approach is somewhat inefficient; you're only looking for one person, but everyone in the company has to listen to the message. This is essentially how Ethernet broadcasting is implemented.

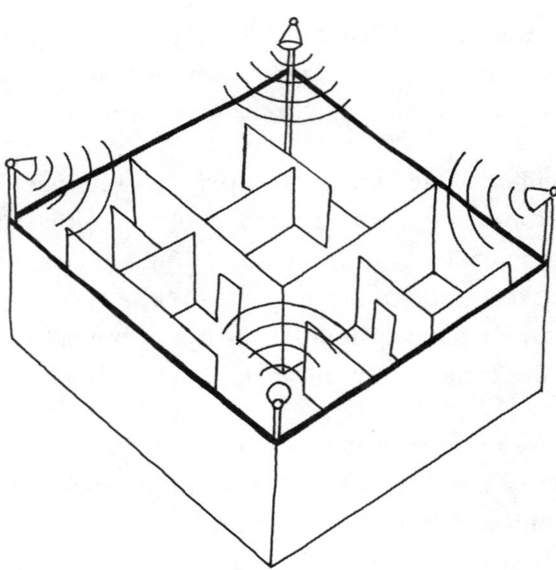

Figure 8.27

Ethernet broadcasts are like company-wide paging that is trying to locate one person.

Compared to other protocols, it's probably fair to say that AppleTalk generates more broadcast messages. In fact, in the early days of Phase 1 EtherTalk, AppleTalk started to get a bad reputation for being excessively "chatty" for this very reason. What annoyed some people was that these AppleTalk-generated broadcasts were being sent to all devices on a given Ethernet—regardless of whether that device even spoke AppleTalk protocols. Thus, the owners of minicomputers, PCs, and UNIX workstations started to complain that their machines were spending an inordinate amount of time responding to broadcasts not intended for their machines. Just imagine how annoying it would be if the same group of people were being continually paged and you always had to listen to the messages since you sat right next to the loudspeaker.

The solution is to be more specific with the broadcast messages. Imagine if the pages were made on a departmental basis (see figure 8.28). If you need to have someone paged, the phone operator asks you for the department of the pagee. When the page is made, only those loudspeakers in the specific department are used. The rest of the employees are spared from having to hear the irrelevant message. This is the concept behind *multicasting*. Each networking protocol that supports multicasting has a unique multicasting address assigned. This address is similar to the department name used in the prior example. An AppleTalk multicast is only "heard" by other AppleTalk nodes. A TCP/IP multicast is only heard by other TCP/IP nodes. With Phase 2, AppleTalk traffic is also more efficient through multicasting, since Phase 2 multicasts are contained within a given zone, even though there may be only one cable segment containing other zones.

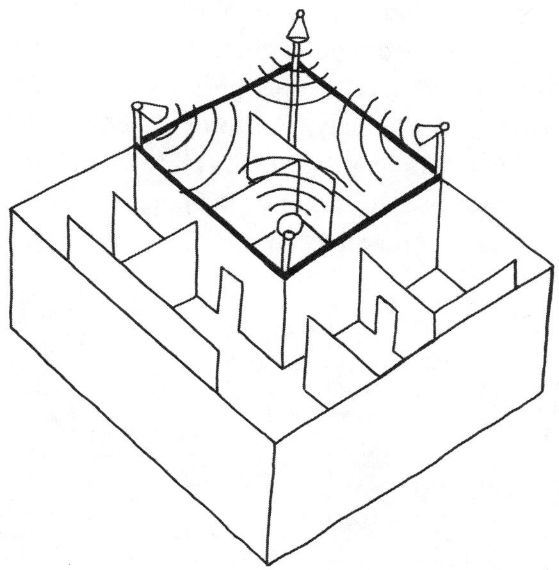

Figure 8.28
Ethernet Multicasts are similar to department-wide paging that is trying to locate one person.

How Does the Chooser Work?

The Chooser is one of the coolest, least understood aspects of the Macintosh. With it, a user can find and select network (and local) services in an easy and consistent manner. The Chooser does many interesting things behind the scenes. It dynamically generates a list of available network zones. When you choose a particular service by clicking on an icon, the Chooser then generates a list of those devices that meet the selection criteria. Finally, once you've selected a particular named service, the Chooser proceeds to discover the AppleTalk address of the chosen service. (You see, the names in the Chooser are for your benefit, while the network addresses are for the benefit of the Macintosh.)

The Unknown Address

We've discussed how AppleTalk dynamically assigns a node number to a device. This was a wonderful achievement, but Apple had an additional problem to solve. Each AppleTalk device automatically generates a unique node number, but initially it's only known by that device. Nodes don't automatically know the node numbers of other devices. With other protocols, such as DECnet, this problem is solved manually. Someone (usually the DECnet administrator) uses a utility program to create a database of node addresses. This database, exemplified in figure 8.29, is required on every DECnet node in order for that node to communicate with the other nodes.

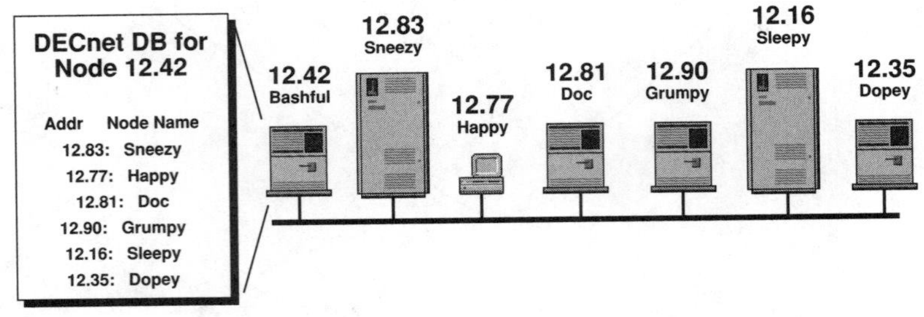

Figure 8.29 Unlike AppleTalk, which dynamically discovers network addresses and services, DECnet requires a specific listing of available nodes before communication can be established.

Apple, desiring a plug-and-play environment, decided that this manual creation of node lists was not in keeping with the spirit of Macintosh. An alternative approach was developed to solve the problem of address determination. Let's consider a Mac that needs to print a document to a particular LaserWriter on the network.

The Mac doesn't have any idea of the other nodes on the network. Therefore, it must go through a process of discovery to identify the available services. This is done by the AppleTalk protocol known as the *Name Binding Protocol*, or NBP.

The process is simple. When a user opens the Chooser and clicks on a service icon (such as the LaserWriter icon), the Macintosh first acquires a list of zones from the nearest routers with the Zone Information Protocol (ZIP). It then sends out a NBP Lookup Request packet. (Actually, it doesn't simply send it out, it broadcasts—or multicasts—the request to all devices on the cable. This makes sense because the Mac has no idea who to send the request to anyway.) Essentially, the NBP Lookup Request packet contains information on the requested named service. A name in the AppleTalk system is called a *Network Visible Entity*, or NVE.

AppleTalk Names and the NVE

NVEs aren't nodes; rather, they are the services offered by nodes. These services are identified by their socket numbers. One AppleTalk node could support a number of services, each with a socket number and a corresponding NVE. The NVE consists of three components along with delimiters and some special symbols. Each name (object, type and zone) is a 32 character case-insensitive alphanumeric name. The syntax is: Object:Type@Zone.

The Object name is the name of the entity that is usually assigned by a person. For a Mac, the object name is defined in the Macintosh Name field of the Sharing Setup Control Panel. LaserWriter object names are established by the Namer utility program. Examples of object names include: `Jim's Mac`, `3rd Floor LaserWriter`, and `Joe's File Server`.

The Type name is the generic name of the service. Apple maintains a registry of these names. For Macs and LaserWriters, the type name has traditionally been the model name of the device. Some examples include `Macintosh IIci`, `LaserWriter Pro 630`, and `PowerBook 180`. Other, more generic type names include `AFPServer` and `PAPSpooler`. Remember, since NVEs and type names are based on sockets, it is possible (and likely) that a single node will have several NVEs.

The last field of the NVE is the zone name where the service can be found. Zone names, as explained earlier, are created by the network administrator and exist within the AppleTalk network routers.

Here are some examples of NVEs:

- `Jim's Mac:Quadra 950@Office Zone`
- `The Group's Printer:LaserWriter@New York City`

In addition to the names, there are special wildcard characters that can be applied to the NVE:

- An equal sign (=) in the Object or Type fields means all objects, regardless of Object (or Type) names.
- An asterisk (*) in the zone field indicates the current zone of the requesting node.

Let's review some examples of NVEs with wildcard characters. `=:=@*` means all objects, of all types, in the current zone. `=:AFPServer@*` means all objects of type AFPServer in the current zone. `=:LaserWriter@Blue` means all objects of type LaserWriter in the Blue zone.

Now, with a basic understanding of the NVE, we can return to the Chooser. When you click on the LaserWriter icon (see figure 8.30), the Macintosh generates an NVE that corresponds to the service and the currently selected zone. The NVE takes the form `=:LaserWriter@*`.

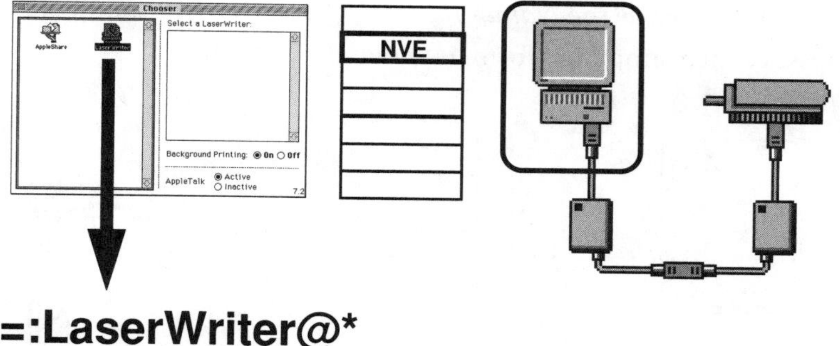

Figure 8.30
When you click on the LaserWriter icon, the Macintosh generates an NVE (Network Visible Entity), shown above. This happens at the Presentation layer.

Deciphering this NVE, we can establish that the Macintosh is looking for all names of type `LaserWriter` in the current selected zone.

This NVE is then referenced within the NBP Lookup Request (see figure 8.31). Remembering that NBP is a Transport layer protocol, the next layer down is the Network layer of DDP. Thus, the NBP Lookup Request is then handed down to DDP.

Figure 8.31
The NVE is placed within an NBP Lookup Request packet. This takes place in the Transport layer.

Next, the DDP datagram must be addressed. The "From" part of the address is easy. The sending Macintosh simply uses its own network and node number. A socket number is chosen at random from the pool of available socket numbers. The "To" part of the address contains the network number, the broadcast/multicast node number of 255, and a special reserved socket number of 2, which is known as the *Names Information Socket.* The complete message, in a simplified form, is shown in figure 8.32.

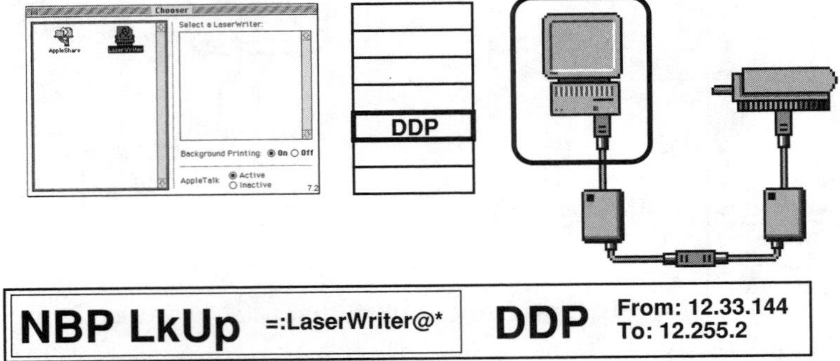

Figure 8.32 DDP Datagram Addressing. The NVE is placed within an NBP Lookup Request packet. This takes place at the Transport layer.

`From: 12.33.144` (the Macintosh)

`To: 12.255.2` (Anyone who will listen)

`NBP LkUp`

`=:LaserWriter@*`

Let's translate this into English:

"Hey there, all you AppleTalk nodes! This is device 12.33 communicating over socket 144. I'm broadcasting to everyone in network number 12 and I'm particularly interested in names. I'm looking for all the names of LaserWriters in the current zone."

The DDP datagram, which contains the NBP request, is then placed in a network frame (see figure 8.33). This frame is then sent out over the cable to all the devices.

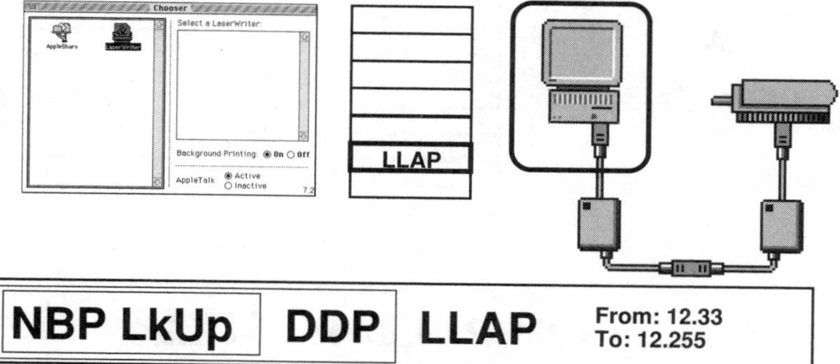

Figure 8.33 The DDP datagram is placed inside an LLAP frame. Since LocalTalk doesn't use physical addresses, LLAP uses the logical AppleTalk addresses.

A device might discard the message if it doesn't apply, but if the NBP request is sent to a device where the NVE matches, such as a LaserWriter, it accepts the datagram, opens it and processes the NBP request (see figures 8.34 through 8.40).

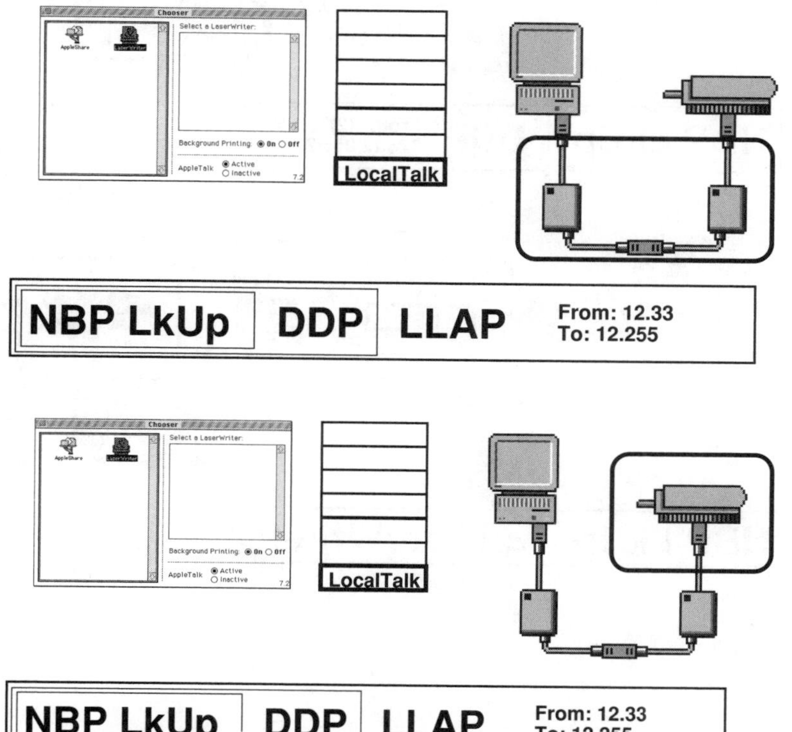

Figure 8.34 The entire contents of the LLAP frame is then broadcast onto the cable segment.

Figure 8.35 Since the message was broadcast over the network, the LaserWriter (and other nodes) process the LocalTalk frame.

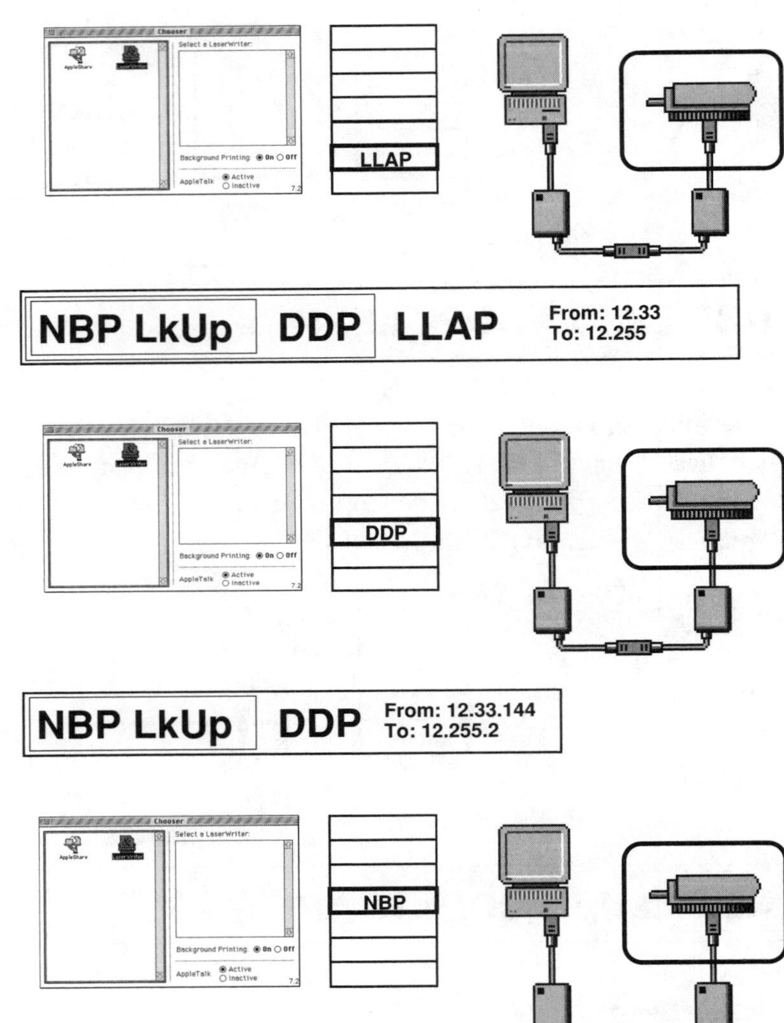

Figure 8.36
The LaserWriter inspects the LLAP frame it received from the LocalTalk broadcast.

Figure 8.37
The LaserWriter strips off the LLAP frame to reveal the DDP Datagram. Now the LaserWriter knows who sent the message.

Figure 8.38
Finally, the LaserWriter uncovered the NBP Lookup request and knows that the device 12.33.144 is interested in names.

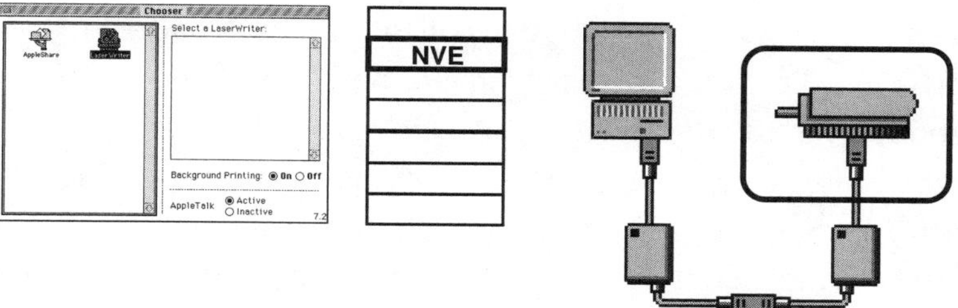

=:LaserWriter@*

Figure 8.39 The LaserWriter inspects the NVE and proceeds to fulfill the NBP Lookup Request.

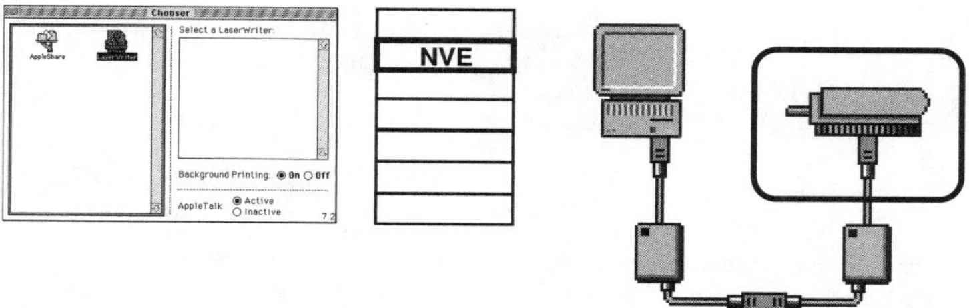

Deb's Dreamy LaserWriter:LaserWriter@*

Figure 8.40 The LaserWriter completes the NVE by adding its name to the NVE.

When a LaserWriter responds to this request, it generates a NBP Response such as `Deb's Dreamy LaserWriter:LaserWriter@*`, which is shown in figure 8.41.

Deb's Dreamy LaserWriter :LaserWriter@*	NBP Response

Figure 8.41 The LaserWriter puts the completed NVE into an NBP Response packet.

The responding devices essentially fill in the blanks of their respective NVEs. Then, the process reverses order. After a LaserWriter responds, its NBP Response is placed into a DDP datagram. The "From" address is simply the address of the LaserWriter, which it already knows; the "To" address is referenced from the source address of the incoming request previously received. The complete message looks like the one shown in figure 8.42.

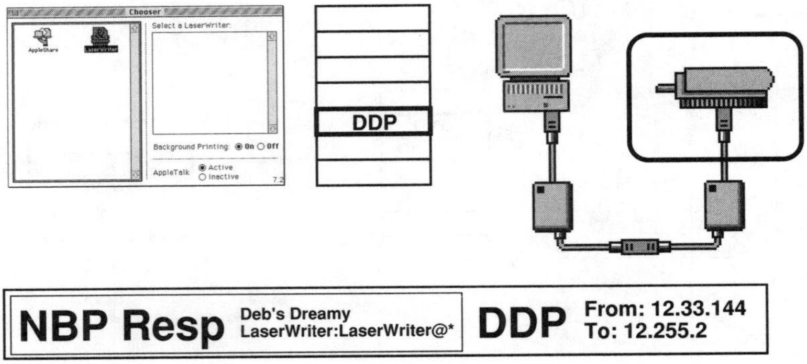

Figure 8.42
The LaserWriter puts the completed NBP Response into a DDP Datagram. The datagram is addressed to the sender of the original message.

Thus, the response is:

`From: 12.144.133` (the LaserWriter)

`To: 12.33.144` (the Macintosh)

`NBP Resp`

`Deb's Dreamy LaserWriter:LaserWriter@*`

Again, let's translate this response into English.

"OK, I hear you, Macintosh! I'm a LaserWriter in your current zone; my name is "Deb's Dreamy LaserWriter" and my address is 12.144.133. Since you told me what address you are when you sent your NBP Lookup Request, I'll send this information to you right away."

Of course, multiple LaserWriters can respond to the NBP Lookup Request, and as they do, your Macintosh displays their names in the Chooser (see figure 8.43). Then, when you select a printer, the Macintosh simply remembers the name of the currently selected printer. This name is then stored in the memory of the Macintosh. This is why, for example, when someone moves their PowerBook from the office network to their home network, the office printer will still be selected. To solve this problem, the LaserWriter must be reselected from the Chooser.

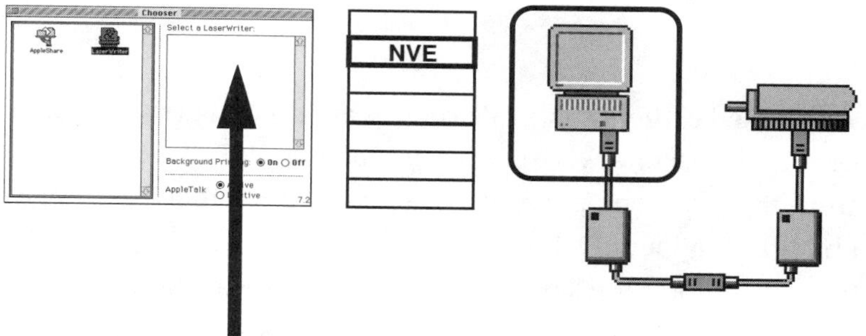

Figure 8.43 After performing a similar process to the LaserWriter, the Mac processes the LLAP and NBP and then places the name of the LaserWriter (and any other responding LWs) into the Macintosh Chooser.

This process also offers an explanation for the rare event that occasionally happens when someone selects a printer on Friday, then the network is altered over the weekend and the printer just so happens to choose a new node number for itself. When Monday comes, the user receives a "...can't locate printer" message. Again, reselecting the printer from the Chooser solves the problem.

This NBP request/response conversation happens every time a Macintosh user selects a service from the Chooser. Because the NBP delivery mechanism involves broadcasting (or multicasting), NBP traffic can be a significant part of AppleTalk network traffic.

AppleTalk Routing

Big AppleTalk internetworks are created by connecting little AppleTalk networks. Routers are the devices that are used to connect the networks. AppleTalk routers are an important part of many AppleTalk networks. In addition to providing a mechanism for growth, they also are used to provide traffic isolation and a means for logically grouping (organizing) network services. In this section, we'll explore how AppleTalk routers accomplish these basic tasks.

Routing Tables

As discussed earlier, AppleTalk routers are used to physically and logically connect network segments. Each AppleTalk network that connects to a port on the router is assigned a number, or a range of numbers, that identify that particular network. These AppleTalk network numbers are key to the operation of the router.

AppleTalk routers rely on tables, stored within the router, to forward AppleTalk datagrams from one network to another. The routing tables keep track of all networks by containing an entry for each network number. For each network number on the internet, the routing table includes the distance of each network (measured in hops, which is the number of routers between the router and the destination network), which port on the router should be used to connect the destination network, and the AppleTalk node ID of the next router. This is shown in Table 8.2.

Table 8.2 A simple routing table.

Net #	*Distance*	*Port*	*Next Router #*
10	0	1	0
20	0	2	0

Net #	*Distance*	*Port*	*Next Router #*
30	1	3	12
40	2	3	12

RTMP, or the *Routing Table Maintenance Protocol*, was Apple's only protocol that maintained routing tables among the routers of an AppleTalk internet. With RTMP, these routing tables are regularly updated every 10 seconds. This is accomplished by each router exchanging routing tables with the other routers on the network. When a router receives a new routing table, it compares it to the existing table. If a new network has been added, or a network distance has been changed, the router updates its table.

RTMP traffic is normally present only between the routers on the internet, but still represents a certain percentage of the total traffic on the network. One of the problems with RTMP is the regular transmission of the routing tables, which occurs even when the network is stable and the network numbers and the routing tables remain unchanged.

To better understand the function of RTMP, let's return to the classroom analogy. As shown in figure 8.44, when the students pass notes between themselves, they frequently have to use an intermediate student as a router. Let's consider that a student is a two-port router (her arms represent network ports). The students who are acting as routers need to know the names of other students and the corresponding student-routers to which they are connected. These student-routers also need to know which hand (port) to use.

Figure 8.44
The students in the class pass their messages through routers.

To solve this problem, each student-router creates a special kind of note that lists all the note recipients, the number of intervening student-routers, which arm to use, and the name of the next student-router in the note-passing chain. Then, once all the student-routers have their own list, they pass it to the other student-routers, who check the notes for updates. These routing lists are shown in figure 8.45. This process continues at regular intervals regardless of classroom changes.

Figure 8.45
Each student router, Pat and Paula, has her own routing information that she uses to route the other students' messages.

Of course, under certain conditions, the note passing between the student-routers can become a problem. The same is true in the real AppleTalk world, as this continual RTMP traffic can become a burden on large networks with many routers (particularly when the routers are connected to WAN links of limited bandwidth).

This routing technique, which uses a list of destination networks with their corresponding distances and the next router in the chain, is called *vector-distance routing*, or *Bellman-Ford* routing. It is a simple routing algorithm (as illustrated in figure 8.46), that attempts to find the shortest path for a datagram by minimizing the number of hops. Other protocols, such as DECnet and TCP/IP, use other routing algorithms that may be more efficient under certain circumstances. Apple is currently investigating other routing algorithms for possible future adoption and inclusion into AppleTalk.

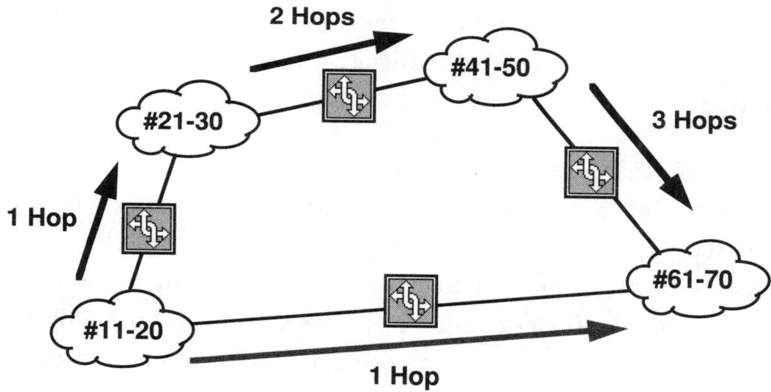

Figure 8.46
AppleTalk datagrams are routed by attempting to minimize the number of hops. In this example, datagrams travel directly from #11-20 to #61-70.

The problem with vector-distance routing is that minimizing the number of hops doesn't always route the datagram through the quicker path. Consider the example shown in figure 8.47. Network #61-70 is one hop away from Network #11-20, but this connection is made through a relatively slow 9600 baud network link. If we can also reach Network #61-70 by making three hops over Ethernet connections, the throughput will be dramatically improved. With our student analogy, it might be faster to pass a note through the three hyperactive students who eat chocolate all day instead of waiting for one sleepy-eyed student to act.

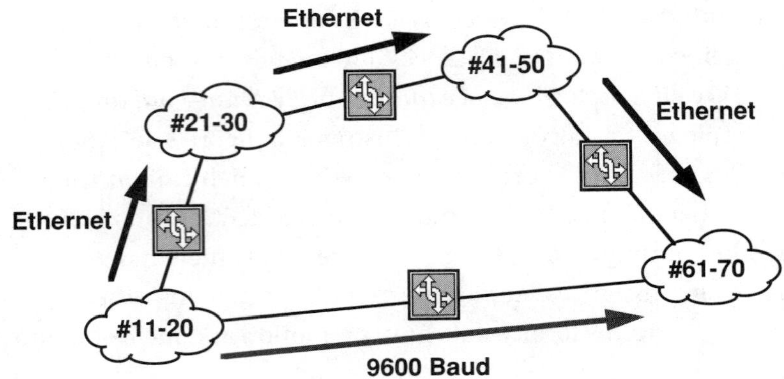

Figure 8.47
AppleTalk datagrams might go faster over a route that has more hops. Therefore, a method of artificial hop adjustment is often required.

AppleTalk datagrams might go faster over a route that has more hops. Therefore, a method of artificial hop adjustment is often required.

Some AppleTalk routers permit the artificial adjustment of a datagram's hop count. Instead of the datagram's hop count being increased by one when going through the router, it could be increased by two, which could force network traffic to take another less costly, more efficient path. Apple's new Apple Internet Router (AIR) also adjusts hop counts in large networks so as not to exceed the limit of 15 hops (see figure 8.48).

Remember that a key aspect of this routing technique is that the routers are not aware of the entire route for any given datagram destination. All that any given router knows for sure is the next router in the chain.

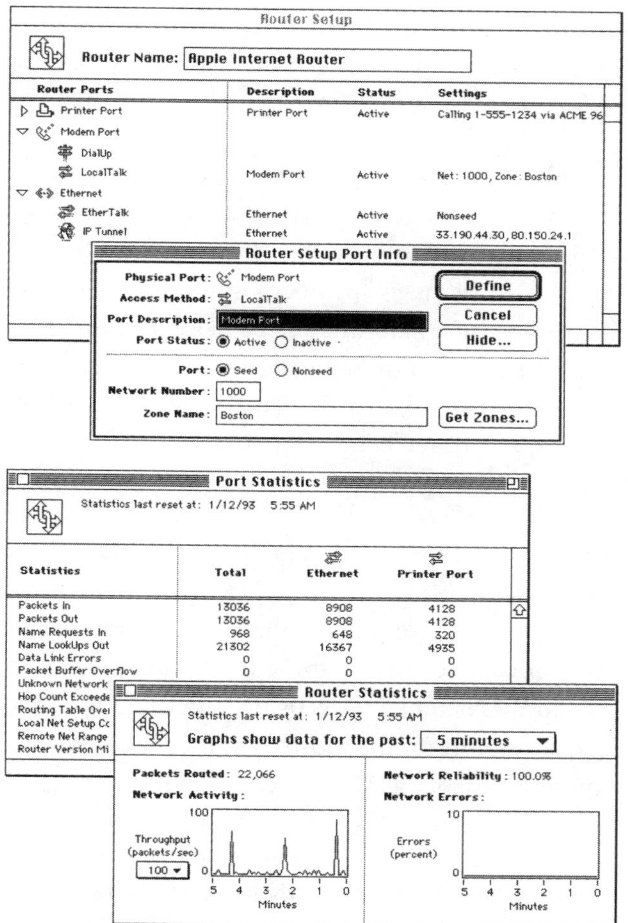

Figure 8.48

Sample screens from the Apple Internet Router.

RTMP versus AURP

To help solve the problem of excessive RTMP traffic, particularly on WANs, Apple has developed a new routing protocol called the *Apple Update Routing Protocol*, or AURP. AURP updates the routing tables only when a change has been made to the network. (Typically, this means whenever a new network has been added to the internet.) With AURP, our student-routers would only exchange routing notes when new students are added to the classroom. AURP is not intended to replace RTMP, which remains a viable protocol for small- and medium-sized LANs; rather, AURP is seen as a complement to RTMP.

Apple describes RTMP as a "no news is bad news" type of routing protocol. This means that if the RTMP updates aren't seen every ten seconds, then something's wrong. Instead, AURP is categorized as a "no news is good news" protocol, since as long as things are quiet, the routing information must be okay. The AURP protocol also defines a method of tunneling, or encapsulating, AppleTalk datagrams within other networking protocols. (The idea behind protocol encapsulation will be covered in the next section.)

The first product to support AURP is the Apple Internet Router (AIR). This new product supersedes the AppleTalk Internet Router 2.0. AIR, like its predecessor, runs on a suitably-configured Macintosh. System 7 is required, along with a minimum of 4 MB of RAM. PowerBooks are not recommended. AIR fully supports AURP over LAN and WAN connections using a modular approach. AIR also includes support for the industry standard Simple Network Management Protocol (SNMP) which provides for remote management.

The standard network supported by AIR is dial-up access over standard phone lines (see figure 8.49). For a dial-up connection, Apple recommends a minimum of a pair of V.32/9600 baud modems. Obviously, the faster the modem, the faster and more responsive the AppleTalk connection will be. Since AIR was developed in a modular fashion, additional capabilities can be simply plugged in as needed. Apple offers several optional products including an AppleTalk/X.25 and AppleTalk/IP extension.

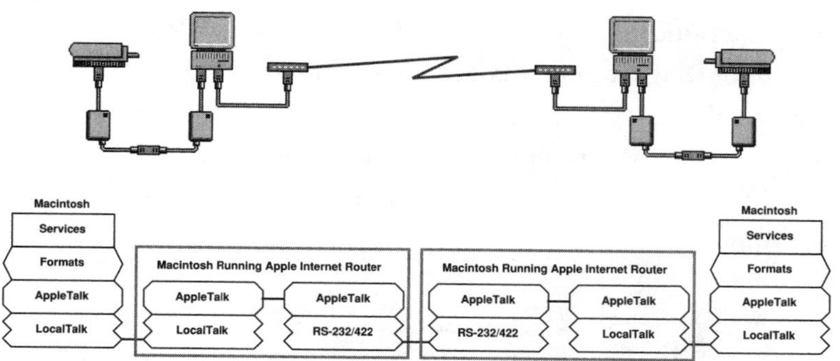

Figure 8.49

A NetPICT diagram of the Apple Internet Router working over conventional dial-up lines.

The AppleTalk/X.25 Wide Area Extension, shown in figure 8.50, enables multiple AppleTalk networks to communicate through an X.25 wide area network. Apple's Serial NuBus card is required to connect to the X.25 service. X.25 will be covered later on; briefly, X.25 is a wide-area networking service that is offered by service providers world-wide. These providers (such as Tymnet and Telenet) can offer customers local phone numbers that are used to connect to the system. One chief advantage of X.25 connections is that, unlike conventional phone lines which are billed solely based on time regardless of traffic, X.25 uses traffic as a prime determining factor in billing. Considering that most network traffic is not continual and tends to be "bursty," X.25 is very often a cost-effective alternative to traditional dial-up lines. A familiar example of X.25 networking can be found at most banks, since many ATM machines use X.25 links to provide wide-area access to your financial data.

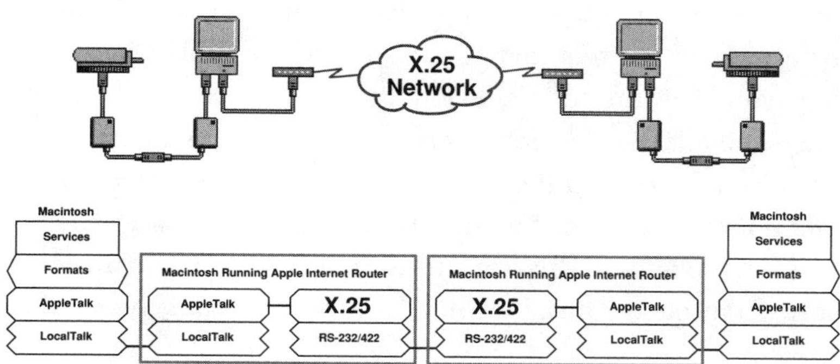

Figure 8.50

A NetPICT diagram of the Apple Internet Router using X.25 networking.

The other optional AIR module is the AppleTalk/IP Wide Area Extension. Diagrammed in figure 8.51, it links multiple AppleTalk networks over a TCP/IP network. The AppleTalk/IP extension is supported on Ethernet or Token Ring cabling. As with the X.25 option, the IP option relies on a networking trick known as tunneling.

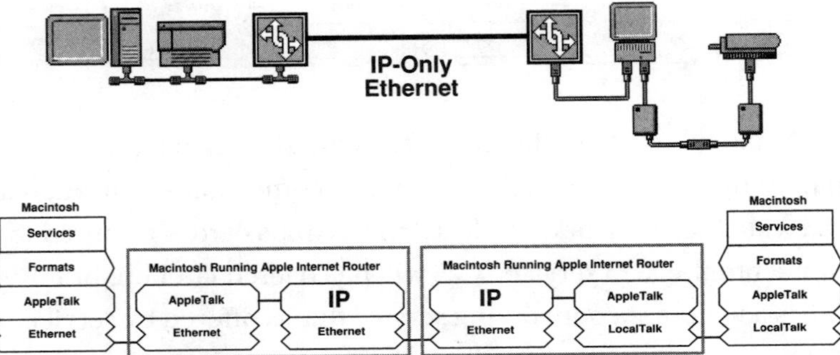

Figure 8.51
A NetPICT diagram of the Apple Internet Router using IP tunneling.

Protocol Encapsulation and Tunneling

Using figure 8.52 as an example, imagine that you want to send a letter to your uncle, who lives on a mountain across the country, as quickly as possible. You could send the letter with an overnight carrier, but for some reason, the carrier won't deliver the letter up the mountain. The regular mail service does go up the mountain; unfortunately, sending it this way would take two weeks for delivery. You then remember that you have a cousin that lives in the town at the base of the mountain who can receive the overnight delivery service. So you proceed to address the letter to your uncle and affix the required postage for regular mail delivery. Then, you place the addressed letter inside the overnight delivery pouch and address it to your cousin. You don't want to make your cousin go up the mountain, so you place a note inside the overnight pouch instructing him to simply drop the enclosed letter into the nearest mailbox. This way, the local mail will deliver the letter within a day or so. Thus, the total delivery time is only two or three days.

Figure 8.52
Sending a letter to your uncle.

This scenario can be directly applied to networking as well. The process of placing one transport protocol inside another is called *protocol encapsulation* or *tunneling*. Tunneling AppleTalk inside of another protocol, such as TCP/IP or DECnet, might be necessary or desirable for several reasons.

One reason could be that an organization's wide-area network only supports a certain protocol. This has been fairly common in the past because a number of routers have only supported a single protocol. For example, many companies that have extensive wide-area DECnet networks interconnect them with DECnet-specific routers. For these companies to be able to offer AppleTalk services over the network, they would have to scrap all their existing DECnet routers and replace them with multiprotocol AppleTalk/DECnet routers.

Alternatively, they can tunnel AppleTalk protocols inside the DECnet protocol. In this case, an AppleTalk datagram that is directed to a distant network is wrapped inside a DECnet packet by a special device and routed over the wide-area DECnet network to another special device, where its AppleTalk datagram is then extracted from its DECnet encapsulation and then passed along using AppleTalk protocols to its final destination.

In the case of AppleTalk/DECnet tunneling, the special device happens to be a DEC VAX that's running the AppleTalk for VMS and DECnet protocols simultaneously (see figure 8.53). The AppleTalk for VMS software establishes a connection with the DECnet software and performs the encapsulation and decapsulation of the AppleTalk datagrams.

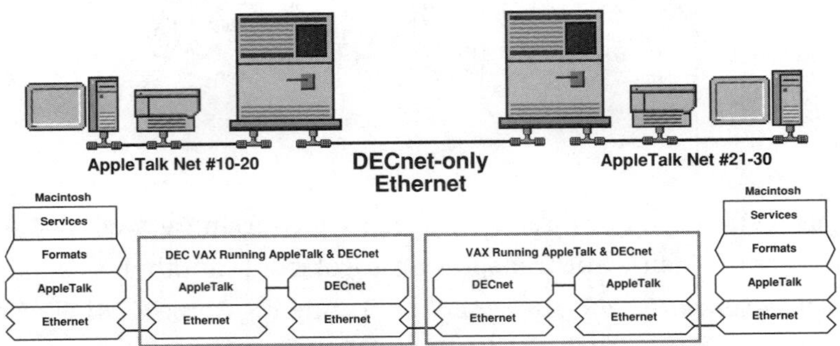

Figure 8.53
A NetPICT diagram of the AppleTalk/DECnet tunnel. In this example, each VAX has two Ethernet controllers. The tunnel acts as an AppleTalk router, so network numbers must be unique.

As mentioned before, with the new Apple Internet Router, tunneling is also possible with X.25 and TCP/IP networks. The concept remains the same—AppleTalk datagrams are placed inside the foreign protocol and then routed accordingly to the corresponding Apple Internet Router (AIR) over the wide-area connection.

Routers that link an AppleTalk network to the foreign protocol network are called *exterior routers.* Routers that perform AppleTalk-to-AppleTalk routing within the internetwork are called *interior routers.*

When the AIR (or any AURP-compliant router) is used in a tunnel configuration, the tunnel side of the connection of the exterior routers appears as an end node of the encapsulating protocol. Using IP encapsulation as an example, when two AURP-compliant routers communicate over a TCP/IP link, they appear as two native TCP/IP devices. On the interior side of the connection, however, the routers must appear as Phase 2 routers that speak RTMP to the other interior routers.

Whenever an AppleTalk datagram is encapsulated in a foreign protocol, the AURP-compliant router adds a special AURP header in addition to the addressing header of the foreign protocol. This special variable length AURP header is called a *domain header* or DI. Technically, the AURP domain header extends the standard 32-bit AppleTalk address (network, node and socket) and creates a complete AURP wide area address.

Before AURP, one of the key rules of AppleTalk network configuration was the uniqueness of AppleTalk network numbers. With the addition of the AURP DI number, it is no longer a requirement that the network number must be globally unique (although it's still a good idea). Now, with the addition of the DI the complete address is `domain(network.node.socket)`.

Adding the DI is similar to adding an area code to a phone number. For example, the phone number 555-1212 is certainly not unique in the whole US phone system. But, by adding a unique three-digit area code to the beginning of the number, it becomes a valid directory assistance number for any area code.

To better illustrate this point, let's use an example of two unconnected LANs. Figure 8.54 shows one LAN in Philadelphia having a Phase 2 network range of 10 to 20. The other LAN in San Francisco has a range of 15 to 50. Under the pre-AURP Phase 2 rules, these two networks could not be linked together because their network numbers overlapped. Both LANs have a network number 15, and therefore a conflict would occur. With AURP DIs, each LAN could have a unique domain number. Philadelphia's domain number could be 1 and San Francisco's domain could be 2. This would create unique addresses for both sides. 1(15.22.129) is now different from 2(15.22.129). Of course, the DIs must be unique on the tunnel. If the tunnel is a TCP/IP tunnel, one sure way to insure that the DIs are unique is to use TCP/IP addresses as the DIs.

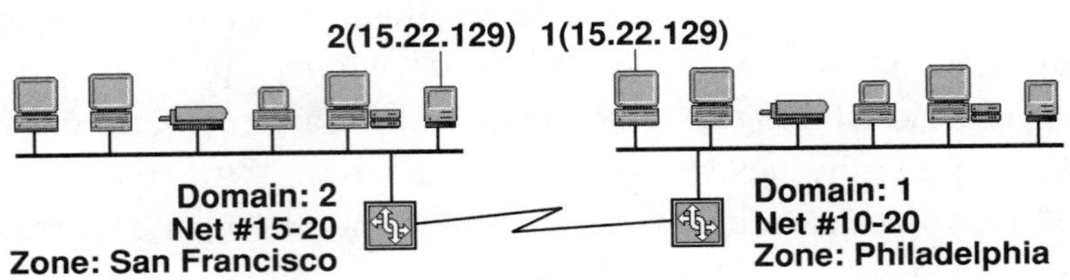

Figure 8.54 With the AURP Domains, AppleTalk network numbers do not necessarily have to be unique. In this example, there are two devices using the 15.22.129 address. The addition of the QURP Domain makes them unique.

Conclusion

The Macintosh supports a number of transport protocols. Its native protocol, AppleTalk, provides plug-and-play connectivity. AppleTalk nodes use dynamic node addressing and name binding to self-configure, which avoids the manual configuration required by other protocols such as DECnet and TCP/IP. Since its inception, Apple has continued to evolve AppleTalk, the most recent changes providing enhanced routing over wide-area networks.

9

Macintosh Media/Cabling

One of the more visible aspects of a Macintosh network is the medium used to make the connection. This chapter covers the various connection media, such as LocalTalk and Ethernet. It covers the advantages and disadvantages of each medium, giving you the knowledge to choose the right medium—or combination of mediums—for your network.

LocalTalk/Phone-Type Connectors

LocalTalk, along with its phone-type variants, is one reason for the popularity of Macintosh networking. Its low cost and easy installation has set the standard for desktop networking. Although LocalTalk is rapidly being supplanted by Ethernet, it still offers a viable solution for many Macintosh users.

Figure 9.1 Apple's LocalTalk connector system. (Courtesy of Apple Computer, Inc.).

LocalTalk

LocalTalk (see figure 9.2) was the first network cabling system available for the Macintosh. Introduced in 1985 along with the LaserWriter printer, LocalTalk was a low-cost plug-and-play solution in a world of thousand-dollar Ethernet cards. LocalTalk and its variants are still used today, but its use is rapidly declining. LocalTalk provides a bandwidth of 230.4 Kbps, which is pretty quick compared to a 9600 baud modem connection. Compared to a 10 Mbps Ethernet connection or a 100 Mbps FDDI connection, however, it's pretty slow.

The LocalTalk cabling system normally connects to a Mac's Printer serial port (shown in figure 9.3), and to the appropriate LocalTalk ports of other devices.

> **NOTE:** The Modem port is not used for LocalTalk connections unless you intend to run router software (such as the Apple Internet Router) on your Mac to route between two LocalTalk segments.

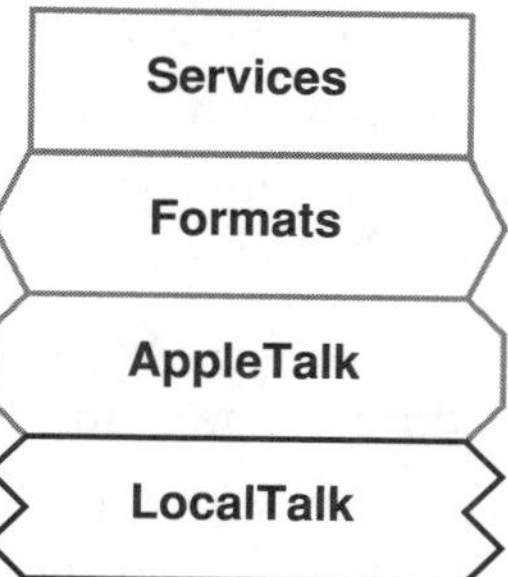

Figure 9.2
LocalTalk resides at the Cabling layer of the NetPICT.

Figure 9.3
Both the Modem and Printer ports are serial ports; however, only the Printer port can be used for LocalTalk.

The heart of LocalTalk is the small connector box which contains a small transformer that electrically isolates the network connection. It has three connections. One side of the box has a length of wire and a connector (either a circular 8-pin DIN8 connector or a D-shaped 9-pin DB9 connector) that is used to connect to the AppleTalk node. The other side of the LocalTalk box has two receptacles that are used to connect the node to the chain of other LocalTalk devices.

Apple's LocalTalk connectors are rarely used today for several reasons. First, when a LocalTalk network is indicated, it usually makes sense to consider the LocalTalk-compatible phone-type connectors. Farallon's PhoneNET, which uses twisted-pair telephone-type wiring, is one such alternative. Another reason is that the LocalTalk connectors do not have a positive locking arrangement—they can be easily pulled out or disrupted. People have been known to wrap electrical tape around the boxes or even Crazy Glue the connectors in place to avoid this problem. Perhaps the most important reason for the decline and fall of LocalTalk is that it's rapidly being replaced by Ethernet. The price of Ethernet connections has dropped dramatically over the past few years, so the cost differential is not as great as it was in the past.

LocalTalk does have cable shielding, so in electrically noisy areas, LocalTalk might be better than the unshielded twisted-pair wiring used by the phone-type connectors. For most small installations where the anticipated network traffic is modest, you'll want to consider the phone-type devices.

PhoneNET and Other Phone-Type Connectors

Farallon was the first company to offer a functional replacement for LocalTalk. They replaced the DIN8 connectors of LocalTalk with the positive locking RJ-11 connectors found on most telephones (see figure 9.4). They also replaced the expensive shielded LocalTalk cable with conventional twisted-pair phone wiring. The PhoneNET connectors were, and remain, completely compatible with the LocalTalk Link Access Protocol (LLAP), so switching over to PhoneNET from LocalTalk requires no software changes or special configuration.

Figure 9.4
The Farallon PhoneNET Connector uses telephone-style RJ-11 locking connectors. (Courtesy of Farallon Computing.)

The success of PhoneNET and similar products was twofold. Small companies were able to create a simple, inexpensive LANs in an hour or so by simply going to Radio Shack and buying a spool of phone wire, a box of RJ-11 connectors, and a $15 crimping tool. Large companies soon found that it was possible to integrate the PhoneNET connectors into their existing wiring schemes—wiring schemes previously used for connecting "dumb" terminals to mainframes and minicomputers over twisted-pair RS-232 wiring.

The PhoneNET connectors also made it possible to move to a star topology (or radial topology), instead of the daisy-chain topology of LocalTalk. PhoneNET currently supports two kinds of stars: *passive stars*, in which each of the segments is interconnected at a panel or junction block, and *active stars*, where the segments join at a LocalTalk repeater. Farallon's first repeater was called the StarController.

Since the star topology only requires a single connection at the node, only one RJ-11 receptacle is required. When a PhoneNET connector is used, the extra receptacle is filled with a terminating resistor. Other brands are self-terminating and don't require a separate resistor. Farallon also offers a single-receptacle connector called the StarConnector. This small connector (see figure 9.5), plugs directly into the printer port of a Macintosh, and is ideally suited for star networks. StarConnectors are also useful in pairs, where they can be used to connect two devices (a PowerBook and a desktop Mac, for example) with a single RJ-11 cable.

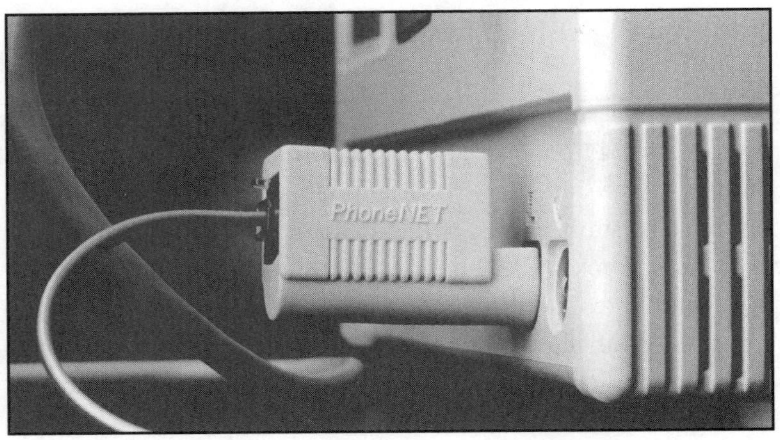

Figure 9.5
The Farallon PhoneNET StarConnector plugs directly into the Printer port. Used in star networks, the device is self-terminating. (Courtesy of Farallon Computing.)

Today, there are many LocalTalk-compatible products. In addition to Farallon, there are several companies that make the phone-type connectors and products.

Design Considerations

If your network consists of a dozen or so nodes in a centralized location, and your bandwidth requirements are modest, then a LocalTalk or PhoneNET daisy-chain might make sense. With either device, you'll be able to add nodes to the ends of the chain, but if you need to add an additional connection somewhere in the middle, the entire network will be disrupted.

A more flexible solution for small workgroups is to use a bus topology. With this system, a single cable is used as a backbone. Each phone-type connector then plugs into the bus. Connections can be made and broken at any time without disruption to the network. This is only possible with the phone-type connectors, such as PhoneNET, and will not work with the LocalTalk connectors.

The next step up is to go with a star topology. The choice of a passive star can be limiting, with restriction on the number of devices and distances. In most cases, passive stars are problematic and not worth the trouble. The other option is to go with an active star. The active star involves the use of a LocalTalk multiport repeater. Products such as the Farallon StarController (shown in figure 9.6) and the Focus TurboStar avoid the problems found in the passive star topologies. These repeaters are a good choice for the LocalTalk network that is spread out through a large building. They're even a better choice if you're able to use existing twisted-pair wiring.

Figure 9.6
The Farallon PhoneNET StarController is an example of a multiport LocalTalk repeater. (Courtesy of Farallon Computing.)

Planning Ahead

If you're going to go the twisted-pair phone-type connector route, be sure to use twisted-pair wiring that's capable of supporting twisted-pair Ethernet. Phone-type connectors require a single twisted pair, while twisted-pair Ethernet requires two twisted pairs. LocalTalk signaling will work over the Ethernet twisted-pair wiring, but not vice-versa. So plan for the future and wire for Ethernet. The additional cost of the cable should be negligible compared to the installation cost. Just make sure you use the appropriate twisted-pair wiring, as there are different kinds of wiring for different applications.

As you consider a LocalTalk or phone-type connector network, keep in mind that the additional cost of the LocalTalk hub increases the per-device cost. Now that Ethernet connections are so inexpensive, you may want to consider spending just a bit more to go Ethernet. If all your devices—present and planned—are equipped with LocalTalk, then choosing it as a cabling system may not be a bad choice. But if you plan to add other PCs, workstations, or printers that don't offer LocalTalk options, maybe it's better to opt for Ethernet at the outset.

When Ethernet is chosen as a backbone cabling system, it used to be that the only option for connecting LocalTalk-only devices (such as LaserWriters) was to install a LocalTalk-EtherTalk router. This is an expensive cure when you may only have a limited number of LocalTalk devices to connect. It also adds the administrative overhead and performance concerns of adding another router to the network. Several years ago Dayna Communication introduced a device called EtherPrint. It acted as a LocalTalk-to-Ethernet bridge. It essentially adapted the LocalTalk device to the Ethernet network. Today, these devices, diagrammed in figure 9.7, have gained in popularity and functionality.

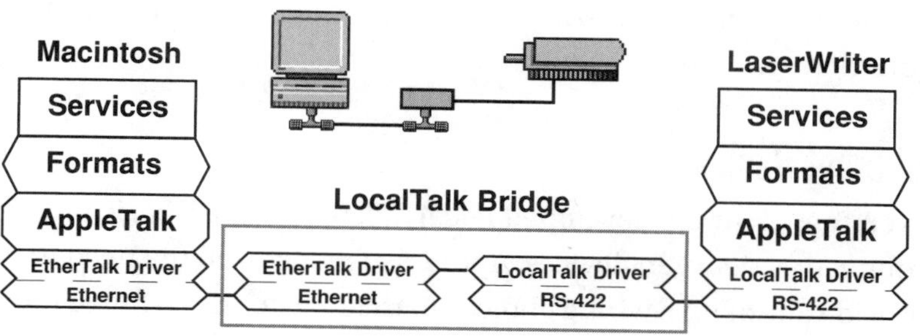

Figure 9.7 Several companies provide LocalTalk-to-EtherTalk bridges (adapters) that can be used to connect LocalTalk-only devices, such as LaserWriters and PowerBooks, to the Ethernet.

Companies such as, Asanté (AsantéPrint), Compatible Systems (EtherWrite), Dayna (EtherPrint Plus), Farallon (LocalPath), Sonic Systems (SuperBridge) and Digital Products (SprintTALK) make LocalTalk-Ethernet bridges. The new generation of devices is able to connect multiple LocalTalk devices—Macs and PowerBooks included. The Farallon and Sonic Systems offerings are software solutions that run on a Mac with the appropriate network interfaces. The Farallon product can even connect devices to Token Ring networks. Many of these devices support security features that can limit access to the LocalTalk device.

Ethernet/EtherTalk

At one time, Ethernet was to cabling systems what FDDI is today—it was expensive and offered a bandwidth well beyond the requirements of most applications. Today, Ethernet is fast becoming the modern equivalent of RS-232. Nearly all computer systems offer Ethernet connections. With the advent of very large-scale intergration, the Ethernet components have been reduced to a single chip, which has driven the cost of Ethernet cards down to less than $200. Fortunately, these price reductions aren't limited to the PC world, as Macintosh Ethernet cards are fast becoming a hot commodity.

Ethernet Basics

Even though Apple developed LocalTalk to provide a basic physical connection between devices, Apple also recognized the need to provide alternative wiring choices to their customers. One of the most popular local area networks (LANs) is Ethernet (see figure 9.8). Originally developed by Xerox in collaboration with Digital and Intel, Ethernet is used by many computer vendors as a wiring media for networking. Companies such as Digital and Sun use Ethernet to run a variety of networking protocols. In fact, Ethernet was developed with multiprotocol support in mind. A single Ethernet network can support many different protocols at the same time.

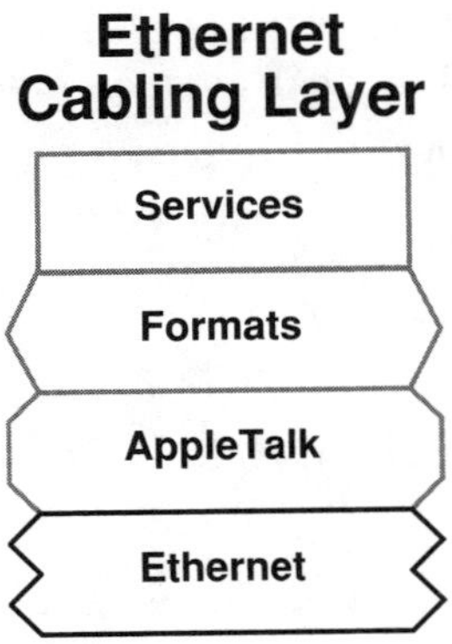

Figure 9.8
Ethernet resides at the Cabling layer of the NetPICT.

When AppleTalk protocols run over Ethernet cables, Apple calls this EtherTalk. Whereas LocalTalk cables have a bandwidth of 230.4 Kbps, Ethernet has a bandwidth of 10 Mbps. So instead of being limited to 32 nodes, as with LocalTalk, EtherTalk networks can support thousands of devices. Theoretically, with the latest version of AppleTalk (Phase 2), a network can have over 16 million devices. Of course, on a single cable you would run out of room to connect all those devices, but Ethernet cables are often "connected" by network bridges, microwave links, and even satellites to other Ethernet networks to create an "extended" Ethernet LAN. Many large companies have extensive world-wide Ethernet LANs with thousands of computers produced by different companies.

The throughput of an Ethernet network is higher than LocalTalk. Actual transmission rates will depend on many factors, such as network traffic, size of the transmitted file, and performance of the individual Ethernet controller. On average, you can expect an Ethernet network to perform three to five times better than a LocalTalk network. Why such a difference? The factors limiting Ethernet throughput are numerous and complex, but the speed of the Macintosh CPU, hard disk, and Ethernet hardware, coupled with network configuration, application performance, and other network traffic all play a role in Ethernet performance.

All Macs and LaserWriters come standard with the hardware to support LocalTalk communications. Some Macs (such as the Quadra family) and LaserWriters (such as the LaserWriter IIG and LaserWriter Pro 630) come equipped with built-in Ethernet hardware. For those Macs that don't have Ethernet, connections are made with the addition of a networking card. LocalTalk LaserWriters, such as the LaserWriter IINT, can connect to Ethernet with adapter devices, such as Dayna's EtherPrint device.

Ethernet cards for Macs with card slots are made by Apple and other vendors (see figure 9.9). The cost varies between $200 and $400. Several companies also sell SCSI/Ethernet adapters for those Macs, such as the Classic and the PowerBook family, without card slots. These devices connect to the SCSI port of the Macintosh, just like any other SCSI device, and then connect to the Ethernet network.

Figure 9.9
A sampling of Ethernet cards. The two-piece units are for the Macintosh SE and SE/30. The one-piece unit is for any NuBus-equipped Macintosh. (Courtesy of Farallon Computing.)

ELAP software drivers are included with both the Ethernet cards and the SCSI/Ethernet devices. This software provides new network driver programs that give you the option, through the Control Panel, to choose between LocalTalk and EtherTalk. Unless you turn your Mac into a router, the AppleTalk traffic can only go through one port at a time.

There are several variants of Ethernet cabling. Even though the cabling is different, the electrical signaling remains the same. Because of this, all Ethernet cable variations use the same ELAP drivers. The only significant difference is the cable type and the connectors.

Thickwire 10Base-5

Thickwire Ethernet (see figure 9.10), is a stiff coaxial (one wire inside another wire) cable about 3/8" in diameter; it employs a 15-pin D-style connector. The cable is terminated at both ends with special resistive fittings that minimize signal reflections that would otherwise degrade communications. Usually thickwire Ethernet is employed as a central "backbone" running throughout a building, although fiber-optic Ethernet is rapidly replacing thickwire as a backbone media. Thickwire Ethernet permits a maximum of 200 devices on a 1,640 foot segment. Thickwire Ethernet is often referred to as 10Base-5 wiring.

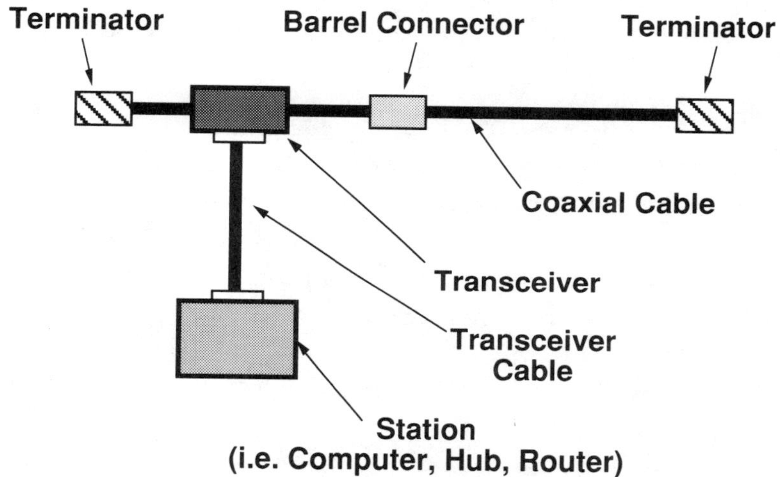

Figure 9.10
Thickwire (10Base-5) Ethernet components.

Thickwire connections are established by clamping a device called a *transceiver* to the cable. Most transceivers are installed by drilling a small hole in the cable with a special tool. This is followed by clamping the transceiver, which pierces the cable with sharp contact pins that make electrical contact. This method of connection is sometimes referred to as a "vampire tap." These taps can only be made at regular intervals along the cable. Most cables have indicator markings every 2.5 meters to help position the transceivers.

Adding transceivers to a backbone cable is not difficult, but this is not a cost-effective way to make a single network connection. Usually transceivers are used to connect hubs (or repeaters), which support the connection of multiple devices through a single transceiver connection to the backbone.

In the 10Base-5 nomenclature, the 10 refers to the bandwidth. All Ethernet implementations have a 10 megabit bandwidth. The term "Base" refers to baseband (as opposed to broadband). Baseband means that the cable only supports a single communications channel. The value of 5 refers to the maximum length of the cable segment, which for 10Base-5 is 500 meters. There is a specification for broadband Ethernet called 10Broad-36. It runs over a coaxial cable and has a maximum segment length of 3,800 meters.

Thinwire 10Base-2

Thinwire Ethernet (see figure 9.11) is thinner (about 3/16 ") and considerably more flexible than the original thickwire. It used to be a popular choice to connect desktop devices and workstations. Today, however, thinwire is being rapidly replaced by twisted-pair Ethernet for desktop connections.

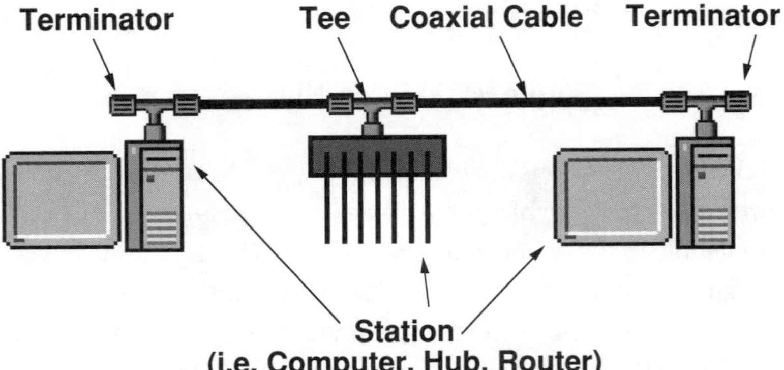

Figure 9.11
Thinwire (10Base-2) Ethernet components.

Thinwire Ethernet uses BNC (twist and lock) type connections and allows 30 devices per 656 foot segment, over a maximum network length of 3,281 feet. Thinwire is often referred to as "Cheapernet," or its more formal name of 10Base-2. This designation is similar to that of thickwire; the 2 indicates a maximum segment length of 200 meters (actually, the maximum segment length is 185 meters, but I guess they didn't want to call it 10Base-1.8).

Connections are made with a tee connector, similar to LocalTalk. One branch of the tee connects to the network device, while the other two connections are used to connect to the network. When thinwire is connected in a daisy-chain, the free ends of the last tees must be terminated with special resistive end caps. Adding more devices to a thinwire daisy-chain disrupts the network because the chain must be broken. It is possible to disconnect a device at the attachment point without disrupting the network chain.

Thinwire can also be configured in a star topology using a thinwire Ethernet repeater. Here, each tee at the end of each branch of the star must be terminated. The use of thinwire star topologies is rapidly declining, due to the arrival of the newer, more flexible twisted-pair Ethernet.

Twisted Pair 10Base-T

Lately, another Ethernet variant has started to become popular. Twisted-pair Ethernet (see figure 9.12) has been around for several years, but during the past two years it has virtually dominated the desktop. With this system, Ethernet can be implemented on standard unshielded twisted-pair wiring. Thinwire Ethernet requires two pairs of wires that meet certain industry requirements.

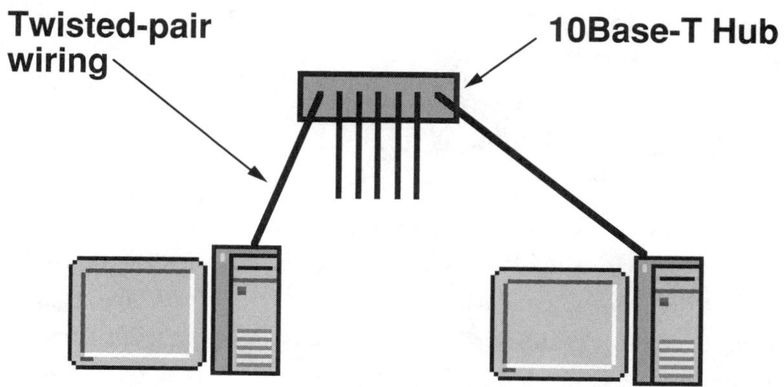

Figure 9.12 Twisted-pair (10Base-T) Ethernet components.

The choice of wire may depend on local building or electrical codes, or on the recommendations of suppliers. It's always best to check with the various codes and suppliers for detailed cabling specifications. As mentioned earlier, it's always wise to cable for thinwire Ethernet even if you're planning to use LocalTalk. It also may be prudent to consider the anticipated wiring standards for the newer high-speed cabling systems such as FDDI (Fiber Data Distributed Interface). There is currently work underway to implement FDDI over copper twisted-pair wiring and to develop a 100 Mbps version of Ethernet that runs over four twisted-pairs. Often, if your wiring strategy covers the most stringent wiring scenario, you'll be able to design for future growth and enhancements.

Unlike thickwire or thinwire that can be connected in a bus or daisy-chain, twisted-pair Ethernet requires the use of a hub. These hubs come in a wide variety of prices and configurations with a varying number of ports and extra features. Some hubs offer a modular construction that make it easy to provide additional connections as required.

All the Ethernet card vendors for the Macintosh offer twisted-pair Ethernet versions, with many cards offering multiple connectors (thick, thin and twisted-pair) on one card. Twisted-pair Ethernet underwent some changes during its early years, and there have been several implementations, but now the standard is set and is widely known as 10Base-T.

Apple's Ethernet Cabling System

In January of 1990, Apple announced a new line of low-cost Ethernet cards. The two new cards (one for the Macs with NuBus slots and one for the Macintosh LC) use a separate attachment unit, known as an Apple AUI (Attachment Unit Unterface) that attaches to either thickwire, thinwire, or twisted-pair Ethernet (see figure 9.13). Resembling LocalTalk connectors, these connectors attach to the Mac or LaserWriter with a new style of connector.

This permits Apple to use these new compact connectors on the motherboards of all their new machines. The appropriate attachment unit (either thick, thin, or twisted-pair) is then connected to the device. This approach offers Apple a single, compact connector for their new products, while still offering the flexibility of three attachment options. Apple has provided the specifications for Apple AUI, so these new connectors are also offered by third-party suppliers. These new devices will bring the ease-of-installation and low cost of LocalTalk to Ethernet networks.

Figure 9.13
Apple's Ethernet NuBus card (and computers so equipped) can connect to Apple's thick, thin or twisted-pair transceivers.

Design Considerations

As with any network design, the physical location is an important determining factor. If all your AppleTalk nodes are in the same room, then 10Base-2 thinwire easily can be daisy-chained among the devices, and will most likely be the cheapest solution. The other option is to use 10Base-T twisted-pair Ethernet. If you choose 10Base-T, you'll need a hub to interconnect the devices. If you have just a few devices to connect, there are a number of vendors that offer small, affordable hubs with anywhere from three to eight ports. The additional price of the hub may make this approach more expensive than thinwire, but the cabling should be slightly cheaper and you may be able to assemble your own cables more easily than thinwire.

If your network is large and spans many rooms or floors, a backbone Ethernet is probably needed. With this approach, a 10Base-5 or fiber optic cable is strategically placed through the building. Often, the cable runs between wiring closets, where network equipment such as hubs, routers, and gateways are located. These wiring closets are often used for phone connections as well. (Some networking vendors offer integrated networking equipment to consolidate the management of voice and data connections.)

With most extensive EtherTalk networks, a major design consideration is the routing and isolation of traffic. Deciding where to place routers and how best to link EtherTalk LANs to wide-area connections is frequently an important concern.

Other Cabling Systems

LocalTalk and Ethernet are the most popular cabling choices for the Macintosh, but the Mac also supports a wide range of other industry standard cabling systems.

Token Ring

Token Ring networks (see figure 9.14) operate using a different principal than Ethernet. As discussed earlier, Ethernet devices listen to the cable before transmitting, whereas Token Ring devices wait their turn until an electronic token comes their way. Because of this fundamental difference, Token Ring networks enjoy certain benefits over Ethernet networks.

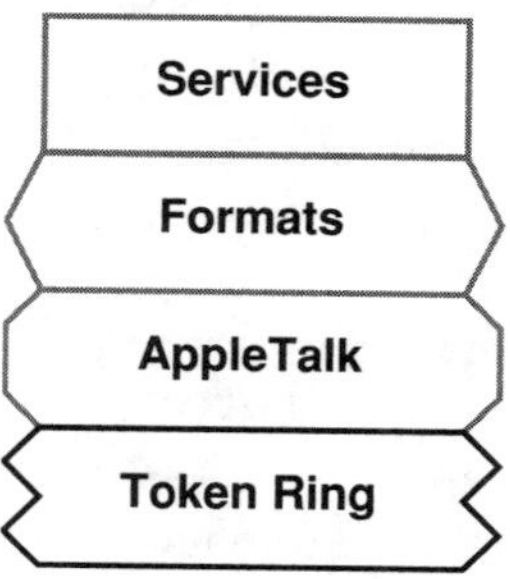

Figure 9.14

Token Ring NetPICT.

First, when it comes to traffic, Token Ring networks are self-limiting. Unlike Ethernet networks, which degrade when excessive traffic causes collisions and retransmissions, Token Ring networks simply reach their maximum throughput and then level out. Another advantage of Token Ring is that a node is always guaranteed access to the cable within a finite period of time. Ethernet nodes play a statistical game where access to the cable is not guaranteed. This makes Token Ring networks appealing for time-critical, real-time, and process control applications.

Most decisions to select Token Ring technology (other than FDDI) are not made because of its technical advantage, but rather to connect to the IBM environment, where Token Ring is a popular choice. There are currently two implementations of Token Ring—a 4 Mbps version and a 16 Mbps version.

Token Ring cards are more expensive than their Ethernet counterparts. Prices range from $500 to $800 per card. Apple and several third-party vendors offer NuBus Token Ring cards.

FDDI

Likely to succeed Ethernet, FDDI (Fiber Distributed Data Interface) is an ANSI and ISO standard network based on dual fiber optic rings (see figure 9.15). FDDI has a bandwidth (data throughput rate) of 100 Mbps. This is 10 times the bandwidth of Ethernet. Just as Apple offered EtherTalk and TokenTalk drivers for Ethernet and Token Ring wiring systems, they have also developed FDDITalk drivers. The Apple drivers currently support AppleTalk Phase 2 and MacTCP. FDDI networks can contain 1,000 nodes no more than 2 kilometers apart, for a total aggregate distance of 100 kilometers.

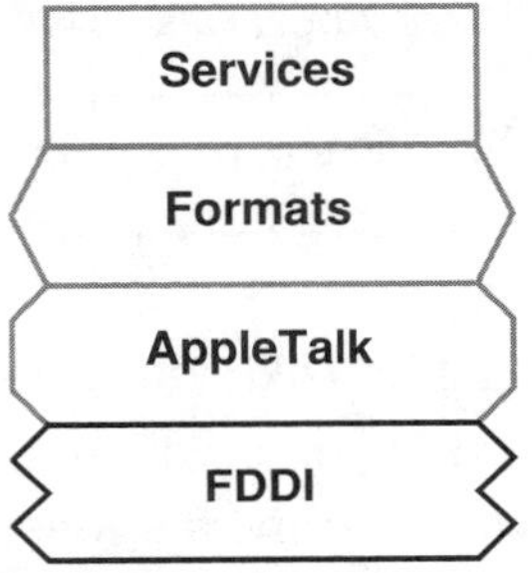

Figure 9.15
FDDI NetPICT.

FDDI cards (see figure 9.16) are still a bit on the expensive side at over $1,000 per card, but just as the cost of Ethernet cards dropped, the price of FDDI cards will come down as well. FDDI cards are currently offerred by several companies; Codenoll and Impulse Technology are two examples. While FDDI is still rare on the desktop, it's becoming increasly prevalent as a backbone cabling system.

Figure 9.16
A FDDI card for NuBus-equipped Macs. (Courtesy of Codenoll Technology Corp.)

Although FDDI is gaining in popularity, there are other upcoming standards vying for acceptance. A proposed "CDDI" standard would offer the performance of FDDI over less-costly copper cabling. HP and AT&T are proposing an upgrade to the Ethernet standard to achieve FDDI performance levels (100 Mbps) over 10Base-T twisted-pair wiring. Instead of two twisted pairs, this approach requires four twisted pairs.

Serial RS-232/422

Serial communications only recently have become a popular cabling medium for AppleTalk. Starting with Apple's Remote Access Protocol (ARAP), many Macintosh users are using serial connections and modems to dial in to remote Macintosh computers. ARAP uses data compression and buffering techniques to coax the most out of the relatively slow dial-up links (see figure 9.17).

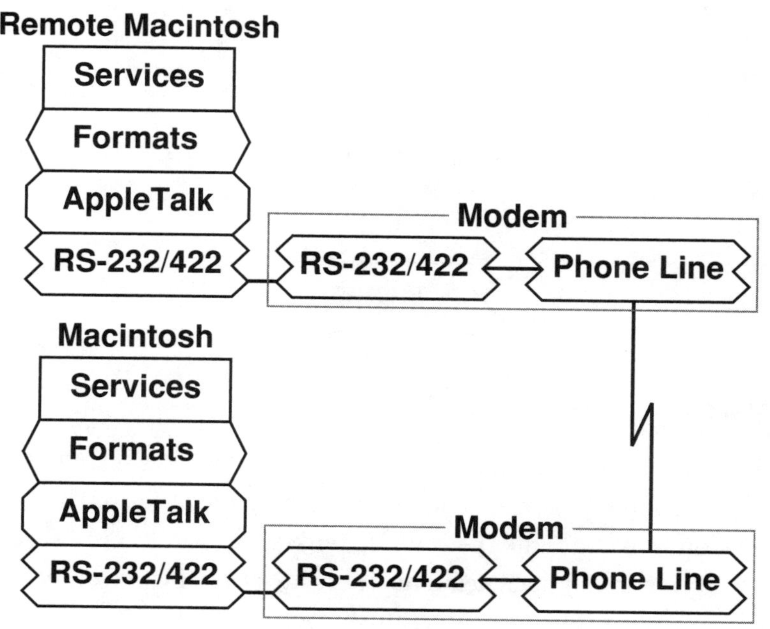

Figure 9.17
AppleTalk Remote Access NetPICT.

ARAP uses the client/server model to make the remote connection. A Macintosh running the client portion of Remote Access dials in to a Remote Access server. With Apple's software, the server is a Macintosh. There are other servers from third-party vendors that use dedicated hardware devices. These servers, such as Shiva's LANrover, connect to multiple dial-up lines and also make a network connection to LocalTalk or Ethernet networks.

ARCNET

ARCNET is a cabling system that is popular on IBM PCs (see figure 9.18). It runs over twisted-pair or coaxial cabling at a bandwidth of 2.5 Mbps. A Macintosh version of this cabling system is now available, along with software that provides the ARCNET data link drivers (ARCNET Link Access Protocol). For more detailed information on ARCNET, refer to Chapter 10, "Living in an Intel/DOS World."

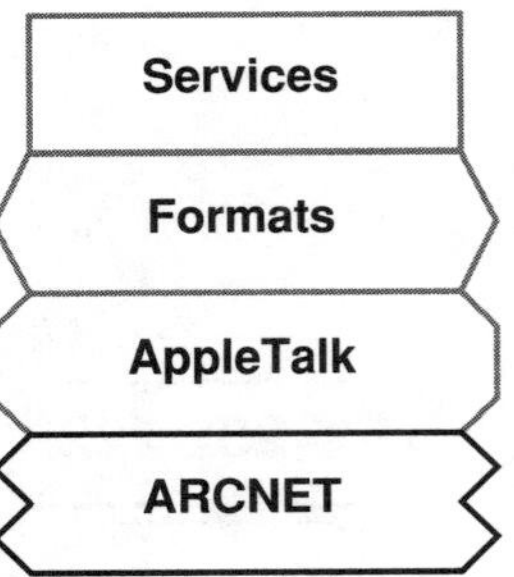

Figure 9.18
ARCNET NetPICT.

Wireless

As computers get smaller and smaller, the cabling systems that used to connect them also tie them down to the desktop. The solution is to eliminate the cabling. Wireless networks are a recent development that does just that. There are several wireless technologies available for the Macintosh.

One option for a wireless network is to use Apple's Remote Access with a celluar phone/modem combination (see figure 9.19). This makes sense for wide-area network connections for a limited number of devices. For LAN connectivity, wireless technology may be useful in locations where conventional wiring is difficult or impossible to run. Motorola, the leading manufacturer of cellular telephones, has a Macintosh product called EMBARC which provides a one-way wireless messaging service for remote Mac users.

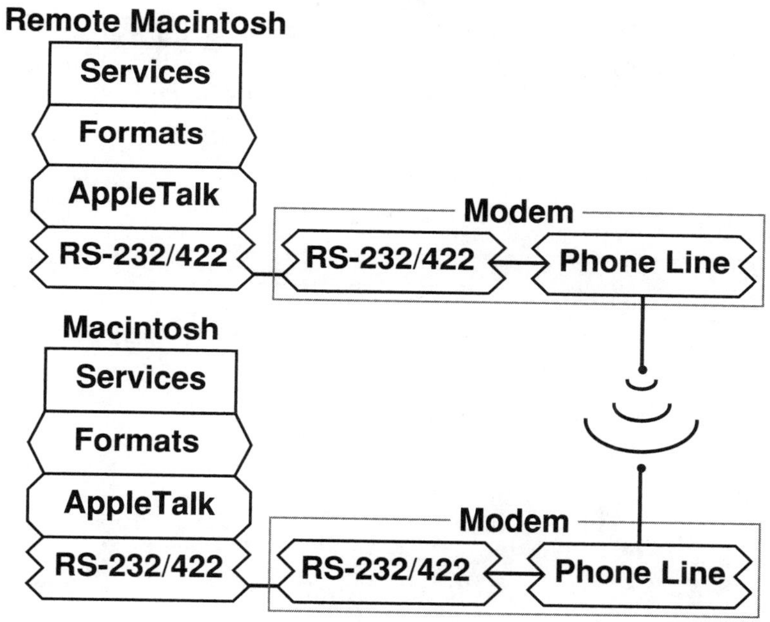

Figure 9.19
Cellular Modem/ARA NetPICT.

There are also options for LAN mediums such as LocalTalk and Ethernet. Photonics makes LocalTalk devices that use reflected infrared to link a number of nodes (see figure 9.20). The infrared devices focus their energy at a single point on the ceiling.

Motorola has developed a wireless version of Ethernet called Altair II (see figure 9.21). These devices use low-power radio waves as a transmission medium. Altair's transmission rate of 5.7 Mbps is somewhat less than Ethernet bandwidth. Setup is easy. Each Ethernet device connects to a small desktop send/receive module.

These desktop modules transmit radio waves to control modules that connect to walls or cubicle partitions. The send/receive modules support all kinds of Ethernet adapters and cost around $1,200. The control module can be used alone or connected to a conventional Ethernet cable. These devices can handle up to 50 wireless devices.

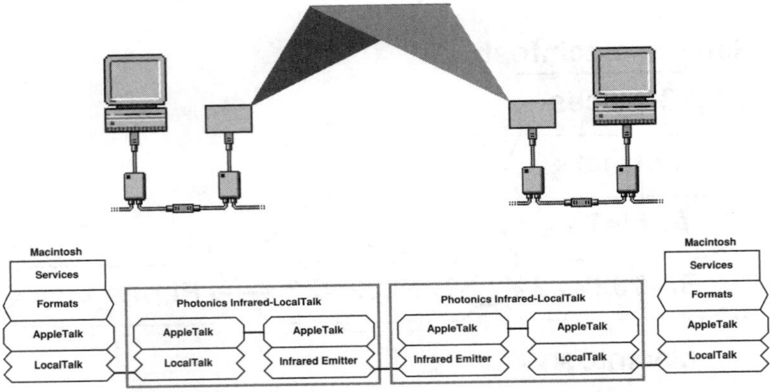

Figure 9.20
Photonics makes a LocalTalk device that uses infrared waves as a connection medium.

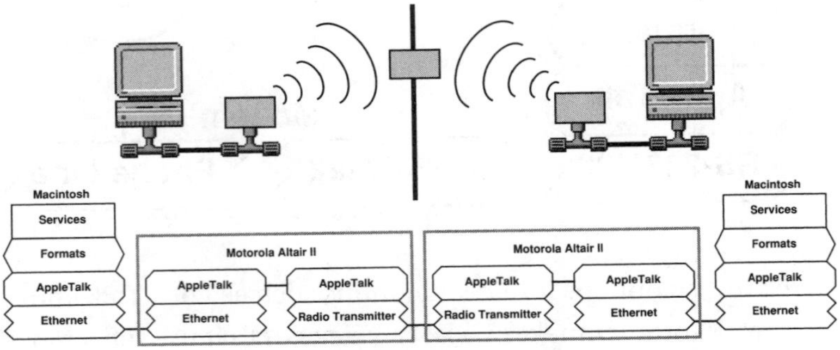

Figure 9.21
Motorola's Altair II technology uses radio waves to carry Ethernet transmissions.

Compared to conventional wired networks, these new technologies are still somewhat expensive and are only cost-effective in those cases where wiring is difficult or where rewiring costs would exceed the cost of the wireless components. Expect wireless communications to continue to increase in popularity as Apple's Newton technology and other handheld computers become popular.

WAN Media

The cabling systems mentioned previously are typically used by LANs. But when Macs need to be networked over longer distances, other technologies are needed. However, compared to the cost and convenience of LAN connections, WAN options are often limited and expensive.

Conventional Dial-Up

Modem access was discussed earlier in the context of remote access. A Macintosh user dials into a server on the LAN and connects to services using a pair of modems. This is fine for the single user, but what about connecting two (or more) LANs over a dial-up connection?

There are modem-based products that work over conventional analog dial-up lines that can be used to link multiple AppleTalk LANs. An example of this can be found in Apple's Internet Router (AIR). In its standard configuration, as shown in figure 9.22, it offers dial-up access over standard phone lines. Apple recommends a pair of V.32/9600 baud modems as a minimum configuration. Farallon, Shiva and other companies make similar products.

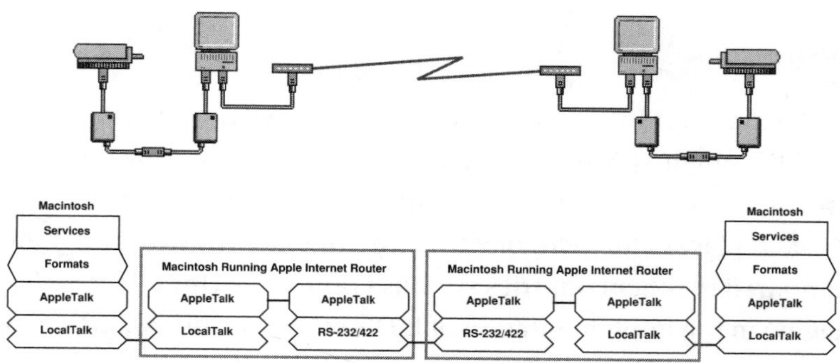

Figure 9.22
The Apple Internet Router can be used to link two remote LocalTalk networks over a dial-up line.

The problem with these products is the relatively slow dial-up connection. This type of connection is slow even for the single

Remote Access user, and more so for a number of LAN users. Conventional dial-up connections are also plagued by noise and disconnections that are more likely to occur with lengthy connection times.

Switched 56K

A faster and more reliable dial-up service is Switched 56K Service. This is a digital 56 Kbps service provided by AT&T over their ACCUNET system, by US Sprint, and others. Obviously this is much faster than a conventional 9600 baud dial-up line; it's also much more reliable. This kind of service is very well suited to connecting remote AppleTalk LANs. Engage Communication Inc. offers an AppleTalk router (SyncRouter LTNT) that connects to Switched 56K services. A NetPICT of the SyncRouter is shown in figure 9.23.

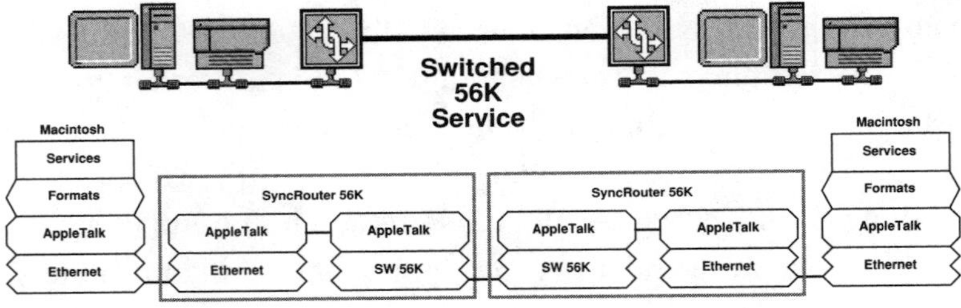

Figure 9.23
Engage's SyncRouter can perform AppleTalk routing over Switched 56K lines.

ISDN

ISDN stands for Integrated Services Digital Network. The promise of ISDN is high-speed, digital communications that provides network, voice, and video to consumers. Think of ISDN as the digital replacement technology for your telephone. Unfortunately, compared to other countries such as France, the United States is lagging in the implementation of ISDN services. This is starting to change as certain areas are now starting to get ISDN.

ISDN uses three channels: two 64 Kbps "B" channels and a single 16 Kbps "D" channel. The "B" channel carries voice and data, while the "D" channel carries signalling data and can be used for lower-speed transmissions. As ISDN services become more readily available they should begin to displace conventional modems as means of connecting AppleTalk services. Engage Communications Inc. has just announced AppleTalk routers that use ISDN as a link (see figure 9.24). They offer a LocalTalk version that provides 64 Kbps throughput and an EtherTalk version that uses both channels and can achieve a throughput of 128 Kbps.

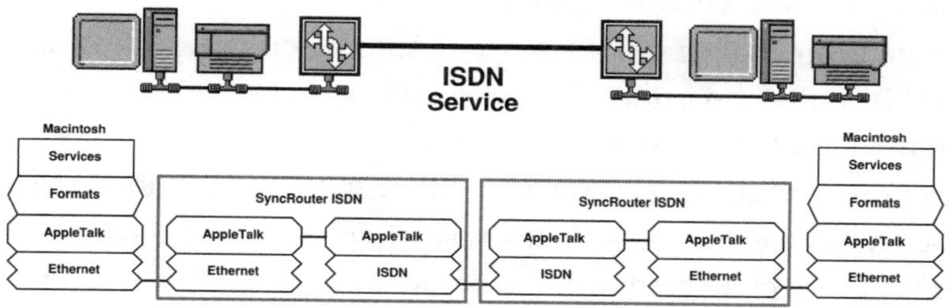

Figure 9.24 Engage's SyncRouter can perform AppleTalk routing over ISDN lines.

Leased Services

Other high-speed services are leased for a specific period of time. These services are incrementally based with T1 services offering a bandwidth of 1.544 Mbps, T2 with 6.312 Mbps, and T3 with 44.736 Mbps. These high speeds come with high price tags as well, making them suitable only for large organizations with demanding traffic requirements.

These leased-line services are usually coupled with high-speed multiprotocol routers from companies such as Cisco, Wellfleet, DEC, and IBM. All these vendors provide AppleTalk routing over leased lines. These multiprotocol routers cost anywhere between $3,000 and $20,000. They provide anything from a single WAN and Ethernet connection to units that have multiple WAN and LAN connections over Ethernet, Token Ring, and FDDI. Figure 9.25 shows a NetPICT of a T1-connected WAN.

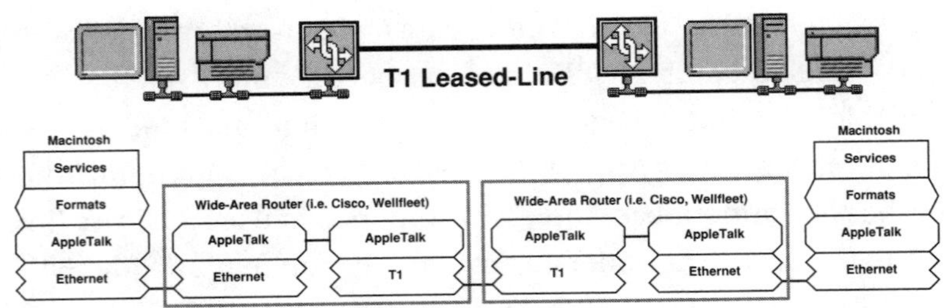

Figure 9.25 Many vendors (such as Cisco, Wellfleet, DEC, and IBM) make routers that support high-speed T1 Leased-Line WAN connections.

X.25 Packet Switched Services

Chances are that when you use your Automated Teller Machine (ATM) you're also using the services of a packet switched network known as X.25. ATM machines enable customers to access their checking and saving accounts anywhere in the world. Obviously, each ATM machine doesn't have everyone's personal account information contained within; instead, it accesses your account information from a centralized location. Other examples of packet switched networks are bulletin board services such as AppleLink and CompuServe. Users of these systems connect to the system over local phone connections.

This is all made possible with X.25 networking. In an X.25 network, services are locally provided over local phone lines. Once connected, the service provides a logical connection to anywhere on the entire system.

In the past, packet switched networking was unsuited for AppleTalk networking because of the overhead imposed by the RTMP routing protocol. Now, with AURP, packet switching has become a viable alternative for AppleTalk WANs. X.25 routing is being offered as an optional extension to Apple's Internet Router.

One primary advantage of an X.25 connection is that the costs are primarily based on usage rather than connect time. In contrast, with a conventional dial-up line, cost is mainly based on connect time. The phone company doesn't care whether you say anything—they'll still bill you. This is the reason why X.25

AppleTalk connections have been long in coming; the continual RTMP traffic made their use uneconomical. X.25 bandwidths range from modem speeds (1200 baud) to special high-speed connections at 2 Mbps. Figure 9.26 shows a NetPICT of a X.25-connected WAN.

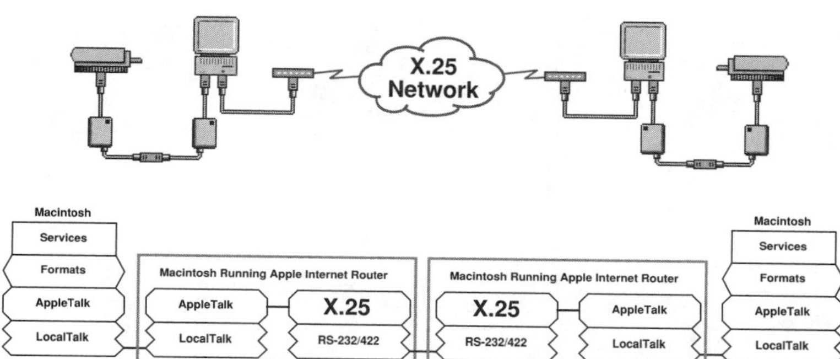

Figure 9.26
The Apple Internet router can be used to link two remote networks over an X.25 network.

Other Packet Switched Services

In addition to X.25, there are other packet switched technologies that show promise. Frame Relay is similar to X.25 but will provide improved performance due to reduced overhead. SMDS (Switched Multimegabit Data Service) is another packet switched service that shows great promise. It differs from X.25 and Frame Relay by employing a datagram approach that is more in keeping with the AppleTalk protocol.

Conclusion

The Macintosh, LaserWriter, and many other peripherals have a built-in networking capability known as LocalTalk. It is a low-cost cabling system that works over twisted-pair cabling. AppleTalk protocols aren't limited to LocalTalk; they can be sent over Ethernet, Token Ring, and most other media. While AppleTalk has been extremely popular on LANs, it has only recently begun to be accepted as a viable WAN protocol.

“Three”

Macintosh is a team player

Networks are often used to connect

Networks are often used to connect different computer systems. When it comes to multivendor networks, the Macintosh is a team player. It supports a wide variety of network Services, Formats, Transports, and Media. AppleTalk is also fast becoming a de-facto industry standard that is supported on many different computers, from the IBM PC to Digital’s VAX mincomputer.

systems. When it comes to multiven
Macintosh is a team player. It supp
network Services, Formats, Transpo
AppleTalk is also fast becoming a de
standard that is supported on many
computers, from the IBM PC to Dig
mincomputer.

Multivendor Networks

pports a wide variety of
ork Services, Formats,
sports, and Media.

10

Living in an Intel/DOS World

Macintosh computers and PCs, when connected, form the most common type of multivendor network. Exchanging documents and sharing resources between Macs and PCs is becoming more commonplace; software developers increasingly are offering separate Macintosh and Windows versions of their applications. With all the attention and focus on these two platforms, it's not surprising that there are so many networking choices available. This chapter will describe the leading choices for putting your Macintosh computers and PCs on speaking terms. Since PCs are the most common network companions, we'll also use this chapter to introduce some generic concepts and utilities that will apply to other networked peers as well.

Services: Application-Based

During the past several years, Macs and PCs have reached an equal stature in the eyes of many users. Many applications and services are supported on both platforms, and since the advent of Microsoft

Windows 3.0, the distinction between the platforms has narrowed considerably. Therefore, it's hardly surprising that there's a strong desire to share and exchange data between these two machines.

Applications

Many new application programs are being written for both the Mac and PC platforms. The applications from Microsoft are the best example. Nearly all their products—Word, Excel, Mail, PowerPoint, Project, and even Flight Simulator—are available for both platforms. In the majority of cases, the binary file formats of these applications are the same, and therefore are interchangable. Other examples of this cross-platform support are Lotus 1-2-3, Autodesk's AutoCAD, WordPerfect, and Claris's FileMaker Pro and ClarisWorks.

The application support extends beyond simple applications, as evidenced by Apple's recent announcement of QuickTime for Windows and Microsoft's adoption of TrueType fonts. With the QuickTime toolkit, Windows developers can create, edit, and display QuickTime files within their applications. Microsoft's inclusion of TrueType might make it a bit easier to move documents between the platforms without the font alteration that often occurs when competing font technologies are used.

This cross-platform trend can only increase, as developments are underway to make it even easier for developers to create either Windows or Mac versions of their applications through the advanced object-oriented compilers. These compilers will be able to substitute the appropriate platform-dependent user interface elements as necessary.

Other Services

Besides applications, there are other services that can be shared by both Macs and PCs (see figure 10.1). These include file, print, database, and mail services. Sharing these services is a somewhat more complex issue than simply sharing application files. With many of these services a specific format and transport layer are often required. For example, a PC can access an AFP file server, but only if equipped with the AppleTalk protocols. Both Macs and PCs can access an NFS file server—but only if both machines have the transport layer of TCP/IP. NFS and most of the other services common to the UNIX environment can also be installed on a suitably equipped PC. This chapter will just touch on a few of these options. For a more complete discusssion of TCP/IP services and protocols, refer to the next chapter. Regardless of the platform, it's often a process of finding a mutually acceptable service that uses compatible formats, transports, and cabling.

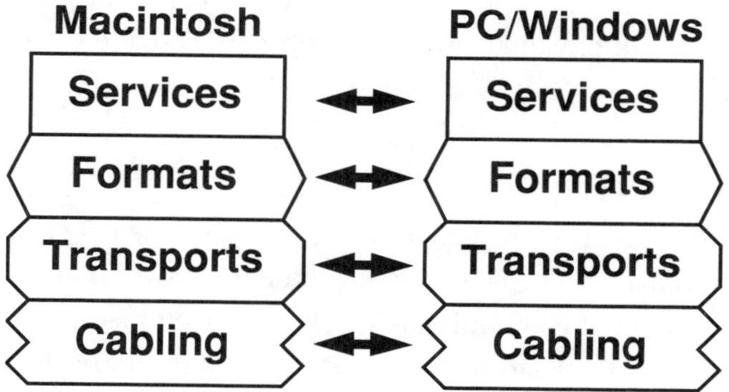

Figure 10.1
Macintosh/PC Services
NetPICT.

Formats: ASCII, EPS, Binary Compatible

The ultimate success of Macintosh/PC integration is largely determined by the formats. Fortunately, there are many shared and compatible file formats. Since the advent of Windows, the number of applications and formats that are shared by both platforms has increased dramatically. There are also a number of mutually acceptable standards, such as Encapsulated PostScript

(EPS) and Rich Text Format (RTF), that can be seamlessly moved between the Macintosh and PC platforms.

ASCII

The IBM PC was IBM's first computer that used the ASCII code instead of their EBCDIC code. Thus, Macs and PCs speak the same format when it comes to text files. Both the Mac and PC have numerous applications that can read and write this format. The only occasional stumbling block is that sometimes PC text files have additional line feed characters at the end of each line of text. These line feeds can often be filtered with special utility programs or text editors. The key aspect of ASCII is that it's often used as the basis for other higher-level formats, such as DXF, IGES, PostScript, and RenderMan (a 3D photorealistic rendering format). All Mac and PC text editors and word processors can read and write ASCII text files.

Word Processing

Many word processors, such as Microsoft Word, usually provide a built-in translation capability to facilitate the movement of documents between the PC and Macintosh. Microsoft has also developed an interchange format called Rich Text Format (RTF) that attempts to preserve certain formatting attributes between the Mac and Windows applications. If the PC word processing document was not created by an application that also runs on the Mac, or cannot be directly imported by a Mac program, then it must be converted. MacLinkPlus, from DataViz, is a utility program that can convert most PC word processing formats into formats that are supported on the Mac. This process is shown in figure 10.2.

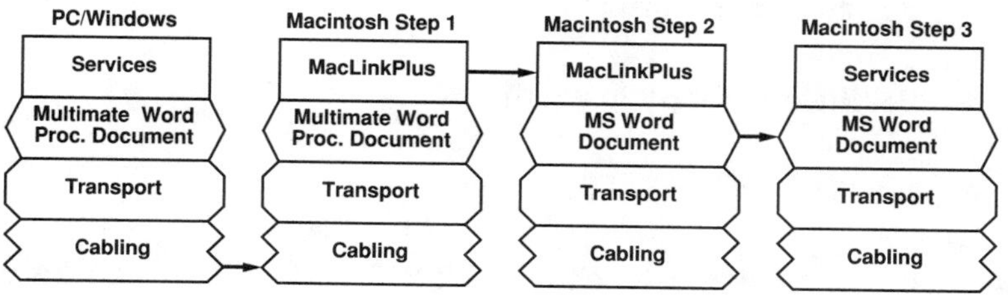

Figure 10.2
Converting a PC Multimate word processing document into a Macintosh Microsoft Word document with MacLinkPlus.

The Last Resort

Of course one option, as shown in figure 10.3, is to save the Mac or PC document that you wish to transport as an ASCII file. You'll lose all the formatting, graphics, and font information, but at least you'll have the document in a form that can be universally read. Use this technique as a last resort.

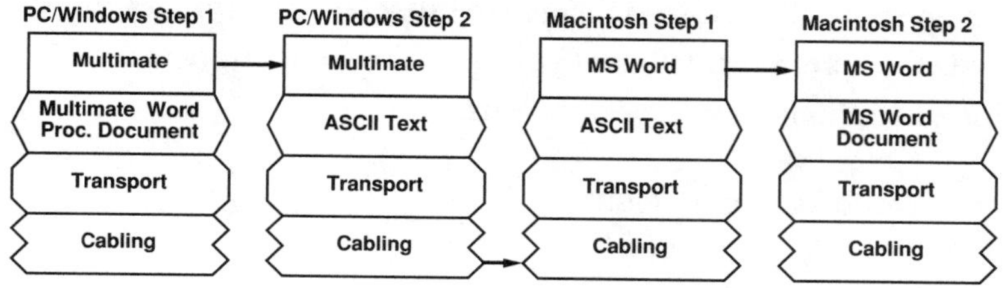

Figure 10.3
ASCII is being used as a neutral exchange format between word processors on the PC and Macintosh.

Graphics

When it comes to graphics, the situation gets even more complicated. There are dozens of different graphic formats that are supported on the Mac or PC. Some of these formats are bitmapped or pixel-based; others are object-oriented, containing object descriptions (such as line, circle, and rectangle) and coordinate data.

The leading graphic formats on the Mac are:

- MacPaint-style 72 dpi (dot per inch) bitmaps

- PICT and PICT2 formats
- EPS (Encapsulated PostScript)
- TIFF (Tagged Image File Format)

Of these, the MacPaint-type bitmap, PICT, and PICT2 formats are somewhat Macintosh-specific, although many Windows applications support these file types directly without translation. The other formats—EPS and TIFF—have become industry standards; they're frequently supported by applications on both platforms. Just be sure to check the specific applications in question.

On the Windows/PC side, there are numerous graphics formats, and with the possible exception of EPSF, TIFF, and some Windows-specific formats, they are quite often specific to a particular application. Listed below are but a few examples of the myriad graphics formats that you're likely to encounter on a PC, along with their DOS file extensions.

- Windows bitmap (`.BMP`)
- Windows Metafile (`.WMF`)
- DrawPerfect (`.WPG`)
- Computer Graphics Metafile (`.CGM`)
- Encapsulated PostScript (`.EPS`)
- Lotus 1-2-3 Graphics (`.PIC`)
- Initial Graphics Exchange Specification (`.IGS`)
- AutoCAD Drawing Exchange Format (`.DXF`)

- Micrografx Designer/Draw (`.DRW`)
- Tagged Image File (`.TIF`)

With the exception of Encapsulated PostScript and Tagged Image File Format (TIFF) files, there are few PC/Windows graphic formats that are uniformly supported in the Macintosh world. Going from the Mac to the PC is much easier because support for the PICT format is common in the PC world; support for the numerous application-specific PC graphic formats by Macintosh applications is unlikely.

One solution, shown in figure 10.4, is to use a PC graphics conversion program, such as Hijaak from Inset Systems. It can convert most PC formats into one of the predominant Macintosh formats (such as MacPaint or PICT). While Hijaak runs on the PC, the flip side of that approach is to do the conversion on the Mac by using the MacLinkPlus graphics translators. They support the conversion of most popular PC graphics formats into the PICT format.

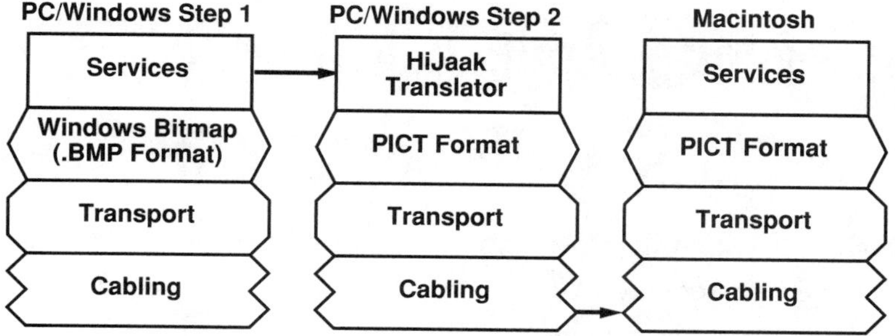

Figure 10.4 PC/Windows graphics files are translated into Macintosh formats with Hijaak from Inset Systems.

For CAD/CAM and technical graphics, there are two formats that are widely supported on both the Mac and the PC. The industry standard IGES is a standard format that can be binary, but is usually ASCII text. DXF is a standard developed by Autodesk, developers of the popular AutoCAD program. It too comes in a binary format, but the most popular format is regular ASCII text. Both of these formats are commonly supported by both Macintosh and PC CAD applications and utility programs. These files can be readily transported between the platforms. In particular, Macintosh/PC users desiring cross-platform conversion should examine the CADMOVER translation program from Kandu Software of Arlington, Virginia. As shown in figure 10.5, CADMOVER can read and write IGES and DXF and convert these formats into a variety of Macintosh graphic formats, such as PICT and EPSF.

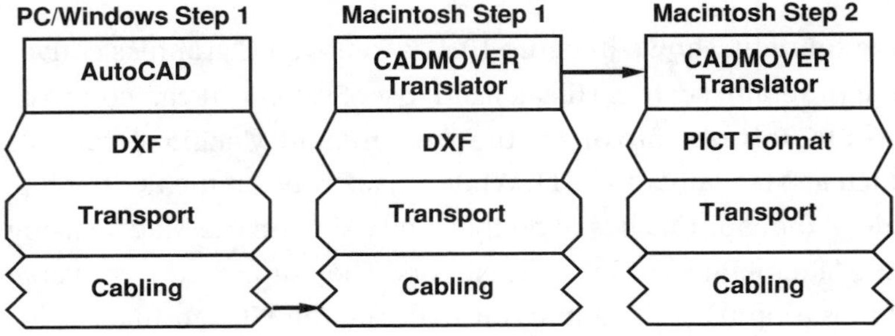

Figure 10.5
PC CAD graphics are translated into Macintosh formats with CADMOVER from Kandu Software.

Transports: AppleTalk (PhoneNET PC), MacIPX, DECnet, TCP/IP

Assuming your Macintosh and PCs are physically networked, what transport protocol will you use to logically connect the machines? At a certain level the choices are simple. You can equip the PC with the AppleTalk protocols, equip the Mac with Novell-compatible protocols, or be a total non-conformist and put foreign protocols (such as DECnet or TCP/IP) on both machines.

The Choices

The choice of a suitable transport protocol is often complicated by the fact that not all services support every transport. Therefore, the selection of a transport often begins at the top of the stack, at the Service layer. If the desired service is AFP file services, then you're somewhat limited to choosing AppleTalk as a transport. In most cases, there aren't too many choices when it comes to transports. All too often, a given service only supports a single transport protocol. The basic choices are simple: Either make the PC speak the Mac transport of AppleTalk, make the Mac speak a PC transport such as Novell IPX, or make both the Mac and PC speak a "foreign" protocol such as TCP/IP or DECnet. The only other options are to use a gateway or use an intermediate computer to act as an exchange agent. Let's explore the options.

AppleTalk on the PC

If you have a network where Macs are predominant and there are just a few PCs, then consider turning those PCs into AppleTalk nodes. One way to do this is with Farallon's PhoneNET PC. It equips a DOS or Windows PC with the AppleTalk protocol stack and also provides the equivalent of the Chooser (see figure 10.6), so that the user is able to select AppleTalk network services (such as AFP file services, System 7 File Sharing, and PAP print services). PhoneNET PC works either with a LocalTalk/PhoneNET card (offered by Apple, Dayna, COPS Inc., and Farallon), most common PC Ethernet cards, and IBM Token Ring 16/4 cards. Figure 10.7 shows various NetPICT diagrams of a PC running PhoneNET PC over different cabling mediums.

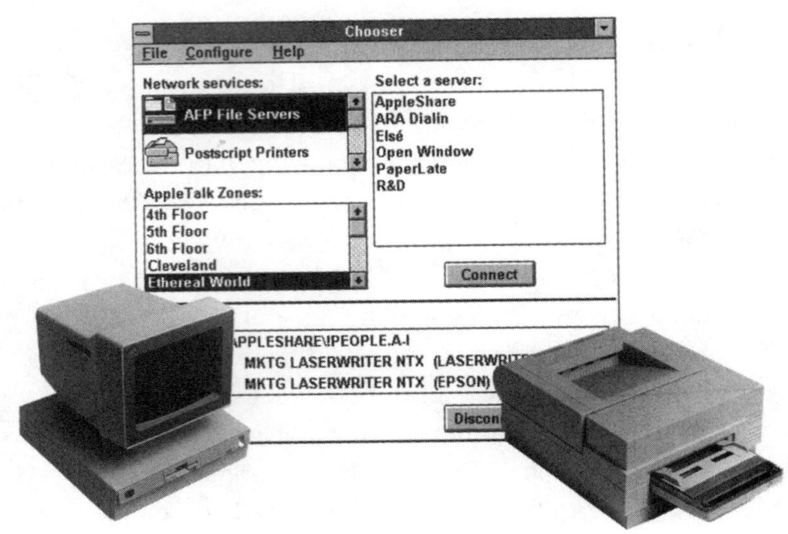

Figure 10.6 Farallon's PhoneNET PC puts the AppleTalk protocol and a Chooser-equivalent onto the PC.

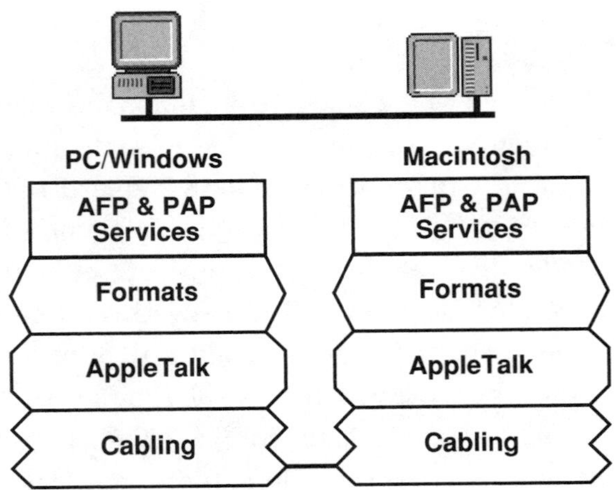

Figure 10.7 Farallon's PhoneNET PC supports AppleTalk over different kinds of cabling.

In addition to the AFP and PAP services supported by PhoneNET PC, various application services are supported by the product as well. A listing of the currently supported PC application appears below.

- Farallon Timbuktu (PhoneNET PC is included with all versions of Timbuktu for Windows)

- Microsoft Mail 3.0 and 3.1
- QuickMail from CE Software
- Lotus cc:Mail
- WordPerfect Office
- Claris FileMaker Pro 2.0
- Blyth Omnis 7 (Can access DAL services)
- Microsoft FoxBase+

As shown in figure 10.8, putting PhoneNET PC on a PC doesn't restrict it from running other protocols, as PhoneNET PC runs concurrently with Novell NetWare IPX and TCP/IP. One advantage of turning your PCs into AppleTalk nodes is that, like the Macintosh, your PC will self-configure its network address. Your PC will also be visible to AppleTalk network management and troubleshooting utilities such as Apple's Inter•Poll.

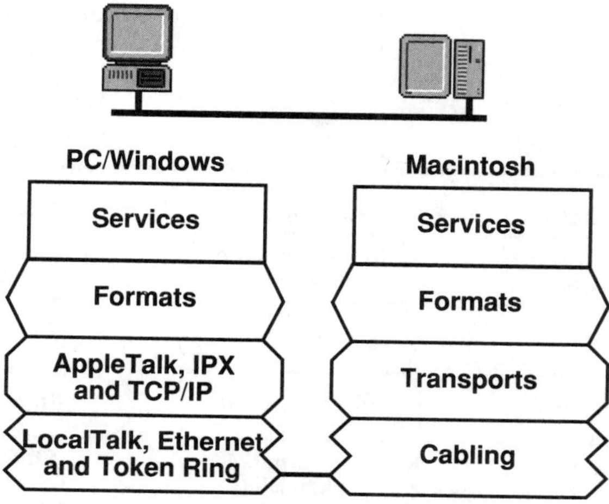

Figure 10.8
Farallon's PhoneNET PC supports the concurrent use of Novel IPX and TCP/IP in addition to AppleTalk; it is supported on PC LocalTalk cards, Ethernet, and Token Ring.

In addition to the Farallon products, another company, CoOperative Printing Solutions Inc. (COPS Inc.), has a number of AppleTalk PC solutions. COPSTalk for DOS and COPSTalk for Windows puts the AppleTalk protocols on a DOS- or Windows-equipped PC. Other products include PServe, which provides unified print queuing for Macs and PCs, and the COPS EasyServer, which turns a PC into an AFP file server.

Yet another PC AFP solution is MacLAN Connect Gold from Miramar Systems Inc. This product connects LocalTalk, Ethernet, or Token Ring users to file and print services. It also supports the recently announced Microsoft Windows for Workgroups.

Novell Solutions

Novell, the networking giant, offers two approaches to Macintosh PC connectivity. First, Novell NetWare servers can be configured as AFP file servers. As shown in figure 10.9, Macs access these services with the AppleTalk transport; PC users access the same server with Novell IPX protocols. Normally it's not recommended, but it is possible for the two environments to share a common file space. Thus, it is possible to share files between the two environments.

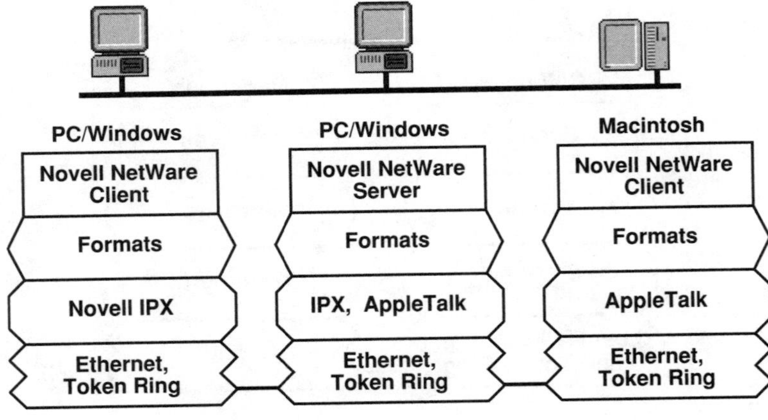

Figure 10.9 Novell's NetWare for Macintosh adds AppleTalk, AFP, and PAP support to PC/Windows computers.

Dayna offers an alternative for the Novell environment, one that turns a Mac into a full-fledged NetWare client running the Novell IPX protocol. As shown in figure 10.10, with Dayna's NetMounter, the AppleTalk protocol stack is replaced with a version of Novell IPX. A Chooser-level driver is used to select and log on to the server. With this approach, the Mac appears as a PC client, so you won't have to purchase the NetWare for Macintosh module. NetMounter also includes a utility that will assign Macintosh creator and type codes to particular DOS file extensions. This makes it possible to copy a Microsoft Excel spreadsheet from a NetWare DOS server and have its Macintosh icon available for subsequent double-clicking.

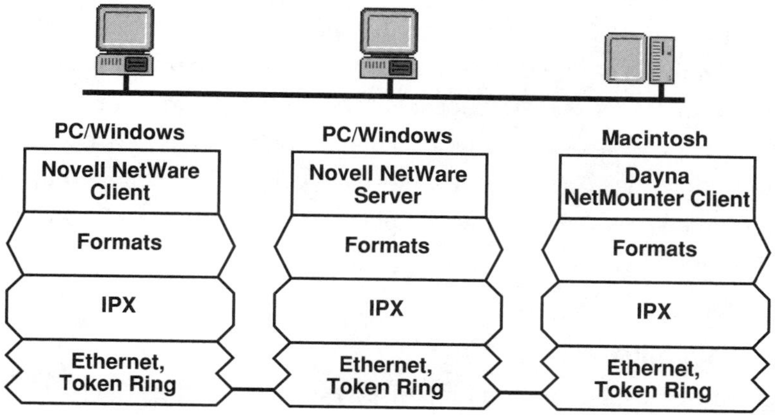

Figure 10.10 Dayna's NetMounter equips Macs with the IPX transport layer and enables them to directly access any NetWare server.

In the past, Novell concentrated on the file service support for the Mac, but Novell has recently begun to develop another approach. MacIPX, shown in figure 10.11, involves placing Novell's IPX protocol on the Macintosh. Intended for developers, MacIPX will provide an avenue for cross-platform peer-to-peer communications between applications on the two platforms. MacIPX should help the Macintosh make inroads into environments where PCs and Novell networks prevail.

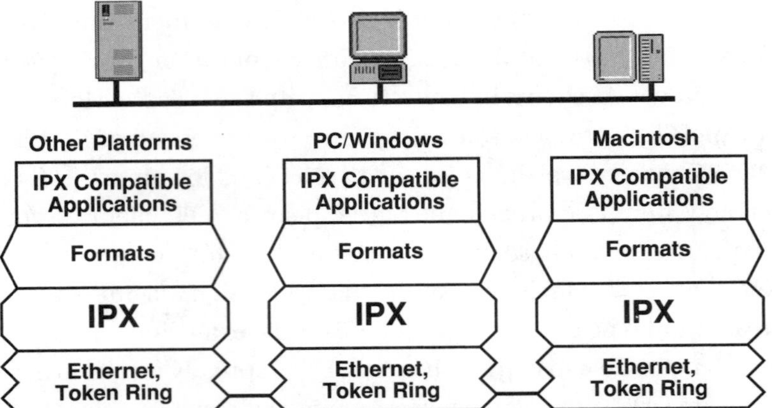

Figure 10.11
Novell's MacIPX transport provides cross-platform peer-to-peer access.

Another Novell Macintosh solution is DataClub, which was recently acquired by Novell from International Business Software Inc. DataClub is a distributed file service that transparently aggregates and manages disk space from the individual workstations. This virtual disk space is made available to the network users as mountable disk volumes. DataClub was originally developed for Macintosh networks, but Novell plans to add support for DOS, Windows, and UNIX.

Banyan Vines

Banyan Vines, a popular enterprise-wide networking system, offers client support for Macintosh workstations, allowing them to share resources with DOS, OS/2, and Windows workstations on the same network. Vines supports the AppleTalk filing protocol and the Printer Access Protocol from their Intel/PC-based Vines server. In addition, AppleTalk tunneling through Vines enables disjointed AppleTalk networks to be connected with each other via the Vines network.

DECnet on the Mac and PC

While the appeal of DECnet is somewhat limited to those sites with DEC VAX computers, another transport alternative is to use

DECnet. When DEC got into the PC clone business, they quickly saw the potential of integrating PCs into their network environment. To achieve this goal, DEC created DECnet DOS, which equips the PC with the DECnet protocol stack. They also developed a number of Service layer applications so that the PC user can engage in terminal emulation, file copying, and printing within a VAX computing environment.

DECnet for the Macintosh is now offered as a component of PATHWORKS for Macintosh, the product that grew out of the Apple/DEC alliance. DECnet for the Mac performs a similar function to its DOS counterpart and enables a Mac to perform services such as file copying, E-mail and terminal services in a DECnet environment.

Because both the Mac and PC support the DECnet transport protocol and the file copy services (see figure 10.12), they can use this mechanism to move files between the two platforms, even when there's no VAX involved. It should be noted, though, that the common services offered by the Mac and PC versions of DECnet are somewhat basic and are likely to be of interest only to those who already have VAX computers and DECnet networks already in place.

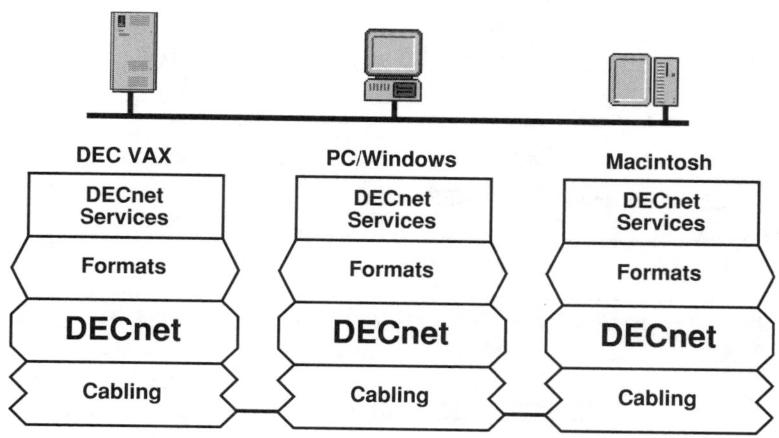

Figure 10.12
Both the Mac and PC can use Digital's DECnet protocol, either with a VAX or separately.

TCP/IP on the Mac and PC

If you're still looking to put a "foreign" transport protocol on your Macs and PCs, then another choice is TCP/IP. Common in UNIX circles, TCP/IP stands for Transmission Control Protocol/Internet Protocol. It is widely used in universities, government installations, defense contractors, and many large corporate installations.

MacTCP is an Apple product that equips the Macintosh with the TCP/IP protocol. MacTCP is similar to AppleTalk, in that it's useless without application services. Most of the application services that work with MacTCP are provided by third parties. The popular services are NFS file service, SLIP, and TELNET terminal services, and X-Windows. These services sit atop the MacTCP transport layer.

Using file access as an example in figure 10.13, a Macintosh equipped with MacTCP and NFS (available from either Wollongong and InterCon) can exchange files with a similarly-equipped PC. PC-NFS from Sun Microsystems is a popular implementation of NFS for DOS. FTP Software's product called PC/TCP Plus provides the PC with the TCP/IP transport protocol and NFS in one package. For more information on TCP/IP solutions, refer to the next chapter, which covers UNIX connectivity.

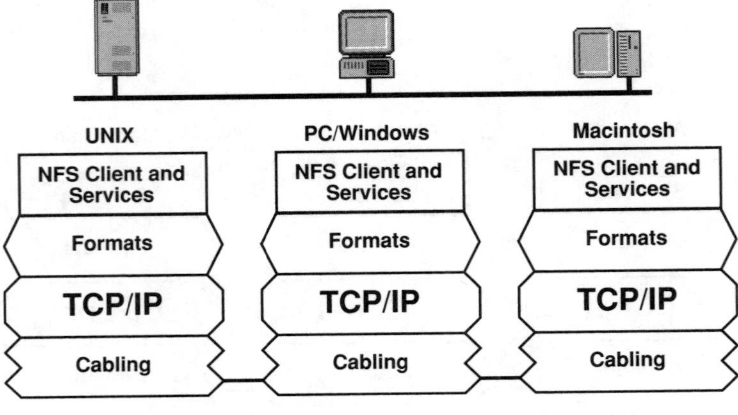

Figure 10.13
The TCP/IP transport is supported on most platforms today, including the Mac and PC. Sun's Network Filing System is a common file service supported by TCP/IP.

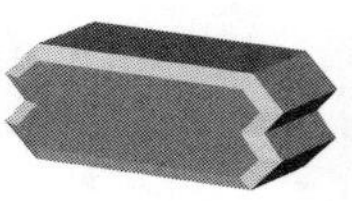

Cabling Options

The choices available for cabling systems for Mac/PC connectivity are as varied as the cabling choices available for the Macintosh. You can choose among LocalTalk, Ethernet, Token Ring, and even the popular PC cabling system, ARCNET.

LocalTalk

The benefits of LocalTalk expressed earlier apply to PCs as they do for Macs. It's cheap and it runs over conventional twisted-pair phone wire. If you're introducing PCs into a largely LocalTalk network, you'll be able to equip your PCs with the LocalTalk hardware. Vendors such as Dayna, Farallon, and COPS Inc. offer such cards. Versions for either the ISA or MicroChannel bus are available.

It probably only makes sense to consider LocalTalk cabling for AppleTalk-only networks. If you're planning a multiprotocol network, you're better off with Ethernet or Token Ring cabling. You will also find that the LocalTalk cards for PCs (see figure 10.14) are nearly the same price as the PC Ethernet cards.

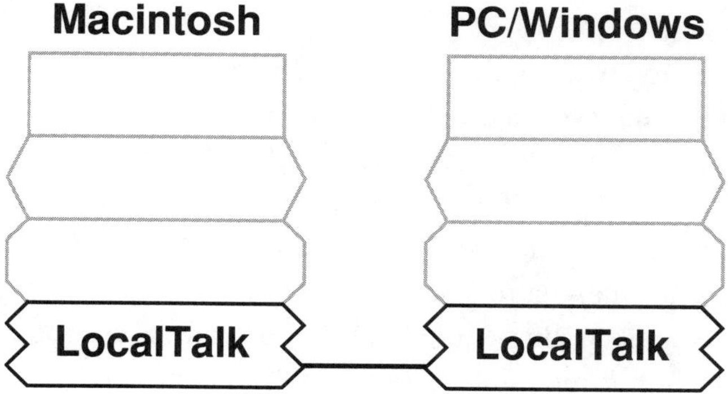

Figure 10.14
LocalTalk on a PC NetPICT.

Ethernet

Ethernet is probably the best choice for a PC/Mac cabling system (see figure 10.15). It's relatively inexpensive, comes in a variety of physical cable types, and (most importantly) it supports a wide variety of networking transport protocols. If you're planning to use multiple protocols, just be sure that all your anticipated protocol drivers support your chosen Ethernet cards. As mentioned before, PhoneNET PC from Farallon supports most Ethernet cards, such as the EtherLink series from 3Com and Novell's NE1000/NE2000, but you may find a card that is not supported. Just be safe; double-check with all vendors and make sure everything's supported.

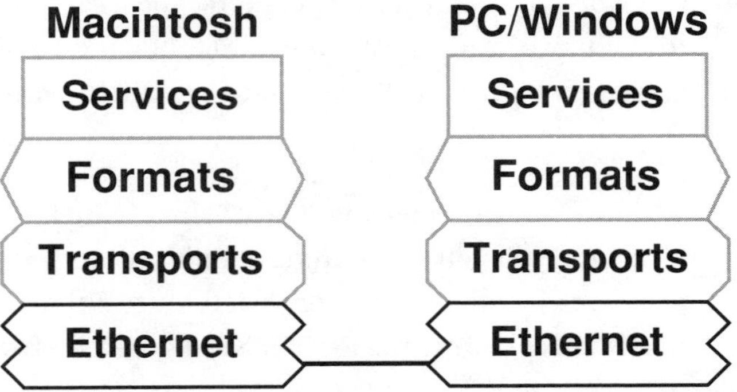

Figure 10.15
Ethernet on a PC NetPICT.

Token Ring

Compared to Ethernet, there's less variety in Token Ring cards. IBM is becoming very agressive in pricing and licensing their Token Ring componentry (see figure 10.16). Prices have already started to drop. Most of the newer cards offer both 4MB and 16MB transmission rates and use the latest integrated circuitry. As with Ethernet, just make sure that the transports you've selected are supported. Token Ring-equipped PCs are likely to be popular in IBM mainframe and minicomputer environments where Token Ring is already in use.

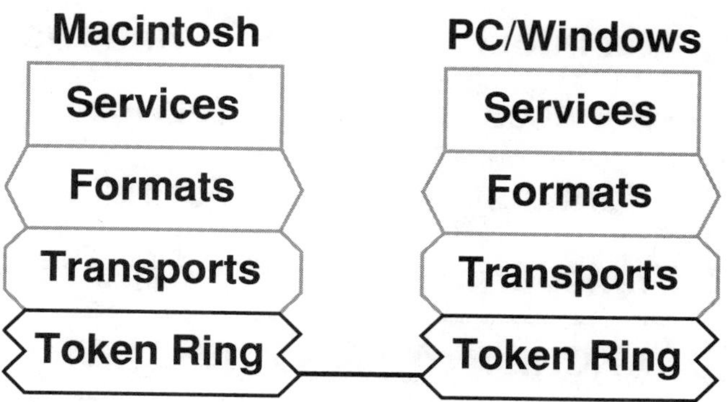

Figure 10.16
Token Ring on a PC NetPICT.

Apple offers a NuBus Token Ring card. This can be used to connect a Macintosh to a Token Ring network directly, or it can be used by a Mac running the Apple Internet Router. When a Mac runs the Apple Internet router, it can be equipped with other networking connections such as LocalTalk and Ethernet. In this case, the router can be used to provide LocalTalk- and Ethernet-equipped Macs access to services on the Token Ring network.

ARCNET

Shortly after the IBM PC was introduced, the ARCNET network system was designed as a low-cost LAN (see figure 10.17). ARCNET is still in widespread use today as a cabling medium for PC networks, particularly NetWare. ARCNET supports two different kinds of cabling (coaxial and twisted-pair) and has a bandwidth of 2.5 Mbps. This places ARCNET between the bandwidths of LocalTalk and Ethernet.

In 1991, ACTINET Systems began to offer a line of ARCNET cards for Macintosh computers. Their ARCTalk cards come in three models: one for NuBus-equipped Macs, one for the Macintosh LC, and one for the SE/30 and IIsi. Included with the cards is ARCTalk software which provides AppleTalk Phase 2 support. Although the original ARCNET specs permit both star and bus topologies, the ARCTalk cards only support the star topology.

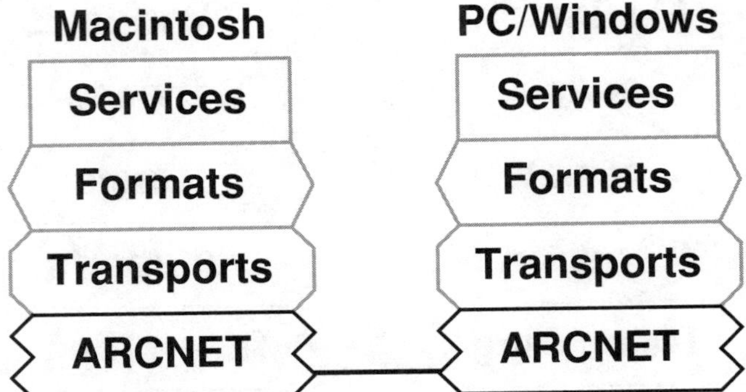

Figure 10.17
ARCNET on a Mac and PC NetPICT.

With the coaxial version of ARCNET, each cable run can be a maximum of 2000 feet. The twisted-pair implementation can run 400 feet (slightly longer than twisted-pair Ethernet). In both cases, an ARCNET hub, available from third-party vendors, is required.

The cards are certified by Novell for use with NetWare for Macintosh and the cards and ARCTalk software are System 7-complient and will run on the Apple Internet Router. Use of the Apple router is important because there are no options for connecting LaserWriters or other LocalTalk devices to an ARCNET network.

Conclusion

There are more networking services, formats, transports, and cabling options available to connect Macs and PCs than with any other platform combination. The key is to first determine the desired services. Then, examine which protocol best delivers that service. Finally, choose a cabling system that balances support for the chosen protocol or protocols with cost and future growth and expansion.

UNIX Connectivity

11

While not as prevalent as the PC or the Mac, UNIX-based workstations and other UNIX computers are very common, particularly in the engineering and technical environments where Macintosh is also very popular. This chapter explores the networking options for Macintosh and UNIX computers.

Services: FTP, NFS, AFP, X-Windows, TELNET

Most of the services in the Macintosh/UNIX world revolve around file access and terminal services. To a seasoned Macintosh user, the services offered in the UNIX-TCP/IP world may seem a bit basic. Many of these services are directed at sophisticated users and programmers. However, new TCP/IP-conversant Macintosh services aimed at a more general audience are being announced every week.

Rather than starting off talking about bringing UNIX services to the Mac, we'll begin by looking at the AppleTalk-based services available for the UNIX environment.

AFP/PAP Services on UNIX Computers

To a Macintosh user, file service means AFP. There are several products that provide this service on UNIX computers. Xinet sells K-AShare, which implements AFP on a Sun or HP UNIX host (see figure 11.1). So, just like with any other AFP server, the Macintosh user accesses UNIX files through the Chooser. The mounted volumes provide access to the UNIX files as if they were local disk files on the Mac. (The Sun or HP running K-AShare could also be set up as an NFS server, so in a sense K-AShare can be thought of as an AFP/NFS gateway.)

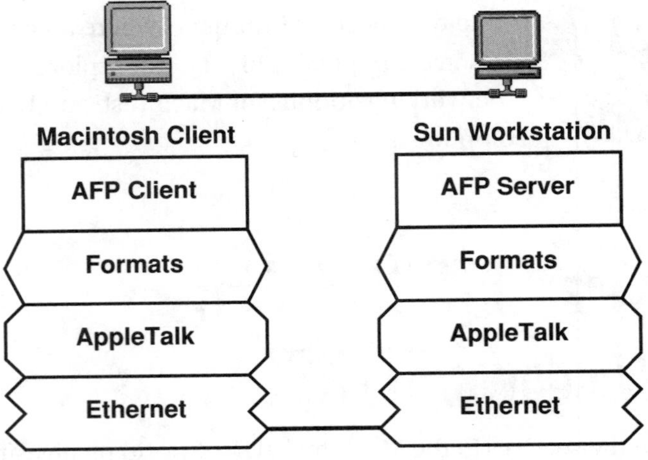

Figure 11.1 Xinet's K-AShare turns a Sun or HP UNIX workstation into an AFP Server.

A companion product from Xinet, K-Spool, provides PAP print spooling services for the Macintosh user. It also acts as a print server and PostScript agent for the UNIX user, forwarding print jobs to a networked LaserWriter.

Diagrammed in figure 11.2, K-Spool's PAP spooler appears to the Macintosh user just as any other LaserWriter. It does this with a special program—a *virtual LaserWriter.* This means that the program accepts and responds to NBP Lookup Requests and Responses. After the NBP process is done and a Macintosh user selects the virtual LaserWriter, the program accepts the PAP commands that contain the PostScript printing instructions. This printing information is placed in a file that is queued until the designated printer is available. This technique avoids the annoying background delays seen when Print Monitor is used to spool the print file on your local Macintosh disk.

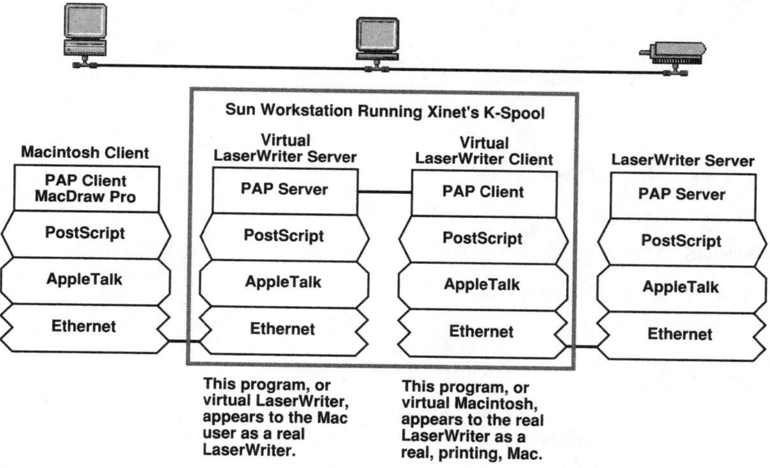

Figure 11.2
Xinet's K-Spool turns a Sun or HP UNIX workstation into a PAP print spooler.

Pacer Software offers PacerShare, shown in figure 11.3, which offers a similar capability for VAX computers equipped with Sun, HP, and DEC Ultrix (DEC's version of UNIX). PacerShare, like K-AShare, maps the AFP file structure onto the native UNIX file structure of the host. PacerPrint provides for LaserWriter printer sharing.

InterCon's InterPrint is another printer utility that provides Chooser-level access to UNIX printers on TCP/IP networks. This utility makes it as easy for a Mac to print to a UNIX PostScript printer as it is to print to a LaserWriter.

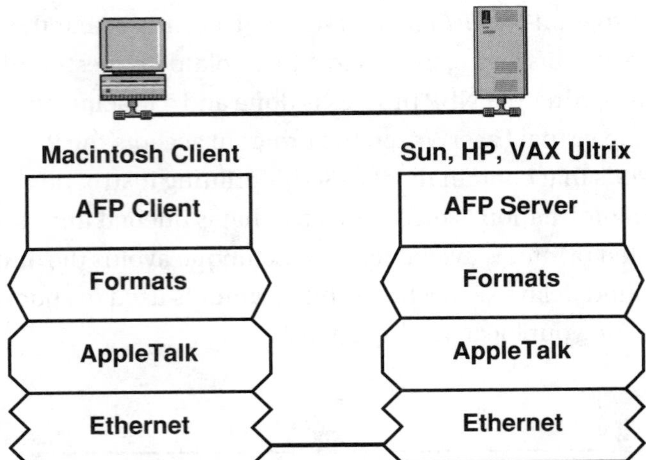

Figure 11.3 PacerShare for UNIX provides AFP file services on Sun, HP, and DEC Ultrix VAX computers.

Data Access Language

DAL services provide access to relational databases on UNIX systems. Apple sells a version of DAL for A/UX equipped Macs, and Pacer offers a DAL server for HP UNIX computers, DEC Ultrix, and Sun's SPARCstation (see figure 11.4). These services use the AppleTalk transport on each of their respective platforms.

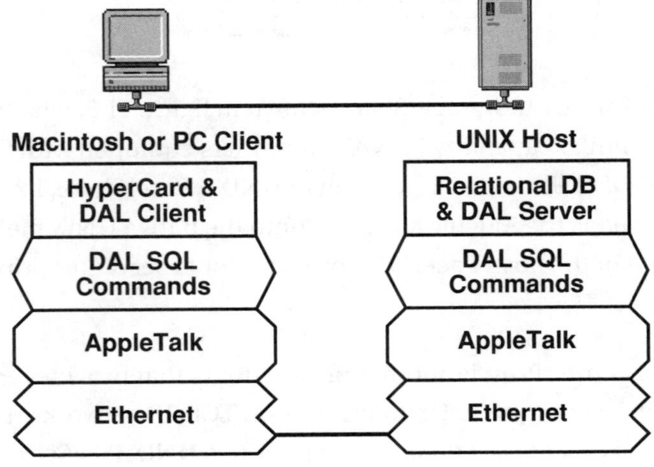

Figure 11.4 Apple and Pacer provide DAL database services on UNIX computers. All UNIX DAL servers use AppleTalk as a transport.

File Transfer Protocol (FTP)

The File Transfer Protocol (FTP) is commonly used in UNIX and TCP/IP networks to move files between nodes. FTP provides directory services, so a user can get a listing of candidate files on a remote machine. It also provides support for a variety of formats (such as ASCII and binary) and insures security by requiring login IDs and passwords. However, some systems offer public access to files without IDs and passwords. This service is known as Anonymous FTP, and many companies, universities, and organizations use it to post information that they wish to distribute freely.

Most implementations of FTP are through terminal-based command line interfaces; any of the TCP/IP compatible terminal services (such as VersaTerm-Pro and NCSA Telnet) can be used to engage in FTP transfers (see figure 11.5). Since the Macintosh has focused attention on the user interface, a number of FTP application services are starting to provide sophisticated interfaces. There's even a freeware HyperCard stack called HyperFTP, written by a Cornell student, that supports the basic set of FTP operations.

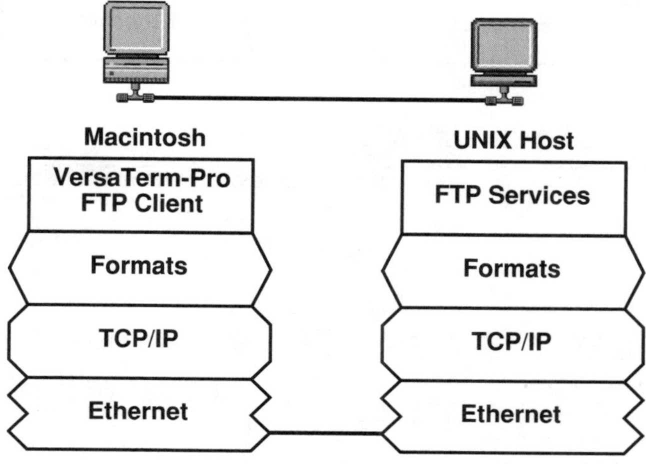

Figure 11.5 Terminal emulators, such as VersaTerm-Pro, provide FTP services to MacTCP-equipped Macs.

FTPShare, from Advanced Software Concepts, is a multi-session FTP server (up to 20 simultaneous sessions) that runs in the background of the Macintosh (see figure 11.6). In many ways, FTPShare can be compared to Apple's System 7 File Sharing. The FTPShare setup screens, shown in figure 11.7, resemble the screens used under System 7 File Sharing, so it should be easy for Macintosh users to adapt. FTPShare also includes a monitoring application that monitors the connected users and gives an indication of FTP activity.

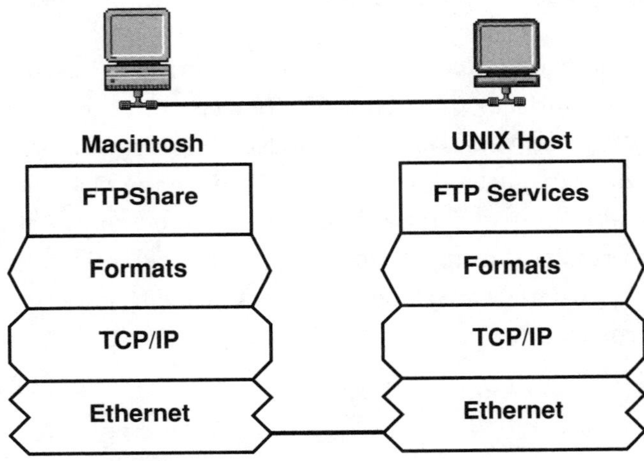

Figure 11.6
FTPShare from Advanced Software Concepts uses FTP to provide Macs with a File Sharing-like capability.

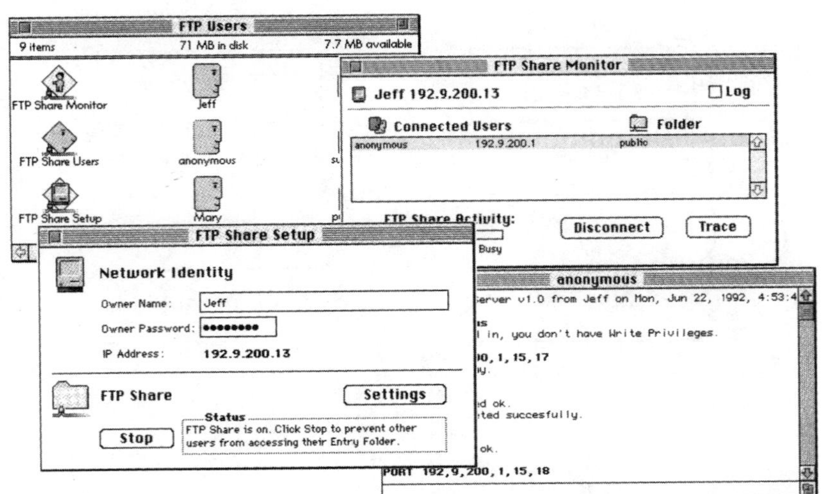

Figure 11.7
FTPShare puts the look and feel of Macintosh File Sharing onto FTP transfers.

Network Filing System (NFS)

Developed by Sun Microsystems, NFS provides additional capabilities not found in FTP. It can be used to transfer files between computers, but it also provides a mechanism for distributed applications that are network-aware. There are several implementations of NFS on the Macintosh; two of the more popular products are NFS/Share from InterCon and Pathway NFS from Wollongong. Both of these products, shown in figure 11.8, work with Apple's MacTCP and bring NFS services to the desktop of the Macintosh, thus retaining the ease-of-use of the Mac.

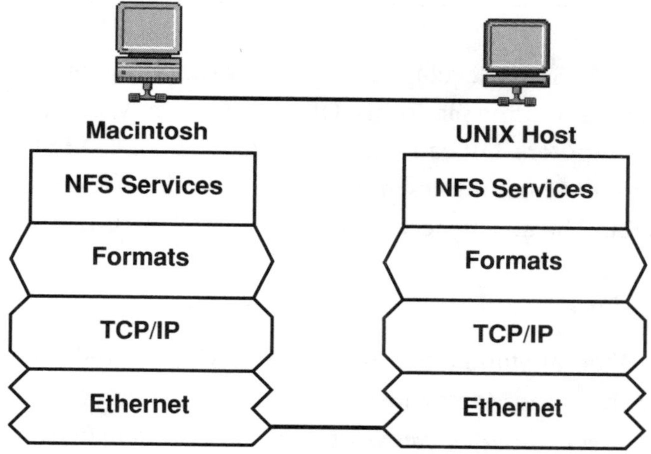

Figure 11.8
InterCon and Wollongong offer NFS services for the Macintosh. They both use the MacTCP transport protocol.

Partner, from IPT, takes another approach to Macintosh/UNIX connectivity. It works in both directions between a Macintosh and Sun SPARC systems. Macintosh users access SPARC files as AFP server volumes; SPARC users access the Macintosh files as if they were NFS volumes (see figure 11.9). IPT also provides PAP print spooling with a variety of UNIX print services and a mail gateway. The Partner application resides on the Sun SPARC machine and does all the necessary transport and service layer conversion; no special software is required on the Macintosh.

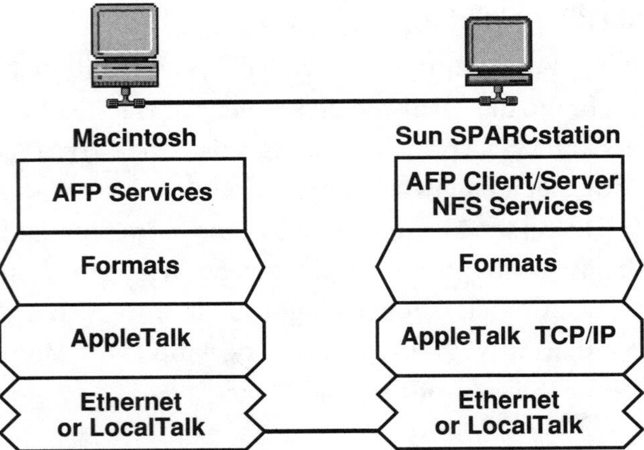

Figure 11.9 IPT's Partner provides bi-directional access of Mac and Sun SPARC files over the network. Mac users see the SPARCstation as an AFP server, while Sun users see the Mac as just another NFS server.

Although NFS was developed by Sun, it is supported on many different computing platforms. Of course, it's most common on UNIX computers, but can also be found on PCs (PC-NFS), DEC VAX and IBM mainframes and minicomputers. Any NFS-equipped Mac should be able to access these other NFS platforms as well.

X-Window

The X-Window standard, also called X or X11, evolved from initial work done at the Massachusetts Institute of Technology. It is a client/server windowing environment that is extensible and customizable. DEC's implementation of X, known as DECwindows, is used as their standard windowing environment on their VAX/VMS computers and UNIX-based workstations. Motif is the name of the X implementation by the Open Software Foundation (OSF). However, the concept and underlying messaging used by these different flavors of X is the same. The user interfaces are slightly different, with different styles of windows, buttons and controls.

X is popular in UNIX (and therefore TCP/IP) networks. However, it should be mentioned that X is not limited to computers running the UNIX operating system or the TCP/IP transport. The X-Window service can be run on many different kinds of computers and network transports.

X works on a client/server model. The computer that displays the image is called the server and the computer that runs the application code is called the client. This is a little confusing because we're accustomed to calling the desktop device the client, but with X the terms client and server reflect how the underlying software operates.

Many companies make X-Window terminals, or servers. These stand-alone devices have just enough processing power to run the X server display software (see figure 11.10). These terminals connect to X client programs running on other computers. Most UNIX workstations can act as both X clients and servers. Sometimes the client and server even run on the same machine, but the system is flexible enough to permit connections locally or remotely.

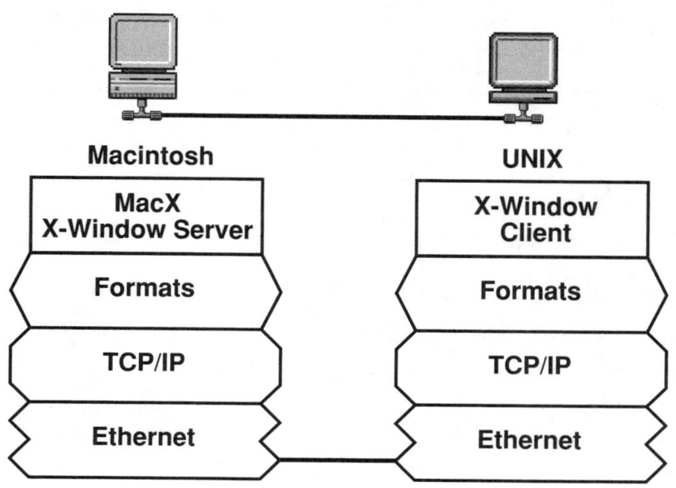

Figure 11.10
X-Window terminals, or display servers, work in conjunction with X-Window clients. The clients are the application programs, which use the display servers to do their graphical work. X-Window clients and servers can be distributed over a network, or together on the same computer.

There are two X-Window servers for the Macintosh: MacX from Apple and eXodus from White Pine Software. Either one can be used to connect to X-Window client applications that run on UNIX computers (or any other platforms that support the X standard). These applications make it possible to display X-Window applications side-by-side with Macintosh windows.

Planet X, from InterCon, is an X-Window client for the Macintosh. It allows a user to view and operate a Macintosh remotely from any X-Window server. As shown in figure 11.11, this server could be a UNIX workstation or even another Mac running MacX. When a session is established, the user operating the X-Window server sees the Macintosh desktop in a separate window. Planet X supports the cutting, copying, and pasting of graphics between the two environments.

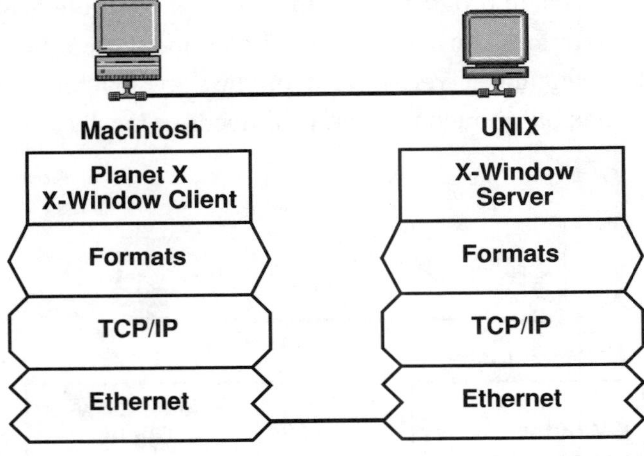

Figure 11.11
Planet X is the opposite of MacX. It turns a Mac into an X-Window client, making it accessible from other X-Window servers.

For all its flexibility, X has yet to really take off. The number of X applications continues to grow, but at a slow pace. The bulk of X applications can be found in the scientific and technical world where UNIX is an established standard. X is also reasonably popular in its DECwindows guise, where Digital continues to migrate its traditionally VT terminal-based applications over to X.

Terminal Services

The most basic of TCP/IP services is the Telnet terminal service. This is a simple protocol that allows a user to remotely connect to a server as if he were using a local terminal. There are several popular terminal emulators that offer Telnet and work in concert with MacTCP (see figure 11.12). Two examples are NCSA Telnet and VersaTerm Pro. With these applications, you can log on to remote TCP/IP hosts over a dial-up connection, or over a network connection such as Ethernet.

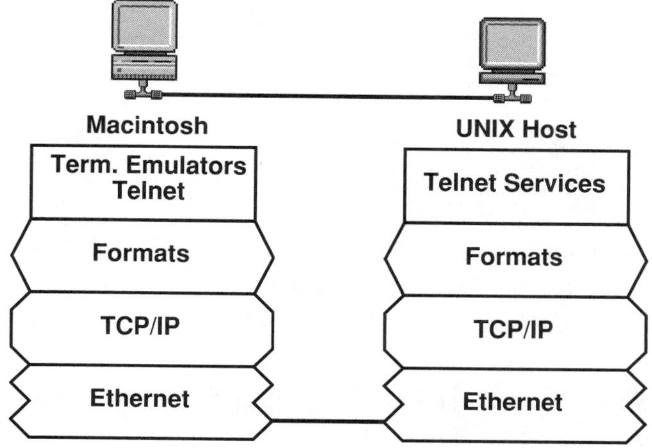

Figure 11.12 Telnet is a popular UNIX terminal service. Many Macintosh terminal emulators support it, using MacTCP as the transport.

Other terminal services use the Macintosh Communications Toolbox (MCT) with MacTCP to provide other kinds of terminal services. Advanced Software Concepts has an entire family of terminal emulation products that work through MacTCP. asc5250 is a MCT terminal emulation tool that allows you to communicate with IBM AS/400 minicomputers over a TCP/IP network. asc3270 is used to enable Macs to communicate with IBM mainframes, using MacTCP (see figure 11.13). This seems weird—TCP/IP has been associated with UNIX workstations for quite a while—but it's becoming more commonplace as TCP/IP begins to displace IBM's non-routable SNA protocol.

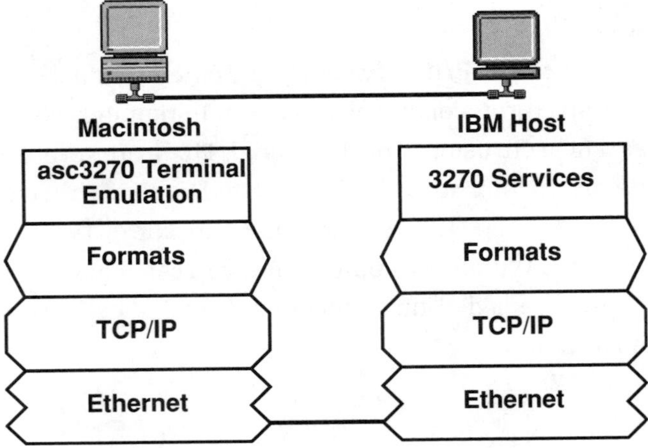

Figure 11.13 NetPICT of an unlikely trio. A Macintosh is running ASC's IBM 3270 terminal emulator using MacTCP as a transport.

Formats

Similar to the formats supported by the PC, UNIX computers are able to share ASCII text files and those application formats that are binary compatible. As an example, let's imagine we have three computers—a Mac, a Sun workstation, and a PC networked with Ethernet. Autodesk makes a version of their AutoCAD CAD program for each of these computing platforms. Each computer has TCP/IP and NFS file services installed. Since AutoCAD uses identical binary formats for all platforms, we're able to freely move AutoCAD files among the different computers. No translation will be required.

Taking this scenario further, imagine we were using Claris CAD on the Macintosh instead of AutoCAD for the Macintosh. Unfortunately, Claris CAD can't directly read the binary format of an

AutoCAD file. In this case we'll have to translate. We can generate an ASCII-based DXF file from the AutoCAD application on the Sun or the PC (see figure 11.14). We then use NFS file services to transfer the DXF file to the Macintosh, where we use the Claris Graphics Translator to convert the DXF format into the native Claris CAD document.

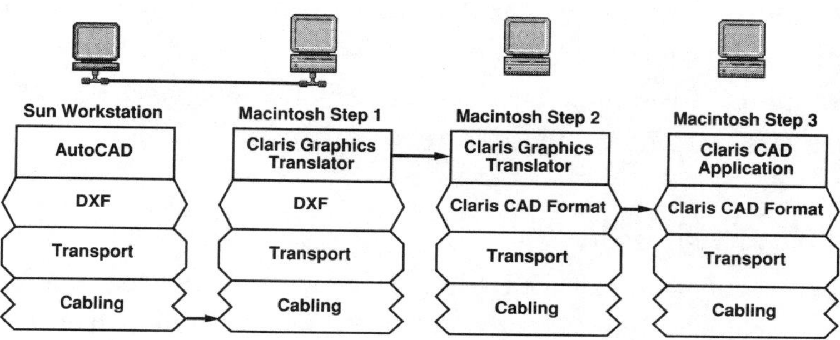

Figure 11.14
A DXF file generated on a Sun workstation is converted into a Claris CAD document with the Claris Graphics Translator.

Many UNIX workstations, particularly those from NeXT, use PostScript as an imaging format. PostScript files from these machines (including the EPSF variety) can be easily exchanged with the Macintosh (see figure 11.15). But, as mentioned before, be aware that EPSF files generated by non-Macintosh applications may not have the PICT preview resource.

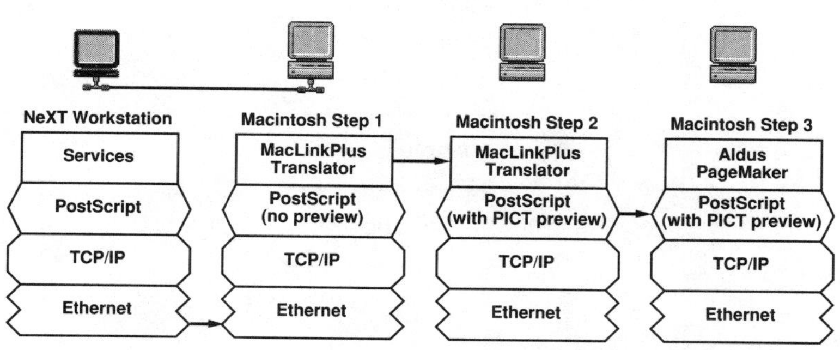

Figure 11.15
A PostScript file (without the PICT preview) is generated by a NeXT application, moved over to the Macintosh, translated into a PostScript file with a PICT preview, and then placed into a PageMaker document.

Transports: AppleTalk, TCP/IP

Mention UNIX networking to most computerphiles and a discussion of TCP/IP will undoubtedly ensue. TCP/IP is an important part of Macintosh/UNIX networking. MacTCP, from Apple, puts the TCP/IP protocol stack onto the Macintosh, giving the Macintosh peer-to-peer capabilities with other IP nodes. The other option is to equip the UNIX machine with AppleTalk protocols. Computers so equipped can serve as AFP file servers, PAP print spoolers and DAL database servers.

AppleTalk for UNIX

Versions of AppleTalk for UNIX have been implemented by Xinet and Pacer (see figure 11.16). These products dovetail with each vendor's respective services (listed previously). Xinet's AppleTalk protocol suite is called K-Talk and is the underlying protocol for their K-AShare AFP server and their K-Spool PAP spooler. Pacer's AppleTalk implementation is used for their PAP and DAL implementations. Both implementations support AppleTalk Phase 2 and must be configured in accordance with the AppleTalk Phase 2 network numbering rules and zone naming conventions.

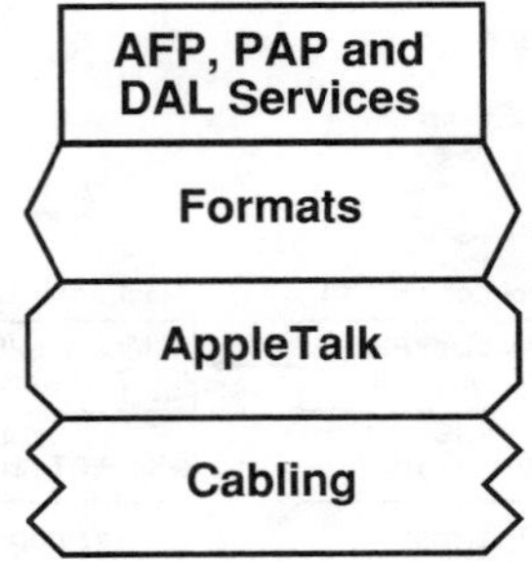

Figure 11.16
The AFP file sharing, PAP print spooling, and DAL database services offered by Xinet and Pacer are all delivered via AppleTalk protocols.

TCP/IP on the Macintosh

The flip side of AppleTalk on UNIX is TCP/IP on the Macintosh. Apple's MacTCP is widely supported by many third-party vendors listed in this chapter—it's the engine that is used by these vendors to create their applications. Figure 11.17 is a diagram of MacTCP transport protocol.

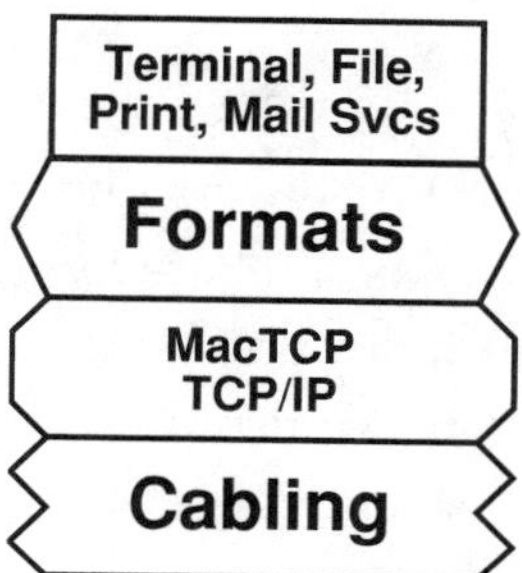

Figure 11.17
MacTCP is Apple's implementation of TCP/IP protocols for the Macintosh.

If you're familiar with TCP/IP networks, configuring MacTCP is a snap. If you're a Mac person and a TCP novice, be prepared for a different world. TCP/IP nodes can obtain their addresses manually or by a dedicated server. There is a mechanism for dynamically assigning addresses, but it's somewhat limited (unlike AppleTalk).

TCP/IP addressing, also referred to as *IP addressing,* uses 32-bit addresses. Unlike AppleTalk addresses, IP addresses can alter the numbers assigned to the network and host identifiers. There are five classes of IP addresses, Class A through E, of which classes A through C are commonly used.

The fundamental difference between the classes is whether you create an address range that provides a small number of networks, each with many nodes; or a range that provides many networks, each with a limited number of nodes. Class A addresses use 7-bit network numbers and 24-bit host numbers. This adds up to 31 bits. (The first bit of a Class A address (0) is reserved and is not used as part of the address.) This provides 128 possible networks, each containing more than 16 million hosts. Class A networks are rare and are used for very large IP networks.

Class B addresses split the 32 bits differently, by using 14-bit network numbers and 16-bit host numbers. (Here, the first two bits (10) are reserved.) Class B networks are common, since they strike a balance between the number of networks and the number of nodes.

Class C addresses use 21-bit network numbers and 8-bit host numbers. The first three bits (110) are reserved. Class C addresses are similar to AppleTalk networks, in the sense that both numbering schemes are based on a large number of networks with a limited number of nodes per network.

The 32-bit IP address is usually written in a four-part decimal notation known as a *dotted quad;* an example is `131.43.3.18`. Each part is eight bits (also called one byte or octet) long. With a Class A address, the first octet (minus the one reserved bit) represents the network ID; the remaining three octets are the host ID.

Class B addresses use the first two octets for the network ID (minus the first two bits). The remaining two octets are used for the host ID.

Class C addresses use the first three octets for the network number (less the first three bits). The remaining octet is used for the host ID.

An exact analogy to AppleTalk addressing is difficult because IP addresses do not specify a particular computer. Since IP addresses contain network numbers and host numbers, they cannot represent single computers that may have multiple connections to different networks. Therefore, an IP router or gateway will have an IP address for each network connection—not each computer.

The name TCP/IP comes from the functions of different parts of the protocol stack. The *Transmission Control Protocol* performs the same tasks as the AppleTalk protocols at the Session and Transport layers of the OSI Reference Model (see figure 11.18). TCP ensures the reliable, sequenced delivery of datagrams. The IP part of TCP stands for the *Internet Protocol*. This corresponds to the Network layer of the OSI model—the layer where AppleTalk DDP protocol resides. The function of this layer is the same in both cases; both IP and DDP are responsible for addressing the source and destination of the message.

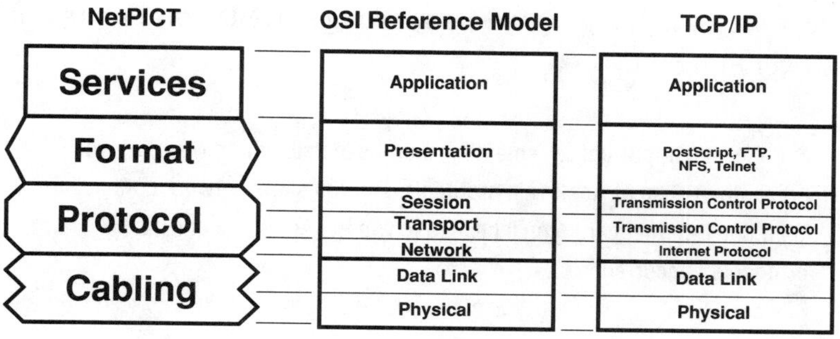

Figure 11.18
TCP/IP gets its name from two protocols that correspond to specific areas of the OSI Reference Model.

AppleTalk DDP datagrams are addressed with network, node, and socket numbers of the source and destination; for example:

DDP Datagram

```
From: 12.22.128

To: 14.43.129
```

IP Datagrams are addressed with the network and host numbers of the source and destination:

IP Datagram

```
From 128.10.2.24

To: 191.5.48.12
```

Cabling: Ethernet, LocalTalk, Token Ring

By far, the majority of the UNIX workstations and computers rely on Ethernet as a cabling medium. There are the exceptions, such as an IBM AS/400 speaking TCP/IP over a Token Ring network. For the most part, though, Macs connecting to UNIX computers will do so over Ethernet.

> **NOTE:** It's important to remember that the installation of MacTCP won't preclude the use of AppleTalk protocols over the same network connection. With one Ethernet card, you'll be able to run the AppleTalk and TCP/IP protocols concurrently.

If you decide to choose an AppleTalk-based service, you have the choice of LocalTalk, Ethernet, or Token Ring as the cabling medium. If you choose LocalTalk, remember that you'll need a router that passes AppleTalk from LocalTalk to Ethernet (see figure 11.19). If you choose TCP/IP on the Mac, you'll be able to use LocalTalk, Ethernet, or Token Ring, but if the UNIX computer doesn't have the same cabling interface you'll need the appropriate IP or multiprotocol router to make the connection (see figure 11.20).

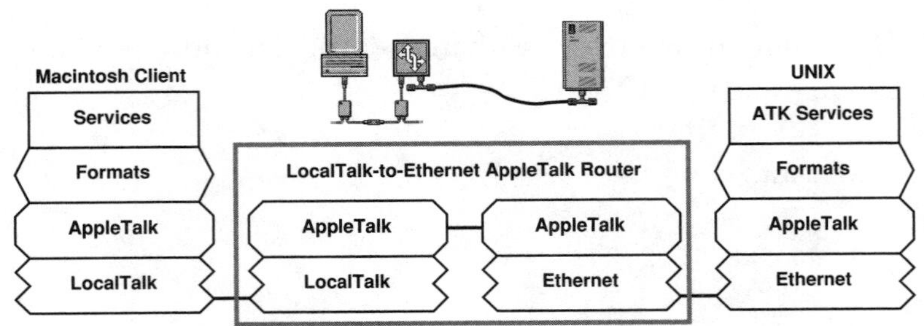

Figure 11.19
LocalTalk Macs communicating with AppleTalk-equipped UNIX computers on Ethernet can use any LocalTalk-to-Ethernet router.

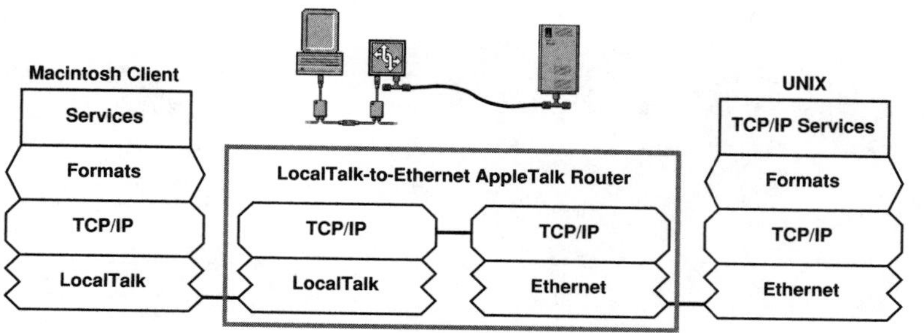

Figure 11.20 LocalTalk Macs using TCP/IP to communicate with UNIX computers on Ethernet must use a LocalTalk-to-Ethernet router that supports IP routing.

Conclusion

The Macintosh can connect to UNIX computers at all levels. UNIX computers can speak the AppleTalk protocol, Macs can speak the TCP/IP protocol, and most UNIX computers and workstations utilize Ethernet cabling, so the integration process is often as simple as installing the right software.

DEC VAX Connectivity

12

Before the famous Apple-IBM Alliance, there was the Apple-Digital Alliance. The collaboration between these two companies resulted in an architecture that combines the best of both worlds. Even though both the VAX and the Macintosh have often been criticized for their so-called "closed architecture," the PATHWORKS for Macintosh environment illustrates that an open architecture is more than a common networking protocol or operating system.

Services: PATHWORKS for Macintosh

The services offered by DEC's PATHWORKS for Macintosh are a combination of products developed by Apple, Digital, and third-party vendors. They address the basic requirements of terminal emulation, X-Window (DECwindows) emulation, AFP file services, PAP print services, DEC print services, DAL database services, and E-mail.

MacTerminal

Traditionally, VAX access has been accomplished with terminals. The ubiquitous VT100 terminal standard (and subsequent versions that are found in nearly all Macintosh terminal emulators) is based on DEC products. MacTerminal is an Apple terminal emulator that comes bundled with PATHWORKS for Macintosh. It provides VT102, VT320, and TTY (an older, basic terminal standard) emulation (see figure 12.1). Compared to other third-party emulators, MacTerminal doesn't offer graphics capabilities, color, macros, or redefinable keys. It provides basic emulation services. It, like most other Macintosh terminal emulators, uses the Macintosh Communications Toolbox (MCT). When purchased separately, MacTerminal provides the basic MCT communication tools of Serial and Modem. With PATHWORKS for Macintosh, additional MCT tools are included that permit terminal emulation over LAT and DECnet connections.

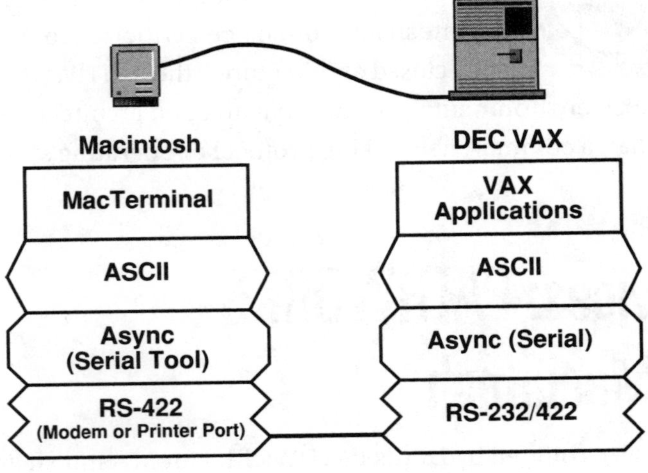

Figure 12.1 MacTerminal provides VT102 and VT320 terminal emulation for Macintosh users connected to DEC VAX computers.

MacX

DECwindows is DEC's implementation of the X-Window standard. Macs equipped with MacX appear as DECwindows terminals (see figure 12.2). MacX fully supports the DECwindow character sets. If you're considering using MacX, plan on picking up a three-button ADB mouse, available from many third-party suppliers (the X-Window system was designed for three-button mice), a minimum of 8 M of RAM, and an Ethernet connection. MacX uses memory and network bandwidth in large quantities.

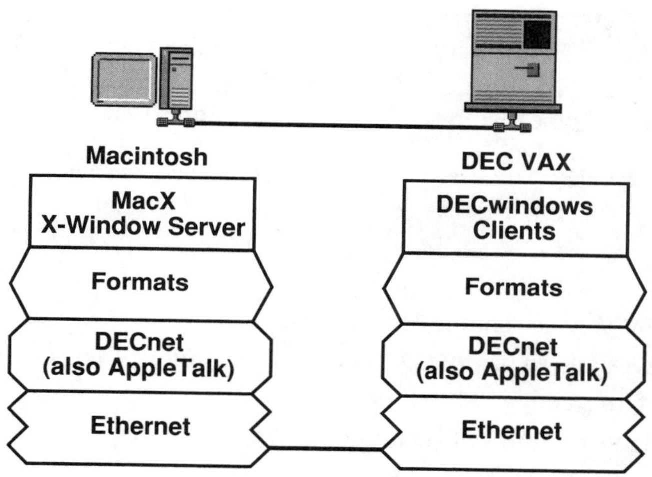

Figure 12.2
MacX provides faithful DECwindows emulation from a Macintosh. In this example, MacX is using DECnet as a transport over Ethernet.

VAXshare File and Print Services

VAXshare is the name given to AFP file services and PAP print services that run on a VAX. The VAXshare file server (see figure 12.3) can be set up to support multiple servers, each potentially with multiple volumes. These volumes can be set up to reference any VMS directory. These directories can contain VMS files (either ASCII or binary) or foreign files, such as those from a PC. This way, Mac users can edit VMS text files with Mac text editors or word processors. They can also exchange binary application files with corresponding VAX or PC applications.

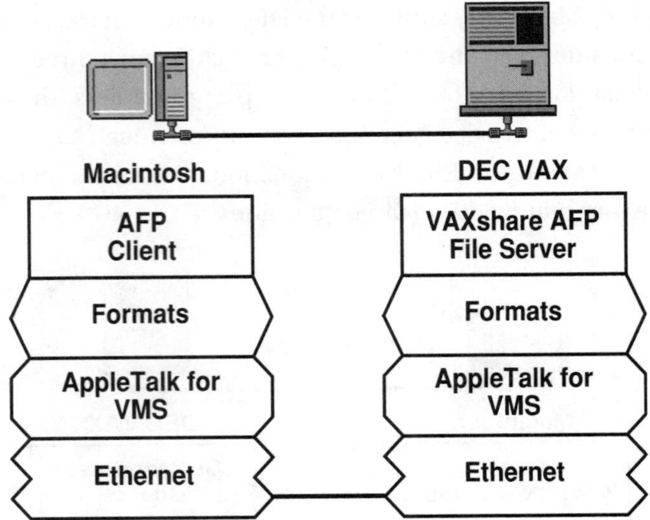

Figure 12.3
DEC's VAXshare file server turns a VAX into an AFP file server. Macintosh users are able to access VAX directories and files.

The print services enable Mac users to spool LaserWriter print jobs to the VAX and to print to DEC PostScript printers; they also enable users of interactive VAX VT terminals to print to Apple LaserWriters through a standard VMS print queue. These are diagrammed in figures 12.4, 12.5, 12.6, and 12.7.

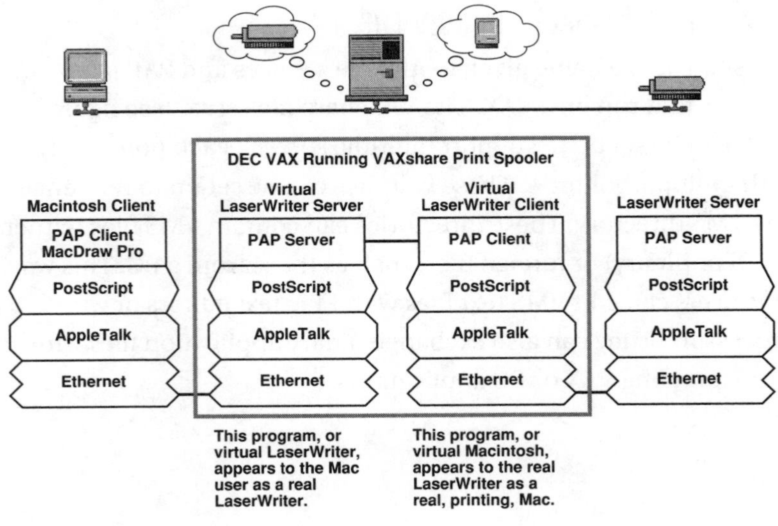

Figure 12.4
One aspect of VAXshare's print services turns a VAX into a PAP print spooler. Macintosh users are able to send print jobs to the VAX. The VAX queues the job and sends it to the "real" printer.

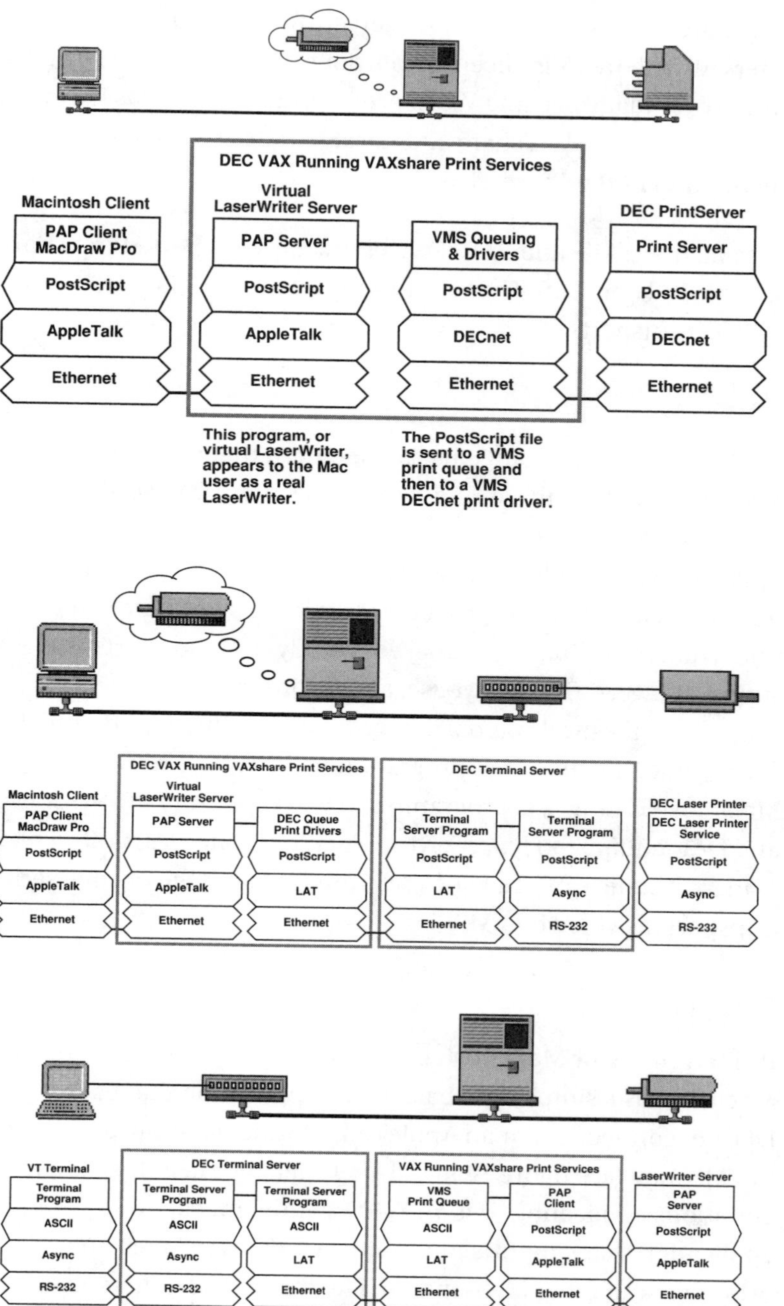

Figure 12.5

Macintosh users are also able to print to DEC PostScript printers. These printers are either directly connected to Ethernet or serially connected to a DEC terminal server.

Figure 12.6

Macintosh printing to DEC PostScript Printer.

Figure 12.7

VMS users (that is, terminal users) can print to Apple LaserWriters as if they were DEC printers.

There are other similar AFP/PAP servers for VMS. Alisa Systems offers AlisaShare (Alisa licensed portions of AlisaShare to Digital, which eventually became VAXshare). Pacer Software has Pacer-Share, which, like VAXshare and AlisaShare, provides AFP file service and PAP print services.

With all these AFP and PAP services, the only supported transport is AppleTalk for VMS. There is no support for the DECnet, LAT, or TCP/IP transports.

DAL

Apple's Data Access Language is a standard that provides a uniform relational database language. Apple offers DAL servers for different platforms. Included with PATHWORKS for Macintosh is Apple's DAL server for VMS (see figure 12.8). When purchased from DEC, it includes support for connections to Digital's relational database, Rdb. If purchased directly from Apple, it also supports Ingres, Oracle, Sybase, and Informix databases. (The support for these additional databases can be purchased directly from Apple.) Included are programming interfaces needed to write Macintosh C or Pascal programs that will support the DAL service and DAL-equipped HyperCard applications. The DAL VMS server works with the AppleTalk for VMS transport and the normal serial transport provided by VMS.

E-Mail

PATHWORKS for Macintosh includes two mail interfaces. Mail for Macintosh is a simple text-based mail application that uses a DECnet connection, or an AppleTalk/DECnet gateway connection, to VMS mail (see figure 12.9). All-In-1 Mail for Macintosh is a more ambitious application. It is an X.400-compliant client/server mail application that supports binary enclosures, return receipts, priorities, and other high-end mail features. (The adherence to the X.400 messaging standard will make it easier to interface with other foreign mail systems that also support the X.400 standard.) DEC also offers companion All-In-1 clients for DECwindows and Windows-equipped PCs. All applications share a similar user-interface.

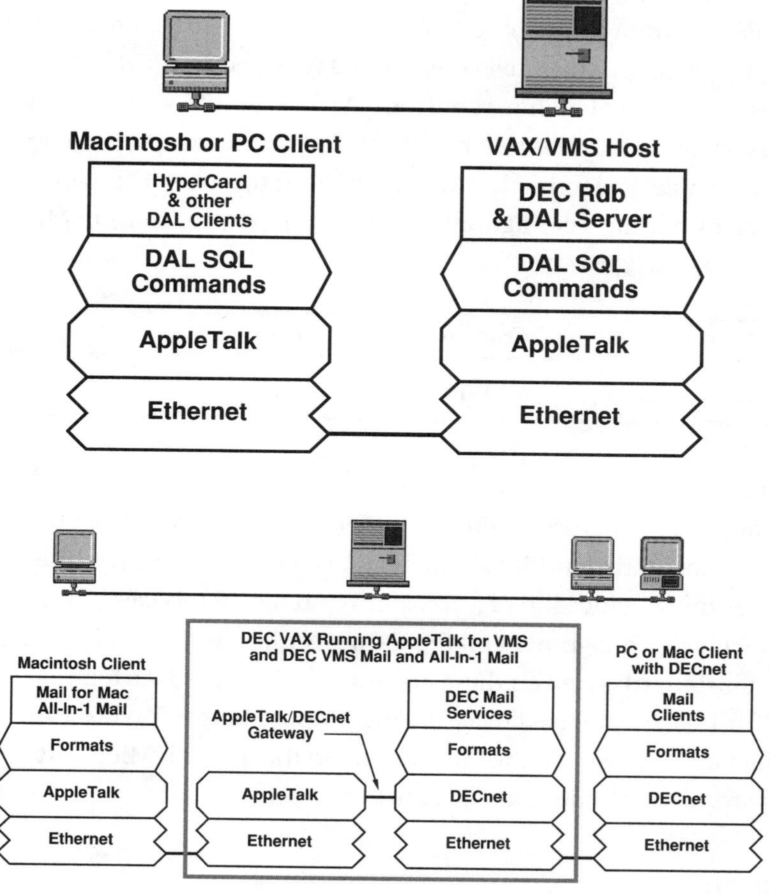

Figure 12.8 Apple's DAL server for VMS is included with PATHWORKS for Macintosh. With it, Mac users can access DEC's Rdb relational database with any DAL client application.

Figure 12.9 Digital offers two mail solutions with PATHWORKS for Mac. Both use DECnet, on the VAX side, as a transport. Macs must either use the DECnet transport or go through an AppleTalk/DECnet gateway.

Formats

Similar to the formats supported by the PC and UNIX computers, the Mac and VAX are able to share ASCII text files and those application formats that are binary-compatible.

ASCII

The old standby, ASCII text, is an important common denominator between the Mac and VAX. With VAXshare, Mac users can freely move ASCII files back and forth. These ASCII files could be VAX command procedures (DCL), VMS source code, PostScript files, or IGES files from a VAX-based CAD/CAM system. VAXshare automatically maps Macintosh creator and type codes to VMS files based on their filename extensions. As an example, you might want all your VMS text files that have a .TXT filename extension to be automatically identified as Microsoft Word text files. This can be done by editing a configuration file that maps extensions to Mac creator and type codes:

Extension	*Creator*	*Type*
.TXT	MSWD	TEXT

In the above example, the .TXT extension is mapped to the creator code of Microsoft Word (MSWD). This code is assigned to Microsoft and identifies all Microsoft Word files. The Type indicates the specific kind of Microsoft Word file, in this case, TEXT. By making this assignment on the VAX, any file with the .TXT filename extension will be given these creator and file types (see figure 12.10). These are used to assign the proper Microsoft Word icon to the file; they also tell the Finder to open the file with Microsoft Word when you double-click the file's icon.

Binary

Just as in the case with the PC and UNIX environments, more and more applications are using the same binary format for their document formats. These files can be seamlessly moved back and forth between the two platforms with no conversion required. When conversion is required, there are several translation utilities available on the VAX. Digital has an interchange standard known as DDIF (see figure 12.11). DDIF supports a number of standard Mac formats, such as MacPaint, PICT, Microsoft Word, and MacWrite. Once these formats are converted (on the VAX) to the DDIF format, they can be incorporated into DEC applications such as DECwrite.

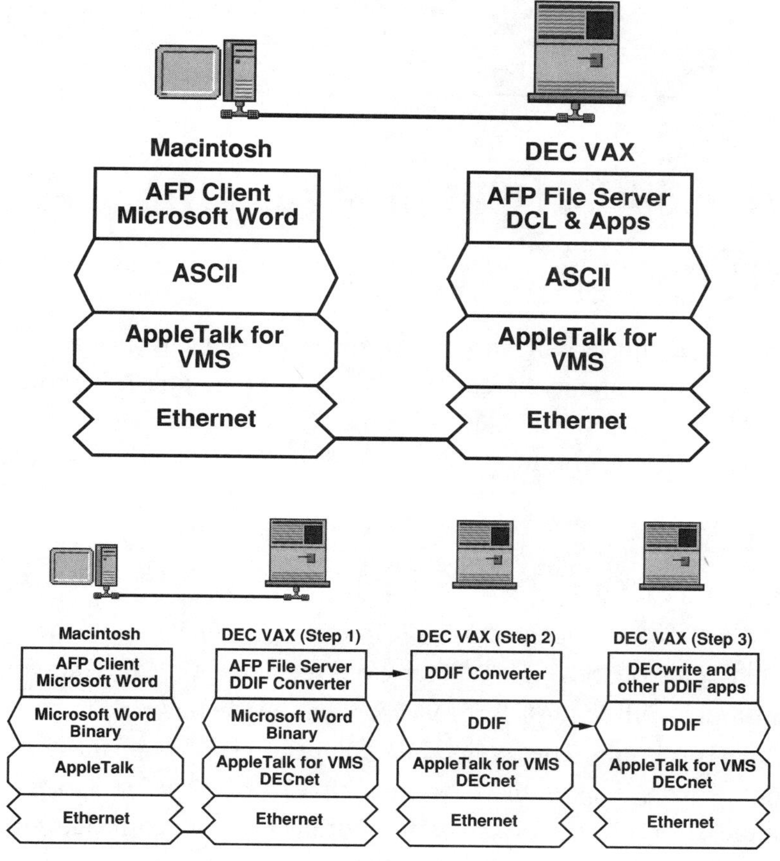

Figure 12.10 ASCII text files can be shared between the Mac and VAX environments.

Figure 12.11 DEC has a common interchange format called DDIF; DEC also offers (not included with PATHWORKS) DDIF conversion tools for MacWrite, PICT, MacPaint and Microsoft Word.

Another approach to conversion is to use explicit conversion utilities to convert one format to another. A good example of this approach can be found in the Keypak line of translators from Keyword Office Technologies (see figure 12.12). Keypak can be used to convert a VAX word processing document format such as WPS+ to a common Mac format such as Microsoft Word.

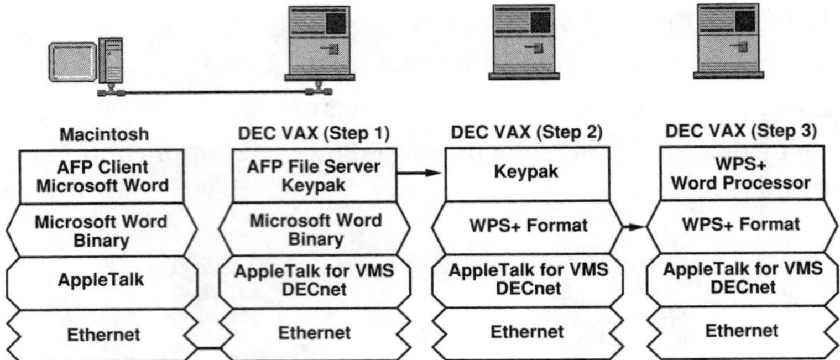

Figure 12.12
Keypak conversion between the DEC WPS+ word processor and MacWrite.

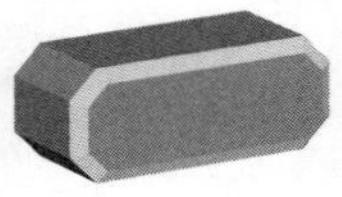

Transports: AppleTalk for VMS, DECnet, LAT

In the Macintosh/VAX world, the transports of each respective platform are equally shared. The VAX speaks the AppleTalk protocol and the Mac speaks DECnet and LAT. As we'll discover, the choice of a transport for the most part is dependent on the desired service.

AppleTalk for VMS

VAXes are able to speak the AppleTalk protocol because they're equipped with the AppleTalk for VMS (see figure 12.13). VAXes equipped with AppleTalk for VMS appear on the network as AppleTalk nodes. The services, VAXshare and DAL, appear as AppleTalk sockets within the node. AppleTalk for VMS supports AppleTalk routing, so VAXes with multiple Ethernet controllers can be set up as AppleTalk Ethernet-to-Ethernet routers.

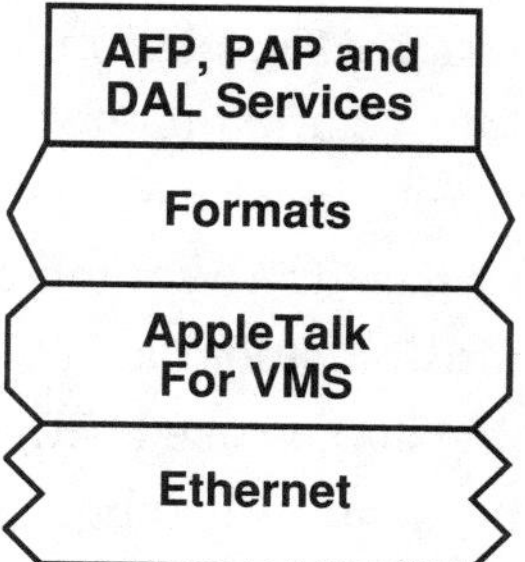

Figure 12.13
AppleTalk for VMS equips a VAX with the AppleTalk protocols. AppleTalk is used by most of the PATHWORKS for Mac services.

DECnet

The most common VAX/VMS transport protocol is DECnet. VAX/VMS systems usually come with DECnet, but Macs do not. So part of the PATHWORKS for Macintosh solution is to install DECnet on the Macintosh (see figure 12.14). DECnet on the Macintosh requires a configuration process that includes the assignment of a DECnet area and node number (similar to an AppleTalk network and node number) and the generation of a list of other DECnet nodes where communication is desired. This explicit address assignment and node listing is contrary to the AppleTalk philosophy of dynamic addressing and name binding using NBP.

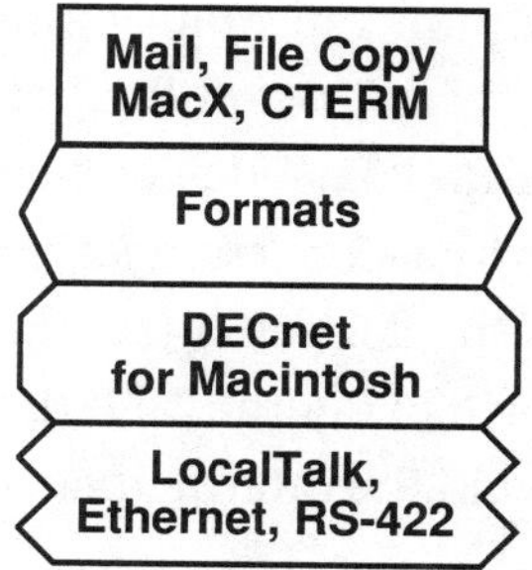

Figure 12.14
DECnet for Macintosh turns a Mac into a DECnet node. A Mac so equipped can be automatically backed up by a VAX on the network.

Despite the extra administrative work, there are reasons for installing DECnet on your Mac. Once so equipped, the Macintosh hard disk can be automatically backed up through DECnet copy commands. The DECnet transport can also be used by MacX, the two mail applications, and terminal emulation. As we'll see in the next section, LAT cannot be routed and therefore will not provide wide-area terminal services. An alternative is the *CTERM* protocol. Part of DECnet, CTERM can be used as a routable terminal protocol. PATHWORKS for Macintosh includes a CTERM Communications Tool (see figure 12.15) that can be used with MacTerminal, or any other Macintosh Communication Toolbox (MCT)-compatible terminal emulator.

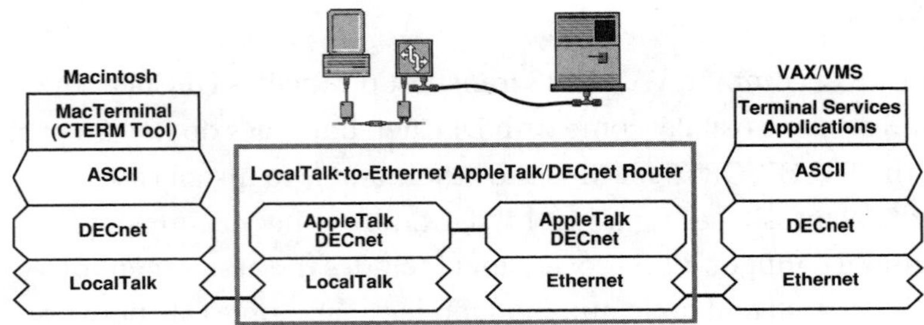

Figure 12.15
CTERM and DECnet provide a routable transport protocol for terminal access in the DEC VAX environment.

LAT

If your Macs are on the same Ethernet as the VAX, you'll be able to use the LAT MCT tool to directly connect to the VAX. Conventional VT terminals, or Macs running terminal emulators over serial lines, aren't capable of speaking LAT over Ethernet; instead, they speak the Async protocol over RS-232. A device called a *terminal server,* or *DECserver,* is used to make the connection between multiple terminals and any LAT-speaking VAX (see figure 12.16). By speaking LAT directly, as shown in figure 12.17, the Macintosh can connect directly and avoid the intermediate service of the terminal server.

As mentioned before, LAT cannot be routed. It was designed for use on a LAN. LAT is a time-critical protocol, so care must be taken when LAT is used on bridged Ethernet. Even though a bridged Ethernet logically appears as a single Ethernet LAN, if the bridge connection introduces a significant delay, LAT may have problems maintaining connections. In these cases, and when a routed network exists, the DECnet CTERM protocol mentioned before might be a better choice.

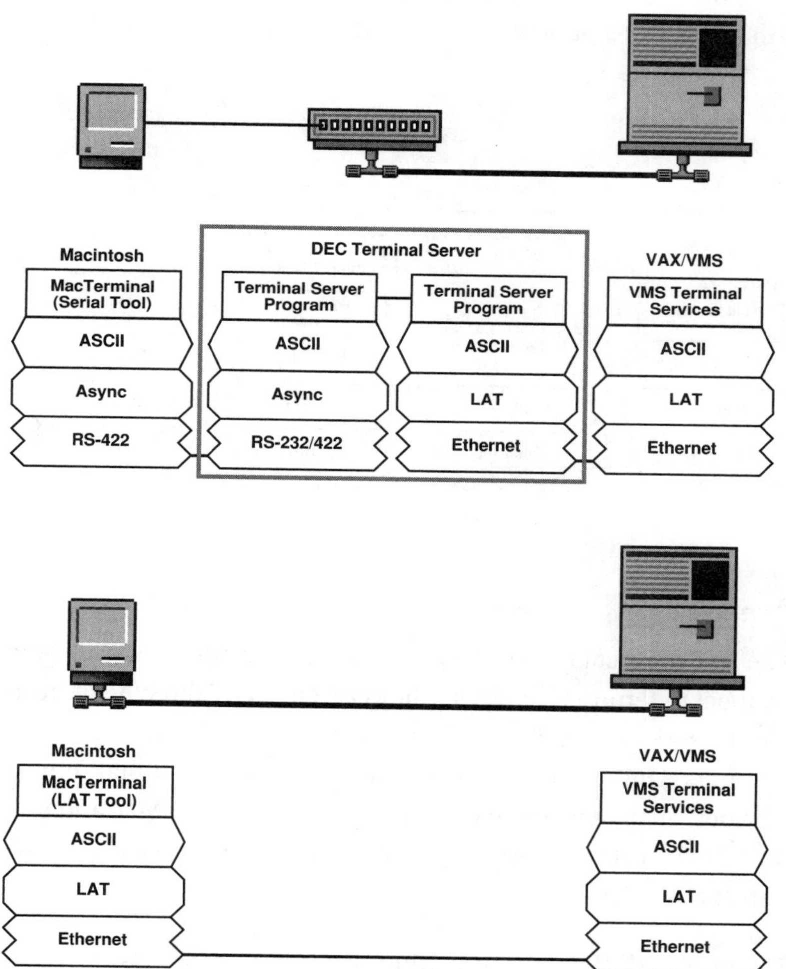

Figure 12.16
In the old days, VAX terminal users relied on terminal servers to connect serial terminals to networked VAXes.

Figure 12.17
Macs on Ethernet that are equipped with the LAT tool bypass the terminal server and can access any LAT host (i.e. DEC VAX) on the Ethernet LAN.

AppleTalk/DECnet Gateway

The AppleTalk/DECnet Gateway converts AppleTalk protocols into the corresponding DECnet protocols. A prime example of its use is with the DECnet-based PATHWORKS mail services (see figure 12.18). Because the VAX mail services are only accessible through DECnet, there are two ways a client Mac can connect: by putting DECnet on the Mac, and by using AppleTalk and going through the gateway. The gateway is selected through the AppleTalk/DECnet MCT tool from within the mail applications.

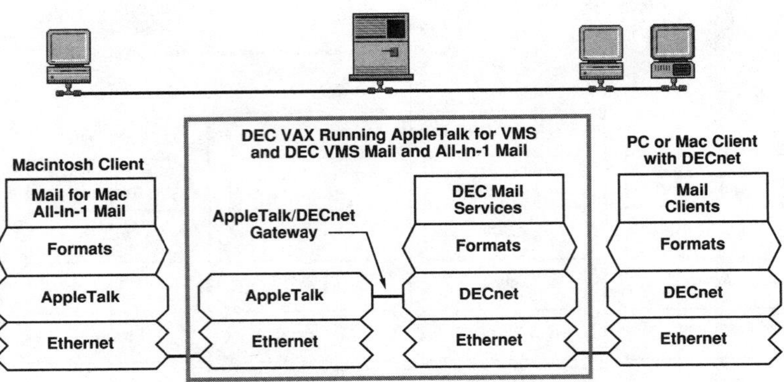

Figure 12.18 The AppleTalk/DECnet Gateway converts AppleTalk protocols into DECnet protocols and vice versa. At the moment, it's main use is to let Macs access DECnet mail services without the administrative overhead of putting DECnet on the Mac.

AppleTalk/LAT Gateway

The LAT protocol is restricted to Ethernet. How do LocalTalk Macs connect to terminal services? They can't use LAT directly because it only works over a direct Ethernet connection. You could use the DECnet CTERM tool and a LocalTalk/Ethernet router that routes DECnet, but you would have to put DECnet on your Mac and put up with the extra administrative overhead associated with DECnet. Fortunately, Apple and DEC came up with another alternative.

The AppleTalk/LAT Gateway runs on a Mac that has LocalTalk and Ethernet connections (see figure 12.19). This effectively turns the Macintosh into a terminal server. The Macs on the LocalTalk side speak the AppleTalk protocol to the server; the server speaks

LAT to the VAX hosts on the Ethernet. Figure 12.20 shows various screens from the AppleTalk/LAT Gateway as well as the client settings of the AppleTalk/LAT Tool.

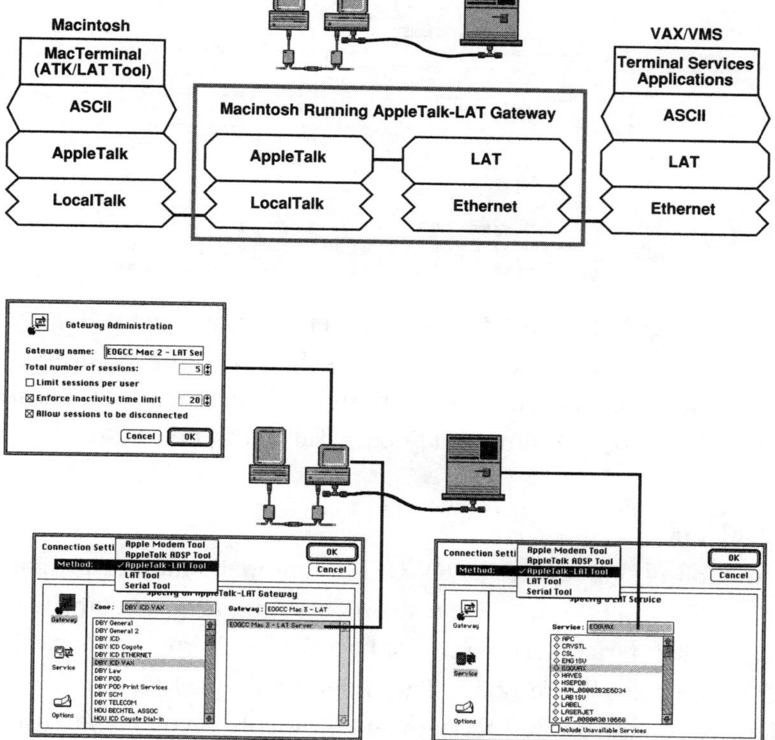

Figure 12.19
Macs connected on LocalTalk can access LAT terminal services by going through the AppleTalk/LAT Gateway.

Figure 12.20
The AppleTalk/LAT Gateway runs on a Macintosh. Client Macs use the AppleTalk/LAT tool to access the gateway.

The gateway is also useful for dial-up users who attach to the network with Apple's Remote Access software (ARA). As shown in figure 12.21, incoming ARA Macs speak AppleTalk. By going through an AppleTalk/LAT Gateway, a remote Mac user can engage in terminal emulation with the VAX, while retaining the capability to access AppleShare file servers and LaserWriter print services.

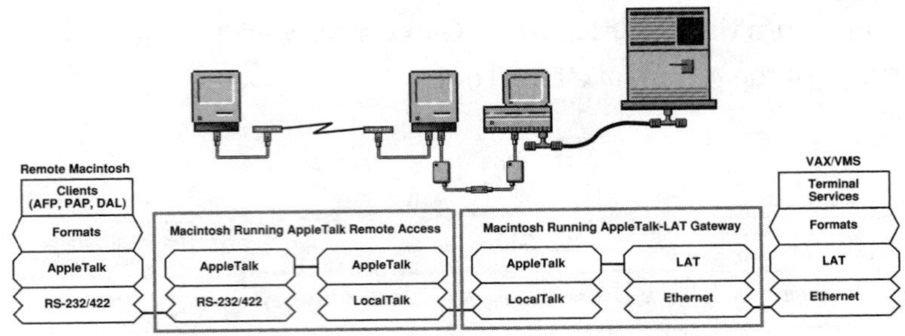

Figure 12.21 The AppleTalk/DECnet Gateway lets remote users engage in terminal emulation at the same time as other AppleTalk services.

Cabling: LocalTalk and Ethernet

The cabling choices for Macs in a VAX environment are primarily LocalTalk and Ethernet. Since it's unlikely that VAXes will ever sport LocalTalk interfaces, the options are few: either put Ethernet on the Macs, or use some sort of LocalTalk/Ethernet router.

LocalTalk

The cabling choices for PATHWORKS-equipped Macs are primarily LocalTalk and Ethernet. Because VAX computers don't come with LocalTalk interfaces, some sort of LocalTalk/Ethernet router will be needed (see figure 12.22). The choice of a LocalTalk router depends on the desired services and protocols. If you plan to use DECnet, then a multiprotocol router capable of routing DECnet will be needed. If you plan to stick to the AppleTalk services, or plan to access the DECnet services (such as E-mail) through AppleTalk, then any generic AppleTalk LocalTalk/Ethernet router will do.

Because most VAX sites have extensive twisted-pair wiring that's used for terminal access, you might want to adapt this wiring to the phone-type LocalTalk connectors, such as Farallon's PhoneNET.

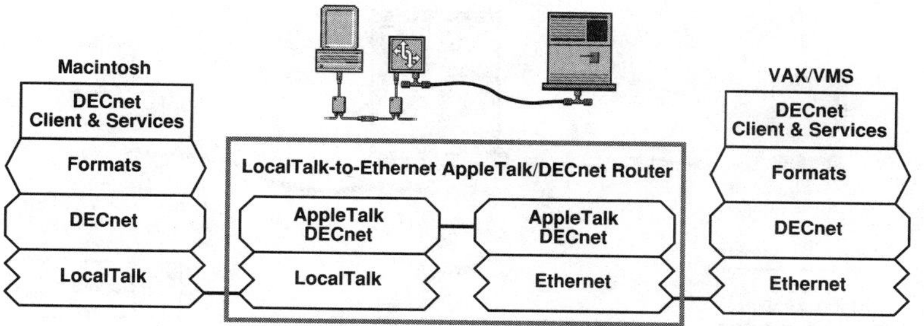

Figure 12.22
Macs with the DECnet transport can still use LocalTalk when a LocalTalk DECnet router is used.

Ethernet

If your VAX network is Ethernet-based, which most are, then it's likely that Ethernet-equipped Macs can be easily incorporated into your network. Digital offers a number of desktop Ethernet products that can be used to connect PCs and Macs to the network. Digital recently announced a line of multiprotocol routers with support for the AppleTalk protocol.

Serial RS-232/Dial-Up

With MacTerminal, Macs can take the place of VT terminals on Ethernet or serial connections. These connections can be made directly to the VAX or through a terminal server.

With serial connections, remote MacTerminal users can use modems and log onto the VAX, but this connection only provides terminal services. Often, remote Mac/VAX users need to access AppleTalk services in addition to terminal services. Apple and DEC don't offer a solution, but Computer Methods Corporation has a product called AsyncServeR that essentially turns the VAX into an AppleTalk Remote Access server (see figure 12.23). Most VAX sites have banks of dial-up modems already in place; AsyncServeR takes advantage of these resources by enabling any Mac with the Remote Access software to dial in and access not only the AppleTalk services on the VAX, but also the services on the entire AppleTalk internet.

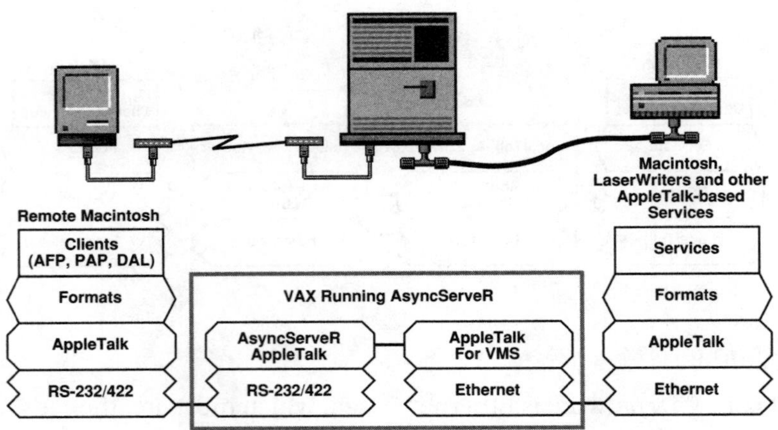

Figure 12.23 AsyncServeR, from Computer Methods, uses the AppleTalk for VMS environment as a foundation for a VAX-based AppleTalk Remote Access Server.

Conclusion

Digital redefined computing in the 1970s; Apple did the same in the 1980s. In the 1990s, Apple and Digital both realize that the network is the common battleground for computing services. Digital, with its PATHWORKS for Macintosh product, has recognized the importance of the Macintosh. They have successfully integrated two supposedly closed architectures by providing terminal emulation, DECwindows (X-Window), AFP file and print services, database access, and two E-mail packages.

IBM Connectivity 13

Still a large part of the corporate world, IBM's mainframe and minicomputers are an important part of Apple's network strategy. Once again, the Macintosh proves its worth as the "universal client," easily connecting to the Big Blue world.

Services: Mainframe and AS/400

The IBM computing world (PCs excluded) is comprised of the large mainframe computers, such as the System 370 (S/370) and 390 (S/390), small mainframes such as the ES/9000, and midrange systems like the AS/400. These systems aren't exactly showcases of client/server technologies, as over the years the typical user-interface has been through terminal emulation.

Terminal Services

In the past, IBM mainframe access was typically made with the 3270 family of terminals. Today, 3270 terminal emulation is commonplace on PCs and Macs (see figure 13.1). As with VT-type terminals, the sales of so-called "dumb" terminals are declining while the use of intelligent workstations is increasing.

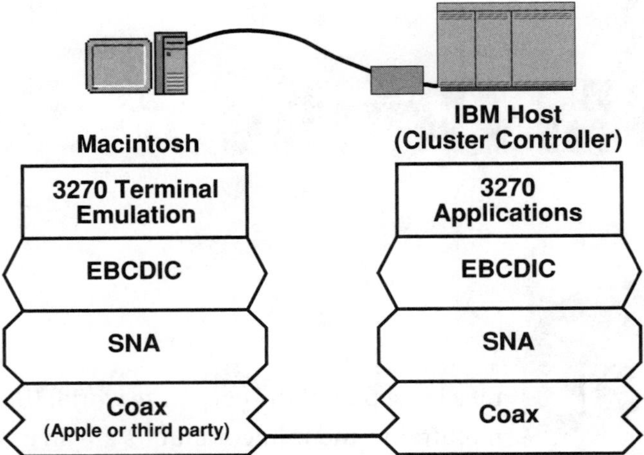

Figure 13.1 A Macintosh running a 3270 emulator over a coaxial connection to the host.

There are a number of 3270 terminal emulators available for the Macintosh. These emulators enable suitably-equipped Macs to access IBM mainframes. Most Mac emulators add value by adding features such as programmable "hot keys" or macro capabilities. Some emulators support keyboard remapping, where 3270 keys can be reassigned to the Macintosh keyboard. A common feature in 3270 emulators is the ability to perform IND$FILE file transfers from within the terminal session. Four popular 3270 emulators include Apple's SNA•ps 3270, DCA's IRMA Workstation for Macintosh, ASC's asc3270, and Avatar's MacMainFrame.

The 3270 standard is used by the large mainframes, while the midrange AS/400 uses the 5250 standard. 5250 emulation on the Mac is not yet as common as emulation of the older 3270. 5250 emulators offer similar features as their 3270 counterparts and are offered by Andrew and ASC (see figure 13.2). Conventional terminal screens can be a bit daunting; to make things a bit easier, IBM terminal sessions can also be front-ended with user-friendly interfaces that interact with the terminal data stream.

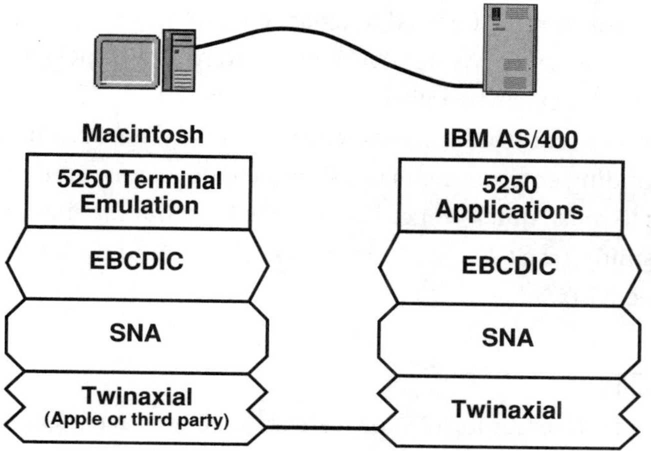

Figure 13.2 A Macintosh running a 5250 emulator over a triaxial connection to the host.

One of the most popular IBM mainframe applications is the PROFS mail environment. Normally, PROFS is accessed with a conventional terminal. However, there are several Mac terminal front ends that put a Mac interface onto PROFS (see figure 13.3). Two of these—MitemVision from Mitem and Executive Workstation from MediaWorks—are HyperCard-based.

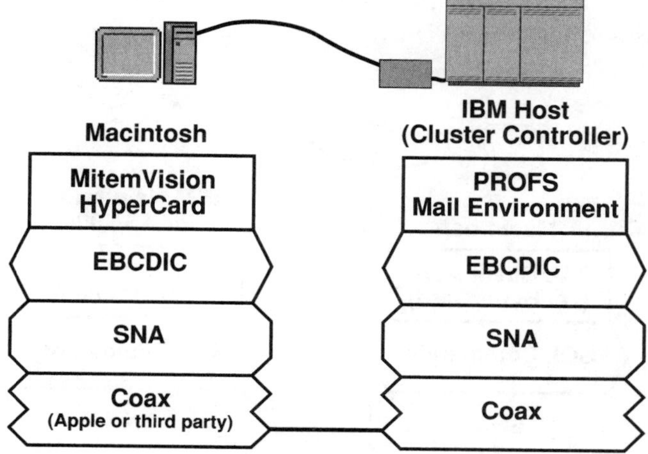

Figure 13.3 PROFS access with MitemVision, a HyperCard-based front end.

HyperCard can also be used to create custom terminal front ends. With products from Avatar, DCA, and Mitem, developers are able to create HyperCard applications using custom XCMDs and XFCNs that provide controlled access to the terminal data stream. Other front-ending environments use their own development environments to make quick work of customized interfaces. These include Blacksmith from CEL, SimMac from Simware, and Both from Connectivité.

Database

Apple's DAL server for IBM provides DAL clients access to IBM DB2 and SQL/DS relational databases (see figure 13.4). Connections to the DAL server can be made through a 3270 terminal connection, serial links, or with IBM's network transport, SNA.

As mentioned elsewhere in this book, DAL clients can be either Mac- or PC-based. They can be developed from scratch with conventional Mac programming environments or authored with HyperCard or Serius. DAL clients can also be used out of the box, since many Macintosh applications, such as spreadsheets and databases, offer built-in DAL support.

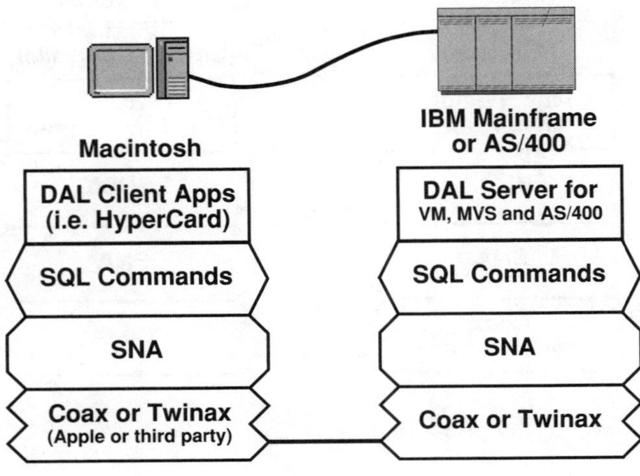

Figure 13.4 Apple's DAL Server for IBM hosts provides Macintosh (and PC) DAL clients access to IBM relational databases such as DB2.

Formats: Mainframe and AS/400

Although the Mac and IBM hosts speak different fundamental languages (ASCII versus EBCDIC) they still enjoy a high degree of interoperability. This is due to the use of standardized terminal formats (as in the case of 3270 terminal emulations) and format translators that provide ASCII to EBCDIC translations in real time.

EBCDIC

The IBM PC was their first computer to use ASCII. Before that, IBM mainframes used EBCDIC (Extended Binary Coded Decimal Interchange Code) which, in a technique similar to that of the ASCII code, uses an eight-bit code to represent characters. Conversions between EBCDIC and ASCII are typically handled by protocol converters that can either be hardware-based (see figure 13.5) or software-based.

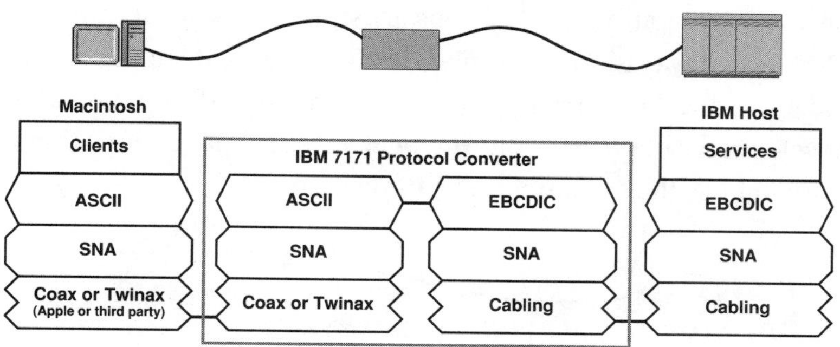

Figure 13.5
IBM's EBCDIC codes are translated into Macintosh ASCII codes with the IBM 7171 Protocol converter.

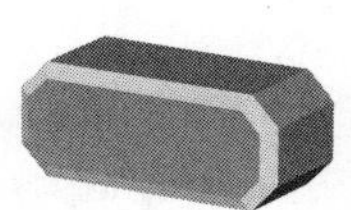

Transports: Mainframe and AS/400

Traditionally, the IBM transports have been unique to the IBM world, focusing on terminal-based applications. During the past several years, as IBM has pursued a peer-to-peer environment, the rest of the industry has started to adopt IBM's new standards. Today, the Macintosh supports all of the major IBM transport protocols, in addition to the IBM-supported industry standards such as TCP/IP.

SAA, SNA, and APPC

SNA stands for *System Network Architecture* and is IBM's primary transport protocol. When a Macintosh runs an IBM terminal emulator, it's relying on a portion of the SNA protocols. SNA is only one part of IBM's networking strategy, known as *System Application Architecture* (SAA). SAA defines an environment that supports peer-to-peer application services, which is a departure from the traditional host-based IBM world.

Part of IBM's SAA/SNA plans include APPC. Standing for *Advanced Program-to-Program Communications,* APPC uses a protocol called LU 6.2 (the LU stands for Logical Unit). Similar enhancements to SNA networking are part of IBM's *Advanced Peer-to-Peer Networking* (APPN) protocol. APPC and APPN are still relatively new, but compatible applications are starting to appear. Apple's SNA•ps gateway is one example (see figure 13.6). It supports both the APPC and APPN protocols and will undoubtedly be used as a development platform for future peer-to-peer applications that work in both the Macintosh and IBM environments.

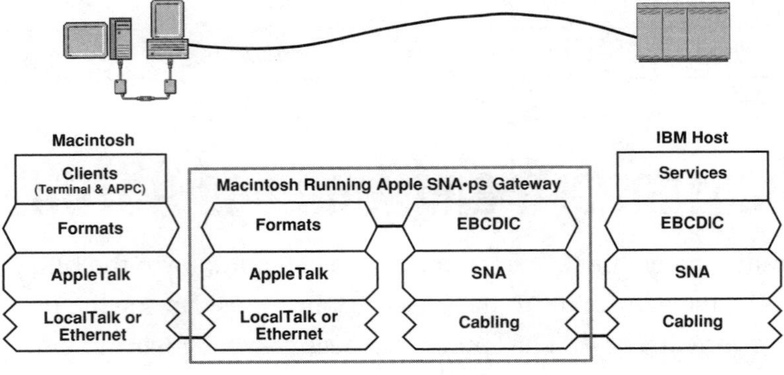

Figure 13.6
Apple's SNA•ps Gateway connects AppleTalk-conversant Macs to an IBM host.

TCP/IP

Many companies, in an attempt to support multi-platform communications, are using the TCP/IP protocol in place of IBM's SNA protocol. TCP/IP provides a common transport protocol that, unlike SNA, is supported on Macs, VAXes, UNIX, and many other platforms. Support for TCP/IP services is beginning to grow as companies such as ASC begin to offer Macintosh terminal emulators that use MacTCP to communicate with similarly equipped IBM hosts (see figure 13.7).

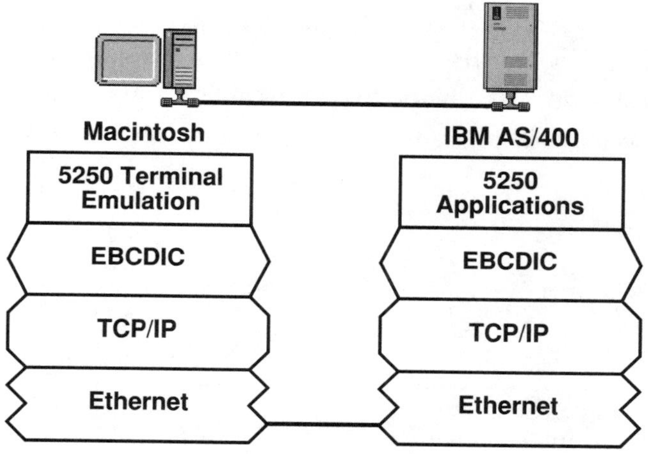

Figure 13.7
5250 terminal emulation with asc5250 over a TCP/IP network connection.

Media: Mainframe and AS/400

There are two primary ways that physical connections are made in the IBM environment. One way is through direct connections, which are primarily used for terminal sessions. These direct connections can be made over coaxial cabling or through a *Synchronous Data Link Control* (SDLC) connection. The other way connections are made is through a LAN, which can be used for a wide variety of services. Token Ring is currently the predominant LAN cabling system in the IBM world, but Ethernet is slowly gaining in acceptance.

Direct Connections

The most common direct connection to an IBM mainframe is made with a coaxial (coax) cable. Traditionally, this has been the method employed by IBM terminals for years; it's also used by Macs and PCs running terminal emulation programs. Because Macs don't come with a coax connection, an expansion card is required. The coax card is usually connected to an intermediate device known as a cluster controller, which is used to connect multiple coax devices to the mainframe. As shown in figure 13.8, terminals directly connected to the IBM AS/400 midrange computer use a variation of coaxial cable called *twinaxial cable.* Unlike coaxial cable, which has a single conductor surrounded by a second shielding conductor, twinaxial cable has two conductors inside. Macintosh coax and twinax cards are available from Apple, Avatar, and DCA.

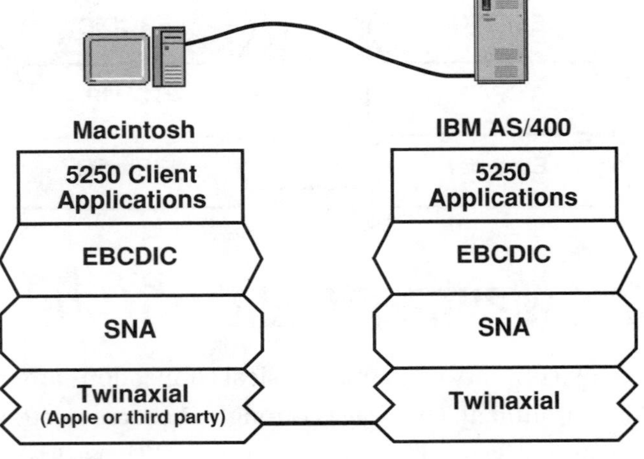

Figure 13.8
A Macintosh connected to an IBM AS/400 host with a twinaxial cable.

SDLC connections are made with high-speed synchronous modems. As shown in figure 13.9, an SDLC card is used to connect the Mac to the modem, which in turn connects to other modems on the mainframe. Apple's Serial NB card can be used to make an SDLC connection. Avatar also offers cards that perform the function.

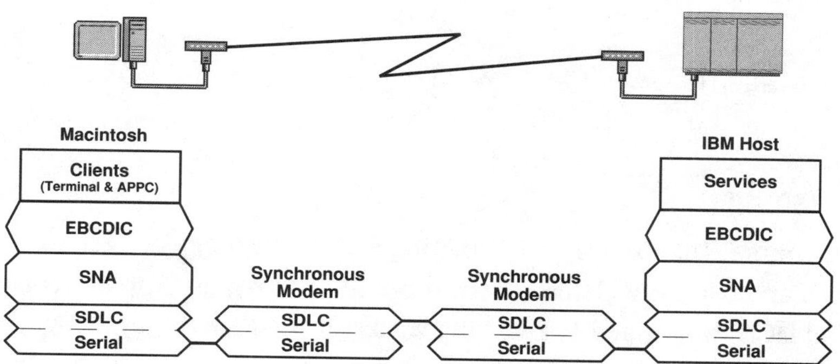

Figure 13.9
A Macintosh connected to an IBM host with synchronous modems and a SDLC connection.

Both the coax and SDLC connections tend to be expensive, either because they require a number of modems (in the case of SDLC) or because the coax connections need available ports on the cluster controller. When ports on the cluster controller are no longer available, another controller is required. To make a number of cost-effective connections to the mainframe, a gateway is often the best option.

Avatar and DCA have software that enable a Macintosh to act as a SNA gateway when coax connections are used. A Mac that acts as a SNA gateway has one coax connection to the cluster controller and another LAN connection to the participating Macs. These Macs run the appropriate vendor's client software and can be on LocalTalk or Ethernet networks. A similar gateway is also used for SDLC connections. A Mac acts a gateway by connecting a LocalTalk or Ethernet LAN to a single, shared SDLC connection (see figure 13.10). An example of this type of gateway can be found in Apple's SNA•ps gateway. In addition to Macs that act as gateways, there are also several dedicated gateway boxes that perform the same function.

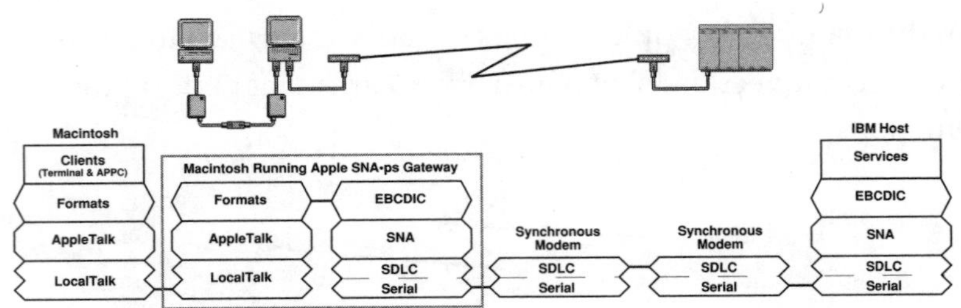

Figure 13.10
A Macintosh connected to an IBM host through an SNA gateway with an SDLC link.

Token Ring

Of course, Token Ring is the leading LAN technology used in the IBM environment. There are number of companies (Apple, Avatar, and DCA) that make Token Ring cards for the Mac. Macs using Token Ring can be attached directly to the mainframe (see figure 13.11), or to a gateway.

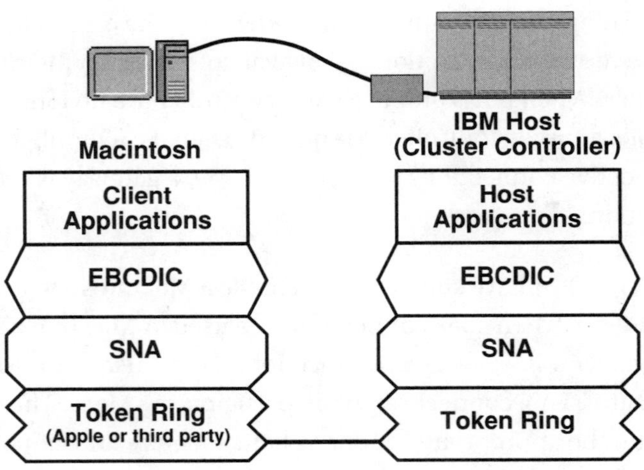

Figure 13.11
A Macintosh connected to an IBM host through a direct Token Ring link.

Ethernet

Ethernet is gaining in popularity in the IBM world, particularly as TCP/IP continues to become more prevalent on IBM mainframes (see figure 13.12). The most popular means of Macintosh Ethernet connections is through a gateway.

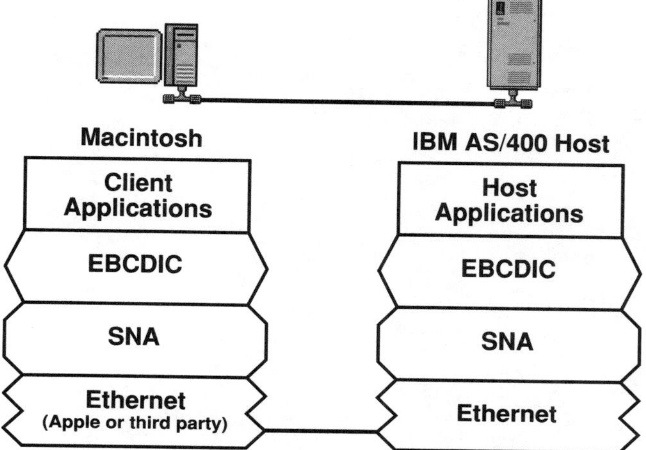

Figure 13.12
A Macintosh connected to an IBM host through a direct Ethernet link.

Conclusion

The IBM mainframe world is changing, but it is still typified by terminal-type applications. The Macintosh can easily adapt to this environment with numerous terminal emulators and front-ending programs. These products support IBM's cabling (coax, twinax, or Token Ring) and protocols (SAA, SNA, APPC, and APPN). They also support non-traditional cabling and protocols such as LocalTalk, Ethernet, TCP/IP, and AppleTalk through the use of gateways.

sign, implementation

"Four"

Part IV brings everything together and outlines the process of design, implementation, and management. First, in Chapter 14, the practical issues centered around network implementation, such as wiring and maintenance, are examined; the NetPICT technique is used to solve specific networking problems. Once a network is in place, the focus shifts to other issues—discussed in Chapter 15—such as keeping track of users and services, troubleshooting, performance monitoring, and security.

Part IV brings everything together and outlines the process of design, implementation, and management.

Network Design, Implementation, and Management

Design and Implementation

14

This chapter covers the basics of network design and implementation. Several common Macintosh network scenarios will be discussed and analyzed. These networking scenarios should make it easy for you to identify your current (or planned) network environment. Also included in this chapter are tips and hints that will streamline your networking tasks.

Top-Down Design Techniques

The NetPICT diagrams used throughout this book conveniently break up networking into four layers. This "divide and conquer" approach, inherent in the layering process, makes it easy to attack networking problems. This is similar to the process in which software projects, or computer programs, are solved by breaking the task into smaller "digestible" components.

Combined, the four layers represent a particular solution to the overall networking problem. However, each separate layer can—and should—be addressed on its own merits.

The process should start at the top. Simply put, this means asking, "What Services are required to do the job?" This should be the driving force behind any network plan. Unfortunately, this is not always the case. All too often, companies start the process from the bottom up. They try to dictate Cabling choices, Transport protocols, and particularly computing hardware in an attempt to achieve some measure of standardization. By starting at the Service layer, it is much easier to stay focused on the users' needs.

Once the question regarding Services is asked, there are a number of other questions that naturally follow. "Do these Services provide for growth? Are we going to be locked into a specific vendor's products?"

Organizations must begin to look at network Services as strategic decisions that can significantly affect their operations. These Services can be as mundane as shared printing to a laser printer, or as pervasive as an enterprise-wide E-mail system. Let's use E-mail as an example.

Let's say that the Ajax company decides that employee communication is a crucial aspect of their business. They decide to implement a corporate-wide E-mail system to facilitate this communication. They decide on an X.400-compatible mail application. One reason that they made this decision was because of the portability of the X.400 standard. They reasoned that widespread support of the X.400 messaging format would enhance their options for future expansion and growth. All in all, a reasonable approach.

Once the Ajax company made the decision to go with the X.400 standard, the rest was comparatively easy. A suitable Transport and Cabling decision is left as the remaining task. It should be obvious that while the decisions of a Transport and Cabling are important, they are secondary to the choice of a Service and Format.

While it's hard to simplify and generalize all networking situations, here are a few suggestions that may help to organize and prioritize your networking plans:

1. Establish and evaluate the required Services. Do they meet your requirements? Are they supportable?

2. During this process, be aware of the limitations and restrictions imposed by the Formats used by the Services you have selected. Will your data be held hostage by the application vendor, or can it be transported to other applications and Services?

3. Once you've chosen the Services, along with their attendant Formats, start thinking about a Transport protocol. Because Services are often protocol-specific, the choice of a Transport protocol may be restricted.

4. While selecting a Transport protocol, familiarize yourself with the administrative requirements inherent in the protocol.

5. Is the candidate Transport protocol supported on likely Cabling mediums?

The preceding five suggestions may be somewhat simplistic, but they help to illustrate and represent the general process of working from the top down during the network design process.

Using NetPICTs to Help with Systems Integration

This book comes with a disk that contains numerous NetPICT symbols. Many of the symbols are duplicated from products discussed in the book; others depict other common networking products.

The disk contains a viewer application called PICTviewer. It is used to view the NetPICT symbols. For each NetPICT symbol there are two files: a PICT file that contains the graphical image, and a text file that contains a textual description of the image. The text file has the same name of the PICT, but with the addition of a ".txt" file extension. For example, the PICT file portion of Apple's Internet Router is named "`Apple Internet Router`," while the text file portion is named "`Apple Internet Router.txt`."

The NetPICT viewer provides an easy means for you to view and read informative data on hundreds of products. Of course, since the symbols are in the PICT format, they can be easily incorporated into documents made by your favorite drawing program. The same can be said for the text (.txt) files. These text files can be added to your drawings to annotate the figures. Many drawing programs, such as MacDraw Pro, can import text files directly. If your drawing program can't directly import text files, then you'll have to copy and paste with a text editor or word processor. By using a drawing program, you'll be able to import those NetPICT symbols that represent the fundamental parts of your present or planned network. You'll be able to see where bridges, routers, gateways, or even format translators are required.

To use the NetPICT viewer, you'll need HyperCard 2.1 (or the HyperCard viewer). You might also want to copy the NetPICT viewer, along with the symbol folder, to a hard disk.

1. Launch the NetPICT viewer by double-clicking its icon.

2. Click several times to close the splash screen.

3. Use the pop-up folder menu to browse through the NetPICT symbol folder hierarchy.

4. Once you've found the appropriate symbol, click once on the name that appears in the window directly beneath the pop-up menu.

   The chosen NetPICT symbol will appear in a separate window to the right of the viewer screen. You can reposition this window at any time. You can even enlarge it to the size of your monitor by clicking on the Zoom box located at the upper right hand corner of the symbol window (see figure 14.1).

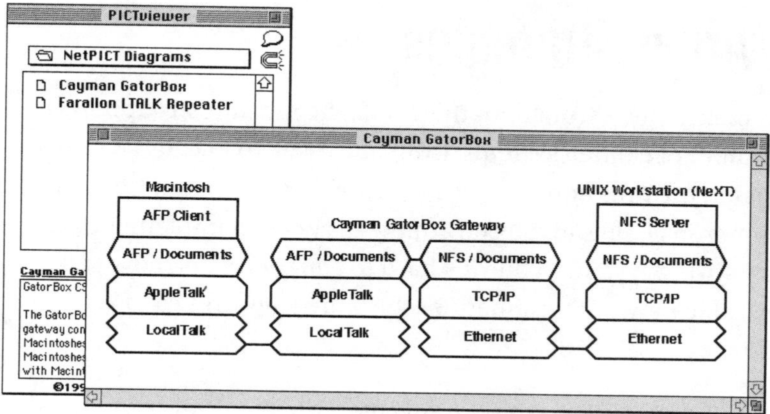

Figure 14.1
The image window of the NetPICT viewer can be repositioned as needed to fully view the NetPICT symbol.

5. To restore the symbol window to the right side of the viewer window, click once on the magnet icon. This will automatically dock the symbol window to its default position at the right of the viewer window (see figure 14.2).

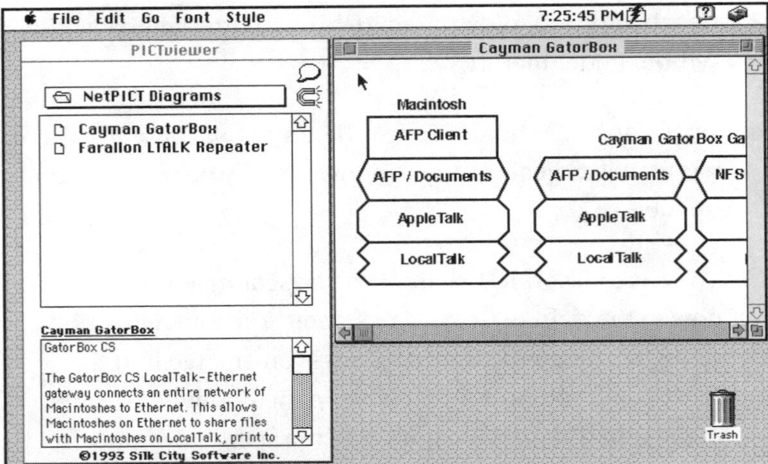

Figure 14.2
The magnet icon re-docks the PICT image at the upper right corner of the viewer application window.

Wiring Strategies

As mentioned throughout this book, the Macintosh supports a number of cabling systems, from LocalTalk to FDDI. We've discussed the pros and cons of each cabling system, but there are numerous issues involved with the design and implementation of any wiring system. While it's hard to generalize and cover all possible networking situations, here are a few things to keep in mind.

- Don't get locked into a specific vendor's proprietary components or cabling scheme. Stay with the accepted industry standards.

> **NOTE:** One exception is Apple's Ethernet system. It uses a special connector to link the device with the external attachment unit. Since the network side of the attachment unit (either 10Base-5, 10Base-2, or 10Base-T) still conforms to industry standards, it's less important that the device side is somewhat non-standard. To their credit, Apple has published and made this standard available for any vendor to use. The Apple Ethernet system has already been adopted by several Macintosh networking vendors. Perhaps other non-Macintosh networking companies will follow suit.

- Don't limit your network and wiring plans just to data. Consider integrating your network plans with other forms of data, such as voice and video. You may be able to save money by installing these different cabling systems at the same time. In many cases, the different systems can use the same face-plate.

- Plan for the future. You may be planning to use only Local-Talk and Ethernet, but you should seriously consider the installation of twisted-pair wiring and fiber backbones that are capable of supporting current and future high-end cabling systems.

Example 1: Four-Pair Twisted Pair

One such industry standard involves the use of four pairs (10Base-T Ethernet requires two pairs) of Unshielded Twisted-Pair (UTP) wiring. The most encompassing standard for UTP is published by the Electronic Industries Association and the Telecommunications Industry Association (EIA/TIA). The standard is commonly referred to as EIA/TIA 568 and TSB-36, which sets a standard for "Category 5" UTP media. Category 5 UTP anticipates the upcoming standards that will support bandwidths of 100 Mbps (Category 4 UTP supports the conventional Ethernet bandwidth of 10 Mbps). These standards include copper versions of the FDDI standard (CDDI) and 100 Mbps implementations of Ethernet. This cabling is also sometimes referred to as "Level 5" cabling.

Example 2: Fiber-Optics

Another example of planning for the future is the choice of fiber-optic cabling. Fiber optic cabling is becoming more commonplace as a medium for Ethernet backbones. In fact, a new emerging Ethernet fiber standard, IEEE 802.3—10Base-F—will be published shortly. Fiber can be run over great distances and is immune from most forms of electromagnetic interference (just don't get it too close to a black hole). Fiber optic cabling is also the basis for the FDDI standard. Fortunately, the two standards overlap somewhat and it's desirable to implement fiber networks that conform to the FDDI standard (ANSI X3T9.5: FDDI) as well as the current and planned Ethernet fiber standards. The moral of this story is to plan for FDDI even though you're only going to use lowly Ethernet. You'll appreciate this approach in the future when FDDI cards sell at CompUSA for $129.

- If it appears that your LAN will need to support more than 50 users, plan on implementing a structured wiring approach to your network design. It's money well spent. By implementing such a system, the ongoing costs involved in support, troubleshooting, expansion, and equipment relocation will be minimized.

- In accordance with your budget, plan on running multiple cable runs to each office or cubicle. The incremental cost of the additional cabling is relatively small when compared to the minor increase in labor cost. Also, don't scrimp on the number of jacks provided to an office or cubicle. You can choose faceplates that have a single, double, or quadruple complement of connectors. While it's often possible to daisy-chain within a room, don't plan on this as a part of the design. Consider that you might want to add printers or other networkable peripherals to a room at any time in the future. You might also need to support devices that require multiple connections to the LAN, such as workstations, routers, and gateways. A good rule of thumb is to plan for two times as many connections as you actually require at present.

- Make sure that fiber and copper cable runs are within the specified length limitations, by carefully planning the location and distribution of wiring closets. Be sure to allocate additional cable length for vertical distances (not usually shown on floor plans) and the routing losses that occur when cable is snaked above ceilings and through walls.

- Speaking of wiring closets, plan the layout and design of these rooms carefully. Make sure that the room is well lighted, ventilated, and capable of being securely locked. If the room is large enough, use industry standard 19" racks to contain the network devices. Obviously, since the room may house a number of routers, gateways, and other network devices, adequate electrical service is crucial. If you have the room, you may also find it convenient to install a small desk with a Mac that can be used for troubleshooting and maintenance. This Mac can also be used to maintain network configuration information, wiring diagrams, and problem logs.

- Are your cables routed in such a manner as to avoid electromagnetic interference and undue mechanical stress? For example, don't drape cables around fluorescent light fixtures, and don't hang wet laundry from cables strung from the ceiling. Use common sense and consult the appropriate local codes and requirements.

- Plan to have your wiring tested before use. This is a particularly good idea for large, expensive installations that use structured wiring. The time to discover breaks or discontinuities in the cable is *before* network deployment. If you use a wiring contractor, be sure to include testing and validation as part of the agreement. The devices used for testing can be rather expensive, so it's likely that this task is better handled by the cable installers.

- Adopt an adequate cable marking and identification scheme. Each and every cable should be unambiguously marked—in a location that will be visible after installation. Be sure to mark both ends of the cable. Make sure the marking is permanent and won't easily be erased or detached. There are many adequate marking systems. Some utilize heat-shrinkable tubing, while others use labeled wiring ties.

- Document everything from the outset. Create a logical and physical diagram of your network. If you're using a cabling system that has physical hardware addresses, such as Ethernet, register these numbers along with their location and description. For this task, a spreadsheet or a simple database (such as FileMaker Pro) is ideal.

- Call, without delay, the Black Box Corporation at (800) 552-6816. They'll send you a free catalog that's chock full of many networking products. It's like the "Sears Catalog" for networkers.

Using these twelve suggestions as a guide, let's now examine some common networking scenarios. These scenarios will serve several purposes. First, they will expose you to a number of different wiring schemes, along with their benefits and disadvantages. Next, because the scenarios progress from the simplest to the most complex, you'll be able to establish a growth path for your environment.

Scenario 1a: Single LocalTalk Network Using a Daisy-Chain Topology

The simplest Macintosh network is the single LocalTalk daisy-chain network (see figure 14.3). This network has been around since 1985 and in many cases is still an entirely acceptable network architecture. This network is inexpensive. All that is required is the LocalTalk (or phone-type) connectors and the necessary wiring. In nearly all cases, the phone-type connectors (Farallon's PhoneNET) are recommended. Because these connectors use the telephone-style RJ-11 jacks, you'll be able to make your own cables by purchasing a spool of twisted-pair phone wire, jacks, and a crimping tool. Electronics stores such as Radio Shack should have everything you'll need.

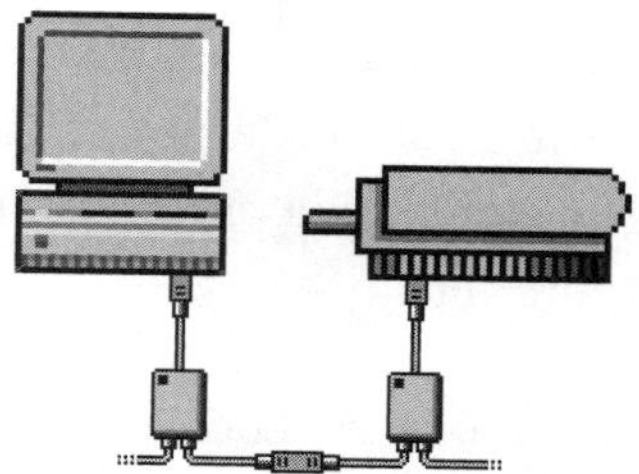

Figure 14.3
A single LocalTalk network with daisy-chain topology.

The cost of this network is the lowest of any of the other scenarios. Expect to pay $25 for each LocalTalk/phone-type connector. With the additional cost of the wiring, the total per-node connection cost should be well under $50.

With this network design, you'll be able to provide modest bandwidth for any number between two and thirty devices. The maximum distance of the network may vary somewhat, but plan on a maximum of 1,000 total feet of wiring. If you need more distance, consider the use of a LocalTalk repeater.

The tradeoffs for this design are the low cost and ease-of-installation versus the limited bandwidth of LocalTalk. If you plan on using services that demand high bandwidth, then the simple LocalTalk is not for you. Applications that demand high bandwidth include networked databases, demanding AFP services where large files are frequently transferred, and demanding print jobs submitted from a number of users. As a rule of thumb, try to avoid putting more than five networked printers on a single segment of LocalTalk. If you need this many printers to service your users, then a routed scenario or a higher bandwidth cabling system is probably required.

This network scenario is ideal for small offices that deal with smaller documents and have modest print requirements. It also helps if the physical layout of the area to be networked can easily support the daisy-chain topology. If the devices are all located within a single room, then the daisy-chain can simply run around the periphery of the room. On the other hand, if your network nodes are distributed throughout a large building that doesn't provide ready wiring access, then a more structured wiring approach might make more sense.

One point to remember about the LocalTalk daisy-chain is that devices can be added to the ends of the chain at any time, but if you need to add a device somewhere in the middle, the network will have to be disconnected to attach the new LocalTalk connector. This addition won't take long, but the users will have to put up with a slight interruption in network services.

These considerations can be summed up as follows:

+ Ideal for small workgroups (2-20 devices) in close proximity
+ Easy to wire
- Limited bandwidth and throughput
- Network disrupted when devices are added
- Limited to approximately 30 devices
● Maximum cabling length of 1,000 feet

Scenario 1b: Single Ethernet Network Using a Daisy-Chain Topology

If you find the simplicity of Scenario 1a appealing, but you're concerned about the limited bandwidth of LocalTalk, then an Ethernet solution may be just the ticket. In this case, we'll use the thinwire variant of Ethernet known as 10Base-2 (see figure 14.4). Although twisted-pair Ethernet (10Base-T) is getting all the attention in the press, a thinwire daisy-chain is still a valid solution for small network installations in one compact area.

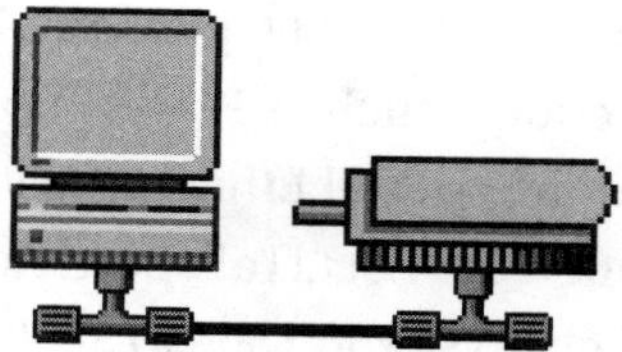

Figure 14.4
A single Ethernet network using thinwire (10Base-2) cabling and a daisy-chain topology.

With the thinwire tee connectors, the nodes simply can be connected one after the other. The total cable length is 185 meters, or about 600 feet. Like the LocalTalk example in Scenario 1a, changes made to the network will cause a brief disruption of services. Apple's thinwire transceivers have a unique self-terminating feature that engages the terminating resistor whenever the connection is broken. With these devices, a break in the middle of a segment will not cause the two segments to fail. Each segment will continue to operate on its own. If you use the conventional thinwire devices, be sure that each free end of the cable has the terminating resistive cap in place.

This scenario is ideal for small workgroups that require more bandwidth than LocalTalk. The Ethernet cabling should provide a 300 to 500 percent improvement in throughput over the LocalTalk cabling. The number of nodes is still somewhat limited, as 30 is the recommended maximum number of devices on a single segment of thinwire.

One difficulty with thinwire is the cabling. Each cable must have the twist-lock BNC connector fittings. You can purchase pre-assembled lengths of these cables, or invest in the bulk fittings and cable and crimp your own. You might need to go to a networking supply house, such as Black Box, to find these components and the proper crimping tools.

The cost of a thinwire network is somewhat more than a LocalTalk network. If your Macs, LaserWriters and other network devices aren't equipped with Ethernet, then Ethernet cards will be required. Expect to pay $200 to $300 per card. Devices that don't offer Ethernet connections (such as PowerBooks and certain LaserWriters) will require special Ethernet devices that connect via the SCSI port or through the LocalTalk port. Add the cost of the cables, and you're likely to spend $300 to $400 per node.

These considerations can be summed up as follows:

+ Ideal for small workgroups in close proximity
+ Easy to wire
+ Improved throughput compared to LocalTalk
- Network disrupted when devices are added
- Segment limited to approximately 30 devices
● Maximum cabling length of about 600 feet

A similar scenario to a single Ethernet network involves the use of FDDI as a cabling medium. Of course, the per-node connection cost is considerably higher. If your network requirements are severe, then this approach should be considered. Perhaps you need to network a number of Quadras in a desktop publishing environment where users are continually transferring 10M Photoshop files, or perhaps you need to upgrade a number of CAD users that are continually taxing the network. In these cases, the extra bandwidth and throughput of Ethernet or FDDI can pay for itself in short order.

If you're planning future network growth and expansion, don't invest heavily in the daisy-chain approach. If you're planning to expand, consider instead scenario 3b, which uses an active Ethernet hub.

Scenario 2: Single LocalTalk Network Using an Active Star Topology

If you plan to stay with LocalTalk but would like to avoid the hassles associated with daisy-chaining, then a star topology is the solution (see figure 14.5). Apple's LocalTalk devices will not work with this topology; you'll need to use the phone-type connectors (PhoneNET or equivalent). (We'll continue to use the term LocalTalk for convenience.) You can also use Farallon's Star-Connectors. They do not require termination and are a bit less expensive than the conventional two-port devices. The easiest and cheapest LocalTalk star is known as a *passive star*. The passive star simply joins together the free ends at a common point. This can be a telephone-style punchdown block or a patch panel.

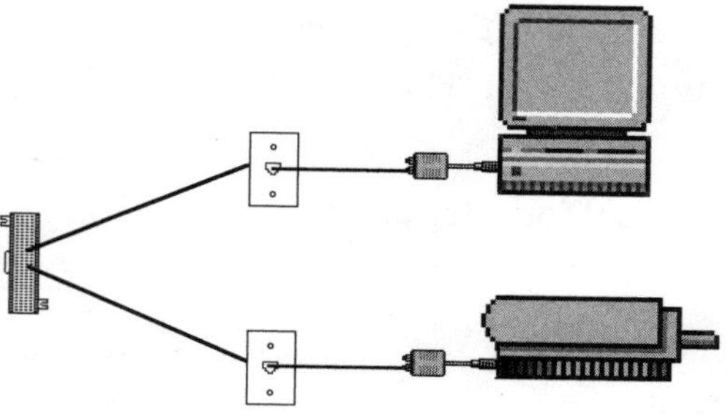

Figure 14.5
A single LocalTalk network with a passive star topology.

This approach makes sense for a small workgroup. You may be able to use existing building wiring to create your passive star. Considering this potential for reduced wiring costs, coupled with the low cost of the StarConnectors, this network scenario can be the most affordable of all. The shortcomings of passive stars are the limits imposed on the number of devices (3 branches with 10 devices each) and the limited extensibility.

To summarize the considerations:

+ Ideal for small workgroups in close proximity
+ Can use existing building wiring

- Restrictive wiring limitations and limited flexibility
- Limited to approximately 30 devices

- Maximum cabling length of 1,000 feet

Scenario 3a: Single LocalTalk Network Using an Active Star Topology

The alternative star topology is the active star (see figure 14.6). It uses a multiport LocalTalk repeater to separately feed each segment of the star. Active stars are generally more reliable and easier to maintain than their passive counterparts. Each cable run has a maximum length of 3,000 feet. For a twelve-port repeater, the maximum cabling distance is 36,000 feet. Most LocalTalk star repeaters are equipped with management software that can enable or disable ports and perform basic line quality testing.

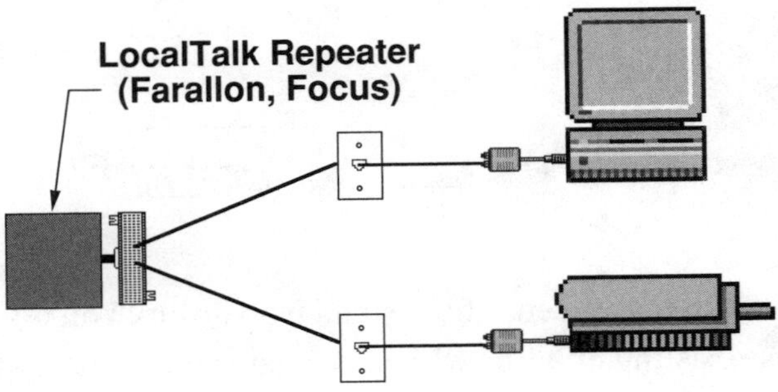

Figure 14.6
A single LocalTalk network using an active star topology.

While it's possible to place forty (or even more) devices on an active star, it's important to remember than the entire star is a single AppleTalk network, sharing the LocalTalk bandwidth of 230.4 Kbps. So, unless your network demands are modest, it's best to limit the number of nodes to 30 or 40.

The cost of an active LocalTalk star network is more than the passive star because you must factor in the cost of the repeater.

Depending on the number of nodes and the cost of the repeater, this could add a considerable amount to the per node cost.

To summarize the considerations:

- + Star topology makes it easier to add and move devices
- + Preferred over passive star topologies in most cases
- + Enhanced reliability
- - Limited to 30 to 40 devices
- - The cost of the repeater increases the cost per node
- ● Maximum cabling length of 3,000 feet per segment

Scenario 3b: Single Ethernet Network Using a Star Topology with 10Base-T Cabling

This scenario provides the bandwidth of the thinwire scenario, with the flexibility of a star wiring topology (see figure 14.7). Twisted-pair (10Base-T) Ethernet networks require a repeater hub. These hubs come in many different sizes and price points. There are even low-cost mini-hubs that have anywhere between four and eight ports.

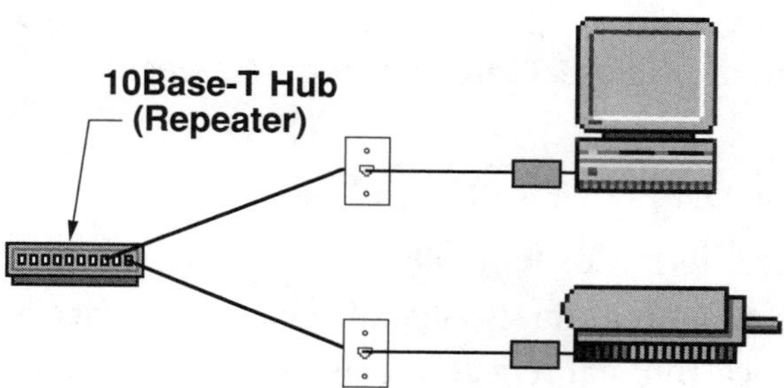

Figure 14.7
A single Ethernet network using a star topology and 10Base-T cabling.

As in the case of the LocalTalk stars, you might be able to use existing building wiring, although 10Base-T wiring requires four pairs of wires that meet certain requirements. If you must create your own wiring, don't worry, it's not too difficult—10Base-T Ethernet uses a larger version (RJ-45) of the RJ-11 connectors used by the phone-type LocalTalk connectors. You can buy the bulk cable, connectors, and proper crimping tools from network supply houses such as Black Box. (Consider the use of Level 5 wiring just in case you plan to migrate to a high-speed network such as 100 Mbps Ethernet or CDDI.)

This single hub approach makes a lot of sense when you need the extra bandwidth of Ethernet and are planning for future growth. When you require additional hubs, the hubs can be linked together with an Ethernet backbone. Of course, the cost of hubs add to the per-node cost, but that's the price of the additional flexibility.

The length of each twisted-pair segment cannot exceed the 100 meter restriction, so the maximum distance between devices (assuming the hub is centrally located) is 200 meters.

To summarize the considerations:

+ The star topology makes it easier to add or move devices

+ Uses low-cost wiring

- Additional cost of the hub adds to the overall cost

● Maximum 10Base-T length of about 325 feet

Scenario 4: Single LocalTalk Network Using a Multiple Star Topology

In an ideal situation, you should only place one device on each port of a LocalTalk star repeater. This way, you'll be able to isolate problem nodes more easily. However, if you place one device per port, you will only be connecting a dozen or so devices per repeater. You can extend this somewhat by linking the star repeaters together (see figure 14.8). For example, by interconnecting three 12-port repeaters, you'll be able to connect 36 LocalTalk devices without having multiple devices per port.

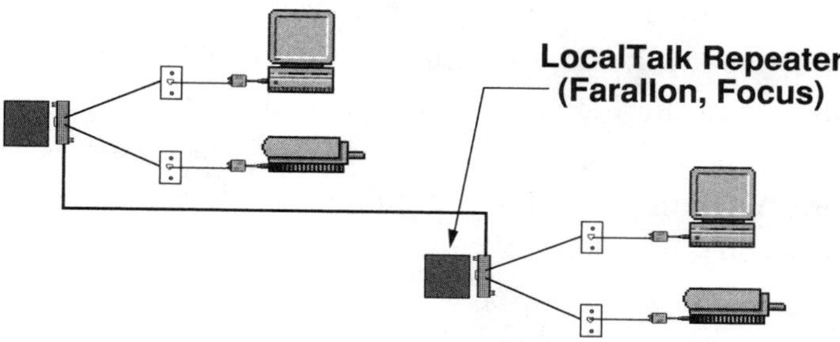

Figure 14.8
A single LocalTalk network using a multiple star topology.

Of course, this is an expensive way to connect LocalTalk nodes. In the example of the three linked repeaters, the per-node cost might exceed $100. Keep in mind that even though multiple repeaters are used, the resultant network is still a single logical LocalTalk segment with a shared bandwidth of 230.4 Kbps. Due to the relatively high per-node cost and the inherent limitations of LocalTalk, be leery of this scenario.

The considerations are:

+ Avoids multiple devices per repeater port
- The LocalTalk bandwidth is shared by all devices
- Still limited in practicality to 30 to 40 devices
- Cost per device is relatively high
● Maximum cabling length of 3,000 feet per segment

Scenario 5: Single LocalTalk Network Using a Bridged Star Topology

An alternative to the LocalTalk repeater is Tribe's LocalTalk bridge (see figure 14.9). This device uses packet switching technology to maximize the limited bandwidth of LocalTalk. If the low-cost and easy installation of LocalTalk appeals to you, but you're finding the LocalTalk bandwidth limiting, then Tribe's LocalSwitch might provide a good alternative. It increases the throughput and extends the number of devices that you can place on your LocalTalk segment. According to Tribe, you should be able to put a total of 60 devices on the bridge.

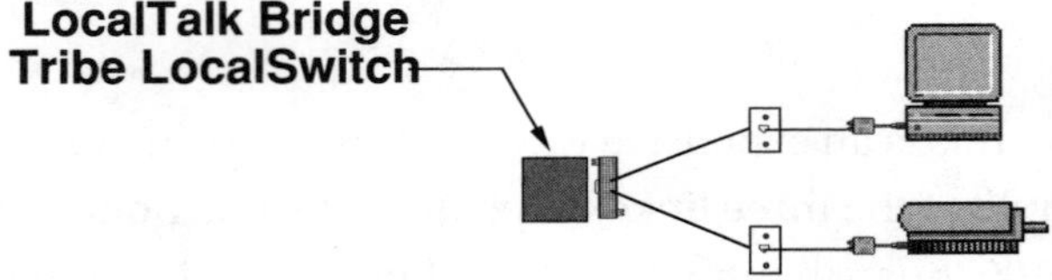

Figure 14.9
A single LocalTalk network using a bridged star topology.

The considerations are:

+ The bridge maximizes the limited LocalTalk bandwidth
+ No router administration is required
- Limited to 40 to 60 devices
- Limited extensiblity without an Ethernet connection
● Maximum cabling length of 3,000 feet per segment

Scenario 6: Multiple LocalTalk Networks Using a Serially Routed Topology

Eventually, as you continue to add LocalTalk devices to the network, you'll reach a point where separate AppleTalk networks are required (see figure 14.10). This might be due to the sheer number of devices or the need for traffic isolation. The key to this scenario is the LocalTalk-to-LocalTalk router. There are a number of companies that make such a router. The router could also be a Macintosh that's running the Apple Internet Router through LocalTalk connectors in the modem and printer ports. In this example, each LocalTalk network is implemented with a repeater or a Tribe bridge.

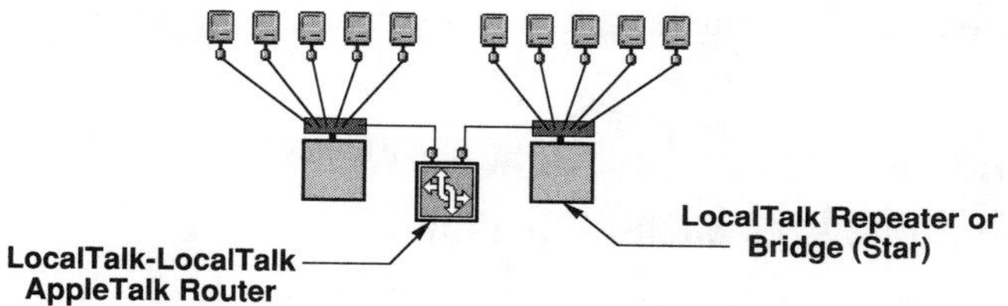

Figure 14.10
Multiple LocalTalk networks serially routed.

The router connects each LocalTalk network in a daisy-chained manner, but it's wise to limit the number of connected networks to a maximum of 4 or 5 networks (3 or 4 routers). Anything more than this increases the risk of network timeouts and delays. (The router introduces a bit of administrative overhead due to the configuration of its network numbers and zone names.)

This scenario makes sense as an upgrade path from the single LocalTalk network that is becoming burdened with traffic. This is particularly the case when the additional traffic can be isolated by the addition of the router. The only shortcoming with this approach is that it's somewhat limited when it comes to expansion. A much better approach is to use an Ethernet network as a backbone (see Scenario 7a below).

To summarize the considerations:

+ The router isolates each LocalTalk segment

● Each LocalTalk network supports 30 to 40 devices (using a repeater)

- Each LocalTalk network supports 40 to 60 devices (using a bridge)
  - Daisy-chaining networks is practically limited to 3 or 4 routers
  - Limited expansion capability
- Maximum cabling length of 3,000 feet per segment

Scenario 7a: Multiple LocalTalk Networks Using a Routed Backbone Topology

When you outgrow your single LocalTalk network, or when you have to connect LocalTalk devices to Ethernet-equipped devices, the easiest way is to link the LocalTalk networks to an Ethernet backbone (see figure 14.11). Each LocalTalk network will connect to the backbone with a LocalTalk-to-Ethernet AppleTalk router.

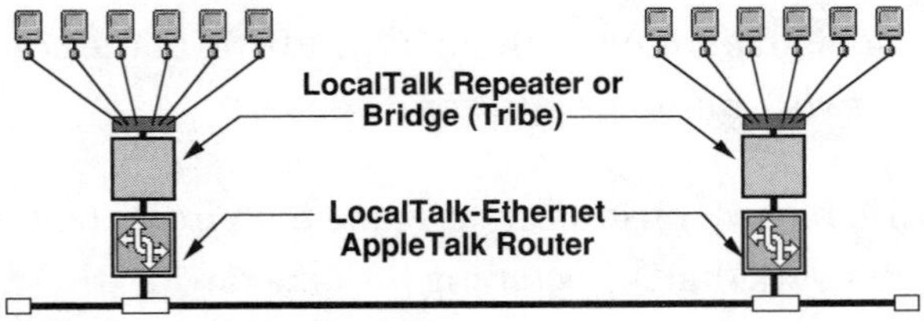

Figure 14.11 Multiple LocalTalk networks using a routed (not bridged) backbone topology.

With this approach, you'll be able to interconnect hundreds of LocalTalk devices. It still makes sense to use some kind of star repeater or bridge in combination with the router. Some vendors (such as Farallon) offer combination devices that merge a LocalTalk-Ethernet router with a star repeater.

As in the prior scenario, some router administration is required. If you plan to connect a number of routers to the backbone, you may want to consider the use of a *seed router*. Seed routers are used to load non-seed routers with network numbers and zone information. Most routers offer this seeding capability, implemented as a part of the router's configuration. The primary advantage of seeding is administrative. Changes made to the backbone's network number range or zone names can be made in a single router instead of changing all the routers on the backbone.

To summarize the considerations:

+ Ethernet backbone provides high-speed path
+ Extensible to many routers and hundreds of devices
+ Traffic isolation with routers
- Router administration required
- LocalTalk bandwidth—no increase in throughput
● Ethernet (thickwire) backbone length approximately 1,500 feet

Scenario 7b: Multiple LocalTalk Networks Using a Bridged Backbone Topology

If you anticipate fewer than 254 devices, then another solution is available from Tribe (see figure 14.12). Their TribeStar bridge has an Ethernet connection in addition to several LocalTalk ports. The TribeStar has the advantage of reduced administration because there are no routers to configure and maintain.

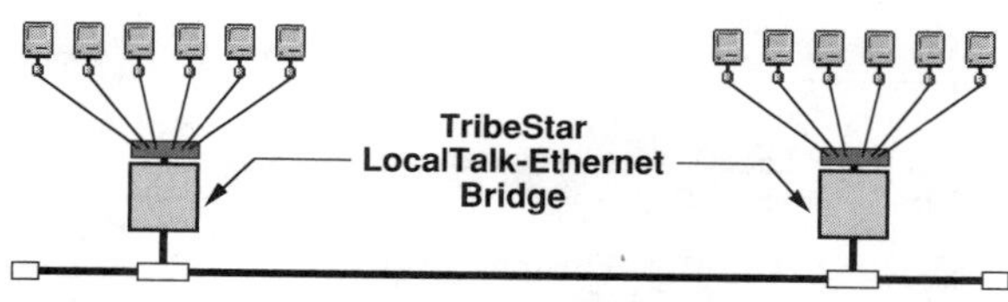

Figure 14.12 Multiple LocalTalk networks using a bridged—not routed—backbone topology.

This scenario makes sense for medium-sized LocalTalk networks where the maximum performance must be obtained for a minimum of administrative overhead. The Ethernet backbone provides a measure of extensibility, so that future bridges (assuming the 254 node limit is not reached) and routers can be added as needed.

The considerations are:

+ The Ethernet backbone provides a high-speed path
+ Extensible to many bridges and hundreds of devices
+ No router administration required
+ Maximizes LocalTalk bandwidth
● Each bridge can support up to 64 devices
- More than 254 nodes requires an AppleTalk router
● Ethernet (thickwire) backbone length of about 1,500 feet

Scenario 8: Ethernet Backbone with Multiple LocalTalk Networks and Direct AppleTalk Nodes

Building on Scenario 7a, you can always add AppleTalk nodes directly to the Ethernet backbone (see figure 14.13). This approach can be used to connect Ethernet-equipped Macs and LaserWriters to the network. It is also widely used to connect other computers, such as UNIX workstations, DEC VAX, and PCs to the network of Macs.

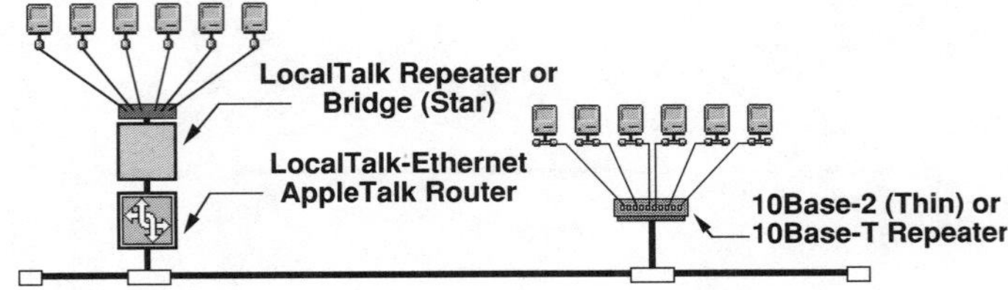

Figure 14.13 Multiple LocalTalk networks and nodes with an Ethernet backbone.

If AppleTalk is to be the transport of choice, then the router can be an AppleTalk-only unit. If other non-AppleTalk nodes are added to the Ethernet, then the router must be a multiprotocol router capable of routing the necessary protocols between the LocalTalk and Ethernet devices.

Keep in mind that the LocalTalk and Ethernet repeaters have different cabling length requirements. LocalTalk runs may approach 3,000 feet, while 10Base-T limits are about one-tenth that distance (100 meters, or about 325 feet).

The considerations are:

+ Ethernet backbone provides a high-speed path
+ Extensible to many routers and hundreds of devices
+ Direct Ethernet connections with thickwire or thinwire hubs

- Ethernet (thickwire) backbone length about 1,500 feet
- 10Base-2 length about 600 feet; 10Base-T length about 325 feet

Scenario 9: Multiple Ethernet Networks Using a Routed Backbone and Star Topology

As the cost of Ethernet connections continue to fall, and as Apple continues to offer built-in Ethernet in more and more Macintosh models, the trend is clearly away from LocalTalk connections. For this reason, solutions like Scenarios 7a and 8 are beginning to become less popular. The direction that most network designers are taking is to use Ethernet to all desktop devices, and then to use an Ethernet segment as a connecting backbone (see figure 14.14). The key component is an Ethernet-to-Ethernet AppleTalk router. These devices are becoming more prevalent. Cayman, for example, has just released such a router; other companies are likely to follow suit. The router could also be a Macintosh with two Ethernet cards running the Apple Internet Router.

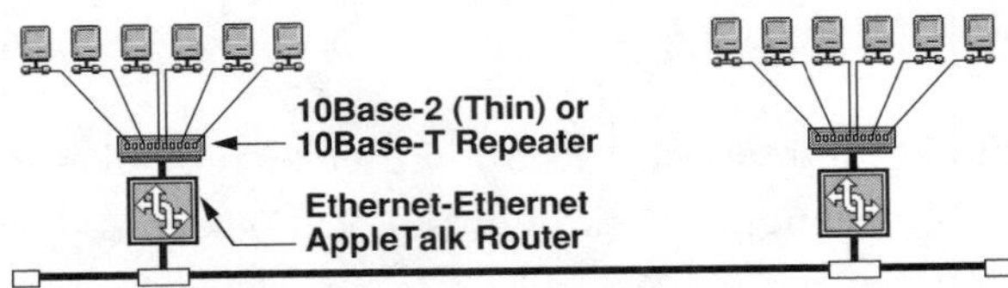

Figure 14.14 Multiple Ethernet networks using a backbone and star topology.

This scenario represents the most flexible and high-performance option for all but the most demanding applications. This scenario also fits in nicely with structured wiring plans, which makes it easy to respond to growth and redistribution of network resources; it also makes it easy to add routers to the network in response to excessive traffic. This approach lends itself to intelligent hubs and concentrators that work in conjunction with, or incorporate, AppleTalk routers. As an example, Cabletron has just announced their intention to incorporate the Cisco 4000 series router into their hubs. Standalone high-performance multiprotocol routers are also likely candidates, as they provide the necessary performance with a wide range of protocol support. These routers are supplied by several vendors; Cisco and Wellfleet are two popular choices.

To summarize the considerations:

+ Ethernet backbone provides a high-speed path
+ Extensible to many routers and hundreds of devices
+ Full Ethernet bandwidth between nodes

- Ethernet (thickwire) backbone length approximately 1,500 feet
- 10Base-2 length about 600 feet; 10Base-T length about 325 feet

Scenario 10: Multiple Ethernet Networks with a FDDI Backbone

As the number of routers increase on an Ethernet backbone, its ability to handle the inter-network traffic plus the inter-router traffic can become strained. For these very large networks, replacing the Ethernet backbone with FDDI is becoming more prevalent (see figure 14.15). For now, the main role of FDDI is likely to be its use as a high-speed backbone medium.

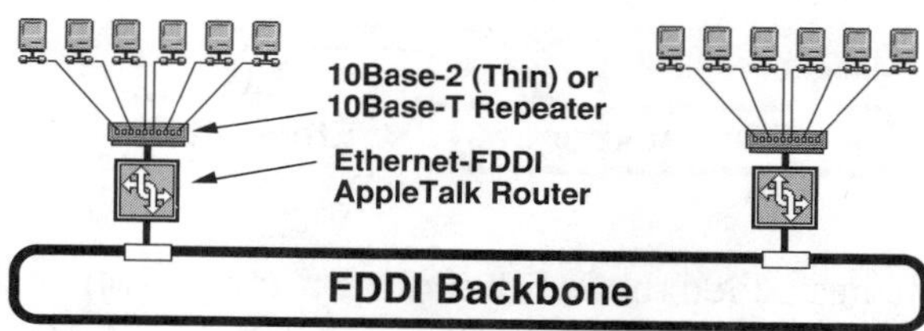

Figure 14.15
Multiple Ethernet networks with a FDDI backbone.

The latest generation of high-speed routers provide, in addition to Ethernet and Token Ring ports, FDDI ports that can provide the connection to the FDDI LAN. Since FDDI LANs can extend over great distances, this scenario is indicated for very large networks with many attached subnetworks.

To summarize the considerations:

- + FDDI backbone provides a high-speed path
- + Extensible to many routers and hundreds of devices
- + Full Ethernet bandwidth between nodes
- ● FDDI supports 1,000 nodes, each up to 2km (over 1 mile) apart, for a total aggregate distance of 100km (over 60 miles)

Scenario 11: Ethernet and FDDI WAN Topology

The last wiring scenario involves the combination of Scenarios 9 and 10 by adding a high-speed WAN connection (see figure 14.16).

These WAN connections are commonly made with the multi-protocol routers mentioned earlier. As mentioned before, one of AppleTalk's past shortcomings was the regular transmission of routing table updates. These updates tended to be burdensome to AppleTalk WAN links. Today, there are many options to solve this problem.

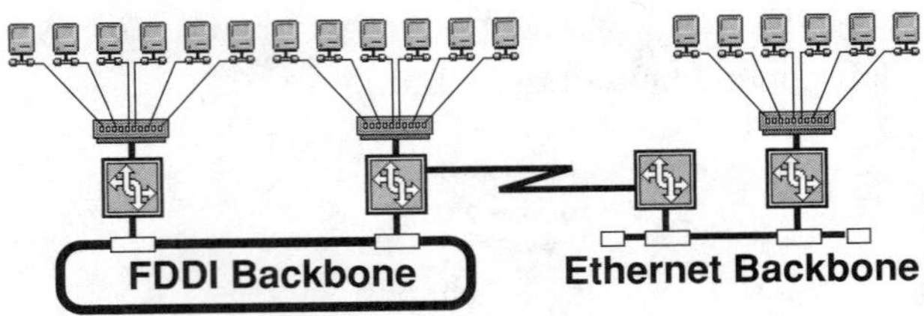

Figure 14.16 Ethernet and FDDI WAN topology.

First, Apple has added the AURP routing protocol, which only sends routing updates when necessary. AURP support is included with Apple's Internet Router, and currently being added to many third-party routers. Another solution for WAN AppleTalk support is through the encapsulation of AppleTalk within another protocol, such as TCP/IP. The process of IP encapsulation of AppleTalk has been recently defined and standardized. Lastly, many high-end router developers offer specialized routing protocols that can be applied to the routing of AppleTalk over the WAN.

It is expected that Apple will take additional steps in the near future to enhance AppleTalk's viability over wide-area networks. These include the support of upcoming Point-to-Point Protocol (PPP), which should enhance remote access and routed connections, and the adoption of other popular routing protocols such as Open Shortest Path First (OSPF), which is popular in large IP internets.

The considerations can be summarized as follows:

+ FDDI backbone provides a high-speed path

+ Extensible to many routers and hundreds of devices

+ Full Ethernet bandwidth between nodes

- FDDI supports 1,000 nodes, each up to 2km (over 1 mile) apart, for a total aggregate distance of 100km (over 60 miles)

Scenario 12: Structured Wiring Example

This last example illustrates a wiring scenario that uses a technique sometimes referred to as a *structured wiring implementation* (see figure 14.17). In this example, a star topology is used to wire all offices and cubicles with several runs of 10Base-T (or even Level 5 compliant) twisted-pair wiring. All wires converge at a master patch panel within a wiring closet. From this patch panel, connections are made to the appropriate wiring devices based on requirements of the connected device.

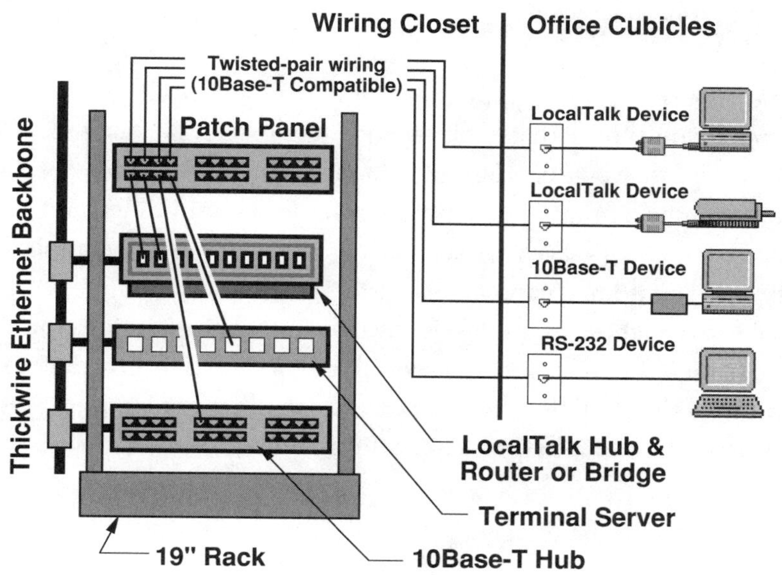

Figure 14.17 An example of a structured wiring implementation.

LocalTalk devices are interconnected to a LocalTalk hub and router; Ethernet devices are connected to an Ethernet hub. While it's not shown in figure 14.16, the 10Base-T hub could also be connected to an Ethernet-to-Ethernet router (as shown in Scenario 9). Serially connected devices are patched to a terminal server. What's important about this scheme is that all devices use identical wiring. Changes are confined to the wiring closet. If a LocalTalk Mac Plus is replaced with an Ethernet Quadra, the only required change is to move a patch cord from the LocalTalk hub to the Ethernet hub.

Some integrated hubs merge the different hubs (such as terminal servers, 10Base-T, and even LocalTalk) into a single, unified chassis. These devices make the wiring process even easier and less cluttered by eliminating the cross-connects that are now part of the hub's backplane.

Conclusion

The development and implementation of an AppleTalk network is not a one-time activity. It is an ongoing process; the network continues to evolve as users are added and technology changes. In this chapter, a number of network scenarios were outlined and discussed. Each successive scenario provided additional complexity—and additional capabilities—over the previous examples. Collectively, these examples delineate a full range of options for the reader; they also illustrate a clear and progressive growth path from the simplest of LocalTalk networks to the most complex combinations of Ethernet, Token Ring, and FDDI cabling.

Management and Troubleshooting 15

How many copies of MacDraw do the users own? Which Macs have enough memory to run System 7? Why can't the users on the second floor print to the LaserWriter? What happens to our network performance at 10 AM every day? Chapter 15 discusses common questions like these—and provides answers to them.

Configuration Management

Keeping track of the software and hardware status of every Macintosh on a network is not an easy task. How much memory does Mary's Mac have? Is everyone using the same version of PageMaker? Many potential problems can be avoided if every user on the network has the same version of important applications and system software, and they all use the same collection of fonts and font technology (TrueType or PostScript). Several products are now on the market that allow you to examine and even install software updates on another Macintosh, using the network to transfer the information. These products are often marketed under the misnomer "network management" tools, perhaps because the person holding the title Network Manager is often responsible for configuration management of every node on the network. These products, while quite useful, do not address the task of actually managing the network itself; they manage the Macs connected to it.

How Do They Work?

A node management product (see figure 15.1) requires that you install a small program, usually called a *responder* or *agent*, on every Macintosh you will manage. The network manager's Macintosh then runs an application which communicates with the responder using a private format. In many products, the responder can also handle the task of copying updated versions of system or application software to the correct location on the remote machine's hard disk. This feature alone can justify the cost of the product, because it will save an enormous amount of time and effort every time you have to upgrade software on every node on your network.

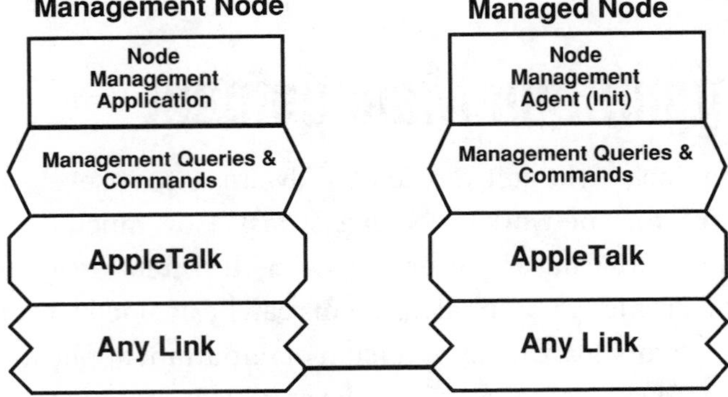

Figure 15.1 "Networked" node management.

Upgrading

Be sure to pick a product that can upgrade the responders, or you might still find yourself roaming the halls with an installer disk a few times a year.

Server and Account Management

Another labor-intensive task is controlling who can use which file servers and printers, who can use the network's dial-out or dial-in services, and reporting when or how often each one has used each service. These resources always have specialized requirements, so each has its own dedicated management tools. Whenever possible, select products which can be managed across the network, instead of those that must be managed locally.

Network Management

At the present time, AppleTalk network management is undergoing significant changes. In the past, AppleTalk management worked with any number of third-party router configuration programs to inspect and modify AppleTalk network numbers and zone names. Several years ago, Apple began development of a management protocol called the Apple Management Protocol, or AMP. During the development process, Apple made the decision to abandon AMP and adopt the industry standard Simple Network Management Protocol, or SNMP. When the promise of SNMP for AppleTalk is fully realized, managers will have a consistent and universal interface for network management.

Simple Network Management Protocol (SNMP)

SNMP is a popular tool for network management in large TCP/IP networks. SNMP provides a means for a management station to query a remote device for configuration information, and in some cases, to load new configuration information. For example, SNMP can be used to examine the Address Mapping Table of an AppleTalk router, or to find out how many DDP packets (or bytes) were sent and received by an AppleTalk node.

The information that SNMP maintains is defined in a data structure definition called the *Management Information Base* (MIB). The complete MIB for AppleTalk is defined in an Internet Engineering Task Force Request For Comment document, RFC-1243.

An SNMP management station communicates with an SNMP agent running on a managed entity (a network node such as a router or gateway). In order for data to be transferred between the devices, it must be described within the MIB. Most MIB elements are currently read-only, so most of the management can be more accurately described as monitoring. As the security features of SNMP improve, more elements in the MIB will allow read-write access from management stations, so active management of AppleTalk network devices using SNMP will become a reality.

For example, the AARP MIB defines access to the information kept in a node's AppleTalk address mapping table. Each entry in the table matches one hardware address to one protocol address, and identifies the port on which the information is used. Since this is the only AMT information in the MIB, it is the only AMT information a management station can request of an SNMP-compliant AppleTalk node.

Similar MIBs are defined for the other lower-layer AppleTalk protocols, such as DDP, RTMP, and ZIP. By examining the MIB definitions, you can see precisely what information is available for each protocol, and what configuration details (if any) can be set remotely.

Because SNMP is a Format layer protocol, there is no reason why it can't be used over AppleTalk instead of TCP/IP. Apple now includes SNMP protocol support in the Macintosh network drivers for LocalTalk, EtherTalk, and TokenTalk. This means that AppleTalk nodes can now maintain statistics on how busy they are and report that information on request to an SNMP management station. Figures 15.2 and 15.3 depict where the differences lie between these two implementations of SNMP.

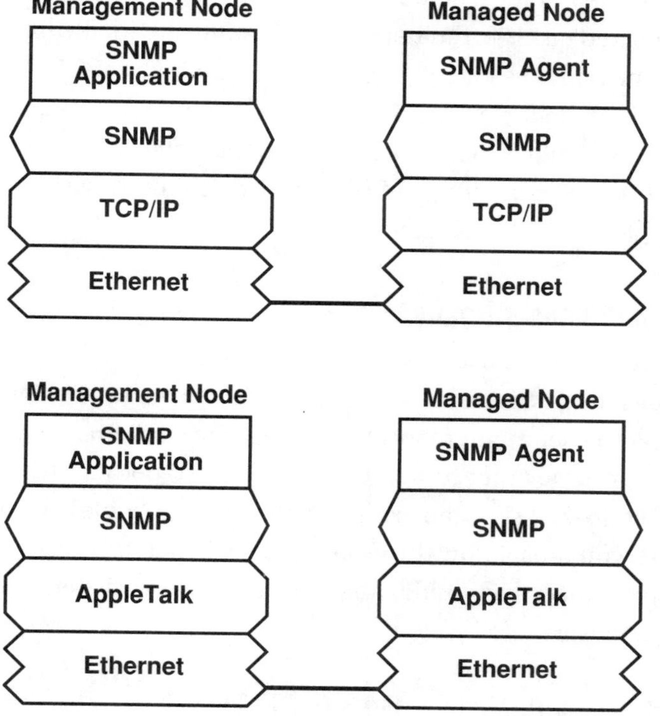

Figure 15.2 SNMP with TCP/IP transport.

Figure 15.3 SNMP with AppleTalk transport.

By sending an alert to the management station, SNMP also provides a means for nodes to notify the network management station of events, such as error conditions. A limited number of these alerts are defined in the current AppleTalk RFC, but the number is expected to grow.

Currently, there is one SNMP management program, called WatchTower from InterCon, that runs on the Macintosh. Because it was developed before a standard was defined for using SNMP over the AppleTalk transport, it uses TCP/IP as the message transport protocol. As SNMP via AppleTalk becomes more popular, SNMP management products using AppleTalk will certainly become available.

Troubleshooting

Diagnosing problems on an AppleTalk network can be a very complicated task. Fortunately, there are software tools that can be a great help in investigating and solving network problems, but no one tool can do the entire job. If you're serious about diagnosing AppleTalk, you'll also need a copy of *Inside AppleTalk, Second Edition*, which contains Apple's official, definitive description of the AppleTalk protocol family.

How the Chooser Really Works

The Chooser is the user's window onto the network, so it often provides the first indication of impending network problems. For example, a user might report that a machine can't find a particular printer or some other resource in the Chooser; perhaps the Chooser doesn't show any zones at all. To solve AppleTalk problem reports, you must know the topology of your network (how the routers connect everything) and you need to know where the affected devices are located.

The Network Census—Who Is Out There?

Apple Computer's Inter•Poll is an easy-to-use network tool (see figure 15.4). This application uses the NBP protocols to obtain both the NVE (the object, type, and zone names) and the logical AppleTalk addresses of the AppleTalk devices found on the network. An accurate NVE and address list is a great help whenever you're looking into a network problem.

However, whenever you use Inter•Poll, keep in mind that NBP is an "unreliable" means of locating every node on the network. The list it produces may not include every node on the network because some devices simply do not respond to NBP Lookups, while others may not respond if they are busy when the lookup message arrives. When Inter•Poll is left to run long enough, and the "Unnamed Devices" option has been selected and added to the search list, you will usually see at least one entry (the unnamed socket number 4) for every active node on the network.

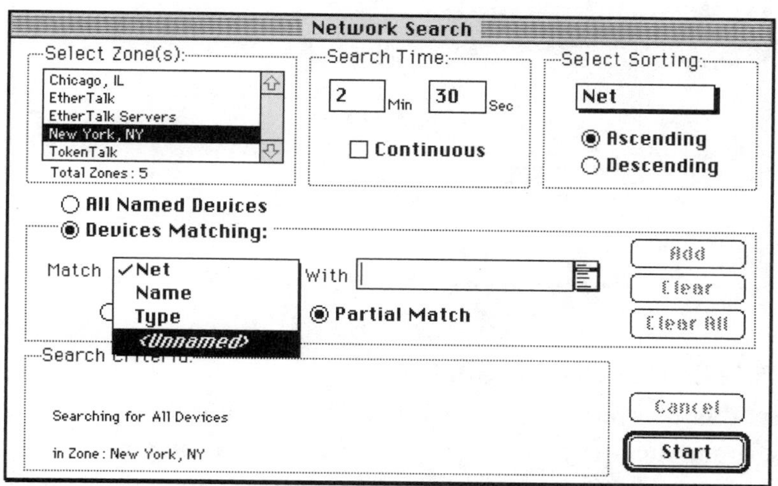

Figure 15.4
Apple's Inter•Poll utility.

If the printer which could not be seen in the Chooser appears in Inter•Poll's list, you can then test how long it takes to send a packet to the printer and back. Within Inter•Poll, this is accomplished by double-clicking on the line containing the name of the printer. A dialog box appears that enables you to send a request for the printer status; Inter•Poll displays the results of the test (see figure 15.5). More importantly, you can send a series of echo packets (the AppleTalk Echo Protocol) to the printer, and Inter•Poll will report how long it took to return each one. Because NBP has a two-second timeout, if packets are lost or take longer than two seconds to return, the Chooser isn't likely to display the printer in its device list. Notice that the display also tells you how many hops the reply message took to return to Inter•Poll. If the number of hops varies widely, the device may be too many router-hops away.

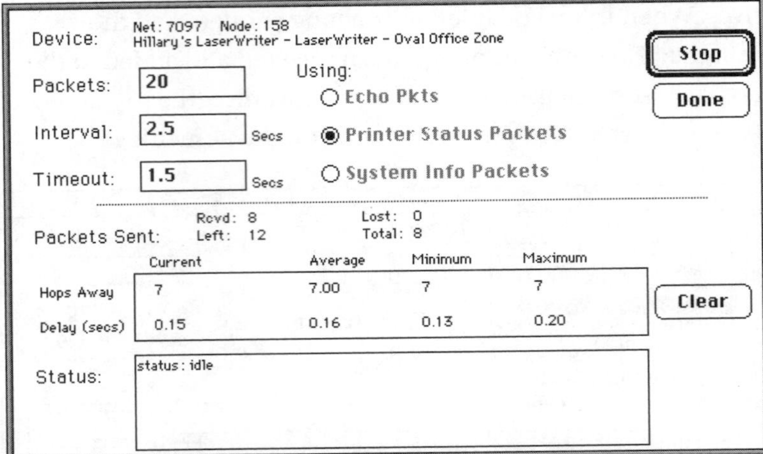

Figure 15.5
Inter•Poll can test how long it takes to send a packet to the printer and back.

Network Mapping Programs

Another very helpful diagnostic tool are programs that draw a map of your network by interrogating devices actually on the network. LANsurveyor from Neon Software, and NetAtlas from Farallon (see figure 15.6), are two Macintosh *network mapping* products. These programs can only create an accurate map if the information they receive from the network's routers is correct. If a mapping program is unable to draw a map of your network, or if it produces something very different than what you expected, you should determine the reason. This technique is often a useful diagnostic aid.

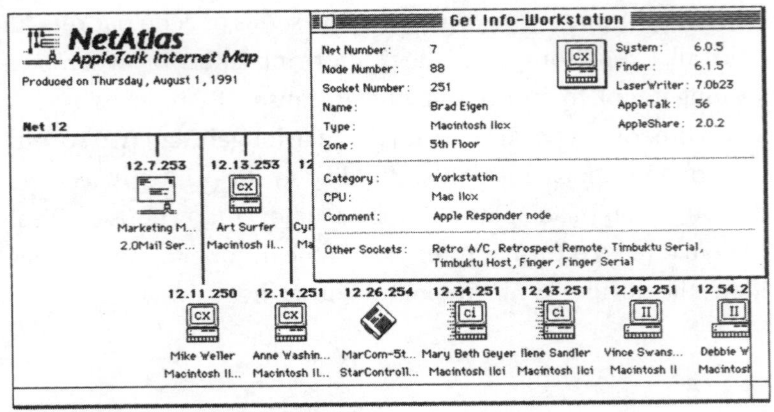

Figure 15.6
Farallon's NetAtlas creates a logical network map of AppleTalk networks.

Router Troubles

As we discussed in earlier chapters, routers play a very important role in the operation of the Chooser, and in network performance in general. As the number of routers on a network increases, so does the challenge in tracing and diagnosing network problems.

Remember that all routers must agree on the network number range and zones list configured on each router port. Every time a new router is added to an active network, there is a chance that it will conflict with the existing routers on the network. If this happens, a product which allows you to examine the active configuration of any router on the network, such as Neon Software's RouterCheck (see figure 15.8), can help you locate the source of the configuration conflict. RouterCheck can also notify you (either on screen or by text pager) whenever a trusted router experiences a network change, such as adding or dropping a routing table entry or zone.

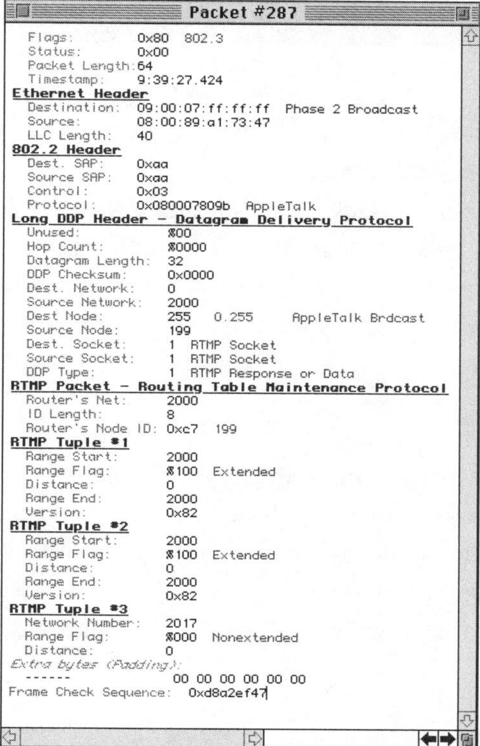

Figure 15.7
A router check using Neon Software's RouterCheck.

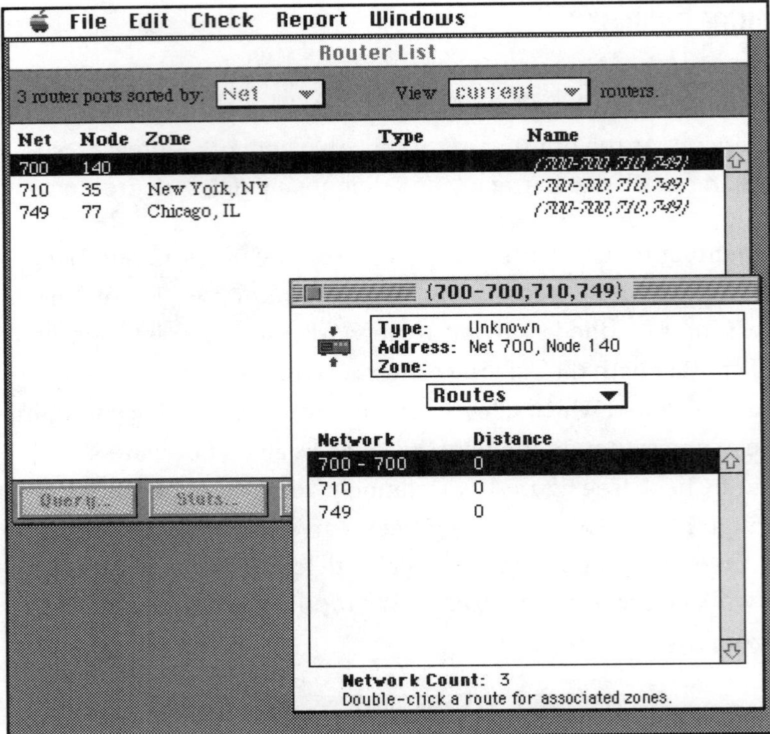

Figure 15.8 EtherPeek capture of a 3-entry RTMP packet. Note the redundant entries. This occurs with the Shiva FastPath routers and does not cause any problems.

Listen and Learn

The most informative network diagnostic tools, sometimes called *network analyzers* or *packet sniffers,* enable you to examine the packets, or frames, that actually appear on the network. Until recently, all network analyzers were very expensive, single-purpose hardware instruments, beyond the budget of the typical manager of a small- to medium-sized network.

Fortunately, there are now very good Macintosh-based network analyzers. These programs convert your ordinary Macintosh into a LocalTalk, Ethernet, or Token Ring network analyzer for a fraction of the cost of the dedicated instruments. NetMinder LocalTalk and NetMinder Ethernet are products of Neon Software; the AG Group's network analyzers are LocalPeek, EtherPeek, and

TokenPeek. As their names imply, these products are Cabling layer- or DataLink layer-specific, and (unlike most Macintosh programs) they aren't expected to work with every possible combination of Macs and networking cards. These programs are typically designed to work with selected high-performance network cards and adapters. Confirm that the hardware requirements of the product match the configuration of the system you intend to use.

A network analyzer is used to capture and examine the packets that are being sent over the network. This is the network equivalent of eavesdropping on someone else's conversation, and we all know how revealing that can be. And yes, these analyzers can be used to read unencrypted data and perhaps learn passwords and other confidential information. Many applications use simple encoding schemes to avoid sending clear-text messages across network links, specifically to make reading packet contents a bit more difficult. This is one area where Apple's Open Collaboration Environment will help. AOCE will provide a new encrypted transport protocol called Apple Secure Data Stream Protocol (ASDSP).

A common problem when adding a new router is that the new router refuses to start, reporting a conflicting network range or zones list. Assuming that you're sure you have configured the new router correctly, how can you determine the source of this conflicting information?

If the network range is in conflict, you can simply capture the Routing Table Maintenance Packets (RTMP), as shown above in figure 15.8, and examine them for conflicting information. Every router broadcasts an RTMP packet every 10 seconds, so it shouldn't take long to find the culprit's physical hardware and logical protocol addresses. You can then use information from Inter•Poll, or use the hardware address, to identify the errant device. Simply rebooting the router may clear the problem, or it may be necessary to reconfigure it.

Diagnosing Chooser Problems

Consider a small EtherTalk network that has several Macs and a LaserWriter. Let's look at what actually happens when you open the Chooser to select a LaserWriter.

You may recall from Chapter 8, "Macintosh Transport: AppleTalk," that the Chooser loads its AppleTalk Zones window by using the Zone Information Protocol (ZIP) to request a list of the reachable zones from a local AppleTalk router. When you click on the LaserWriter icon in the Chooser, it obtains the list of active printers in the selected zone by sending NBP Lookup messages to the selected zone. As NBP Response packets containing the names of currently active printers arrive, the printers' names will be added to the list of names displayed on the right side of the Chooser. Let's examine these Zone Information and Name Binding messages in detail to see exactly how they work.

Figure 15.9 shows a trace (captured by NetMinder Ethernet) of all the messages in and out of a Macintosh as the Chooser was opened and the LaserWriter icon was subsequently selected. This trace is quite small because a filter was used to ignore all the other traffic that was present on the network at the same time.

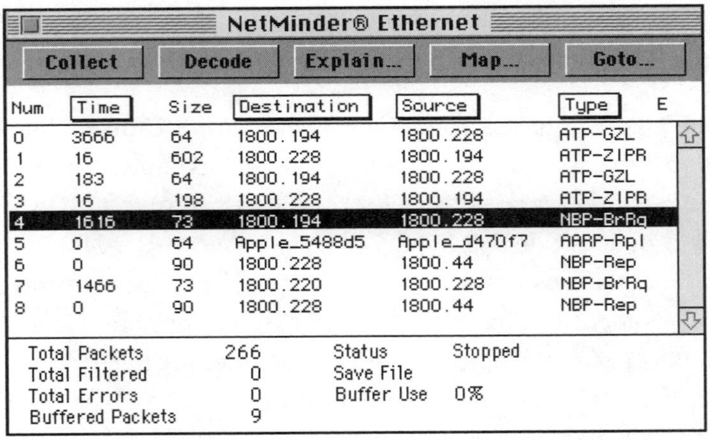

NetMinder® Ethernet

Collect | Decode | Explain... | Map... | Goto...

Num	Time	Size	Destination	Source	Type
0	3666	64	1800.194	1800.228	ATP-GZL
1	16	602	1800.228	1800.194	ATP-ZIPR
2	183	64	1800.194	1800.228	ATP-GZL
3	16	198	1800.228	1800.194	ATP-ZIPR
4	1616	73	1800.194	1800.228	NBP-BrRq
5	0	64	Apple_5488d5	Apple_d470f7	AARP-Rpl
6	0	90	1800.228	1800.44	NBP-Rep
7	1466	73	1800.220	1800.228	NBP-BrRq
8	0	90	1800.228	1800.44	NBP-Rep

Total Packets	266	Status	Stopped
Total Filtered	0	Save File	
Total Errors	0	Buffer Use	0%
Buffered Packets	9		

Figure 15.9
Chooser traffic as viewed by NetMinder.

NetMinder has formatted the headers of the captured packets so we can easily see the address of the node sending the request (source), the address the message was sent to (destination), and the type of packet see figures 15.10 through 15.13).

Packet 0 (figure 15.10) is a "GetZoneList" (GZL) request, sent from node 1800.228 (the Macintosh) to node 1800.194 (an EtherTalk router).

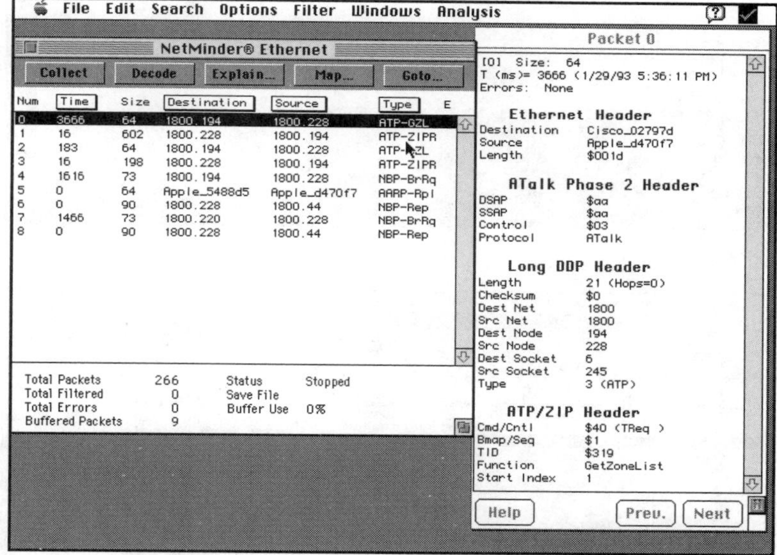

Figure 15.10
Packet 0.

Just 16 milliseconds later, the router sent Packet 1 (figure 15.11), a "ZoneInformationProtocolReply" (ZIPR), which contains the list of zones on this network.

In this case, the entire list could not fit into one reply message (the reply contained 43 zones), so the node sent a second request asking for the next portion of the zone list, starting at number 44; this was Packet 2 (figure 15.12).

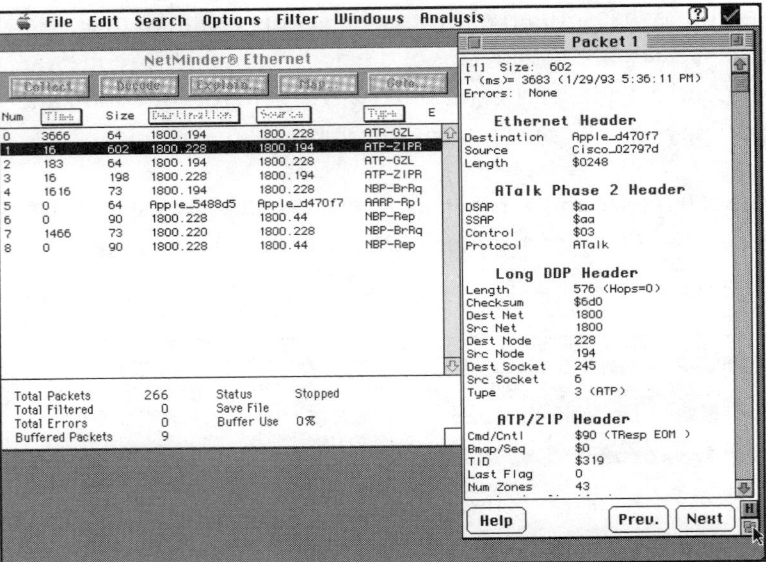

Figure 15.11
Packet 1.

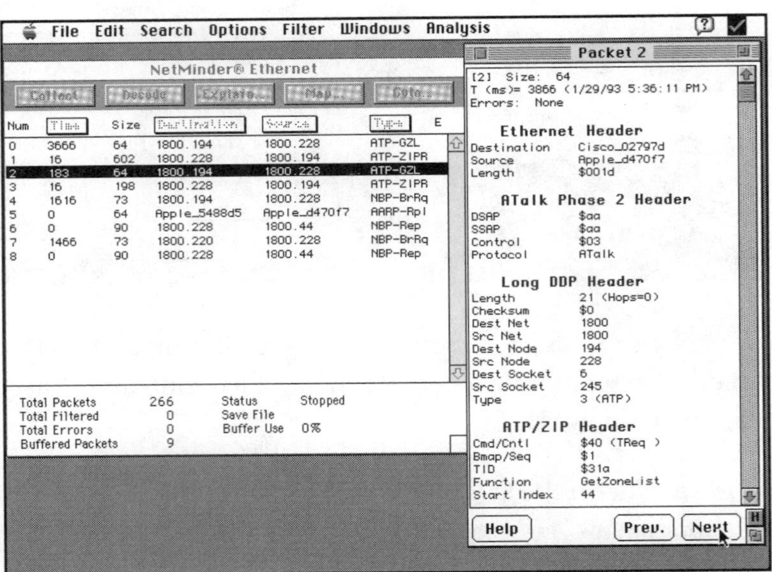

Figure 15.12
Packet 2.

The second reply from the router, Packet 3 (figure 15.13), contained 13 additional zones. At this point, the Chooser has enough information to display a complete zone list.

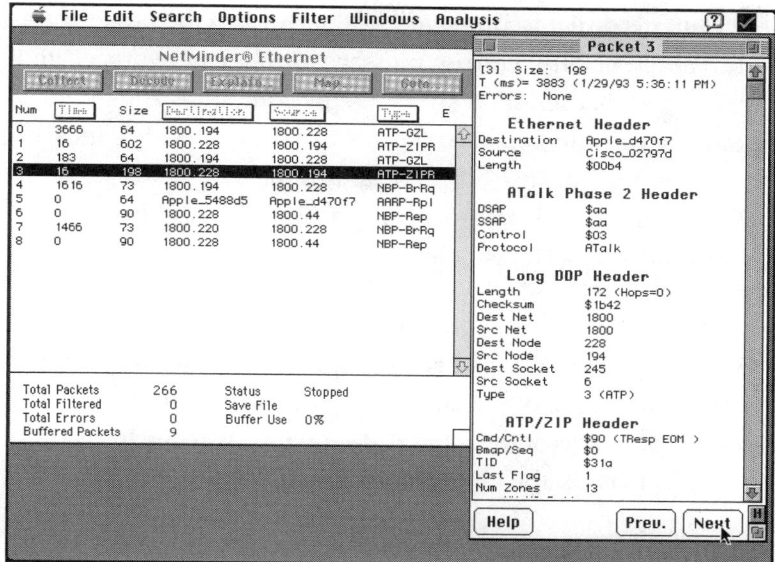

Figure 15.13

Packet 3.

A little more than a second later—1.616 seconds, to be exact—when the user clicked on the LaserWriter icon, an NBP-BrRq (NBP Request) was sent to the router. This was Packet 4 (figure 15.14).

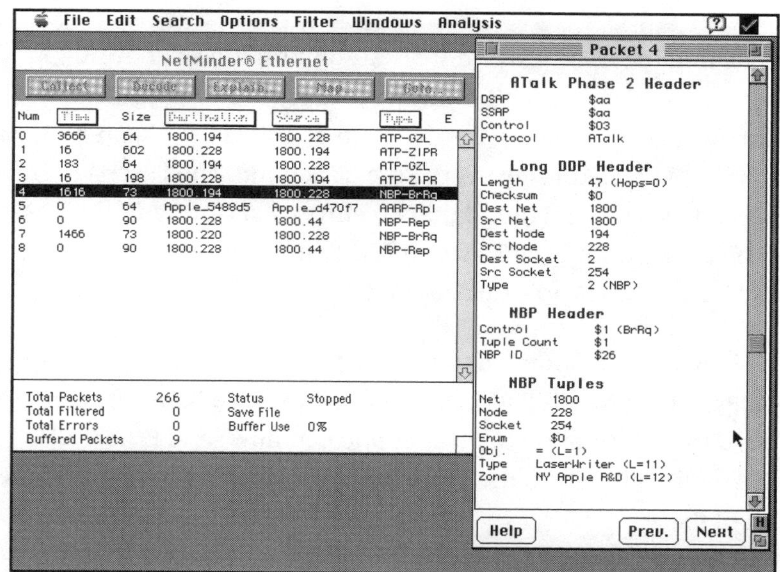

Figure 15.14

Packet 4.

If the router is directly connected to a network in the target zone, it will broadcast an NBP Lookup message onto the network; all active LaserWriters will then send an NBP reply containing their names back to the Macintosh. This trace doesn't show these broadcasts from the router, because for this example we have configured NetMinder Ethernet to capture only messages to and from the Macintosh running NetMinder.

If the routing table in the router contains entries for distant networks using the same zone name, it will forward the NBP Request to those other networks, where a local router will convert the request to a broadcast message and send it out on any local network which is in the target zone.

A LaserWriter on the local network (1800) has heard the router's broadcast, and will now send a reply to the Mac. In order to send an NBP reply directly to the Mac, rather than back through the router, the LaserWriter must learn the correct physical hardware (that is, Ethernet) address to use to send a packet to the Mac's logical protocol address (AppleTalk address 1800.228).

Recall that the AppleTalk Address Resolution Protocol (AARP) is used to associate a node's Ethernet address to its AppleTalk address. The information necessary to do this is kept in an Address Mapping Table (AMT) in every EtherTalk node. The LaserWriter checked its AMT and found that no entry exists for node 1800.228, so the LaserWriter broadcasts an AARP probe/request containing the Mac's logical AppleTalk address.

The Macintosh responded to the AARP request with the AARP reply (`AARP-Rpl`) shown in Packet 5 (figure 15.15). The LaserWriter added the information to its AMT and can now send EtherTalk NBP replies directly to the Macintosh. Packet 6 (figure 15.16) is the first of these.

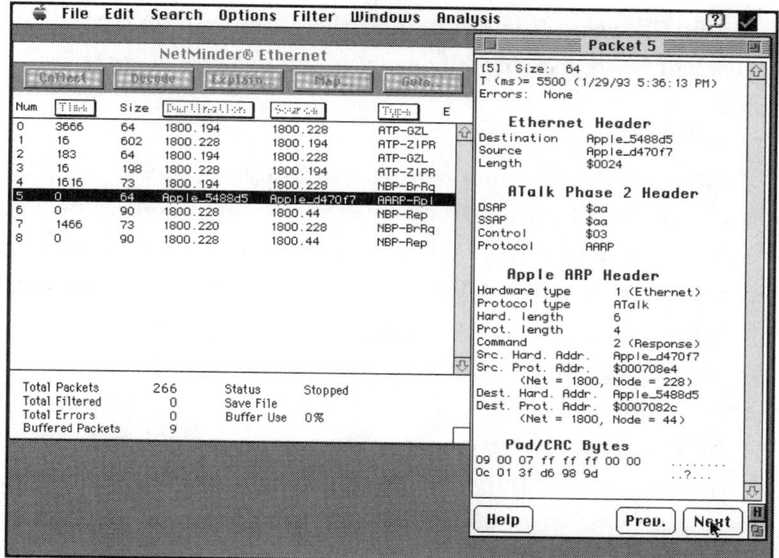

Figure 15.15

Packet 5.

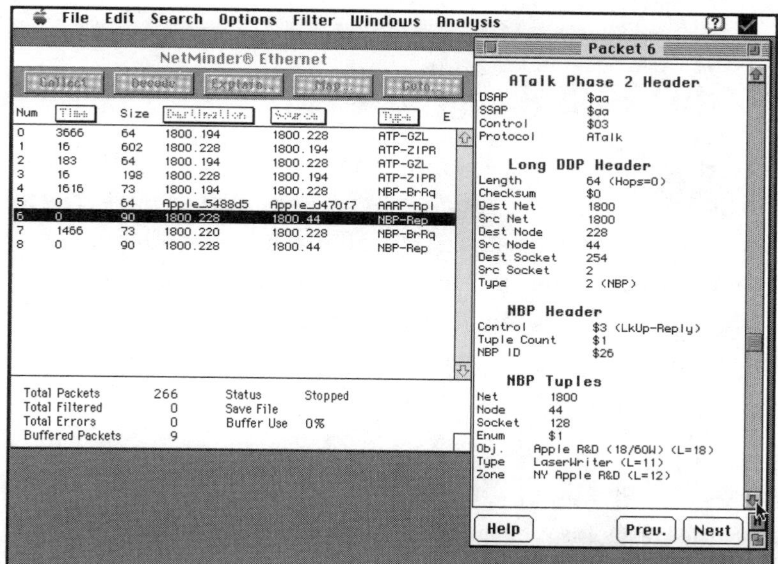

Figure 15.16

Packet 6.

The NBP request and reply packets will continue as long as the Chooser remains open on the Macintosh. Under System 7, the longer the Chooser remains open, the less frequent the NBP request will be sent, eventually dropping to just one every thirty seconds.

With a packet-level view of the network, and perhaps a trace of a normal example to compare against, you can often determine if a problem is caused by the Macintosh, a router that isn't doing what its supposed to, or a device which isn't responding as it should. If the printer doesn't send the NBP reply, then the printer is obviously the problem. If a router doesn't send a zone list when the Mac requests one, then the router is the problem. In cases where the problem conversation crosses networks or zones, it may be necessary to trace the messages at each end (or even on each network along the way) in order to get a complete picture of what is happening.

Performance

Network performance is a complex equation consisting of many variables. Some of these variables, such as bandwidth, are easy to quantify. Other variables, such as traffic, are more ambiguous. Networks are dynamic, unpredictable, complex systems. Optimizing their performance requires a basic understanding of the underlying theory, access to traffic monitoring tools, and the ability to interpret—and act upon—test results.

The Real Meaning of Bandwidth

Everyone wants his computer to operate as quickly as possible. As described in previous chapters, Ethernet is not faster than LocalTalk at the physical level. All signals travel at nearly the speed of light. But not all network interfaces send and receive signals at the same speed. How can both of these statements be true?

Ethernet hardware can create and detect a single electrical state change (corresponding to a binary digit) in 1/40th the time of LocalTalk. So an Ethernet can carry 40 times more information than LocalTalk in a given period of time. But a single Macintosh on Ethernet typically communicates only three or five times faster than on LocalTalk. Why this discrepancy? It's because the Macintosh cannot send and receive data at Ethernet's maximum rate. The most important performance benefit of Ethernet over LocalTalk is that, because each bit can be sent (and received) so quickly, the cable is much more likely to be idle at the moment your computer needs to use it, even with many more nodes on the network.

Traffic Jams

How can you tell if network traffic levels are affecting user performance? A relatively easy way is to use a network analyzer such as EtherPeek or NetMinder to trace the signals on the network. After collecting a sample of all the traffic on your network, these programs will tell you exactly how busy your network really was at that time.

Benchmarks

It's a good idea to do this occasionally when the network is operating normally, so as to obtain benchmarks of your normal network state.

Another technique is to install specialized devices that listen to the traffic on the network and count how many packets and bytes were sent from each node on the network, and to what destination. Dayna sells specialized pods that can be connected to a segment in order to monitor the traffic levels. The pod can be queried by a program called Network Vital Signs, which uses the data reported by the pods to provide information about the monitored network.

Any network which shows a high utilization is likely to force nodes to wait to send data often enough to affect performance. In many cases, network traffic may be high only a few times throughout the day. By learning as much as possible about these traffic peaks, you may be able to distribute or isolate these demands and avoid paying for expensive network upgrades.

Analysis of the trace may show that the majority of the traffic is caused by just a few nodes that talk to each other constantly. In this case, moving these top talkers to their own network may bring performance back to acceptable levels for everyone.

Another means to monitor network utilization by individual nodes is to have each device keep track of how much data they transfer and to report the information, upon request, to a central station that compiles information from many nodes to create an over-all picture of the network's utilization. SNMP management stations can poll SNMP managed nodes regularly throughout the day and compile this information into a time-line analysis of network utilization.

Traffic Cops

On LocalTalk, adding a router between the section with the top talkers and the rest of the network is the most common way to prevent the traffic between certain nodes from delaying traffic among the other nodes. As an alternative, traffic can be isolated by adding a LocalTalk switch or bridge, such as Tribe's LocalSwitch, that dynamically connects multiple LocalTalk segments only when the source and destination of a particular packet requires it. Tribe recently announced a new product called TribeStar. It has eight bridged LocalTalk ports and one Ethernet port.

On Ethernet and Token Ring networks, link-layer bridges can also be used to isolate traffic within limited portions of the network. Chapter 5, "Common Network Components," described how an

Ethernet bridge examines the source and destination of the physical hardware addresses on every packet it hears on each port and maintains a table of known addresses that have been heard on each port. When the bridge receives a packet on one port, it will resend it on the other port unless the destination address is known to be on the same port as the sender. In this case, the bridge does not transmit the packet on the other port, and the traffic level on the rest of the Ethernet is reduced.

Traffic levels across the entire Ethernet can be significantly reduced by moving top-talking pairs onto the same side of strategically placed bridges. Afterwards, the node's connectivity to the rest of the Ethernet will be unchanged. Whenever a packet's destination address is on the other side of the bridge, it will be sent. In effect, the bridge is an invisible gate that allows packets to pass through only on a need-to-go basis.

It is sometimes possible to achieve utilization of 200% to 300% of Ethernet's total bandwidth through the intelligent installation of Ethernet bridges (see figure 15.17).

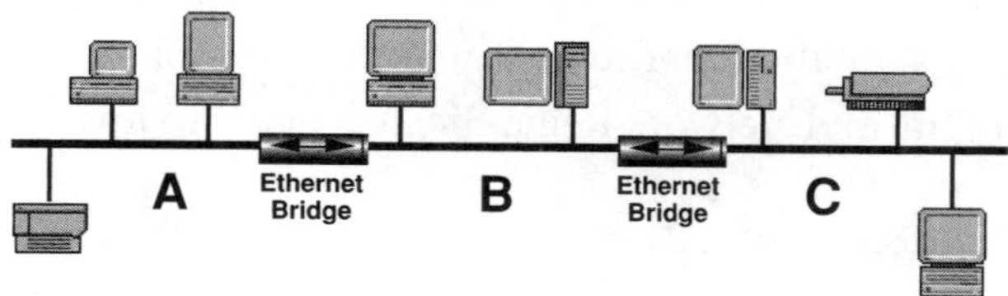

Figure 15.17

Ethernet bridges.

Consider the network diagram in figure 15.17. The three pairs of nodes, A, B, and C, each consume up to 40% of the Ethernet bandwidth communicating with each other, and up to 10% communicating with all the other nodes on the network. Without bridges, this Ethernet would experience peak demands of 150% of the available bandwidth. But, by adding two bridges in the appropriate places, no single section will ever see a demand higher that 60%.

In Token Ring environments, Source Routing Bridges (SRBs) provide a similar opportunity to isolate high volume conversations onto their own ring. Unlike Ethernet bridges, SRBs are not entirely invisible at the link level. Their presence requires some additional overhead because ring-to-ring routing information must be added to every packet. But SRBs are invisible at the AppleTalk protocol level, so they can provide some traffic isolation which is invisible to the user.

Another possible source of performance problems are the routers. As inter-network traffic grows, the routers will become unable to keep up with the demand. Most routers keep simple counters of how many packets are sent and received, and how many were ignored or discarded due to various errors.

Figure 15.18 shows a statistic screen from an Apple Internet Router, running on a Macintosh IIci. The counters indicate that this router is very lightly loaded, but the Recent Network Error Rate is extremely high; the Network Reliability is only 63.4%. Notice that the error counter Local Net Setup Conflicts is already 22 on the Ethernet port. This indicates that there is a router with a conflicting configuration on the Ethernet. Eliminating the conflict will reduce the Error Rate and Network Reliability will begin to improve.

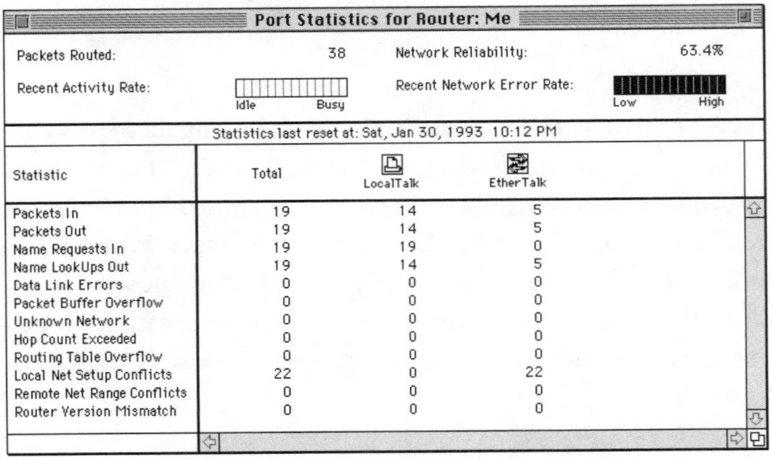

Port Statistics for Router: Me

Packets Routed: 38 Network Reliability: 63.4%

Recent Activity Rate: Idle Busy Recent Network Error Rate: Low High

Statistics last reset at: Sat, Jan 30, 1993 10:12 PM

Statistic	Total	LocalTalk	EtherTalk
Packets In	19	14	5
Packets Out	19	14	5
Name Requests In	19	19	0
Name LookUps Out	19	14	5
Data Link Errors	0	0	0
Packet Buffer Overflow	0	0	0
Unknown Network	0	0	0
Hop Count Exceeded	0	0	0
Routing Table Overflow	0	0	0
Local Net Setup Conflicts	22	0	22
Remote Net Range Conflicts	0	0	0
Router Version Mismatch	0	0	0

Figure 15.18

Router Errors.

One way to determine the source of these conflicts is to capture all the RTMP and ZIP packets on the segment for a few minutes. By examining the RTMPs sent by each router, the one sending a conflicting Network Range can be identified. By examining the Zone Information Protocol (ZIP) messages, a router sending a different zones list can be identified.

Security

On an AppleTalk network, security is primarily the responsibility of the individual devices. AppleTalk File Sharing and AppleTalk Remote Access use the “Users & Groups” file to manage access to a node. AppleShare servers have a more advanced version of the same scheme. At the other end of the spectrum, Apple Laser-Writers (PAP servers) don’t restrict network access at all.

Some network devices also support additional forms of security, restricting what network services can be seen by a particular node. AppleTalk Remote Access can be configured to grant access to “just this node” or the entire network. Some routers can be configured to hide or show any device, or entire class of devices (for example “Joe’s AppleShare” or “All LaserPrinters”) based on the identity of the node seeking the device. Routers from Compatible Systems do this by forwarding NBP messages to and from your node only if you’ve properly identified yourself to the router and if the router’s manager has granted permission for your node to communicate with the device (or device type) of interest.

A similar scheme is utilized by several non-Macintosh AppleTalk Remote Access products. One is AsyncServeR, a software ARA server for VAX/VMS, that supports individualized network access profiles for each dial-in connection account; another is the Shiva LanRover family of dedicated ARA servers.

A few high-end routers, such as those from Cisco, can be configured to perform true zone hiding. In this case, the router hides zones from all the other routers on the network. Over wide-area connections, this feature can be used to limit Chicago's view of Denver's network to a single zone, rather than the thirty-five zones that actually exist in Denver. Instituting a limited view of remote networks can be useful in controlling which devices at one site can communicate with devices in other sites. It can also be used in very large networks to simply reduce the number of zones in the Chooser to a more manageable number.

These schemes have one significant limitation. When a router provides the security, only connections that come through the router can be controlled. Access attempts originating within the local network remain uncontrolled and unrestricted.

A security feature of AOCE (Apple Open Collaboration Environment) will provide an AppleTalk network-wide access control mechanism. AOCE allows a network administrator to grant or deny access to a network device (or type) for an individual user, or group of users.

Conclusion

If you manage an AppleTalk network, there is no substitute for understanding AppleTalk, but there are quite a few tools that, when used together, can help reveal many of AppleTalk's secrets to you. This chapter has described only a small portion of them.

16

The Future of Macintosh Networking

One goal of this book was to give the reader a "gut-level" understanding of the theories, components, and implementation details involved with Macintosh networking. Hopefully, as new services, formats, transports, and cabling systems come along, you'll be better equipped to identify, classify, and evaluate their suitability for your networking environment.

Actually, it seems as if each *week* brings new networking technologies. While it's hard to predict the future, some trends in Macintosh networking are likely to continue.

One such trend is wireless networking. You should expect an explosion in this technology over the next few years. This growth should occur throughout all the various wireless technologies—cellular, radio waves, and infrared. These technologies should primarily affect the implementation of local-area networks and remote users.

Another area to watch in the near future is the continued enhancement of the AppleTalk protocol stack. It's been widely discussed by Apple, and in the press, that the AppleTalk Remote Access Protocol will be enhanced to work over the Point-to-Point Protocol (PPP). This will have the effect of lowering the cost and enhancing the performance of dial-up access. Other AppleTalk changes are likely to affect the routing aspects of the protocol. The newly released AURP routing protocol is likely to undergo continued updates; there's even talk that Apple will adopt more sophisticated routing algorithms such as the OSPF (Open Shortest Path First) protocol.

It's also likely that Apple will continue the enhancement of AppleTalk by making some of the traditional AppleTalk services, such as AFP and PAP, protocol-independent. Perhaps not too far in the distant future, you will be able to access these services over the TCP/IP protocol stack instead of the AppleTalk stack.

Even the Macintosh-compatible cabling systems are likely to evolve over the years. One obvious change is that Apple's inclusion of Ethernet is likely to extend further down the product line into the midrange, and perhaps even into the low-end systems as well. As Ethernet finds its way into the mainstream product lines, expect high-bandwidth replacements for Ethernet to appear. At the moment, it's somewhat unclear which of the new high-speed technologies—either FDDI/CDDI or 100 Mbps Ethernet—is likely to become the dominant LAN cabling system. In either case, the cost is likely to plunge as economies of scale are applied.

All in all, when it comes to networking, Apple's in an extremely strong position for the future. At every layer, Apple has continued to innovate. At the Service layer, Apple has pioneered dynamic service acquisition and continues to provide world-class services. The two most recent examples of this are Publish and Subscribe and AOCE. At the Format layer, Apple has acknowledged the importance of format transportability with the Clipboard, XTND, and EasyOpen. Apple's attention to the Transport layer is well known. From AppleTalk's dynamic addressing to MacTCP's integration, Apple consistently provides transport excellence. Even at the Cabling layer, Apple continues to provide innovation, with LocalTalk, Ethernet, and with various wireless technologies.

Glossary of Networking Terminology

n the following section, you might notice the icons beside many of the definitions. The icons are representations of the four layers of the NetPICT model:

 Services layer

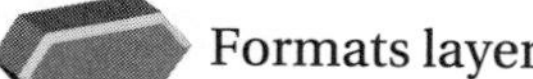 Formats layer

 Protocol layer

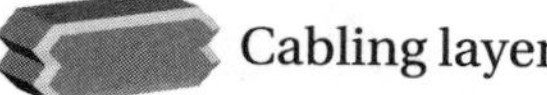 Cabling layer

Each icon indicates the layer of the NetPICT model to which the defined term belongs. Using these icons, you can easily determine where each term fits in the networking universe. If a term can be specifically placed within the seven-layer OSI Reference model, then its OSI layer is indicated within the definition.

10Base-2 An Ethernet implementation that uses a thin coaxial cable. 10Base-2, like other Ethernet implementations, has a bandwidth of 10 Mbps. The maximum cable segment length is 185 meters.

10Base-5 The original Ethernet medium, 10Base-5 uses a heavy shielded coaxial cable. The cable has an approximate diameter of 3/8". It has a bandwidth of 10 Mbps. The maximum segment length is 500 meters.

10Base-T An implementation of the Ethernet standard that runs over two pairs of unshielded twisted-pair wiring. Like the other Ethernet implementations, 10Base-T has a bandwidth of 10Mbps. The maximum segment length from the hub to the device is 100 meters.

802.3 An IEEE standard that defines the CSMA/CD (Carrier Sense Multiple Access/Collision Detection) method of network access. CSMA/CD is used by Ethernet networks.

802.5 An IEEE standard that defines the Token Ring network access method.

-A-

AARP See AppleTalk Address Resolution Protocol.

AAUI See Apple Attachment Unit Interface.

access privileges Controls placed upon network services that limit and control user access.

active star A network with a multiport repeater at the center. Each device connects to the repeater. Active stars do not perform network addressing—network packets seen on one branch of the star are seen on all branches.

address A sequence of bits used to identify devices on a network. Each network device must have a unique address. Addresses fall in two categories: physical hardware addresses (Ethernet), and logical protocol addresses (AppleTalk).

Address Mapping Table (AMT) A table that associates physical hardware addresses with corresponding logical protocol addresses. In the case of AppleTalk, the AMT is updated and maintained by the AppleTalk Address Resolution Protocol (AARP).

address resolution The association of physical hardware addresses (Ethernet) with logical protocol addresses (AppleTalk). See also Address Mapping Table.

Address Resolution Protocol (ARP) A TCP/IP protocol used to map logical IP addresses onto physical hardware addresses (Ethernet). Similar to Apple's AARP.

ADSP See AppleTalk Data Stream Protocol.

AEP See AppleTalk Echo Protocol.

AFP See AppleTalk Filing Protocol.

amplitude The magnitude of an electrical signal. Measured by subtracting the minimum voltage from the maximum voltage of an electrical signal.

AMT See Address Mapping Table.

analog A method of data transmission where (unlike digital transmissions) the data is continually modulated over an infinite voltage range.

Apple Attachment Unit Interface (AAUI) Apple's physical Ethernet interface. AAUI uses a special connector and uses an external transceiver, either thickwire, thinwire, or twisted pair, to connect to the network.

AppleShare file server A Macintosh product from Apple that runs the AppleTalk Filing Protocol (AFP).

AppleTalk Apple's networking software that provides reliable delivery of data between clients and servers. There are implementations of AppleTalk on many different computers.

AppleTalk address A three-part number that uniquely identifies a particular network, node, and socket on an AppleTalk network.

AppleTalk Address Resolution Protocol (AARP) Apple's protocol that maps the logical AppleTalk node addresses to the physical hardware addresses.

AppleTalk Data Stream Protocol (ADSP) A connection-oriented Session layer protocol that provides a reliable, bi-directional stream of data between two sockets in an AppleTalk network.

AppleTalk Echo Protocol (AEP) An AppleTalk Transport layer protocol that enables a node to send a special packet to another node and to receive an echoed response in return. Used to determine round-trip delivery times and reachability.

AppleTalk Filing Protocol (AFP) The AppleTalk Presentation layer protocol that defines shared file access. Platform-independent, AFP is the basis for Apple's AppleShare product.

AppleTalk for VMS An implementation of the AppleTalk network protocol suite that runs on a DEC VAX under the VMS operating system. It essentially turns a VAX into an AppleTalk node. Application services, such as the VAXshare file server, are seen as AppleTalk sockets.

AppleTalk Session Protocol (ASP) An AppleTalk Session layer protocol that provides for the creation of a network session. It also keeps the communications in the proper sequence.

AppleTalk Transaction Protocol (ATP) An AppleTalk Transport layer protocol that manages the give and take of a network transaction.

AppleTalk-LAT connection tool A CTB (Communications Tool Box) tool that is used in conjunction with the AppleTalk-LAT Gateway. It passes AppleTalk protocols to the gateway, where they are then converted into DEC's LAT protocol. Used to access LAT terminal services over LocalTalk or AppleTalk Remote Access sessions.

AppleTalk-LAT Gateway A software gateway that runs on a Macintosh and is used to translate AppleTalk protocols into LAT protocols. The AppleTalk-LAT Gateway is part of DEC's PATHWORKS for Macintosh product.

AppleTalk/DECnet Transport Gateway A software gateway that is included with AppleTalk for VMS. It provides Mac users with access to DECnet-based applications, such as E-mail and DECwindows.

Application layer The topmost layer of the ISO's OSI Reference Model; it corresponds to the Service layer of the NetPICT model. It defines the protocols and connections for applications. See OSI Reference Model.

ARCNET Originally developed by Datapoint Corporation, ARCNET (which stands for Attached Resource Computer NETwork) is a popular LAN in the IBM PC world. ARCNET uses a token-passing scheme and runs on coaxial or twisted-pair wiring. Several vendors make ARCNET cards for the Macintosh.

ARP See Address Resolution Protocol.

ASCII ASCII (which stands for American Standard Code for Information Interchange) is a commonly used coding scheme that uses 8 bits of data to encode alphanumeric characters and special control characters. In many ways, ASCII text files are a common denominator among many computers and programs.

ASP See AppleTalk Session Protocol.

Asynchronous communication (Also known as async communication.) A technique of data transmission that sends one character at a time without waiting for an acknowledgment.

ATP See AppleTalk Transaction Protocol.

attenuation The loss or diminution of an electrical signal that occurs during transmission.

AWG AWG (which stands for American Wire Gauge) is the US standard for specifying the diameter of a wire conductor.

-B-

backbone network A network topology where devices connect to a single cable. Thickwire Ethernet networks are commonly used as backbone networks.

bandwidth The total message-carrying capacity of a medium. Bandwidth is typically measured in bits per second. It is not an indication of speed.

baseband A kind of network transmission that uses the entire bandwidth of a medium to transmit a signal. Baseband communications are commonly used by most LAN cabling systems, such as LocalTalk, Ethernet, and Token Ring.

bits per second (bps) A unit that measures the message-carrying capacity of a medium. A kilobit per second (Kbps) is one thousand bits per second; a megabit per second (Mbps) is one million bits per second.

bps See bits per second.

bridge A network device used to connect two networks at the Data Link layer. Bridges are essentially unaware of the logical protocol address, although some bridges can block protocols by filtering their type codes.

broadband A kind of network transmission that splits the bandwidth of a medium to support multiple channels of communication. This technique is used by cable television.

broadcast transmission A network transmission that is sent to all network devices.

brouter A network device that routes the routable protocols and bridges the non-routable protocols. It essentially merges the functionality of bridges and routers.

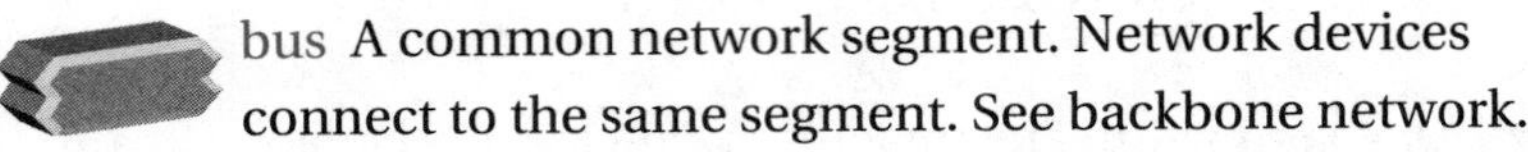

bus A common network segment. Network devices connect to the same segment. See backbone network.

bus topology A network scheme that uses a single cable to connect devices. Unlike ring topologies, the cable does not connect to itself. See backbone network.

-C-

Carrier Sense Multiple Access with Collision Avoidance (CSMA/CA) A cable access technique used by LocalTalk. Devices listen for the presence of a carrier before transmitting. Nodes try to avoid collisions by backing off for a random period of time whenever a message is not successfully transmitted. LocalTalk doesn't have the detection and recovery circuitry found in CSMA/CD networks.

Carrier Sense Multiple Access with Collision Detection (CSMA/CD) A cable access technique used by Ethernet that allows devices to gain access to a transmission medium by listening for the presence of a carrier. If no carrier is detected, the data is transmitted. Each node is capable of detecting collisions and retransmitting as required.

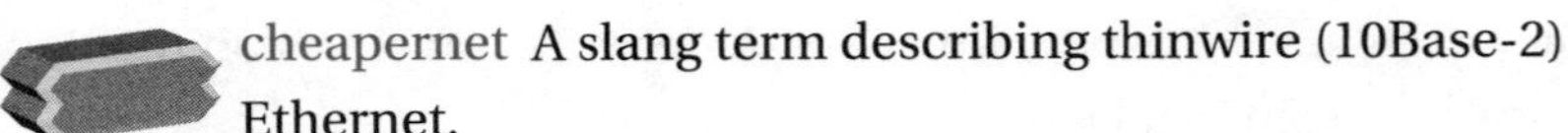

cheapernet A slang term describing thinwire (10Base-2) Ethernet.

Chooser The Macintosh desk accessory used to select AppleTalk (and other) services.

client A client is a process or entity that employs the services of other processes or entities known as servers. For example, a Macintosh uses AFP client software to access AFP servers.

client/server A term given to the interaction of software processes that function in a cooperative manner. Clients make requests of servers.

coax See coaxial cable.

coaxial cable A cable that contains two conductors, one inside the other. Coaxial cables, sometimes called coax, are used in thickwire and thinwire Ethernet and in IBM terminal connections.

collision The condition that results when two network devices transmit at nearly the same time. The transmissions collide, rendering the message unusable.

Control Panel A Macintosh utility that enables you to change various aspects of the Macintosh. The Network control panel is used to select from different network data links. This is where the cabling choice (such as EtherTalk, LocalTalk, TokenTalk, or FDDITalk) is made.

CSMA/CA See Carrier Sense Multiple Access with Collision Avoidance.

CSMA/CD See Carrier Sense Multiple Access with Collision Detection.

-D-

Data Link layer The second layer from the bottom of the OSI Reference Model. The Data Link layer corresponds to the top half of the Cabling layer of the NetPICT model. The Data Link layer defines the protocols that manage the creation of network frames, such as LLAP (LocalTalk Link Access Protocol). See OSI Reference Model.

datagram A packet of data, unique to a specific protocol. Datagrams are placed within network frames for delivery over the network. With AppleTalk, the Datagram Delivery Protocol (DDP) is used to encapsulate higher-level AppleTalk protocols within an addressable unit.

Datagram Delivery Protocol (DDP) The Network layer protocol that provides the ultimate addressing of AppleTalk datagrams (network, node, socket) over an AppleTalk network.

DECnet A suite of networking protocols developed by Digital Equipment Corporation for use on VAX/VMS, PDP-11, PCs, and other computers. Versions of DECnet are available for the Mac from Digital and Thursby Software Systems.

DECnet tunnel A technique used by AppleTalk for VMS and DECnet, which encapsulates AppleTalk datagrams within DECnet packets for delivery over a DECnet link.

default zone The AppleTalk zone that a device belongs to by default when it's placed on an extended (Phase 2) network. The default zone of a Mac can be changed by double-clicking on the current network icon in the Network Control Panel.

dynamic node addressing A technique Apple uses whereby AppleTalk nodes automatically pick unique network addresses. This is in direct contrast to other protocols, such as DECnet, that maintain a listing of node addresses for each node.

-E-

EBCDIC EBCDIC (which stands for Extended Binary Coded Decimal Interchange Code) is a coding system that uses 8 bits of data to represent alphanumeric characters and control sequences. Used by IBM mainframes.

ELAP See EtherTalk Link Access Protocol.

emulation See terminal emulation.

entity type The part of an NVE (Network Visible Entity) that identifies the generic class to which the entity belongs. Examples include "AFPServer" or "LaserWriter." The entity type is assigned by Apple Computer, who maintains a registry.

Ethernet A LAN cabling system originally developed by Xerox, Intel, and Digital. Ethernet has a bandwidth of 10Mbps and uses the CSMA/CD access method. Ethernet supports many different networking protocols, including AppleTalk.

EtherTalk Apple's implementation of AppleTalk protocols on Ethernet. EtherTalk places the DDP datagrams into Ethernet frames.

EtherTalk Line Access Protocol (ELAP) The specific data link protocol used by EtherTalk.

-F-G-

FDDI FDDI (which stands for Fiber Distributed Data Interface) is a 100 Mbps LAN technology that uses a token-passing access method. FDDI uses dual fiber-optic rings. There are several FDDI cards available for the Macintosh. A variation of FDDI that uses copper wiring, called CDDI, is currently under development.

file server Software that provides network users with shared, controlled access to files. In the Macintosh environment, the standard for file service is the AFP file server.

File Transfer Protocol (FTP) A Service layer protocol common in the TCP/IP world. It is used to copy files between network devices.

frame A data link structure for conveying information over a transmission medium.

frequency The number of times in a unit of time (usually a second) that a signal cycles between minimum and maximum voltage.

FTP See File Transfer Protocol.

gateway A device (or software process) that translates entire protocol stacks.

-H-

half-router A pair of routers connected with a communication link. This tandem acts as a single routing device. AppleTalk half-routers require unique network numbers on each side.

hardware address The unique physical address determined at the Physical and Data Link layers. For example, each Ethernet card has a unique hardware address that's stored within the card.

hop A unit of distance that measures the passage of a datagram through a router. The distance between networks is often measured by the number of hops.

hop count The number of routers that a datagram travels through on the way to its destination. AppleTalk permits a maximum of 15 hops, although hop count adjustment can be used to provide routing flexibility.

-I-

International Standards Organization (ISO) An international standards-making body responsible for numerous standards, including film speed and the OSI Reference Model.

internet The term applied to multiple AppleTalk networks that are connected by AppleTalk routers. Also called an internetwork.

internet router (IR) A device that connects AppleTalk networks by using network numbering to pass, or deny passage of a datagram.

Internet Protocol (IP) The Network layer protocol of the TCP/IP protocol suite. Analogous to Apple's DDP.

Internetwork Packet Exchange (IPX) A Network layer protocol used by Novell NetWare that provides addressing, routing, and switching packets.

IP See Internet Protocol.

IPX See Internetwork Packet Exchange.

IR See internet router.

ISDN ISDN (which stands for Integrated Services Digital Network) is a digital communications standard that integrates voice and data. ISDN services are just beginning to become common in the US. It offers the promise of affordable high-speed WAN communications.

ISO See International Standards Organization.

-K-L-

Kbps Kilobits per second. See bits per second.

LAN See Local Area Network.

LAP See Link Access Protocol.

LLAP See LocalTalk Link Access Protocol.

Local Area Network (LAN) A network in one area, such as a building or a group of buildings.

Local Area Transport (LAT) DEC's proprietary, licensed Ethernet protocol, used to connect terminal devices to host computers. Macs can speak the LAT protocol directly with the LAT Communications Tool. At the present time, LAT's use is limited to terminal emulators and terminal front-ends.

LocalTalk Apple's low-cost LAN network that runs over twisted-pair wiring. LocalTalk has a bandwidth of 230,400 bps (230.4 Kbps).

LocalTalk Link Access Protocol (LLAP) The Data Link level protocol that manages the delivery of data on a LocalTalk network.

-M-

Management Information Base (MIB) A database used by SNMP for maintaining the status and control for a network device. Each network device has its own specific MIB. Data within the MIB is used by an SNMP agent as part of a network management application. AppleTalk MIBs have been recently defined by Apple and are currently being implemented by most AppleTalk networking vendors.

Mbps Megabits per second. See bits per second.

MIB See Management Information Base.

modem A device that converts digital data from a computer into analog data, which can then be transmitted over a telephone line. This process is called modulation. It also performs the opposite process, demodulation, to convert incoming analog signals into digital data that the computer can understand.

multicasting Multicasting is similar to broadcasting, but it provides a protocol-specific method of identifying network devices. Each protocol, such as AppleTalk, has its own multicast address.

-N-

Name Binding Protocol (NBP) The AppleTalk Transport level protocol that maps the NVE onto the corresponding AppleTalk address. NBP provides AppleTalk with a way to dynamically find named services on the network.

NBP See Name Binding Protocol.

Network File System (NFS) A Presentation layer protocol developed by Sun Microsystems to provide TCP/IP networks with file services. NFS is similar in scope to Apple's AFP.

Network interface controller (NIC) A networking card, such as an Ethernet, Token Ring or FDDI, for a computer.

Network layer The layer of the OSI Reference Model that controls network addressing. The Network layer corresponds to the bottom third of the Protocol layer of the NetPICT model. With AppleTalk, the Network layer is defined by DDP. IP is the Network layer for TCP/IP networks.

network number A 16-bit number used to identify the AppleTalk network to which a node is assigned. Nodes choose their network number from an AppleTalk router; when no router is present they choose a number from a pre-defined range known as the startup range.

network number range A range of network numbers that have been established within the routers for use on Phase 2 extended network segments. Non-extended networks, such as LocalTalk, are restricted to single network numbers.

Network-Visible Entity (NVE) An AppleTalk concept that names devices by their name, generic type, and zone. Examples include “My Mac:Macintosh Quadra 950@BlueZone” and “Joe’s Printer:LaserWriter@NYC Zone.”

NFS See Network File System.

node An addressable entity on a network, such as a Mac or a LaserWriter.

node identifier (node ID) An 8-bit number that uniquely identifies each node on a single AppleTalk network number.

non-extended network An AppleTalk network that supports addressing of up to 254 nodes and supports only one zone. A LocalTalk network is an example of a non-extended network.

NVE See Network-Visible Entity.

-O-P-

OSI Reference Model A model put forward by the International Standards Organization (ISO) that provides a standard point of reference for networking protocols. It uses seven layers to break down the network process into independent processes. (OSI stands for Open Systems Interconnection).

packet An organized sequence of binary data that includes data and control structures.

PAP See Printer Access Protocol.

passive star A network topology where every branch is connected to a common point. Unlike active stars, passive stars have no repeater at the center to actively retransmit signals.

peer A network device that is treated as the communicative equal to another device on the network. Networks that let devices communicate with each other as equals are sometimes referred to as peer-to-peer networks.

Physical layer The level at which the actual delivery medium is realized. For example, the three different kinds of Ethernet and two different kinds of Token Ring cable are defined in this layer. The Physical layer of the OSI reference model corresponds to the bottom half of the Cabling layer of the NetPICT model.

Point-to-Point Protocol (PPP) A protocol that supplants the Serial Line Internet Protocol (SLIP). It provides remote access to IP networks via asynchronous and synchronous links. It is similar to Apple's Remote Access Protocol. There is some discussion that PPP might be adapted to provide remote AppleTalk protocol access.

port The connection between a router and a network. Routers can have multiple ports.

PPP See Point-to-Point Protocol.

Presentation layer The layer of the OSI Reference Model that establishes data formats and requisite conversions. The Presentation layer corresponds to the Format layer of the NetPICT model.

print spooler A service that queues print jobs and manages the submission of these jobs to the printer. This relieves the client workstation from this task.

Printer Access Protocol (PAP) The AppleTalk protocol that controls the communication between clients (Macs) and print servers (LaserWriters).

protocol A set of rules for information exchange over a communication medium. The set of protocols used by a particular networking protocol, such as AppleTalk, is called a family or suite of protocols.

protocol stack (or suite) An implementation of a specific networking protocol consisting of multiple individual protocols.

punchdown block A wiring device used in telephone and network installations for interconnecting many wires. Most phone-type punchdown blocks have fifty rows of four contacts each. The contacts accept the wires, which are "punched down," to make electrical contact. A tool, called a punchdown tool, is used to push the wire onto the contact.

-R-

repeater A network device that repeats the signals on a network. Repeaters operate at the Physical layer of the OSI Reference Model. Repeaters amplify weak signals from one segment and repeat them on another segment.

ring topology A network organization in which all the nodes are connected in a ring. Data passes around the ring from node to node. Each node retransmits the messages to the next node in the ring.

RIP See Routing Information Protocol.

router A network device that connects networks by maintaining logical protocol information for each network.

Routing Information Protocol (RIP) A protocol used to update routing tables on TCP/IP networks. Similar to Apple's RTMP.

routing table A table, maintained by an AppleTalk router, that maps the AppleTalk internet by specifying the path and distance (in hops) between itself and the networks. Routers use these tables to determine whether or not a datagram should be forwarded.

Routing Table Maintenance Protocol (RTMP) An AppleTalk protocol used by the routers to establish and maintain the routing tables used by the AppleTalk routers on the network. RTMP packets are sent at regular intervals by the routers. RTMP was recently supplanted by AURP, which only sends routing information when network changes make it necessary.

RTMP See Routing Table Maintenance Protocol.

-S-

SDLC See Synchronous Data Link Control.

seed router An AppleTalk router that contains the network numbers and zone information that is used by non-seed AppleTalk routers on the network.

segment A length of network cable. A segment can be connected to the port of a repeater, bridge, router, or gateway.

Sequenced Packet Exchange (SPX) The Transport layer protocol used by Novell NetWare. Provides a connection-oriented, guaranteed delivery link between Novell NetWare nodes.

server A network device or process that provides a service to networked clients. In the AppleTalk environment, examples of servers include AppleShare file servers and LaserWriter print servers.

session A logical connection between two network devices. In an AppleTalk network, the AppleTalk Session Protocol (ASP) is used to establish, maintain, and discontinue sessions.

Session layer The layer of the OSI Reference Model that establishes a logical connection between network devices. The Session layer corresponds to the upper third of the Protocol layer of the NetPICT model.

Serial Line Internet Protocol (SLIP) A TCP/IP-based protocol used to run IP over serial lines such as dial-up phone lines. Similar to Apple's Remote Access Protocol.

shielded cable A cable that is surrounded by a grounded metallic material. It minimizes disruption of the signal by external electrical noise and prevents the cable from emitting unwanted electrical signals.

Simple Network Management Protocol (SNMP) A management protocol used to maintain and query network entities. SNMP uses agents on managed nodes to maintain a database known as a MIB (Management Information Base). The data stored within the MIB can be transmitted to the management software upon request.

Single Mail Transfer Protocol (SMTP) An electronic mail service common on TCP/IP networks.

SLIP See Serial Line Internet Protocol.

SMDS See Switched Multimegabit Data Service.

SMTP See Single Mail Transfer Protocol.

SNA See Systems Network Architecture.

SNMP See Simple Network Management Protocol.

socket An addressable entity within an AppleTalk node. Sockets can be thought of as network processes.

socket number An 8-bit number that uniquely identifies a socket. With AppleTalk, there are 256 sockets. 0 and 255 aren't used, leaving 254 available for use. Numbers 1-127 are reserved by Apple; 128-254 are available for use by applications.

split-horizon routing A technique for maintaining routing tables that was introduced with AppleTalk Phase 2. Routing information is only forwarded to those routers that can use the information.

SPX See Sequenced Packet Exchange.

SQL See Structured Query Language.

star topology A centralized network with a hub, concentrator, or repeater at the center of the network.

Structured Query Language (SQL) A language, standardized by ANSI, used to manipulate relational databases. Apple's Data Access Language (DAL) uses a variation of SQL to access relational data through DAL servers.

Switched Multimegabit Data Service (SMDS) A relatively new high-speed WAN networking technology offered by telephone companies and service providers.

Synchronous Data Link Control (SDLC) A Data Link Layer protocol used by IBM's SNA networks.

Systems Network Architecture (SNA) A suite of communications protocols developed by IBM. Analogous to the AppleTalk protocol suite.

-T-

TCP/IP TCP/IP (which stands for Transmission Control Protocol/Internet Protocol) is a set of networking protocols commonly found on, but not limited to, UNIX computers.

TELNET A Service layer protocol common to TCP/IP networks that provides terminal services.

terminal emulation A program, usually on a personal computer, that masquerades as a computer terminal. The most common terminals that are emulated are the VT series established by DEC and the 3270 series from IBM.

terminator A resistive device attached to the ends of a cable to minimize unwanted signal reflections from the cable segment.

thickwire A type of Ethernet cabling, also known as 10Base-5, that uses a thick (approximately 3/8") coaxial cable. Primarily used as a backbone to which thinwire or twisted-pair hubs are connected.

thinwire A type of Ethernet cabling, also known as 10Base-2, that uses coaxial cable and BNC connectors.

TLAP See TokenTalk Link Access Protocol.

Token Ring A cabling system, common in the IBM world, that connects network devices in a ring topology. It uses the method of token passing to enable nodes to access the network.

TokenTalk Apple's product that puts the AppleTalk protocols onto a Token Ring network.

TokenTalk Link Access Protocol (TLAP) The data link access protocol used in a TokenTalk network. TLAP puts AppleTalk protocols onto a Token Ring network.

topology The physical connective structure of a network. Common topologies include bus, ring, and star.

transceiver An interface between a node and the network. Transceivers transmit and receive network messages.

Transport layer The layer of the OSI reference model that ensures that the message is correctly transmitted. If one portion of the communication transmission is lost or garbled, it's the job of the Transport layer to retransmit the necessary portion. The Transport layer of the OSI model corresponds to the middle third of the Protocol layer in the NetPICT model.

tunneling A process that enables one protocol's datagram to be encapsulated within another protocol's datagram.

twisted-pair Wiring that consists of two insulated copper multi-stranded conductors twisted around each other to reduce electrical interference. Twisted-pair wiring can be used by phone-type LocalTalk connectors, Ethernet, ARCNET, and other cabling systems.

VAX A line of computers manufactured by Digital Equipment Corporation (DEC). VAX stands for Virtual Address eXtension.

VAXshare Part of DEC's PATHWORKS for Macintosh software that enables a VAX to act as an AFP file server and PAP print spooler.

Vines Banyan's network operating system. "Vines" is an acronym for VIrtual NEtwork Software.

VMS An operating system used by Digital Equipment Corporation for its line of VAX computers. VMS stands for Virtual Memory System.

volume A disk that appears on the Mac desktop. A volume could be a hard disk, floppy disk, or a network file server disk.

-W-Z-

Wide Area Network (WAN) A network that spans distances beyond the range served by LANs. WAN distances are usually measured in miles instead of feet.

ZIP See Zone Information Protocol.

ZIT See Zone Information Table.

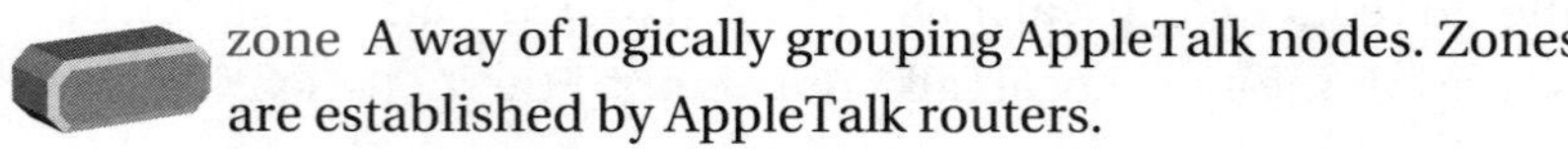

zone A way of logically grouping AppleTalk nodes. Zones are established by AppleTalk routers.

Zone Information Protocol (ZIP) The AppleTalk Session layer protocol that maintains the mapping of AppleTalk network numbers to zone names. ZIP is used by the Chooser to obtain a list of zone names.

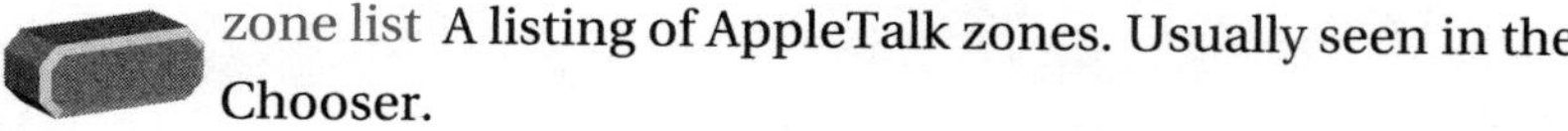

Zone Information Table (ZIT) A listing of zones maintained by AppleTalk routers that relates zone names to the ports of a router.

zone list A listing of AppleTalk zones. Usually seen in the Chooser.

zone name A name assigned to an AppleTalk network zone. Can be 32 characters long and is case-insensitive.

NetPICT Encyclopedia

This appendix contains a sampling of key NetPICT diagrams that have been used throughout the book. These diagrams are also included on the disk that comes with this book.

AppleShare Server

AFP Server

Formats

AppleTalk

Ethernet

AFP Server (Ethernet)

An AFP server on an Ethernet network, such as a Macintosh running AppleShare or a VAX running VAXshare.

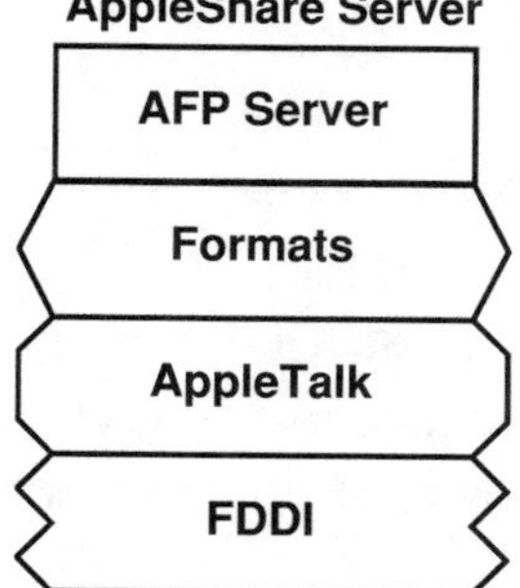

AFP Server (FDDI)

An AFP server on a FDDI network. An example of such a device is a Macintosh running AppleShare with a FDDI card and the FDDITalk protocols.

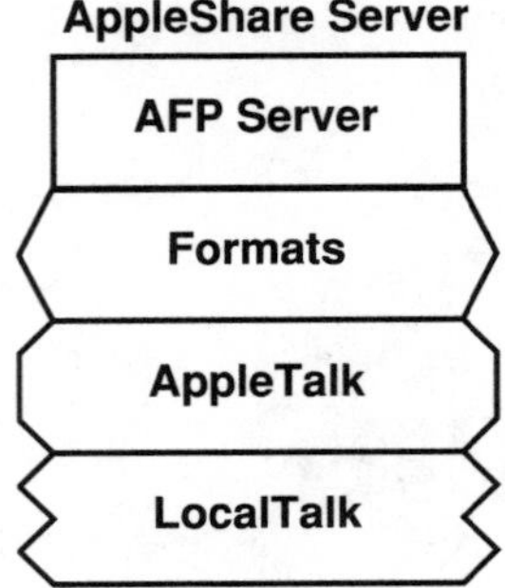

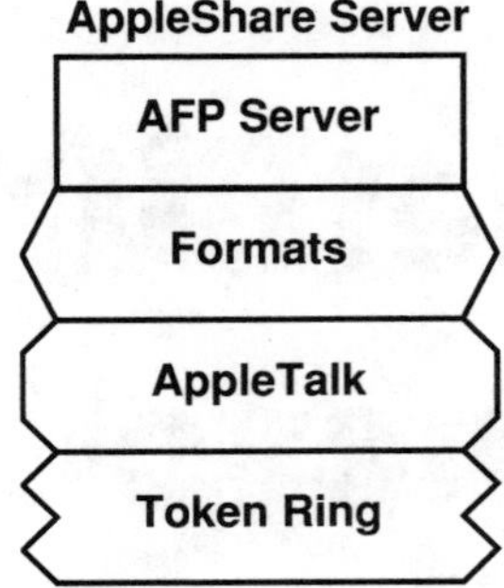

AFP Server (LocalTalk)

An AFP server on a LocalTalk network, such as a Macintosh running AppleShare.

AFP Server (Token Ring)

An AFP server on a Token Ring network. An example would be a Macintosh running AppleShare with a Token Ring card and the TokenTalk protocols.

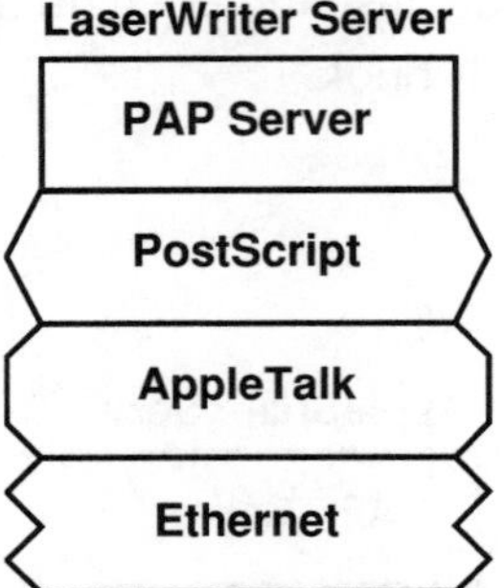

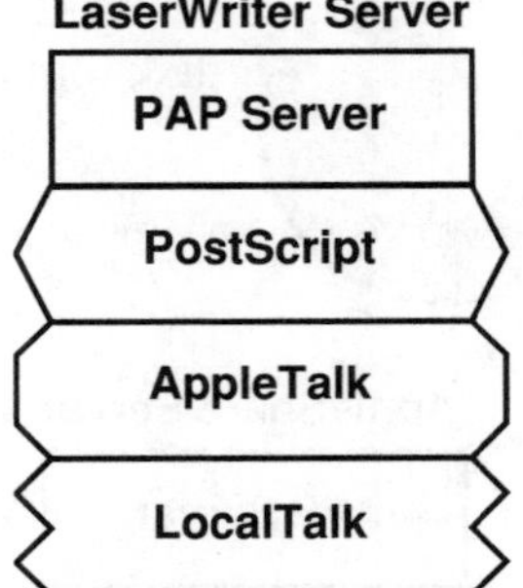

Apple LaserWriter (Ethernet)

Some laser printers come equipped with Ethernet interfaces. Examples include Apple's LaserWriter IIg and LaserWriter Pro 630.

Apple LaserWriter (LocalTalk)

Some Apple laser printers come equipped with LocalTalk interfaces. Examples include Apple's original LaserWriter and the LaserWriter IINT.

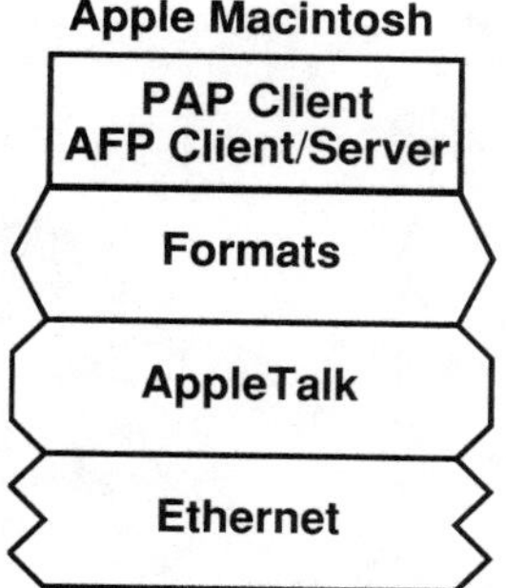

Apple Macintosh (Ethernet)

Some Apple Macintosh computers come equipped with Ethernet interfaces as standard equipment (such as the Quadra 950); add-on Ethernet cards can be purchased for Macs without built-in Ethernet.

Apple Macintosh
PAP Client
AFP Client/Server
Formats
AppleTalk
FDDI

Apple Macintosh (FDDI)

An Apple Macintosh with a third-party FDDI NuBus card installed, along with the FDDITalk protocols.

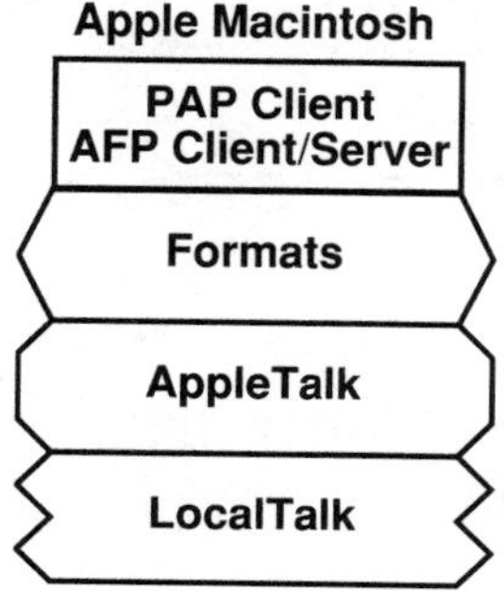

Apple Macintosh (LocalTalk)

All Apple Macintosh computers come equipped with LocalTalk as standard equipment.

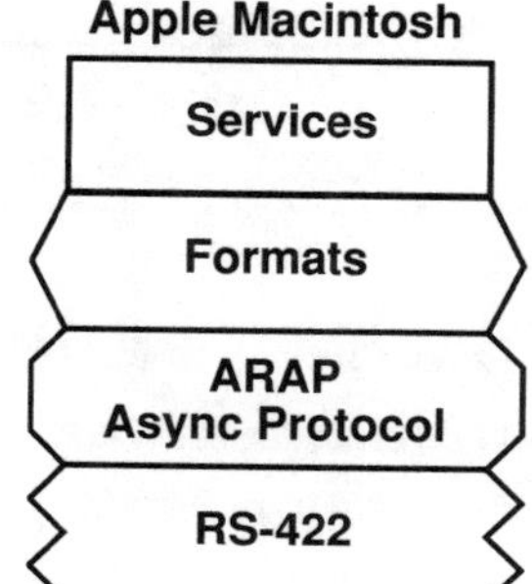

Apple Macintosh (RS-422)

Any Apple Macintosh can use either of its two serial ports (RS-422) for asynchronous services, such as ARAP.

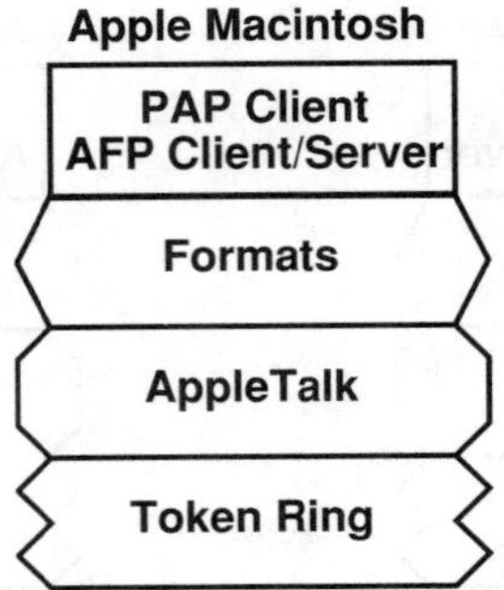

Apple Macintosh (Token Ring)

An Apple Macintosh with a Token Ring NuBus card installed, along with the TokenTalk protocols.

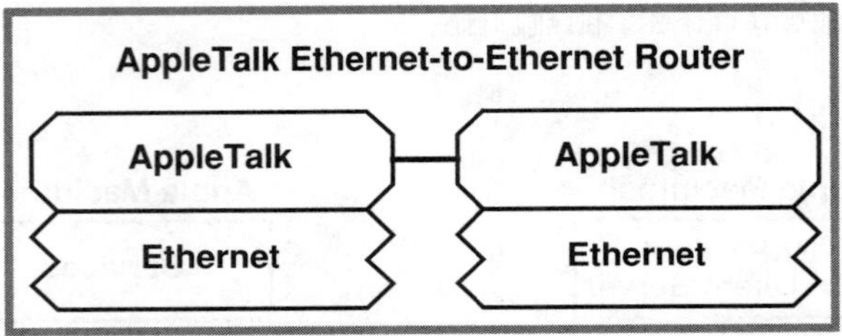

AppleTalk Ethernet-to-Ethernet Router

An AppleTalk router that connects two Ethernet networks together. Examples include Apple's Internet Router (equipped with two Ethernet cards), or even a VAX running AppleTalk for VMS over two Ethernet controllers.

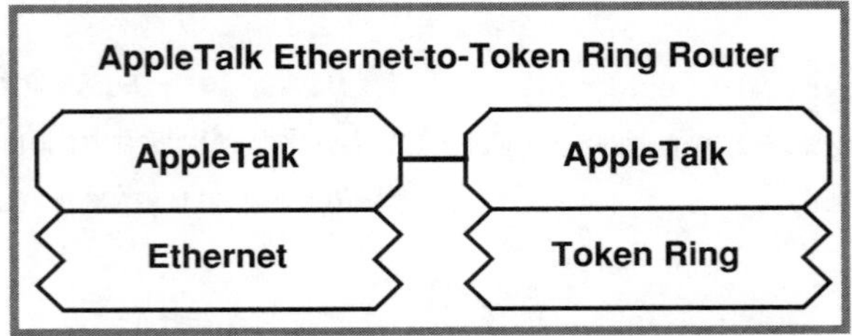

AppleTalk Ethernet-to-Token Ring Router

An AppleTalk router that connects an Ethernet network and a Token Ring network. The best example of such a device is Apple's Internet Router (equipped with an Ethernet card and a Token Ring card).

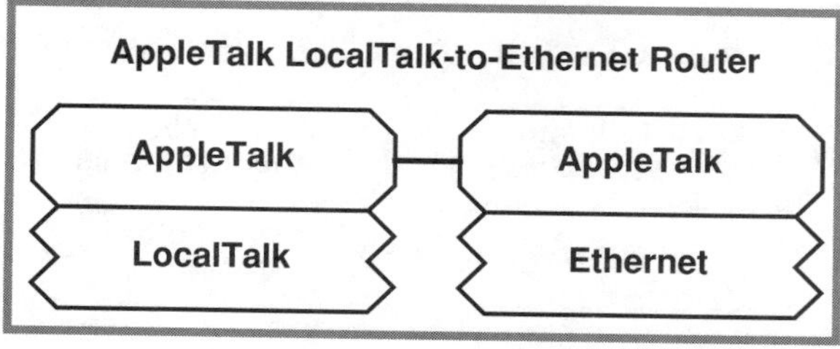

AppleTalk LocalTalk-to-Ethernet Router

An AppleTalk router that connects a LocalTalk network and an Ethernet network. Examples include Apple's Internet Router (using a LocalTalk connector and an Ethernet card) and dedicated routers such as Shiva's FastPath 5.

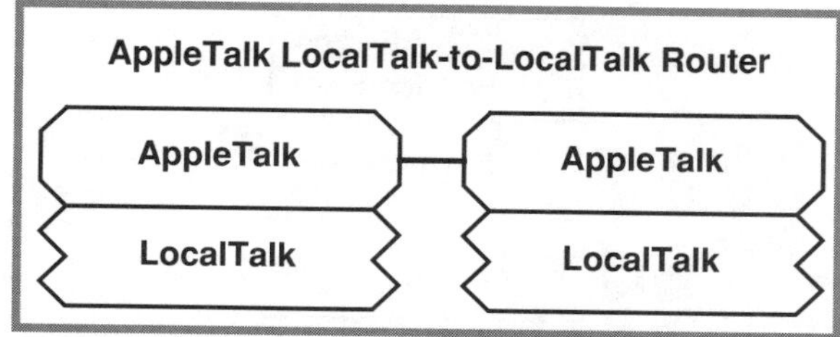

AppleTalk LocalTalk-to-LocalTalk Router

An AppleTalk router that connects two LocalTalk networks. The best example is Apple's Internet Router (using both the printer and modem ports for LocalTalk connections).

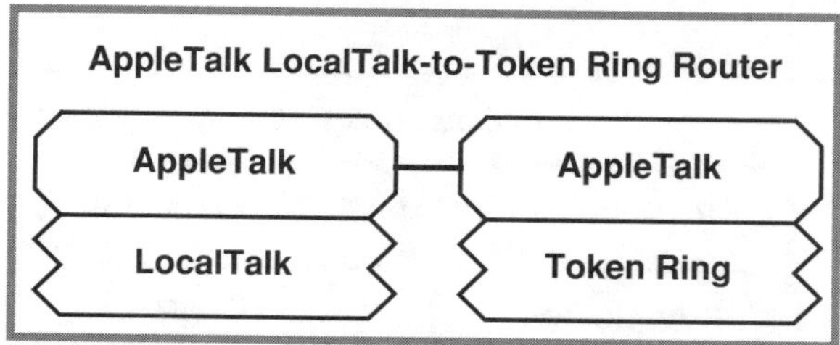

AppleTalk LocalTalk-to-Token Ring Router

This diagram represents an AppleTalk router that connects a LocalTalk network and a Token Ring network. The best example of such a device is Apple's Internet Router (equipped with a LocalTalk connector and a Token Ring card).

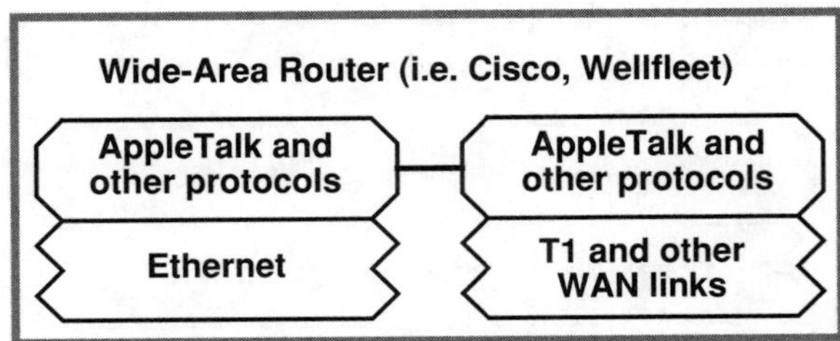

AppleTalk multiprotocol WAN router

An AppleTalk (multiprotocol) router that connects an Ethernet network to a WAN connection (such as a T1 link). Examples include multiprotocol routers from Cisco, Wellfleet, and IBM.

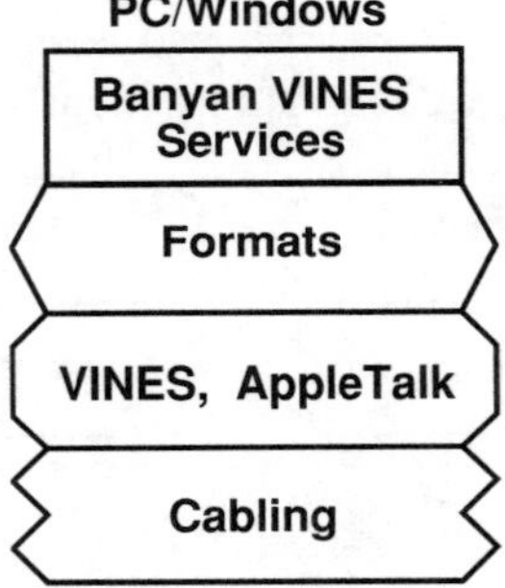

Banyan VINES server

A Banyan VINES server running on a PC host. Notice that in addition to the VINES protocol, the AppleTalk protocol is also installed on the host. This system also supports the encapsulation of AppleTalk within VINES datagrams.

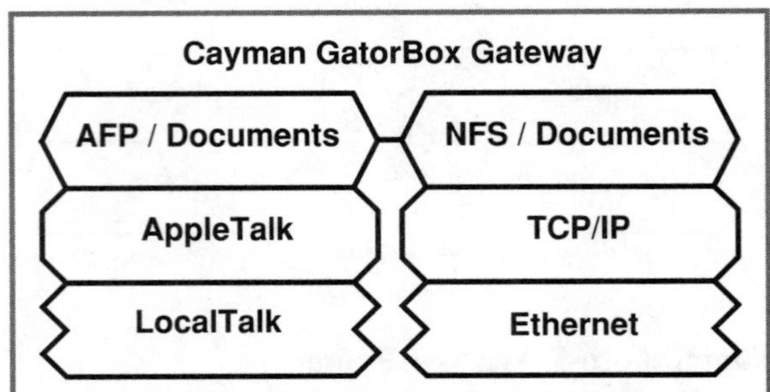

Cayman GatorBox

The Cayman GatorBox is an AFP-to-NFS gateway. Devices on the AFP side see the GatorBox as an AFP server, while devices on the NFS side see the GatorBox as just another NFS client.

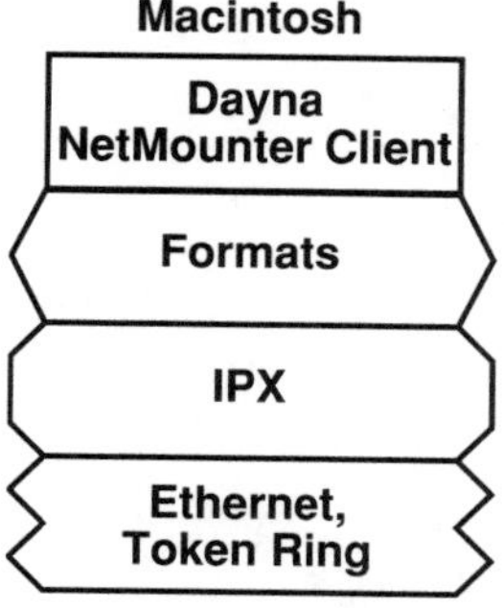

Dayna NetMounter

The Dayna NetMounter equips a Macintosh with the Novell transport protocols, making it appear like any other DOS client on the network. This is an alternative to the NetWare for Macintosh product from Novell.

Macintosh
DECnet Services
Formats
DECnet
LocalTalk, Ethernet, RS-422

DECnet for Macintosh

Part of the PATHWORKS for Macintosh solution is to provide the option to turn Macintosh computers into DECnet nodes. DECnet for Mac provides E-mail, file services, DECwindow, and backup services over LocalTalk, Ethernet, and RS-422 cabling.

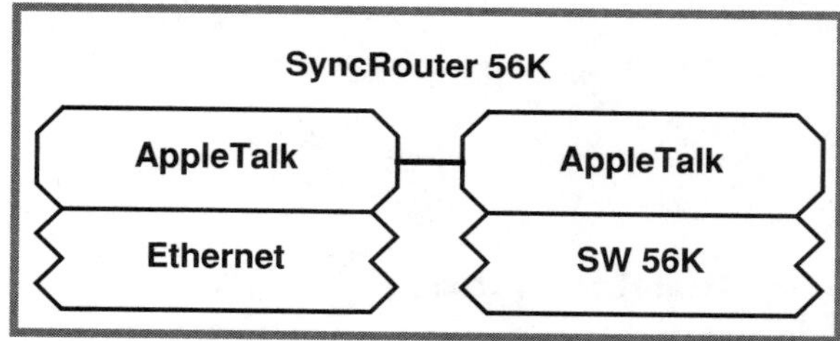

Engage SyncRouter 56K

Engage's AppleTalk router, which connects an Ethernet LAN to a switched 56K WAN link. This device works in tandem with another identical unit.

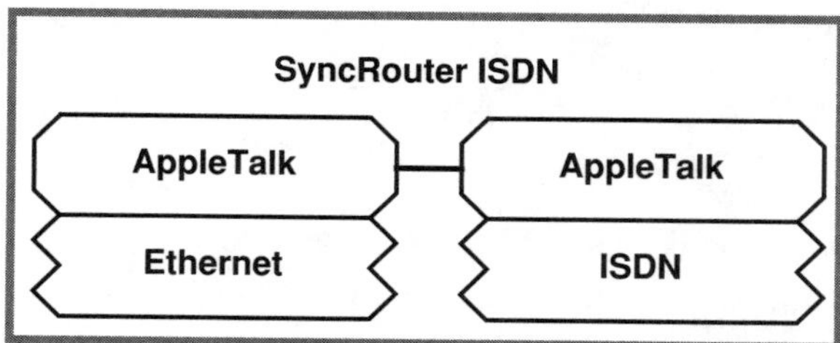

Engage SyncRouter ISDN

Engage's AppleTalk router, which connects an Ethernet LAN to an ISDN WAN link. This device works in tandem with another identical unit.

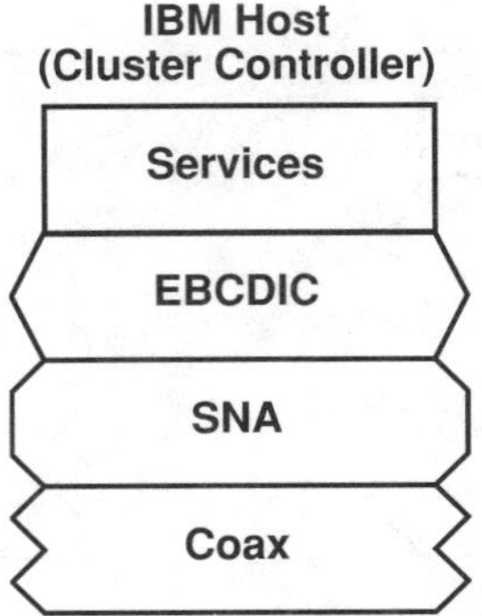

IBM Mainframe

An IBM mainframe environment (with the cluster controller).

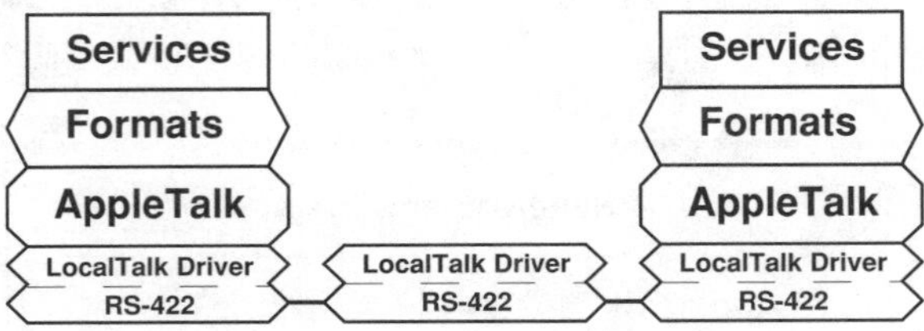

LocalTalk Bridge (Tribe LocalSwitch)

The LocalTalk bridge operates at the Data Link layer. It does not provide a routing capability. By rapidly switching between devices on the LocalTalk segment, the modest bandwidth of LocalTalk is maximized.

LocalTalk Repeater (Farallon PhoneNET Repeater)

The LocalTalk repeater operates at the physical layer by electrically duplicating signals from one side of the connection to the other. It's used to extend the range of LocalTalk segments.

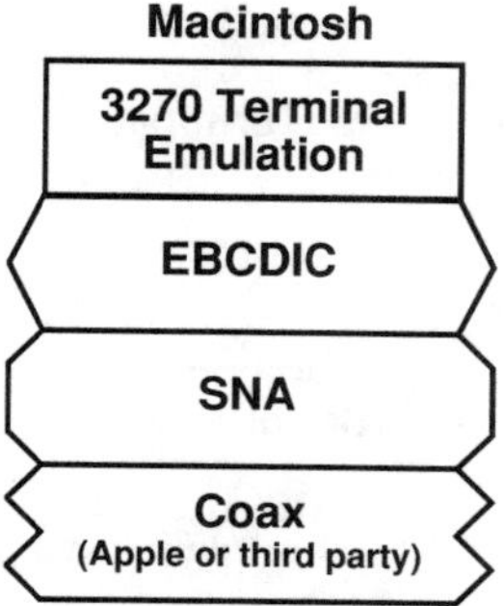

Macintosh IBM 3270 Client

A Macintosh 3270 terminal emulator running over a coax card. An example of this is the MacIRMA emulator and card.

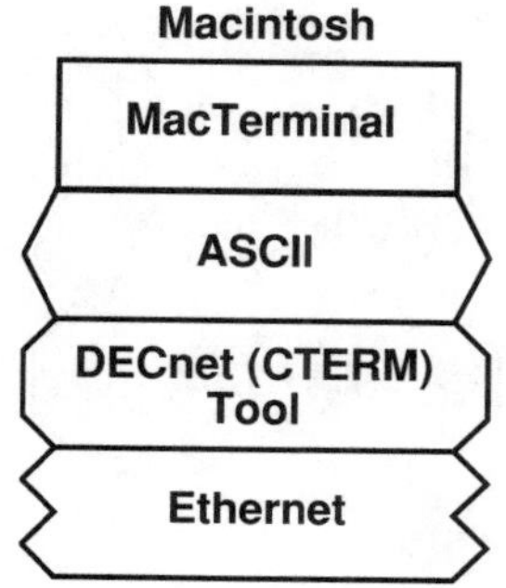

MacTerminal DECnet (CTERM) over Ethernet

Here, a Macintosh is used to run a terminal emulation session with the CTERM protocol (part of the DECnet protocol) over an Ethernet network. The selection of the CTERM protocol is made through the Macintosh Communications Toolbox.

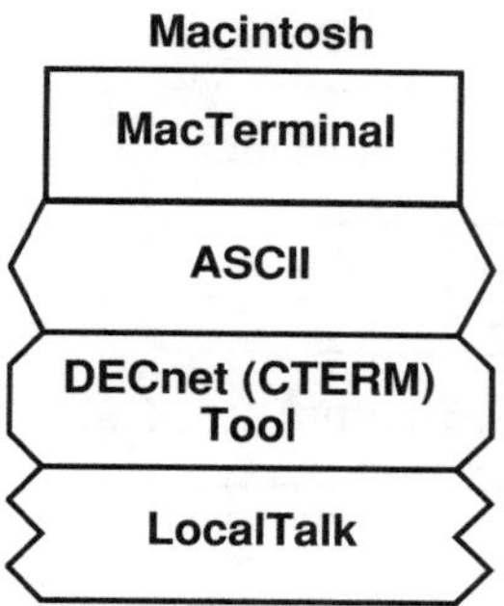

MacTerminal DECnet (CTERM) over LocalTalk

Here, a Macintosh is used to run a terminal emulation session using the CTERM protocol (part of the DECnet protocol) over a LocalTalk network. Of course, the Ethernet-resident host VAX computer must be accessible through a LocalTalk-to-Ethernet router that routes the DECnet protocol.

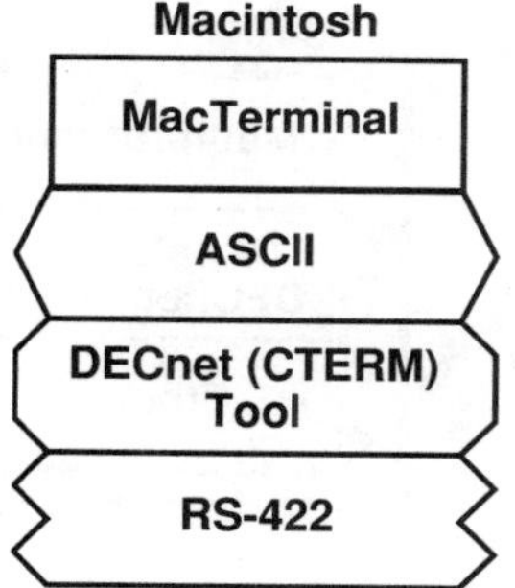

MacTerminal DECnet (CTERM) over RS-422

Here, a Macintosh is used to run a terminal emulation session using the CTERM protocol (part of the DECnet protocol) over a serial connection through the Mac's RS-422 (printer or modem) port.

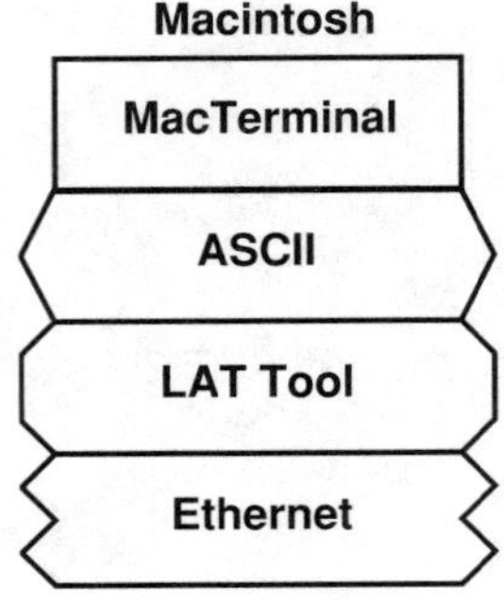

MacTerminal Local Area Transport (LAT) over Ethernet

Here, a Macintosh is being used to run a terminal emulation session using the LAT protocol over a Ethernet network. The host VAX is also speaking the LAT transport protocol. The selection of LAT is made through the Macintosh Communications Toolbox.

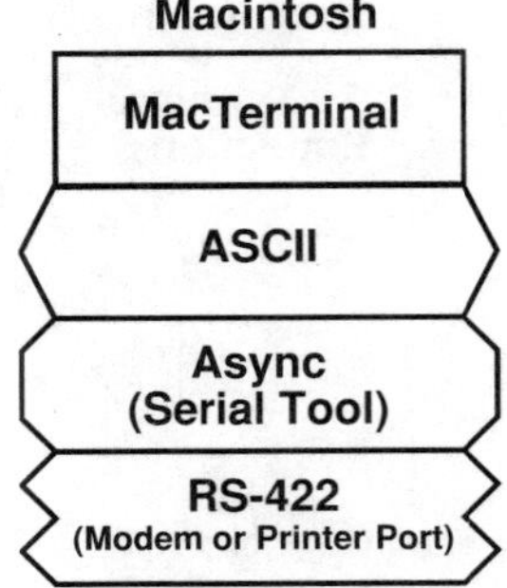

MacTerminal Asynchronous Protocol over RS-422

In this diagram a Macintosh is used to run a terminal emulation session using the "async" protocol over an RS-422 connection (made through the modem or printer port). This is representative of most terminal emulators that use async dial-up lines.

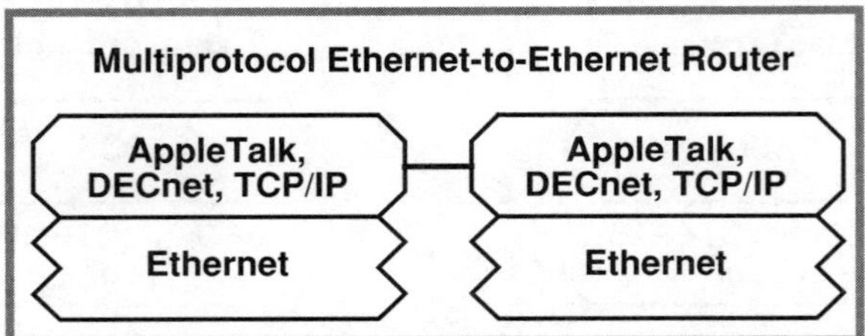

Multiprotocol Ethernet-to-Ethernet Router

A multiprotocol router (AppleTalk, DECnet, and TCP/IP) used to connect two Ethernet segments. Examples include routers from Cisco and Wellfleet.

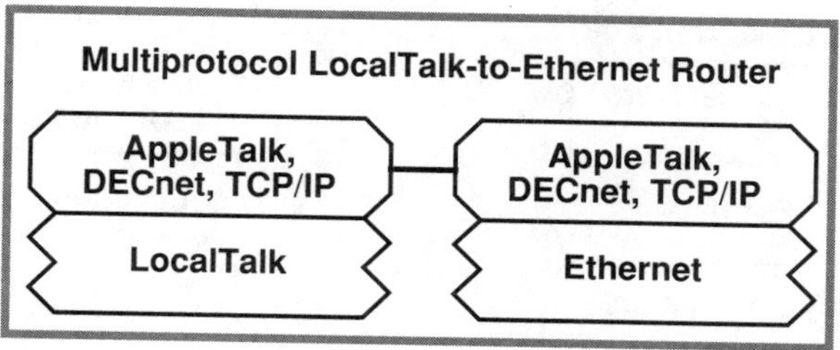

Multiprotocol LocalTalk-to-Ethernet Router

A multiprotocol router (AppleTalk, DECnet, and TCP/IP) used to connect a LocalTalk network to an Ethernet segment. Examples include routers from Shiva, Webster, and Cayman.

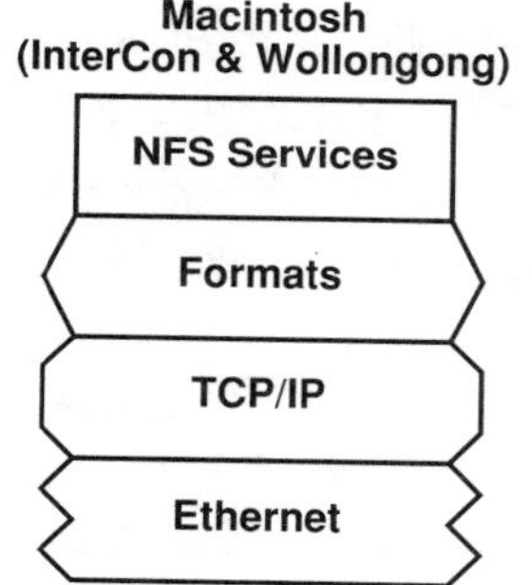

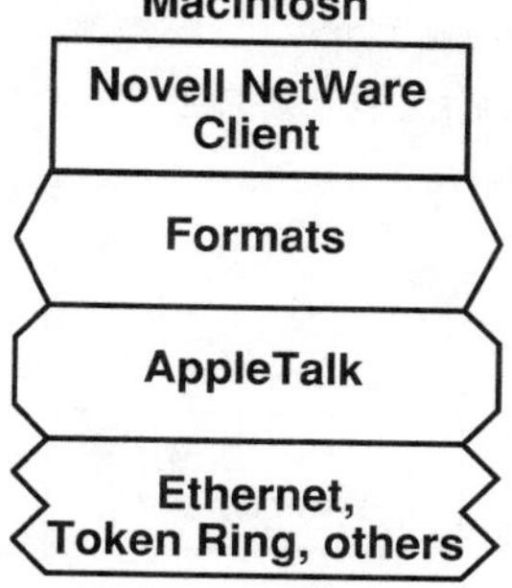

NFS Services on a Macintosh

A Macintosh equipped with Apple's MacTCP can support higher level protocols such as Sun's Network Filing System (NFS). Implementations of NFS for the Mac are provided by InterCon and Wollongong.

Novell NetWare for Macintosh Client

NetWare for the Mac relies on the AppleTalk transport to deliver NetWare services to the desktop. Because it uses the AppleTalk transport, any cabling system or router that is supported by both the Mac and the PC is supported by NetWare for the Mac.

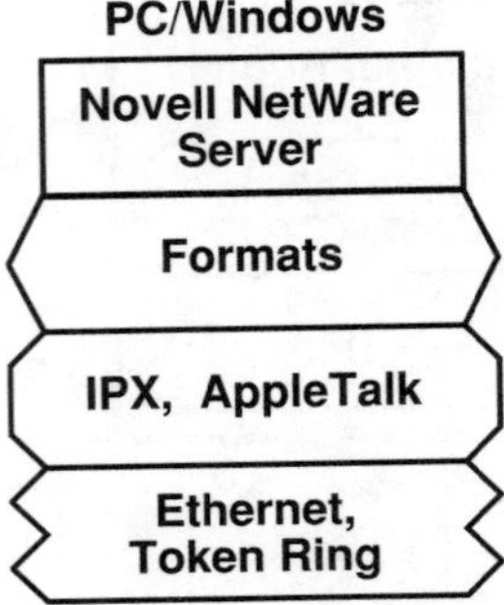

Novell NetWare for Macintosh Server

NetWare for Macintosh services are implemented on a PC server with a NetWare Loadable Module (NLM). The NLM also provides the PC with the AppleTalk protocol suite.

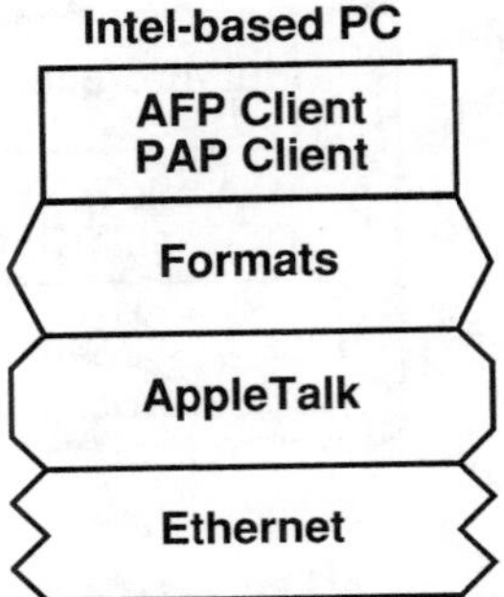

PC with AppleTalk and an Ethernet Card (PhoneNET PC)

This PC supports AFP and PAP protocols with the AppleTalk protocol stack over an Ethernet connection. The best example is Farallon's PhoneNET PC product, which supports Ethernet connectivity (in addition to LocalTalk and Token Ring).

PC with AppleTalk and a LocalTalk Card (PhoneNET PC)

This PC supports AFP and PAP protocols with the AppleTalk protocol stack over a LocalTalk connection. The best example is Farallon's PhoneNET PC product which supports Ethernet connectivity (in addition to LocalTalk and Token Ring).

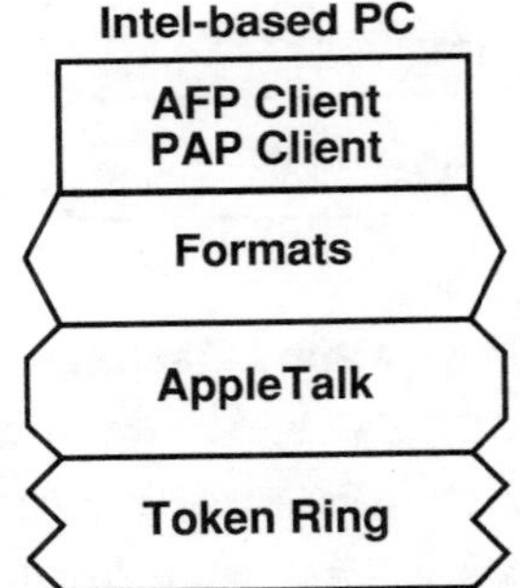

PC with AppleTalk and a Token Ring Card (PhoneNET PC)

This PC supports AFP and PAP protocols with the AppleTalk protocol stack over a Token Ring connection. Again, the best example is Farallon's PhoneNET PC product.

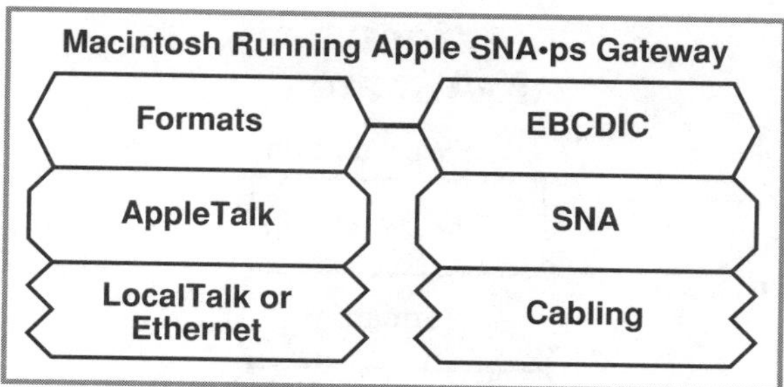

SNA•ps Gateway

This represents a Macintosh running Apple's SNA•ps gateway. It is used to connect members on an AppleTalk network to an IBM host.

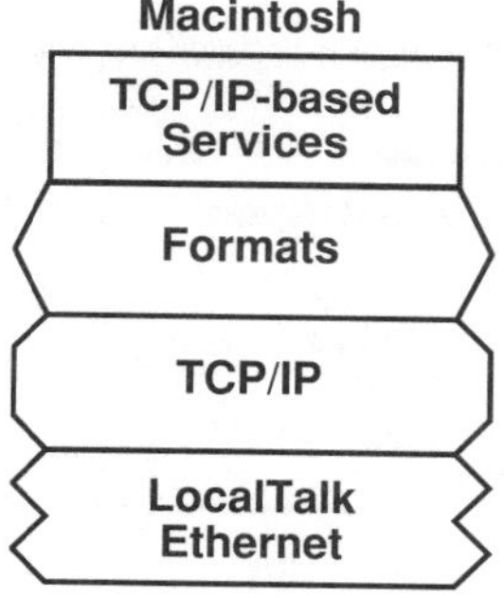

TCP/IP on the Macintosh

This Macintosh has been equipped with Apple's MacTCP, which puts the TCP/IP protocol stack on the Mac, enabling it to participate in IP network services over LocalTalk or Ethernet.

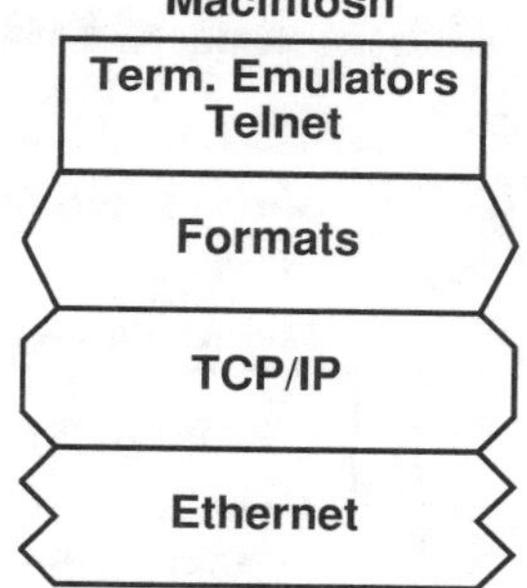

Telnet Services for the Macintosh

One popular IP service is the Telnet terminal protocol that sits atop the TCP/IP protocol stack. An example of this would be running the VersaTerm-Pro terminal emulator over LocalTalk or Ethernet.

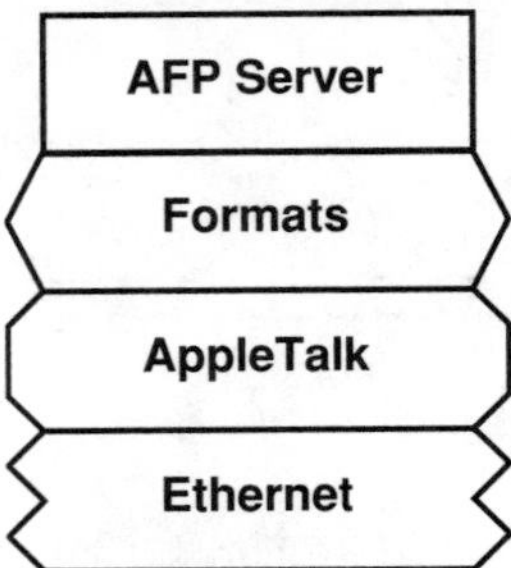

Xinet K-AShare

Xinet's K-AShare turns a Sun workstation into an AFP server. Notice that the Sun has the AppleTalk protocol stack installed.

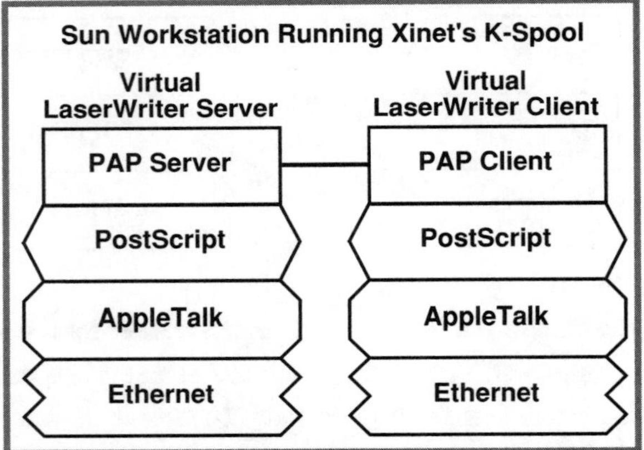

Xinet K-Spool

Xinet's K-Spool turns a Sun workstation into a PAP print spooler. The spooler accepts Mac print jobs, spools them, and sends them to the appropriate network printer.

Listing of Macintosh Networking Companies

B

3Com Corporation

5400 Bayfront Plaza
Santa Clara, CA 95052
(800) 638-3266
(408) 764-5000

-A-

Actinet Systems, Inc.

360 Cowper Avenue
Suite 11
Palo Alto, CA 94301
(415) 326-1321

AESP, Inc.

1810 NE 144th St.
North Miami Beach, FL 33181
(800) 446-2377
(305) 944-7710

AG Group

22540 Camino Diablo
Suite 202
Walnut Creek, CA 94596
(510) 937-7900

Alisa Systems, Inc.

221 East Walnut Street
Suite 175
Pasadena, CA 91101
(818) 792-9474

Andrew Corporation

4301 Westbank Drive
Suite A-100
Austin, TX 78746
(800) 531-5167
(512) 314-3000

Apple Computer, Inc.

20525 Mariani Avenue
Cupertino, CA 95014
(408) 996-1010

Applied Engineering

P.O. Box 5100
Carrollton, TX 75011
(800) 554-6227

APT Communications, Inc.

9607 Dr. Perry Road
Ijamsville, MD 21754
(301) 831-1182

Artisoft Inc.

691 River Road
Tucson, AZ 85704
(602) 293-4000

Asanté Technologies

404 Tasman Drive
Sunnyvale, CA 94089
(408) 752-8388

AT&T

295 North Maple Avenue
Basking Ridge, NJ 07920
(908) 221-6153

Avatar Corporation

65 South Street
Hopkinton, MA 01748
(508) 435-3000 East
(408) 727-3270 West

-B-

Banyan Systems, Inc.

120 Flanders Road
Westboro, MA 01581
(508) 898-1000

Blyth Software

1065 East Hillsdale Boulevard
Foster City, CA 94404
(415) 571-0222

Brio Technology, Inc.

444 Castro Street
Suite 700
Mountain View, CA 94041
(415) 961-4110

BT Tymnet

P.O. Box 49019
560 North First Street
San Jose, CA 95161-9019
(408) 922-7583

-C-

Cabletron Systems

35 Industrial Way
Rochester, NH 03867
(603) 332-9400

Cactus Computer, Inc.

1120 Metrocrest Drive
Suite 103
Carrollton, TX 75006
(214) 416-0525

Caravelle Networks Corporation

301 Moodie Drive
Suite 306
Nepean, ON 2H 9C4
Canada
(613) 596-2802

Cayman Systems, Inc.

26 Landsdowne Street
Cambridge, MA 02139
(617) 494-1999

cc:Mail, Division of Lotus Corporation

2141 Landings Drive
Mountain View, CA 94043
(415) 961-8800

CEL Software

P.O. Box 8339
Station F
Edmonton, Alberta T6H 4W6
Canada
(403) 463-9090

Cisco Systems Inc.

1525 O'Brien Drive
Menlo Park, CA 94025
(415) 326-1941

Claris Corporation

5201 Patrick Henry Drive
Santa Clara, CA 95052
(408) 727-8227

Clear Access Corporation

200 West Lowe Street
Fairfield, IA 52556
(515) 472-7077
(800) 522-4252

Codenoll Technology Corporation

1086 North Broadway
Yonkers, NY 10701
(914) 965-6300

Compatible Systems Corporation

P.O. Drawer 17220
Boulder, CO 80308
(800) 356-0283
(303) 444-9532

Computer Methods Corporation

525 Route 73 South
Suite 300
Marlton, NJ 08053
(609) 596-4360

Connectivité Corporation

220 White Plains Road
Tarrytown, NY 10591
(914) 631-5365

CSG Technologies

530 William Penn Place
Suite 329
Pittsburgh, PA 15219
(412) 471-7170
(800) 366-4622

-D-

Data Spec

9410 Owensmouth Avenue
Chatsworth, CA 91311
(818) 772-9977

DataViz

55 Corporate Drive
Trumbull, CT 06611
(203) 268-0030

Dayna Communications, Inc.

50 South Main Street
Fifth Floor
Salt Lake City, UT 84144
(801) 531-0203

Digital Communications Association, Inc.

1000 Alderman Dr.
Alpharetta, GA 30202
(404) 442-4000

Digital Equipment Corporation

146 Main Street
Maynard, MA 01754
(508) 493-5111

Digital Products Inc.

411 Waverley Oaks Road
Waltham, MA 02154
(617) 647-1234

-E-

EDI Communications Corporation

20440 Town Center Lane
Suite 4E1
Cupertino, CA 95014
(408) 996-1343

EMAC Division of Everex Systems, Inc.

48431 Milmont Drive
Fremont, CA 94538
(800) 628-3837

Engage, Inc.

9053 Soquel Drive
Aptos, CA 95003
(408) 688-1021

Everywhere Development Corporation

2176 Torquay Mews
Mississaugua, ON LSN 2M6
Canada
(416) 819-1173

-F-

Fairfield Software, Inc.

200 West Lowe Street
Fairfield, IA 52556
(515) 472-7077

Farallon Computing, Inc.

2000 Powell Street
Suite 600
Emeryville, CA 94608
(800) 998-7761
(510) 596-9100

Focus, Inc.

800 West Cummings Park
Suite 4500
Woburn, MA 01801
(800) 538-8866
(617) 938-8088

-H-

Hayes Microcomputer Products, Inc.

P.O. Box 105203
Atlanta, GA 30348
(404) 840-9200

Helios USA
10601 South DeAnza Blvd.
Suite 103
Cupertino, CA 95014
(408) 864-0690

Hewlett-Packard Co.
5301 Stevens Creed Boulevard
Santa Clara, CA 95052
(800) 752-0900

-I-

IBM Corporation
1133 Westchester Avenue
White Plains, NY 10604
(800) 426-3333

IDEAssociates, Inc.
29 Dunham Road
Billerica, MA 01821
(508) 663-6878

Impulse Technology
210 Dahlonega Street
Suite 206
Cumming, GA 30130
(404) 889-8294

Infotek, Inc.
56 Camille Lane
East Patchogue, NY 11772
(516) 289-9682

InterCon Systems Corp.
950 Herndon Parkway
Suite 420
Herndon, VA 22070
(703) 709-9890

International Transware, Inc.
1503 Grand Road
Suite 155
Mountain View, CA 94040
(800) 999-6387
(415) 903-2300

IPT - Information Presentation Technologies
555 Chorro Street
San Luis Obispo, CA 93405
(805) 541-3000

Kandu Software Corp.
2305 North Kentucky Street
Arlington, VA 22205
(703) 532-0213

Keywork Technologies

2816 Eleventh Street, NE
Calgary, Alberta T2E 7S7
Canada
(403) 250-1770

-M-

Marietta Systems International

29 El Cerrito Avenue
San Mateo, CA 94402
(415) 344-1519

MCI

1111 19th Street NW
Suite 500
Washington, DC 20036
(800) 444-6245

MDG Computer Services

634 South Dunton
Arlington Heights, IL
60005-2544
(708) 818-9991
(708) 453-6330

Microsoft Corporation

One Microsoft Way
Redmond, WA 98052-6399
(206) 882-8080

Miramar Systems

201 North Salsipuedes
Suite 204
Santa Barbara, CA 93103
(805) 965-5161

Mitem Corporation

2105 Hamilton Avenue
Suite 350
San Jose, CA 95125
(408) 559-8801

Motorola Computer Group

10700 North De Anza Boulevard
Cupertino, CA 95014
(800) 759-1107 Ext. MU

MultiAccess Computing Corporation

5350 Hollister Avenue
Suite C
Santa Barbara, CA 93111
(805) 964-2332

-N-

National Semiconductor Corporation

2900 Semiconductor Drive
P.O. Box 58090
Santa Clara, CA 95052-8090
(408) 721-5000

Neon Software, Inc.

1009 Oak Hill Road
Suite 203
Lafayette, CA 94549
(510) 283-9771

Network General Corporation

4200 Bohannon Drive
Menlo Park, CA 94025
(415) 688-2700

Network Resources Corporation

736 South Hillview Drive
Milpitas, CA 95035
(408) 263-8100

Nevada Western

615 North Tasman Drive
Sunnyvale, CA 94089-1950
(408) 734-8727

Novell, Inc.

122 East 1700 South
Provo, UT 84606
(800) 638-9273
(801) 379-5900

-O-

ON Technology, Inc.

155 Second Street
Cambridge, MA 02141
(617) 876-0900

Oracle Corporation

500 Oracle Parkway
Redwood Shores, CA 94065
(415) 506-7000

-P-

Pacer Software, Inc.

7911 Herschel Avenue
Suite 402
La Jolla, CA 92037
(619) 454-0565

Photonics Corporation

200 East Hacienda Avenue
Campbell, CA 95008
(408) 370-3033

-R-

Racal-Interlan, Inc.

155 Swanson Road
Foxborough, MA 01719
(508) 263-9929

-S-

Shiva Corporation

One Cambridge Center
Cambridge, MA 02142
(800) 458-3550
(617) 252-6300

Sitka Corporation

950 Marina Village Parkway
Alameda, CA 94501
(800) 445-8677
(510) 769-9669

Soft-Switch Inc.

640 Lee Road
Wayne, PA 19087-5698
(215) 640-9600

SoftWriters, Inc.

P.O. Box 1308
Round Rock, TX 78680
(512) 244-3999

Sonic Systems, Inc.

333 West El Camino Real
Suite 280
Sunnyvale, CA 94087
(800) 535-0725
(408) 736-1900

Standard Microsystems Corporation

80 Arkay Drive
Hauppauge, NY 11788
(516) 273-3100

StarNine Technologies, Inc.

2126 Sixth Street
Berkeley, CA 94710
(510) 548-0391

Synergy Software

2457 Perkiomen Avenue
Mt. Penn, PA 19606
(215) 779-0522

-T-

Talaris Systems, Inc.

6059 Cornerstone Court West
San Diego, CA 92121
(619) 587-0787

TechGnosis Inc.

301 Yamato Road
Suite 2200
Boca Raton, FL 33431
(407) 997-6687

TechWorks

4030 Braker Lane West
Suite 350
Austin, TX 78759
(800) 879-7745
(512) 794-8533

Terranetics

1538 North Martel Avenue
Suite 413
Los Angeles, CA 90046
(818) 446-7692

Thomas-Conrad Corporation

1908-R Kramer Lane
Austin, TX 78758
(800) 332-8683
(512) 836-1935

Thursby Software Systems, Inc.

5840 West Interstate 20
Suite 100
Arlington, TX 76017
(817) 478-5070

Tribe Computer Works

1195 Park Avenue
Suite 211
Emeryville, CA 94608
(510) 547-3874

Trik, Inc.

400 West Cummings Park
Suite 2350
Woburn, MA 01801
(800) 766-0356
(617) 933-8810

-U-

Ungermann-Bass, Inc.

3990 Freedom Circle
P.O. Box 58030
Santa Clara, CA 95052
(800) 873-6381
(408) 496-0111

United Data Corporation

3755 Balboa Street
Suite 203
San Francisco, CA 94121
(415) 221-8931

US Sprint Communications

P.O. Box 8417
1200 Main St., 4th Floor
Kansas City, MO 64105
(800) 877-2000

-W-

Webster Computer Corporation

2109 O'Toole Avenue
Suite J
San Jose, CA 95131
(800) 457-0903
(408) 954-8054

White Pine Software

40 Simon Street
Suite 201
Nashua, NH 03060-3043
(603) 886-9050

WilTel

P.O. Box 21348
Tulsa, OK 74121
(800) 642-2299

The Wollongong Group, Inc.

1129 San Antonio Road
Palo Alto, CA 94303
(415) 962-7100

WordPerfect Corporation

1555 North Technology Way
Orem, UT 84057
(801) 225-5000
(800) 451-5151

-X-

Xinet

2560 9th Street
Suite 312
Berkeley, CA 94710
(510) 845-0555

Live Wired

A Guide to Networking Macs

Index

Symbols

A

B

C

D

E

F

G

H

I-J

K

L

M

O

P

Q

R

S

T

U-V

W

X-Z

KEEP UP TO DATE ON MACINTOSH CONNECTIVITY THROUGHOUT THE YEAR. SUBSCRIBE TO

If you're a Macintosh networking and communications professional you need to stay abreast of this fast-moving industry and you should be reading *Connections: The Technical Journal of Macintosh Connectivity. Connections* is the only publication devoted exclusively to issues that are important to people who design and implement Mac connectivity solutions. Whether you're interested in Mac to Mac, Mac to PC, Mac to UNIX, or Mac to mainframe connectivity, *Connections* has valuable information you cannot afford to be without.

Connections is different because of its focus. We don't spend time on video cards, monitors or spreadsheets. We talk about networking. This focus allows us to go beyond the topics found in the monthly and weekly magazines. *Connections* takes you inside the cutting-edge technology of such issues as Apple's Open Collaboration Environment, Wide Area Networking strategies, and Enterprise Network Management techniques. Each issue of *Connections* provides you with approximately thirty-two pages of in-depth tutorials and analysis about the issues you face, and will be facing, on a daily basis. *Connections* does not accept any advertising, so every page contains information you can use. Information this focused on Macintosh networking is not available anywhere else.

Connections costs just $195 a year for eight information-packed issues — a small price to pay for staying on top of the fastest-moving section of the Mac industry.

You can try *Connections: The Technical Journal of Macintosh Connectivity* risk-free. Simply return the card below and you'll receive your first issue absolutely free. If you decide *Connections* isn't an outstanding resource, just write "cancel" on the accompanying invoice and we'll stop the subscription immediately. Also, you can cancel your subscription at any time and we will refund the subscription fee for any remaining issues.

Don't miss another issue. Start your no-risk subscription today! Mail or fax a copy of the card below to:

Winehouse Computer Company
20 North Santa Cruz Avenue — Tel: 408-354-2500
Los Gatos, CA 95030 — Fax: 408-354-2571

YES! Please enter my no-risk subscription and send me a free issue of *Connections.* If I like what I see, I'll pay $195 and get seven more issues for a total of eight. If not, I'll return the bill marked "cancel", keep the free issue, and owe nothing.

❑ Payment Enclosed ❑ US/Canada Subscription: $195 Name ____________

❑ Bill Me ❑ Overseas Subscription: $250 Company ____________

Charge my credit card: ❑ Visa ❑ MasterCard Street ____________

Card Number ____________ City/State/ZIP ____________

Expires ____________ Phone Number ____________

Signature ____________ E-Mail Address ____________

How to Use the Disk

This book comes with a disk that contains an entire library of the NetPICT symbols used throughout the book. For each NetPICT symbol there are two files: a PICT file that contains the graphical image, and a text file that contains a description of the image. The text file has the same name as the PICT, but with the addition of a ".txt" filename extension. For example, the PICT file for Apple's Internet Router is named `Apple Internet Router`, while the text file is named `Apple Internet Router.txt`.

The disk also contains a viewer application, called PICTviewer. PICTviewer is used to view both the NetPICT symbols and the associated text. PICTviewer provides an easy means for you to view and read informative data on hundreds of products. Of course, since the symbols are in the PICT format, they can be easily incorporated into documents made by your favorite drawing program. The same can be said for the text (.txt) files. These text files can be added to your drawings to annotate the figures. Many drawing programs, such as MacDraw Pro, can import text files directly. If your drawing program can't directly import text files, then you'll have to copy and paste the text using a text editor or word processor. By using a drawing program, you'll be able to import those NetPICT symbols that represent the fundamental parts of your present or planned network. You'll be able to see where bridges, routers, gateways, or even format translators are required.

The NetPICT files are compressed to save space. You will have to decompress them and save them to your hard disk in order to use them. (They will take about 3M of disk space when you have extracted them.) Double-click on the `NetPICTs.sea` icon. You will be prompted to choose a location to save the extracted files. When you have done so, click the Save button. The files will self-extract.

To use the NetPICT viewer, you'll need HyperCard 2.1 (or the HyperCard Viewer). You might also want to copy PICTviewer to your hard disk.

1. Launch the NetPICT viewer by double-clicking its icon.

2. Click three times to close the splash screens.

3. Use the pop-up folder menu to browse through the NetPICT symbol folder hierarchy.

4. Once you've found the appropriate symbol, click once on the name that appears in the window directly beneath the pop-up menu.

   The chosen NetPICT symbol will appear in a separate window to the right of the viewer screen. You can reposition this window at any time. You can even enlarge it to the size of your monitor by clicking on the Zoom box located at the upper right hand corner of the symbol window.

5. To restore the symbol window to the right side of the viewer window, click once on the magnet icon. This will automatically dock the symbol window to its default position at the right of the viewer window.